International Marketing Management

Strategies, Concepts and Cases in Europe

by

Mario Glowik
Slawomir Smyczek

Oldenbourg Verlag München

Bibliografische Information der Deutschen Nationalbibliothek

Die Deutsche Nationalbibliothek verzeichnet diese Publikation in der Deutschen Nationalbibliografie; detaillierte bibliografische Daten sind im Internet über http://dnb.d-nb.de abrufbar.

© 2011 Oldenbourg Wissenschaftsverlag GmbH
Rosenheimer Straße 145, D-81671 München
Telefon: (089) 45051-0
www.oldenbourg-verlag.de

Lektorat: Christiane Engel-Haas
Herstellung: Constanze Müller
Titelbild: thinkstockphotos.de
Einbandgestaltung: hauser lacour
Gesamtherstellung: Druckhaus „Thomas Müntzer" GmbH, Bad Langensalza

Dieses Papier ist alterungsbeständig nach DIN/ISO 9706.

ISBN 978-3-486-59749-3

Preface

In recent decades, against the background of integrated global trade patterns, the complexity of international marketing and management has increased enormously. University programs as well as continuing education courses for business practitioners are necessary in order to prepare participants for their professional careers in the global arena. This book aims to meet these educational requirements in the context of international marketing and management issues.

The entire publication is divided into nine chapters. Chapter one provides an introduction to the topic and definitions of international marketing management and the consequences of liberalized trade patterns. Related to the outcomes of globalization, chapter two discusses the contents and importance of social responsibility and business ethics in international marketing and management. Chapter three provides insights into relevant elements of a firm's international market environment. The investigation of a firm's macro and micro environment is of particular importance before deciding on business objectives and constructing a suitable firm strategy; this subject is taken up in chapter four. Chapter five discusses relevant information sources and effective techniques that can be utilized in the course of carrying out international market research. Chapter six introduces the cultural aspects of management and marketing. This discussion continues at a deeper level in chapters seven and eight, which deal with culturally influenced customer behavior and its application in international markets. Chapter nine, which concludes the book, discusses pragmatic issues for operating in international business, such as the elements of an international export contract (e.g., delivery terms, payment conditions, etc.) as well as international distribution and promotion.

Overall, the authors' intention is to combine the latest theoretical concepts with up-to-date examples from a variety of firms. In particular, the book focuses on the European markets, customers, industries, and corresponding societal environments.

The authors would like to take the opportunity to express their sincere thanks to Mrs. Margie Dyer from Texas, U.S.A., for her professional support and valuable comments when proofreading the manuscript. The authors would like to thank Mrs. Christiane Engel-Haas and Mrs. Sarah Voit from the Oldenbourg publishing house in Munich, Germany, for her continued and kind support in the course of the preparation of this publication, *International Marketing Management.*

Mario Glowik

Sławomir Smyczek

Table of Contents

List of Figures

1 Chapter: An introduction to international marketing management

- Describe developments in international trade.

- Explain the internationalization motives of firms.

- Explain the definitions and scope of international marketing.

- Describe the philosophy of a marketing driven company.

- Explain the challenges for marketing executives involved in international business.

- Describe the important elements of the marketing planning process.

1.1   Developments in international trade

Discussions of multinational firms, world trade, and globalization, as frequently found in the mass media and academic research, may give the impression that cross continental trade flow patterns are new. However, porcelain and silk were imported from China to Arab countries and Europe for more than a thousand years. The Knights Templar (the Order of the Temple), maintained a cross-continent trade and a logistics and financing network from the north of Europe to Africa from the 12th until the beginning of the 14th century. Thus if international trading itself is not a unique phenomenon of the 21st century, what makes this century different?

In general, when comparing the term internationalization as used at present with its historical use, it is the **factor of time** that is different, reflected in shortened product life and technology cycles, much faster logistics, and accelerated aging of information and knowledge. One of the major reasons that the factor of time has led to complex competitive forces is trade liberalization. Liberalized trade patterns help firms get involved in international market entry activities more easily, which has made global competition more intensive and led to shorter half-life times of technologies, products, and managerial knowledge. What elements supported the liberalization of global trade and why could cross-country business relations have developed in so promising a way in recent decades?

From 1948 to 1994, the **General Agreement on Tariffs and Trade (GATT)** provided the basis for tariff reductions through a series of multilateral negotiations also named 'GATT rounds'. This first round of GATT negotiations resulted in a package of trade rules and 45,000 tariff concessions affecting trade valued at USD 10 billion, about one fifth of the world's total. The group of GATT nations had expanded to twenty-three by the time the deal was signed on 30 October 1947. The tariff concessions went into effect on 30 June 1948 through a 'Protocol of Provisional Application'. As a result, the 'General Agreement on Tariffs and Trade' was born, with the twenty-three founding members (officially named 'contracting parties'). In the early years, the GATT trade rounds concentrated on further reducing tariffs. Then the Kennedy Round in the mid-sixties brought about a GATT Anti-Dumping Agreement. The Tokyo Round lasted from 1973 to 1979, with 102 countries participating. During this period, efforts to progressively reduce **tariffs** continued. The results included an average one-third cut in customs duties in the world's nine major industrial markets, bringing the average tariff on industrial products down to 4.7 percent. The tariff reductions, phased in over a period of eight years, involved an element of 'harmonization', meaning the higher the tariff, the larger the cut, proportionally. In other issues, the Tokyo Round had mixed results and failed to solve fundamental problems affecting farm trade. Moreover, the GATT system was ineffectively handling increasing 'non-tariff' barriers. **Non-tariff barriers** contain, among other things, subsidies or tax benefits in order to provide competitive advantages for local industries, escalating bureaucracy (e.g., safety standards, hygiene certificates, document presentation, approval procedures, etc.,) or 'buy national campaigns'. In comparison to tariffs, the variations of 'non-tariff' barriers mentioned above are more difficult to prove as 'unfair' by the foreign party. The protection of 'brands' and emerging services industries, where the core product is usually based on 'knowledge' (intellectual property rights), had not been covered by the GATT system and its rules, which remain un-changed since its foundation in 1947. Evidently, starting in the mid-eighties, the GATT sys-tem needed to be modified against the background of new services-based industries and emerging non-tariff hindrances to global trade (WTO, 2010a).

year/period	location / name	subject covered	countries participating
1947	Geneva	tariffs	23
1949	Annecy	tariffs	13
1951	Torquay	tariffs	38
1956	Geneva	tariffs	26
1960-1961	Geneva Dillon Round	tariffs	26
1964-1967	Geneva Kennedy Round	tariffs and anti-dumping measures	62
1973-1979	Geneva Tokyo Round	tariffs, non-tariff measures	102
1986-1994	Geneva Uruguay Round	tariffs, non-tariff measures, services industries, intellectual property rights, dispute settlement procedure, particular topics on agriculture and textile, establishment of WTO	123

Source: WTO (2010a)

Figure 1. GATT trade rounds

As a consequence, the eighth GATT round, named the Uruguay Round of 1986-94, was the last and most extensive of all and finally led to foundation of the World Trade Organiza-tion (WTO). The WTO became effective on the 1st of January 1995. Whereas GATT had mainly dealt with trade in goods, the WTO and its agreements contain important elements such as trade in services, traded inventions, creations and designs (intellectual property rights), and subsidies. Another alteration, compared with the previous GATT, is a dispute settlement system. Trade relations often involve conflicting interests. Agreements, including those painstakingly negotiated in the WTO system, often need interpreting. The most harmonious way to settle these differences is through a neutral procedure based on an agreed upon legal foundation. That is the main purpose behind the dispute settlement process written into the WTO agreements (WTO, 2010a).

The Doha Round, the most recent negotiations of WTO, was launched in Doha (Qatar) in November 2001. The agenda of the Doha Round is much broader than past GATT agreements and is specifically targeted at addressing the needs of developing countries. The focus of negotiations has been on reforming agricultural subsidies, improving access to global markets, and ensuring that new liberalization in the global economy respects the need for sustainable economic growth in developing countries. At the Geneva Ministerial in 2008, the Doha Round came very close to a framework agreement on further tariff cuts for industrial goods and agricultural exports and a comprehensive package of farm reform in developed countries. This package would have gone further than any previous multilateral trade agreement. It would have removed almost all remaining tariffs between developed countries for industrial goods and would have included a proportionate contribution from large emerging economies such as Brazil, China, and India. Unfortunately, the meeting broke down over a disagreement between exporters of agricultural bulk commodities and countries with large numbers of subsistence farmers on the precise terms of a 'special safeguard measure' to protect farmers from surges in imports. At this time, the future of the Doha Round is uncertain (EU_Commission, 2010).

The case: EU priorities in the Doha Round

Concerning market access for the industrial goods sector, the EU wants to create significant new trade flows by cutting tariffs in both developed countries and the growing emerging economies such as China, Brazil, and India. The goal is to create new trade between developed countries, but also between developing countries.

For the agriculture sector, the EU is committed to an agreement that reforms farm subsidy programs throughout the wealthy world in line with the EU's wide-ranging 2003 reform of the Common Agricultural Policy. As part of the Doha Round, the EU has offered to cut farm tariffs by 60 percent, reduce trade-distorting farm subsidies by 80 percent, and eliminate farm export subsidies altogether. The EU also wants to see new market access opportunities for its own processed agricultural exports.

In market access negotiations for the services trade, Doha should bring considerable and real market opportunities for business as well as benefits to consumers worldwide. However, the EU does not seek general deregulation or privatization of sectors where principles of public interest are at stake, and the EU is also committed to defending the right of WTO members to promote cultural diversity.

The EU approaches the Doha Round with the goal of reaching an agreement on a package of development measures, including a special agreement to address trade distortions caused by subsidies to cotton farmers in developed countries, the extension of unlimited market access to all Least Developed Countries by as many countries as possible, a new global package of 'aid for trade' assistance to help the poorest build the capacity to trade, and special measures to help the poorest countries implement any Doha Agreement effectively and without long-term harm to their economies.

In addition, the EU seeks an agreement on a new set of rules to govern the use of trade defense instruments so they are not abused, and a complete update of the WTO's rulebook for trade facilitation, the standard practice for customs and other border-related procedures world wide – a potential source of huge savings for traders, especially in developing countries. The EU also wants to use the Doha Round to improve the protection of geographical indications – the special legal identity given to products like Parma Ham and Roquefort cheese that are closely linked to a particular place and tradition of production.

Source: The EU Commission (2010)

There is no doubt that international business provides many advantages for a firm in times of prosperity but simultaneously increases marketing planning and control complexity. The economic wealth in countries such as Germany, France, or Italy significantly correlates with their export performance. The increasing variety of products often comes along with intensified competition in the markets, often but not necessarily in the consumers' favor. Because of global trade patterns, a market crisis is not restricted anymore to one country or local sales region. **Market uncertainty** easily becomes a country, or even cross-continent, issue in times of crisis. Marketing executives should be aware that banks that invest globally, worldwide procurement sources, and cross-country value adding manufacturing of multinationals lead to accelerated dynamics in business and trade in times when the economic environment is changing. Thus, market response speed along with flexible marketing planning and control mechanisms become a key to gaining competitive advantage.

The economic and financial crisis that began to interrupt the world economy in the closing months of 2008 produced a global recession in 2009 that resulted in the largest decline in world trade in more than seventy years. The rate of trade growth had already slowed from 6.4 percent in 2007 to 2.1 percent in 2008, but the 12.2 percent contraction in 2009 was without precedent in recent history (WTO, 2010b). The development of world trade (variations in percent) for the period 1999-2009 is illustrated in Figure 2.

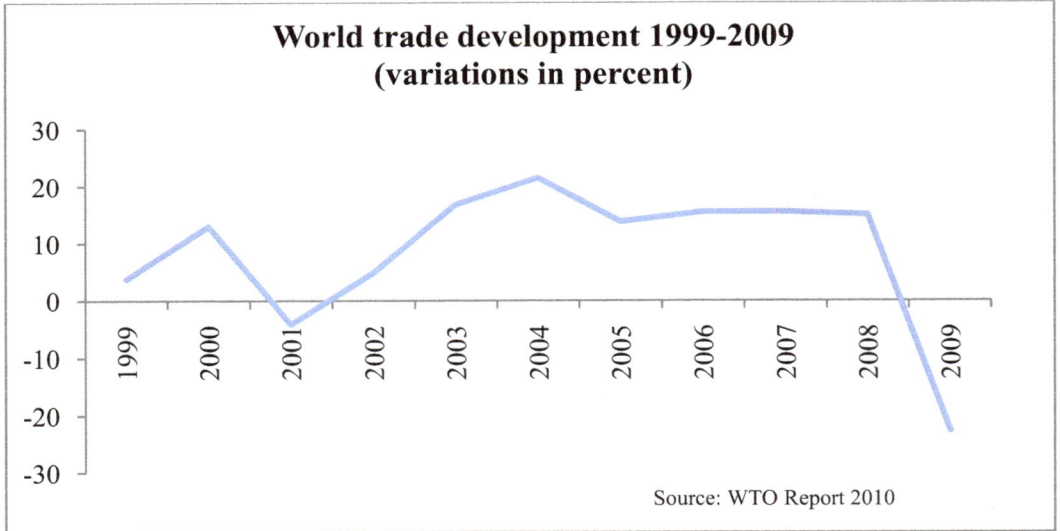

Figure 2. World trade development 1999-2009

In a globalized world, a firm's international marketing manager is confronted with complex and rapidly changing environments. Thus, sophisticated and continuously up-dated market research is of vital importance. Marketing executives should be aware that currently some countries run huge state deficits (e.g., the United States, Japan, and Greece) as an outcome of the recent global financial and economic crisis, which may contribute to more volatile financial market dynamics in the future. Because of the severe earthquake, followed by a tsunami and the nuclear power plant disasters in March 2011 (e.g., Fukushima), the state deficit will further increase in Japan. An overview regarding national 'current account deficit' and the 'general government gross debt' by country ('top ten' in 2010) is given in below Figures 3 and 4 (IMF, 2010).

General government gross debt by country (2010)

■ in percent of GDP

Japan, Lebanon, Greece, Italy, Belgium, Singapore, Ireland, United States, France, Portugal

Source: IMF World Economic Outlook Database (2010)

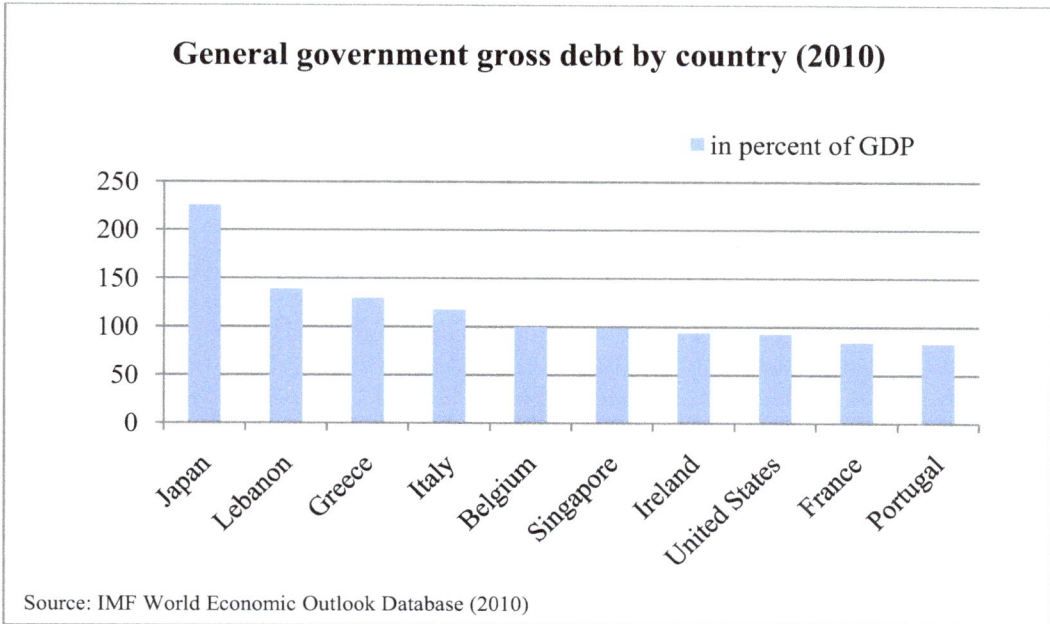

Figure 3. General government gross debt by country: top ten in 2010

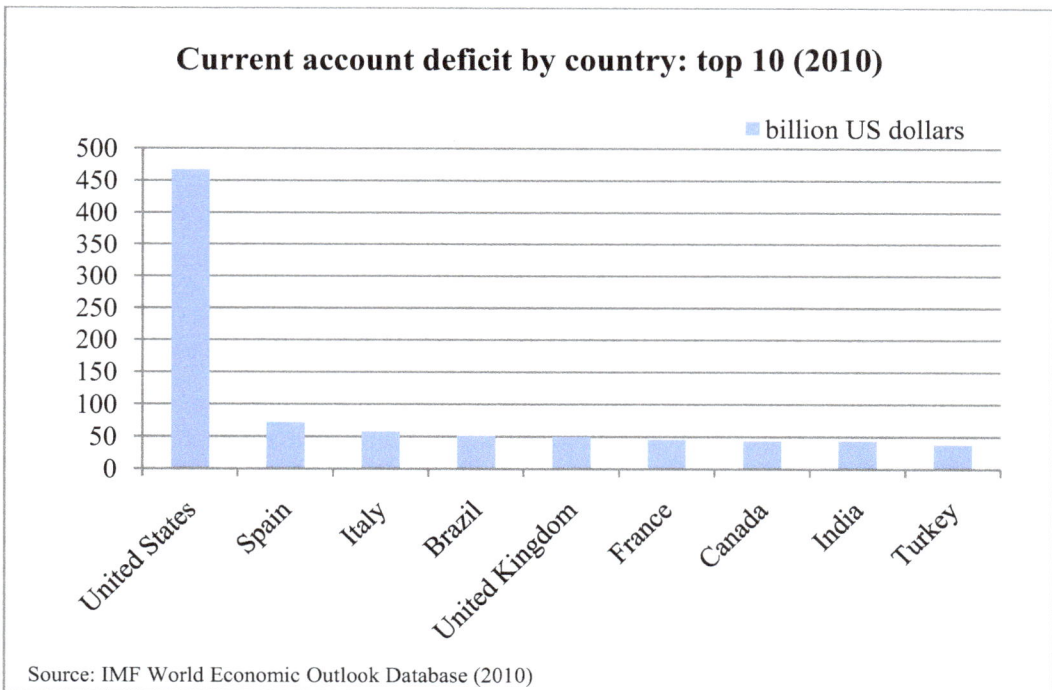

Current account deficit by country: top 10 (2010)

■ billion US dollars

United States, Spain, Italy, Brazil, United Kingdom, France, Canada, India, Turkey

Source: IMF World Economic Outlook Database (2010)

Figure 4. Current account deficit by country: top ten in 2010

Public deficits and accumulated private debts through an 'easy money lending policy' provide fundamental risks for inflation, which finally may reduce the purchasing power of consumers and thus provoke overall market uncertainty in the coming years.

1.2   Internationalization motives

The term **globalization** is complex, often controversially and emotionally discussed, and depending on one's point of view, either interpreted in a negative or positive sense. Critics of globalization make arguments about unrestrained profit maximization by multinationals using their diversified assets around the globe. Globalization is often a synonym for degrading conditions of employment, regional deindustrialization that results in higher unemployment rates, and decreasing salaries. Moreover, discussions about globalization are linked with arguments that countries such as those in Africa or Latin America do not have a ghost of chance to gain competitive positions in the global arena as long as the business rules are dictated by globally operating multinationals originating in the West (e.g., oil production on the Ivory Coast). Another criticism related to globalization arises from huge ecological damage stemming from regionally promising investments (e.g., cutting down the rain forests in Latin America) and the difficulty of controlling compliance with or ignorance of safety standards (e.g., BP's Deepwater Horizon oil spill in the Gulf of Mexico in 2010).

Positive interpretations of globalization usually point out the high mobility of products, services, capital, and technology around the world, which increases market competition and leads to broader product and service offerings and competitive pricing, thus providing various opportunities for end consumers. Globalization provides a further chance for particular industries where the business is connected with the factor of time, such as logistics, information sourcing and exchange, and databank hardware and software management. As a consequence, internationalization is no longer an exclusive issue reserved for large multinationals. These outcomes also allow small and medium-sized firms to start international business and, thus, provide challenging and interesting job opportunities. Smaller firms, often young and innovative, are, compared to the past, in a much better position to initiate international business activities. Internationalization motives seem to be manifold; thus a detailed perspective is necessary to discover the main motives that explain why firms take the international route.

There are five major reasons that firms take the initiative to start internationalization. First, there are **demand oriented internationalization motives**. Foreign markets offer additional sales volumes and, thus, simultaneously provide better prerequisites for economies of scale effects for a firm's procurement and manufacturing costs. A firm's engagement in foreign markets has advantages due to a better customer proximity and improved product and service adaptation to a foreign country's tastes and design expectations. Emerging countries such as the BRIC (Brazil, Russia, India, and China) have demand markets with considerable sales volumes. Consequently, rising demand abroad can compensate for saturated markets at home. Tariff barriers have been reduced between countries and continents or have even disappeared in regions such as Europe. For example, the expansion of the European Union (EU) in 2004 to include Central and Eastern European countries (CEE) opened new business opportunities for Western firms that seek to expand their international activities in these up-coming markets (e.g., Poland, Hungary, and Romania). Particularly firms from Germany, because of its geographical location and strong foreign trade orientation, benefit from the EU expansion to the East. Outside Europe, tremendous dynamics with considerable impacts on worldwide trade patterns are particularly noticeable in Asia. In 2009, China took over the position as a world export champion, followed by Germany, the United States, and Japan. The ten leading merchandise exporters are illustrated in Figure 5 below (WTO, 2010b).

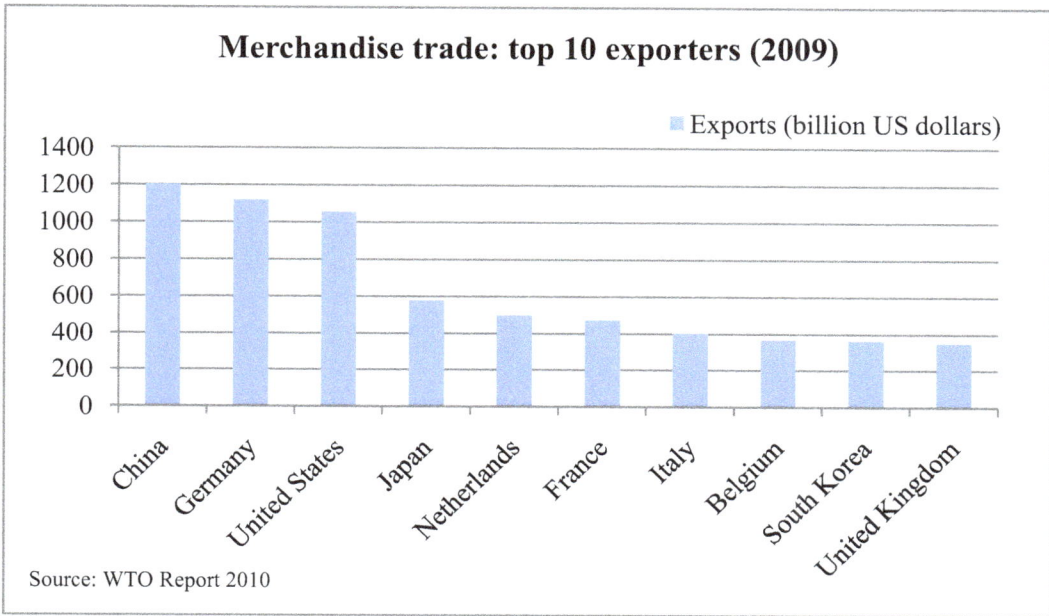

Merchandise trade: top 10 exporters (2009)

■ Exports (billion US dollars)

Source: WTO Report 2010

Figure 5. Leading export countries of merchandise trade in 2009

China has used its strong export surpluses in the past to accumulate foreign exchange re-serves and has become the world's largest foreign exchange reserve holder followed by Japan (compare Figure 6) (IMF, 2010).

Foreign exchange reserves by country: top 10 (2010)

Source: IMF Data Template on International Reserves and Foreign Currency Liquidity

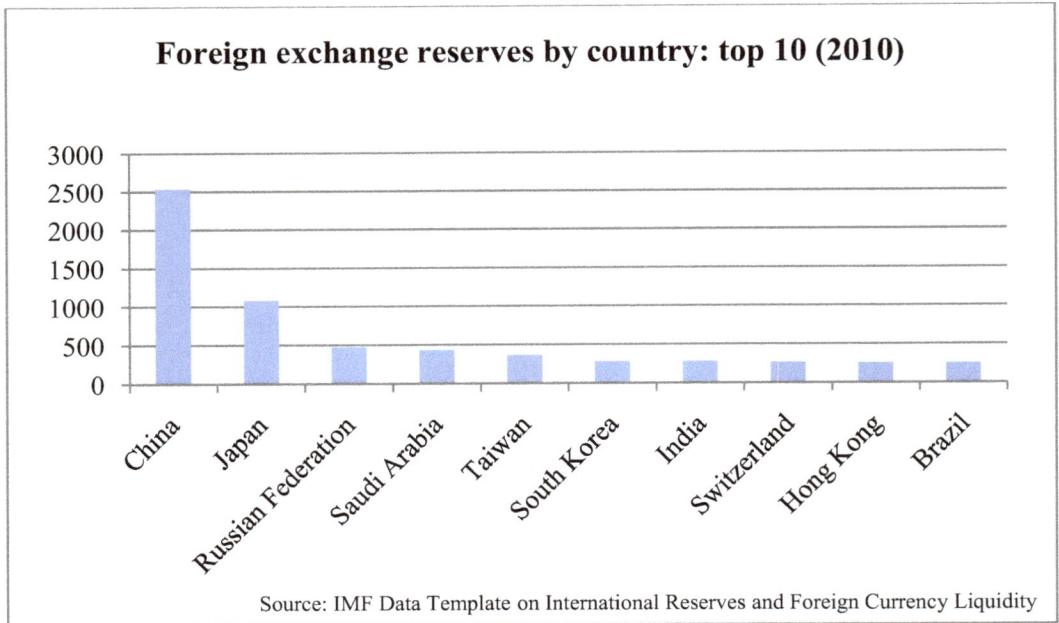

Figure 6. Foreign exchange reserves by country: top ten in 2010

The second reason firms go abroad has its roots in the resource-based view (Fahy, 2002; Penrose, 1995; Wernerfelt, 1984). **Supply oriented internationalization motives** involve a firm's desire to access rare or expensive raw materials; qualified, motivated, and cost efficient human capital; and other valuable resources such as brands, distribution channels, patents, and managerial know-how. These resources sometimes are only available in the target region or, alternatively, seem to be more attractive for cost or quality reasons there, in comparison with the home country. In light of faster technology and product life cycles and knowledge-intensive industries, knowledge-specific factors, such as educated labor forces in the region, R&D center intensity, science and education networks, and linkages between universities and firms, become the focus of management. Firms can make use of liberalized trade patterns and foreign direct investment opportunities, allowing them to supplement their existing technologies and manufacturing processes by expanding internationally to gain access to rare and new knowledge (Chidlow et al., 2009). Newly upcoming technologies, such as data storage and exchange, along with advanced hardware and software information systems help to take advantage of real-time communication with the firm's own entities, suppliers, and customers abroad. Keillor et al. (2001) found empirical evidence that firms, when faced with trade barriers, tend to prefer foreign direct investments (e.g., local manufacturing) in foreign target markets as a viable alternative for successful internationalization instead of contractual relations such as exports.

The case: Nokia to refocus its Japanese operations

November 27, 2008 – Nokia Press Services, Tags: Japan

As part of its effort to sharpen its business focus and priorities, Nokia will discontinue mobile device sales and marketing activities in Japan. These plans will impact approximately 10 percent of Nokia's Japanese employees. Nokia's substantial global R&D and sourcing operations in Japan will continue unaffected. 'In the current global economic climate, we have concluded that the continuation of our investment in Japan-specific product variants is no longer sustainable', said Timo Ihamuotila, executive vice president of Nokia. In Japan, Nokia has an important R&D center, which plays an integral part in Nokia's global product development. These global R&D activities will continue unchanged. Nokia will also continue its significant sourcing activities in Japan. Japanese manufacturers are important partners who play a critical role in Nokia's global supply-chain strategy and with whom Nokia continues to develop its world-class logistics operations. Vertu, Nokia's exclusive line of handcrafted mobile phones, will continue operations in Japan.

Source: Nokia (2008)

The third motive that explains why firms internationalize, called the **follow the customer phenomenon,** has simultaneously arisen in light of globalized supply, manufacturing, and distribution chains (Samiee, 2006). Enterprises often do not independently and autonomously make internationalization decisions because they are integrated in network grids with customers, suppliers, and other stakeholders. Against the background of worldwide integrated value-added chains, a trend is visible in which suppliers are increasingly forced to follow their customers abroad. For example, in 2007, the Japanese consumer electronics giant Sharp started the manufacture of Liquid Crystal Display (LCD) modules near the city of Torun in Poland. The Sharp factory is located in the industrial 'Crystal Park', where Sharp's supplier firms from Japan, such as Sumika Electronic Materials, Tensho Corporation, U-Tec, Sohbi Craft, and Kimoto, established their manufacturing facilities (Repetzki, 2010). Analogous to the follow the customer phenomenon, is the **follow the competitor phenomenon** because firms are embedded in networks. A network is an industrial system of relationships among independent organizations. The industrial system is composed of firms indirectly and directly engaged with other entities, including competitors, which results in mutual interdependencies of the involved participants (Johanson and Mattsson, 1988; Ritter et al., 2004). For example, a competitor's movement to a promising target country for procurement, sales, and/or manufacturing reasons may force a firm to follow its competitor in order to realize economies of scale and/or strategic market positioning (e.g., brand building, product penetration) opportunities. In particular, integration in regional industry clusters, instead of manufacturing alone, provides several competitive advantages as the example of the automotive industry illustrates.

The case: Automotive Cluster – Slovakia

The cluster consists of independent regionally interconnected companies that are competitors; but at in same time, they need to solve similar problems like education of employees, cooperation with R&D institutions, and logistics and supplier access. Through cooperation in these fields, they can solve the problems more easily and quickly, which provides them various competitive advantages. Three global car manufacturers – VW, PSA, and KIA – are engaged in manufacturing in Slovakia in addition to more than 240 automotive industry supplier firms. The Slovakian automotive cluster is co-funded by the South East Europe program and the European Union. The project brings together universities, R&D institutions, small and medium-sized firms, and support from the European Union in order to prepare and create the first automotive network in Southeast Europe.

Source: Autoclusters European Union (2010)

The fourth internationalization motive, **financial resources**, considers firm-level financial characteristics that influence the probability of undertaking internationalization activities. Nations provide through their political-legal and infrastructure environment, and different market attractiveness divergent incentives for investments in their countries. The United Kingdom and France hold the leading position among the European countries with the highest accumulated foreign direct investment (FDI) stock (inward). The U.S. both attracts the most investment inflows from abroad and runs the highest accumulated FDI (inward) stock compared with all other nations wordwide. China is ranked second and has currently the highest investment inflows from abroad behind the U.S. (UNCTAD, 2009; UNCTAD, 2010). An overview of the countries' ranking is provided in Figures 7 and 8.

Foreign direct investment flows (inward) by country in 2009

■ billion US dollars

Source: UNCTADStat (2010)

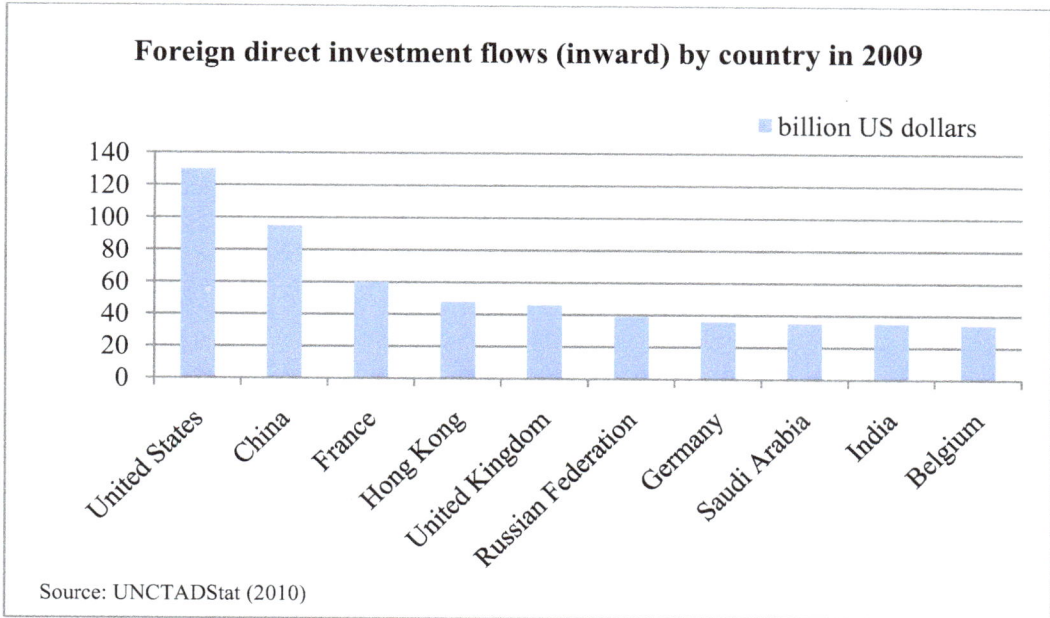

Figure 7. Foreign direct investment flows (inward) in 2009 by country

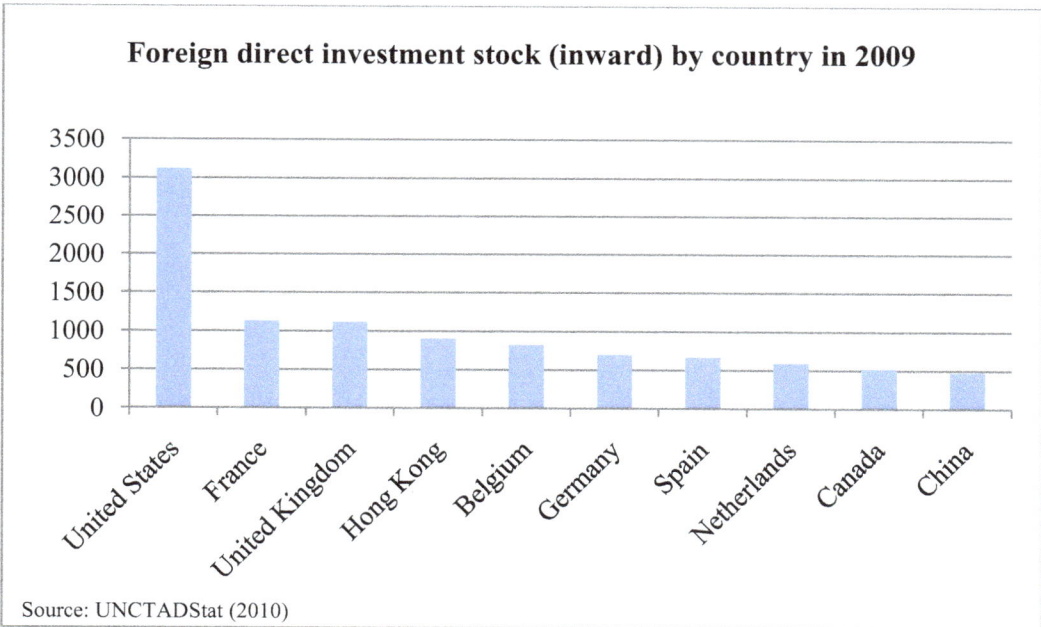

Foreign direct investment stock (inward) by country in 2009

Source: UNCTADStat (2010)

Figure 8. Foreign direct investment stock (FDI inward) in 2009 by country

A firm is more likely to engage abroad when it has access to competitively priced equity and debt; when it has cross-listed its stock in a larger, more liquid equity market; when it enjoys a strong investment grade credit ranking; and when it is able to negotiate reduced taxation and/or attract subsidies in the foreign market. Thus, financial assets are not a 'by-product' of a firm's competitive strength. 'Financial characteristics and proactive financial strategies make a significant contribution towards understanding the decision to make a foreign direct investment' (Forssbaek and Oxelheim, 2008: 640). The major five internationalization motives: demand oriented, supply oriented, follow the customer, follow the competitor, and financial resources, as discussed in the sections above, are summarized and illustrated below.

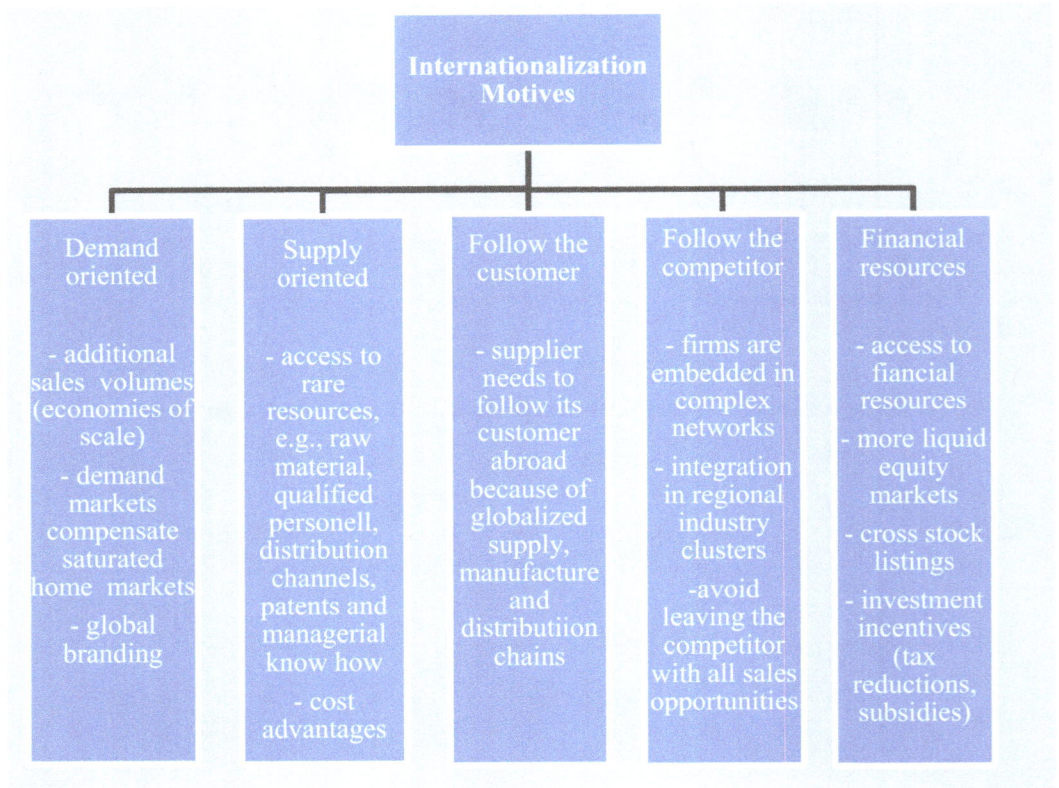

Figure 9. Firm motives for internationalization of a business

International business is not necessarily a forward directed, successful, and linear approach as claimed in traditional internationalization models (Johanson and Vahlne, 1977; Luostarinen, 1980). The complexity of competition amplifies and increases the threat of being logged out of the market, as some firms experienced to their regret. Traditional firms doing business for decades went bankrupt or have been sold (e.g., Volvo, Grundig). Flexible organizations, where the importance of the human factor concerning both the employees and customers is highlighted, should drive the firm culture, which thus provides major potentials for competitive advantage in the global market place. As a consequence, searching for multi-lingual, qualified, loyal, life-long, educated, and motivated personnel (who often value the work atmosphere, intellectual challenges, and work-life balance more than pure monetary incentives), serve as the major challenge for firms engaged in international business, particularly in knowledge-intense industries.

1.3   Impacts on international marketing management

Decades ago, marketing was often seen mainly as advertising a firm's products, finding customers to buy these products at favorable prices, and building suitable and effective distribution channels. However, marketing is a much broader discipline than just selling products; it also encompasses the entire company's market orientation toward its customers and the firms overall competitive environment. In other words, marketing strategies require careful attention to both customers and competitors (Özsomer and Simonin, 1999). Marketing is essentially a creative corporate activity involving the planning and execution of the conception; pricing; promotion; and distribution of ideas, products, and services in an exchange that not only satisfies customers' current needs but also anticipates and creates their future needs (Kotabe and Helsen, 2008). In the long run, a firm gains considerable advantage if its marketing policy is able to balance the corporate social responsibility (society's profits) and the firm's monetary targets (individual firm profits). International trade patterns, relatively unrestricted movement and activities of competitors as well as advanced data storage and communication technologies have resulted in a tremendous increase of marketing complexity in recent decades. As a result, firms' marketing activities have grown from managing pure marketing mix instruments towards interdisciplinary aspects (e.g., technology, ecology, logistics, culture, and psychology).

As a consequence, **international marketing management** includes activities such as permanent scanning of the firm's macro and micro environment, systematic marketing planning, strategy formulation, implementation, and control of marketing activities against the background of worldwide competitive forces that change on a daily basis. Instead of an internal firm perspective, modern marketing philosophy takes the **customer network perspective**. Managing **customer relationships** in turn is the core focus of marketing. There is an interaction between the firm and the customers, as well as relationships among the customers themselves and among customers and **competitors**. Marketing staff have to value the term *relationship* as the key. Marketing efforts are built on each other; and, therefore, a product, service, and the marketers' efforts have to be seen as connected. Marketers should consider any action under the prism 'are customers better off?' (Czinkota and Ronkainen, 2007: 17) and 'how do our competitors serve the customers?'

The successful firm needs to foster **network marketing** activities that consider, in addition to the customers and competitors, diversified interests of shareholders and stakeholders in various countries. While in the past many firms often relied on exporting only, globalized trade patterns provide interesting alternatives for suitable market entry and penetration strategies in foreign markets, including international joint ventures and foreign manufacture. As a consequence, the challenges for marketing executives in their daily jobs have increased and include, among others, lobbying and fostering of network relationships with the firm's stakeholders.

Targeting the highest production outputs, lowest material procurement prices, efficient manufacturing, and flat organization hierarchies are undoubtedly important but become meaningless if the firm makes a product not needed by the market. For that reason, the **marketing driven company**, understood as a firm philosophy rather than as a single marketing tool, moves the **customer** into the center of the firm's interest. Marketing driven means creating a product or service in accordance with the customers' wishes instead of reacting in accordance with the mainstream of competitors in the market. Consequently, the firm's management focuses on a planned and coordinated combination of a marketing mix where the customer needs serve as the major focus of all activities. The marketing driven enterprise integrates the customer into its organizational culture. The management emphasizes striving to create and maintain a solid relationship between the firm, the customer, and the whole company environment (Albaum et al., 2008). Similarly, Czinkota and Kotabe (2005: 4-5) define marketing as an 'organizational function and a set of processes for creating, communicating, delivering, and maintaining value streams to customers and for managing customer relationships in ways that benefit the organization, its stakeholders, and society in the context of a global environment'.

The **marketing scope** expands if the firm procures international business activities. In general, there are four levels of marketing that depend on the firm's degree of involvement in the international market place.

- **Import and export marketing** describes the process whereby the firm engages in purchase activities from foreign areas and/or sells its products and services across national/political boundaries. Products sold in the home and foreign target markets do not differ significantly.
- **International marketing** includes activities in more than one country, where the firm procures international business and engages in activities such as the adaptation of product features and communication policies according to local market requirements (e.g., customer design expectations).
- **Multinational marketing** takes place when all marketing activities are executed by the firm's subsidiary in each and every foreign market; and as a result, different products are set up by the firm's subsidiaries and launched in the markets.
- **Global marketing** represents the most complex level, where the whole organization simultaneously focuses on the suitable selection and exploitation of global marketing instruments and marshals resources around the globe with the objective of achieving global competitive advantage. Global marketing includes standardizing marketing programs across different countries particularly with respect to product offerings, promotion, price, and distribution policy. There are economies of scale effects that usually come along with the benefits of a global brand building. Global integration helps to reduce cost inefficiencies and duplication of efforts among the firm's home market and international target markets (Doole and Lowe, 2008; Kotabe and Helsen, 2008).

These marketing levels do not necessarily reflect a sequence of development that indicates whether a firm is internationally more or less successful. Smaller firms can efficiently procure export business for the entire time of their international activity. In the case of export marketing, executives focus on appropriate pricing and payment security instruments, such as letters of credit. The receipt of customer payments in time is of vital importance, particularly for smaller firms. Due to their limited resources in comparison to large multinationals, multinational marketing or global brand building may not make sense.

Multinational firms do not rely on international trading only. They procure cross-border business activities including assets in diversified countries allowing them to take advantage of internalization of value-added activities and regional environmental supply and demand opportunities (Drori et al., 2006; Dunning, 2000). For multinationals involved in various business activities in regionally diversified markets, the organization of business and marketing management are more complex. The firm's overall strategic predispositions have an impact on its management and marketing philosophy. The 'ethnocentric-polycentric-regiocentric-geocentric' (E.P.R.G) model, originally set forth by Perlmutter (1969), categorizes four dimensions of the firm's internationalization paths. The ethnocentric firm philosophy (type of governance: top down) emphasizes the cultural superiority of the parent firm's country (Kotabe and Helsen, 2008; Wind et al., 1973). The local management consists of expatriates sent by headquarters, and management procedures are transferred from the head office and imposed on regional subsidiaries. Product, price, communication, and distribution policies are taken over from headquarters without modification and implemented in foreign target markets. The polycentric approach (type of governance: bottom up, each local unit sets objectives) recommends behavioral adaptation to regional market circumstances and cultural norms, which results in different organization designs, procedural norms, and reward systems. The mix of marketing activities such as products and services (e.g., design, features), pricing policies, distribution (place), and promotion (e.g., customer loyalty programs) are adjusted in order to better meet local customer requirements. The regiocentric approach (type of governance: mutually negotiated between the regions) emphasizes, due to political-legal or socio-cultural reasons, the existence of diverse regional markets. Trading blocs tend to favor local firms within one region and disfavor those outside, for example through tariff and non-tariff barriers (Doole and Lowe, 2008). Thus manufacturing and administration, such as marketing activities, are individually and locally developed and implemented, according to regionally diversified market conditions. Finally, geocentric firms (type of governance: mutually negotiated within the whole organization) emphasize equal sharing of decision power and responsibility between headquarters and subsidiaries. Management is promoted according to ability rather than nationality (Rugman and Collinson, 2009).

Reflecting Perlmutter (1969), Bartlett and Ghoshal (1990; 1998) developed strategic alternatives. The appropriateness of each strategy varies and depends on the extent of pressure for cost reductions and local responsiveness (Hill, 2009; Welge and Holtbrügge, 2010).

• International strategy: domestic products sold globally with only minimal local customizing, e.g., differing periods of guarantee after purchase.

- **Global standardization strategy**: cost reductions through economies of scale achieved by manufacture of widely standardized products, similar methods of promotion, and selection of distribution channels.
- **Localization strategy**: increasing profitability by local customizing of products (e.g., quality, design, service) and regionally diversified communication.
- **Transnational strategies**: realizes the simultaneous combination of local responsiveness and cost reductions through economies of scale and resource and internalization advantages within the global organization of an MNE.

The concept of transnational strategies describes how to effectively and simultaneously organize resource allocation in diversified regions around the globe where the MNE procures business activities. Company units spread around the world mutually exchange managerial knowledge and market information, capital, raw materials, and other resources. Standardization effects within the organization are intentionally not the primary goal. The transnational concept claims that diversified resource strengths and the corresponding resource exchange within the organization provide the basis for competitive advantages (Ghoshal, 1987; Holtbrügge and Welge, 2010). However, the concept tends to ignore the 'human factor', such as the instinct for self preservation or even resource egotism of the local management, which may hesitate to supply valuable knowledge, for example because of individual career opportunities. 'Local patriotism' increases, particularly in times of crisis when sales figures are falling and profits turn to losses. Consider a situation where two geographically independent manufacturing plants are running accumulated overcapacities; and, therefore, the top management considers shutting down one of these plants. Under such circumstances, the voluntary transfer of strategic resources by the local management is just an unrealistic ideal.

1.4   Marketing as planning

Marketing planning is a systematized way of relating developments in future markets. It allows better management of the effects of often uncontrollable elements of a firm's external environment on the firm's business objectives. Planning is a commitment of resources used to realize the firm's targets. Marketing planning refers to, among other things, the formulation of marketing goals such as turnover, profit per product, number of current and new customers, new product launches, market penetration and entry strategies for new markets, and methods of accomplishing these objectives in a given period of time. A marketing plan commits resources to products and markets to strengthen the firm's competitive position. The plan must blend the permanent changing parameters of external international market environments with internal corporate objectives and capabilities in order to develop efficient and contemporary marketing programs (Cateora et al., 2009).

The more the firm is involved in international business in diversified markets the higher the complexity of environmental impacts stemming from economic and political forces. Simultaneously, challenges for international marketing managers concerning socio-cultural sensitivity in diverse cultural areas and accelerated time for market responses have increased. Marketing managers, having analyzed the characteristics of the foreign target market(s), are in a position to specify the mix, or the **four Ps** (product, price, place, and promotion) of suitable marketing variables that will best suit local customer needs (Perreault and McCarthy, 2005).

Product policy contains these elements.

- Core product: product range, application, new innovation, market run out, model variation, quality, design, functionality, life-cycle, and product durability

- Service: packaging, delivery and payment terms, warranty periods, recycling service, readability and understanding of manuals, eventual product training

Pricing policy determines the cost of the product to the customer, including manufacturing costs, delivery, service and warranties, and sales margins. Rebates and discounts include the seasonal, cash, and quantity allowances granted to the order. Pricing is the only revenue-generating element of the marketing mix (Czinkota and Ronkainen, 2007). Marketing managers when doing price quotations segmented by customer groups should pay attention to a reasonable level of complexity and transparency of price offerings so that price quotations, rebates, and discounts are understandable (Homburg and Krohmer, 2009). The scope of benefits granted should be explicitly communicated between supplier and customer prior to a contract signature so in the future the customer can take advantage of the agreement within the time frame previously agreed to with the supplier.

Distribution policy contains such essentials as the point of sales, terms of delivery (e.g., International Commercial Terms), and the selection of appropriate distribution channels. Commodity products targeting mass markets might preferably be sold through superstores and the Internet. On the other hand, technically complex products that are in need of an explanation, premium, and individually manufactured products are better sold through retail and specialized stores. Product branding is the essential part of **promotion**. Brand building is complex and demanding, and necessarily takes a long-term perspective. Conversely, quality problems usually cause immediate damage to the product brand and the firm's reputation. Marketing people should keep in mind that it takes years to build up a brand that can, however, be easily destroyed over night. Marketing executives in accordance with the overall firm strategy and culture select suitable advertising methods that include the selection of media. Advertising can focus on price and product attributes or, alternatively, on image building campaigns. Promotion refers to the kind, availability, and competence of sales efforts as well as the after sale service.

The **marketing process** consists of four stages: analysis, planning, implementation, and control. **Analysis** involves the data collection, using quantitative and qualitative marketing research techniques. The marketing manager, through the information collected, can better consider external opportunities and threats (market chances) and internal strengths and weaknesses (firm resources). The top management of the firm relies on the efforts and competence of the marketing department, selecting suitable marketing mix combinations in order to gain a competitive advantage. Planning refers to long-term marketing strategies and short-term tactics developed in order to exploit particular market opportunities based on a marketer's prior situation analysis. Implementation includes all activities to determine marketing efforts regarding the product, price, distribution, and promotion policy for the target markets. Marketing plans have to consider expected and difficult foreseeable changes within the firm and external environmental forces. Flexibility and reliable and updated market information allow for changes to occur in implementing the plans. Therefore, marketing control mechanisms are installed to permanently monitor external environmental and internal firm resource changes. Short-term control tools include continuously reviewing the weekly, monthly, and annual sales plans and comparing sales records with sales targets, price, and profitability control. Long-term control is achieved by company-wide or functional audits in order to make sure that marketing not only is doing things right but also is doing the right things. Control outcomes (e.g., sales records versus plans, pre-stage planning failures) provide valuable input for the subsequent planning activities of the marketing department (Czinkota and Ronkainen, 2007). R&D spending mirrored in a high number of patents is just one way to gain competitive advantage. Primarily, the speed of market launches of newly developed products and the time spent reacting to market changes are the keys to competitive advantages in the global arena. Efficient and updated market research supplying reliable and updated market information is crucial for effective marketing planning.

List of References

Albaum, G., Duerr, E. & Strandskov, J., 2008. *International marketing and export management.* Essex: Pearson Education Limited.

Bartlett, C. A. & Ghoshal, S., 1990. *Internationale Unternehmensführung. Innovation, globale Effizienz, differenziertes Marketing.* Frankfurt: Campus.

Bartlett, C. A. & Ghoshal, S., 1998. *Managing across borders: the transnational solution.* Boston: Harvard Press.

Cateora, P. R., Gilly, M. C. & Graham, J. L., 2009. *International Marketing.* Boston: McGraw-Hill Irwin.

Chidlow, A., Salciuviene, L. & Young, S., 2009. Regional determinants of inward FDI distribution in Poland. *International Business Review*, 18: 119-133.

Czinkota, M. R. & Kotabe, M., 2005. *Marketing management.* Cincinnati: Atomic Dog Publishing.

Czinkota, M. R. & Ronkainen, I. A., 2007. *International marketing.* Mason, OH: Thomson Higher education.

Doole, I. & Lowe, R., 2008. *International marketing strategy. Analysis, development and implementation.* London: South-Western Cengage Learning.

Drori, G. S., Meyer, J. W. & Hwang, H., 2006. *Globalization and organization.* Oxford: Oxford University Press.

Dunning, J. H., 2000. The eclectic paradigm as an envelope for economic and business theories of MNE activity. *International Business Review*, 9 (2): 163-190.

Eu_Commission, 2010. The Doha round [online]. [cited 04.10.2010]. Available from World Wide Web:<URL:http://ec.europa.eu/trade/creating-opportunities/eu-and-wto/doha/>.

Fahy, J., 2002. A resource-based analysis of sustainable competitive advantage in a global environment. *International Business Review*, 11: 57-78.

Forssbaek, J. & Oxelheim, L., 2008. Finance-specific factors as drivers of cross-border investment. An empirical investigation. *International Business Review*, 17: 630-641.

Ghoshal, S., 1987. Global strategy: an organizing framework. *Strategic Management Journal*, 8: 425-440.

Hill, C. W. L., 2009. *International business: competing in the global marketplace*. Boston: McGraw-Hill/Irwin.

Holtbrügge, D. & Welge, M. K., 2010. *Internationales Management. Theorien, Funktionen, Fallstudien*. Stuttgart: Schäffer-Poeschel.

Homburg, C. & Krohmer, H., 2009. *Marketingmanagement: Strategie – Instrumente – Umsetzung – Unternehmensführung*. Wiesbaden: Gabler.

Imf, 2010. Time series data on international reserves and foreign currency liquidity official reserve assets and other foreign currency assets [online].[cited 07.11.2010]. Available from World Wide Web: <http://www.imf.org/external/np/sta/ir/IRProcessWeb/data/802P816.pdf>.

Johanson, J. & Mattsson, L.-G., 1988. Internationalization in industrial systems – a network approach. In Hood, N. & Vahlne, J.-E. (Eds.) *Strategies in global competition*: 468-486, New York: Croom Helm.

Johanson, J. & Vahlne, J.-E., 1977. The internationalization process of the firm - a model of knowledge development and increasing foreign market commitments. *Journal of International Business Studies*, 8 (1): 23-32.

Keillor, B., Davila, V. & Hult, T. G., 2001. Market entry strategies and influencing factors: a multi-industry/multi product investigation. *The Marketing Management Journal,* 11: 1-11.

Kotabe, M. & Helsen, K., 2008. *Global marketing management*. Hoboken, NJ: John Wiley & Sons.

Luostarinen, R., 1980. *Internationalization of the firm. An empirical study of the internationalization of firms with small and open domestic markets with special emphasis on lateral rigidity as a behavioral characteristic in strategic decision-making*. Helsinki: The Helsinki School of Economics.

Nokia, 2008. Nokia to refocus its Japanese operations [online]. [cited 15.07.2010]. *Nokia Press Services*. Available from World Wide Web:URL:http://pressbulletinboard.nokia.com/tag/japan/.

Özsomer, A. & Simonin, B., 1999. Antecedents and consequences of market orientation in a subsidiary context. Enhancing knowledge development in marketing. *American marketing association educators proceedings, Summer 1999*.

Penrose, E., 1995. *The theory of the growth of the firm*. New York [first published 1959]: Oxford University Press.

Perlmutter, H. V., 1969. The tortuous evolution of the multinational corporation. *Columbia Journal of World Business*, 4: 9-18.

Perreault, W. & Mccarthy, E. J., 2005. *Basic marketing. A global marketing approach*. Burr Ridge: McGraw-Hill.

Repetzki, B., 2010. Germany Trade and Invest. Polen kaufen mehr Haus-, Audio- und Videogeräte [online]. [cited 18.07.2010]. Available from World Wide Web:<URL:http://www.gtai.de/fdb-SE,MKT200710238001,MSN.html>.

Ritter, T., Wilkinson, I. F. & Johnston, W. J., 2004. Managing in complex business networks. *Industrial Marketing Management*, 33: 175-183.

Rugman, A. M. & Collinson, S., 2009. *International business*. Essex: Pearson Education Limited.

Samiee, S., 2006. Supplier and customer exchange in international industrial markets: an integrative perspective. *Industrial Marketing Management*, 35: 589-599.

Unctad, 2009. United Nations Conference on Trade and Development - Statistics [online]. [cited 17.8.2009]. Available from World Wide Web:<URL:http://www.unctad.org/sections/dite_fdistat/docs/wid_cp_hu_en.pdf>.

Unctad, 2010. Inward and outward foreign direct investment stock, annual, 1980-2009 [online]. [cited 12.12.2010]. Available from World Wide Web: <www.http://unctadstat.unctad.org>.

Union, A. E., 2010. Automotive Cluster - West Slovakia [online]. [cited 18.07.2010]. Available from World Wide Web:<URL:http://www.autoclusters.eu/index.php/partner/127-automotive-cluster-west-slovakia>.

Welge, K. M. & Holtbrügge, D., 2010. *Internationales Management*. Stuttgart: Schäffer-Poeschel Verlag.

Wernerfelt, B., 1984. A resource based view of the firm. *Strategic Management Journal*: 5 (2): 171-180.

Wind, Y., Douglas, S. P. & Perlmuttter, H. V., 1973. Guidelines for developing international marketing strategies. *Journal of Marketing*, 37 (2): 38-46.

Wto, 2010a. Understanding the WTO: The GATT years from Havana to Marrakesh [online]. [cited: 05.10.2010]. Available from World Wide Web:<URL:http://www.wto.org/english/thewto_e/whatis_e/tif_e/fact4_e.htm>.

Wto, 2010b. *World trade report*. Geneva.

2 Chapter: Corporate social responsibility in light of internationalization

- Describe the concepts and strategies of Corporate Social Responsibility.

- Identify the role of mission in building corporate identity of companies in the international market.

- Explain the ethical aspects of companies' activities in the international market.

- Point out the benefits and losses from compliance with consumers' rights by companies in the international market.

- Present the consumer protection models in Europe.

2.1   Corporate social responsibility concept

In the contemporary global economy, one can observe a growing interest among companies (especially the ones operating in the international market) in the problem of **Corporate Social Responsibility (CSR)**. The popularity of the issue is mainly demonstrated through a variety of social initiatives undertaken by an increasing number of companies that, while entering foreign markets, try to coax local communities into using their own brand. These social initiatives are pursued on the basis of mutual benefits, i.e., provision of help to beneficiaries of such programs and achievement of corporate gains through a positive consumer reaction (Smith, 2003). Nonetheless, in practical terms, there are only a few social programs that evoke positive consumer responses (Sen and Bhattacharaya, 2001). Moreover, some of them prove to have a harmful effect on the corporate operation (Yoon, 2003; Yoon and Gurhan-Canli, 2003). The concept of corporate social responsibility has been given a great number and variety of definitions (e.g., Davis, 1960; Friedman, 1970; Fitch, 1976; Carroll, 1979; Zenisek, 1979; Frederick, 1986; Epstein, 1987; McWilliams and Siegel, 2001; Schwartz and Carroll, 2003; Kotler and Lee, 2005) developed during more than fifty years of scientific research (De Bekker et al., 2005). Unfortunately, this multitude of definitions makes the concept of social corporate responsibility quite ambiguous and vague (Vogel, 2005). Therefore, in order to clearly present the nature of CSR, it is necessary to focus on several characteristic definitions of the concept in the order in which they were developed.

The first modern definition of corporate social responsibility was elaborated in 1953 by R. Bowen (Garriga and Mele, 2004), who concluded that social responsibility refers to a businessman's duties, particularly when conducting corporate policy, making decisions, and pursuing activities that are desirable in terms of social values and goals (Carroll, 1999). It is noteworthy that this definition integrates social responsibility into the processes and decisions of managers as individual workers. Thus, social responsibility directly refers to a concrete group of people, to the corporate management, but not to the corporation considered as a whole. R. Bowen maintains that corporate decisions and activities should take certain values and social goals into account (Stieb, 2001). This precursor of the modern approach to the concept of corporate social responsibility clearly highlights the fact that consequences of managerial decisions are measured not only in terms of corporate gain or loss. A similar idea of corporate social responsibility has been proposed by Davis (1960), who has pointed out that CSR refers to certain processes that take place in a company. In his CSR concept, corporate activities and decisions should be undertaken, at least partly, for reasons that go beyond direct economic and technical interests. In addition, Davis (1960) relates the range of social responsibility of companies to their social power and points to consequences of insufficient corporate responsibility in the so-called **Iron Law of Responsibility**, which says that those who do not take responsibility in proportion to their power, are doomed to lose it in the end (Davis, 1967). Later, the same scientist demonstrates that concrete benefits are gained and costs borne for companies as a result of their practical application of the idea of social responsibility (Davis, 1973).

According to Frederick (1986), CSR implies that it is necessary to supervise the working of the economic system in a way that can guarantee fulfillment of social expectations. Consequently, the use of economic production factors should ensure enhancement of socio-economic welfare through production and distribution. Furthermore, Frederick (1986) strongly emphasizes that the manner of allocating production factors should not exclusively serve the narrow interests of individual people and companies. While defining the concept of corporate social responsibility, it is necessary to mention the figure of Friedman (1970), who postulated that the only duty of a company towards society is to increase its profits within a legal framework, an idea contrary to most CSR concepts. It is also worth mentioning the definition of CSR developed by Johnson (1971), who has written that a company can be considered socially responsible when its management balances various interests (Zasuwa, 2009). Instead of concentrating solely on the growth of profits for its shareholders, a responsible company also takes note of its employees, suppliers, recipients, the social community, and the society. Compared to earlier definitions, Johnson's approach focuses on corporate responsibility towards definite interest groups. This idea was further developed by, among others, Freeman and Clarkson in the so-called theory of stakeholders (Zasuwa, 2009).

Within the last several years as well as in previous years, scientists have been emphasizing the existence of corporate freedom in solving social problems. One of the latest definitions says that social responsibility refers to activities undertaken for social sake, reaching beyond corporate interests and beyond the requirements of the legal framework (McWilliams and Siegel, 2001). A similar definition has been proposed by Kotler and Lee (2005), who stated that social responsibility constitutes a commitment to improve societal welfare through discretionary business activities and corporate financial support.

Last, but not least, it is worth noting a proposed CSR definition in the European Union (EU) document, 'Promoting a European Framework for Corporate Social Responsibility. Green Paper'. In this work, it has been assumed that being socially responsible means not only fulfilling legal expectations, but investing 'more' into human capital, the environment, and the relations with stakeholders (European Commission, 2001). One can observe that the EU definition of CSR has been derived from earlier concepts, and CSR relates to activities that go far beyond legal requirements. It focuses on three major areas that should be of special corporate interest: human capital, the natural environment, and relations with stakeholders. Additionally, it is noteworthy that expenses for social responsibility are treated as investments. It should be emphasized that the EU document clearly states that social responsibility should also be promoted in small and medium-sized companies, as they make the greatest contribution to the modern economy (European Commission, 2001). This focus on the application of the principle of social responsibility by small and medium-sized companies seems especially interesting and valuable, since previously CSR had referred to the sector of 'big companies' – i.e., international corporations.

In the endeavor to characterize the concept of social responsibility, it is necessary to concentrate on its different types. An interesting and popular approach to this concept has been put forward by Carroll (1979), who has maintained that a company bears economic, legal, ethical, and discretionary responsibility. The economic responsibility consists in conducting a business activity with a profit, but the profit itself is not of prior importance here. The legal responsibility is concerned with the observation of laws in running the day-to-day business. The ethical responsibility, in turn, requires not only fulfilling legal duties, but going beyond this minimum. The last type of responsibility - discretionary responsibility - consists of corporations sharing their resources with society. It is worth emphasizing that the model assumes some hierarchy of responsibility. Consequently, Carroll (1979) leaves no doubt as to the hierarchy of corporate duties, saying that more than anything else, companies constitute a basic economic unit in our society, and as such are committed to producing goods and services that are necessary for the society and to selling them at a profit. All other corporate roles are based on this fundamental assumption. Similar significance is given to legal responsibility, which should also be demanded of a company. Next in the hierarchy, there is ethical responsibility, which is expected of companies, and discretionary responsibility, which is socially desired. The hierarchy of CSR types reveals the existence of certain levels of social responsibility (Zasuwa, 2009).

The classification of the types of social responsibility presented above is strictly of a theoretical character, which produces some difficulties in research on real corporate activities and which provokes some critical voices (Clarkson, 1995). Due to these imperfections, Carroll and Schwartz (2003) developed a new CSR model, which, unlike the previous concept, assumes a division of social responsibility into three areas: economic, legal, and ethical. The philanthropic responsibility, previously classified as a separate unit, has been incorporated into the economic or the ethical responsibility. Researchers utilizing the new version in contrast to the previous one leave out the assumption of a hierarchy of social responsibility, arguing that, in real terms, the importance of the three areas may vary. Thus, this model may be more easily employed in the description of actual corporate behavior (Schwartz and Carroll, 1995).

The concept of CSR is evolving. In its contemporary approach, it goes back to the 1950s and 1960s (Epstein, 1987). During this period, scientific attention was mainly concentrated on the character and range of corporate responsibility to the society (Wood, 1991a). Consecutive stages of CSR development were concerned with researchers' interests in the ways of implementing the concept in economic practice. It is assumed that these stages comprise social corporate responsiveness, social justice, and social corporate performance (Windsor, 2001; Waddock, 2004). The idea of CSR had its beginnings in 1970 and, as the term implies, is connected to the company's response to social needs (De Bekker et al., 2005). According to Epstein (1987), corporate social responsiveness as a practical matter refers to the development of an organizational process of the decision-making tasks of predicting, responding, and managing all consequences of corporate policy and corporate operation. In this and other approaches, the very essence of corporate social responsiveness is revealed in a set of definite corporate decision-making processes relating to social issues (e.g., Frederick et al., 1992; Wood, 1991a; Ackerman, 1973).

Corporate response to certain social issues may take different forms, from abstaining from resolving social problems to undertaking activities that prevent them. There are four main strategies of corporate responsiveness: reactive, defensive, adaptive, and proactive (Carroll, 1979). An interesting explanation of these strategies has been proposed by Clarkson (1995), who characterizes the strategies of corporate social responsiveness as focusing on the corporate attitude and on the outcome of corporate activities. Accordingly, the reactive strategy appears only when a company 'denies' its responsibility and 'does' less than is expected of it. In the defensive strategy, a company recognizes its responsibility and fulfills social expectations in a minimum way. The adaptive strategy, in turn, consists of corporate acceptance of its commitments and fulfillment of all requirements. In the proactive strategy, a company takes greater responsibility and undertakes more than is expected of it. Watrick and Cochran (1985) present a similar classification of the four strategies. At this point, it is worth mentioning the fact that this typology covers all the possibilities of potential corporate behavior.

The idea of **Corporate Social Rectitude (CSRc)** represents another stage in the development of the social responsibility of a company (Windsor, 2001; Frederick, 1986; Waddock, 2004). The term, social rectitude, has been proposed by Frederick, who developed the concept in 1986 in response to a growing managerial interest in the issue of business ethics during the 1980s (Waddock, 2004). In the author's opinion, corporate social rectitude refers to the problem of the moral correctness of undertaken activities and the formulated policy of a company (Frederick, 1986). The concept of corporate social rectitude seems to reach deeper than the idea of social responsibility or responsiveness. It combines corporate policy and corporate operation with fundamental moral principles, the sources of which can be found in the Christian religion or in humanism (Frederick, 1986). In practice, companies that are honest assume that ethical concerns are fundamental to the company, and are not merely peripheral; that managers are employed and trained to accept and apply ethical principles in their work; that special analytical tools are employed in order to find, predict, and solve ethical problems; and that companies try to connect their current and future policy to basic values (Frederick, 1994). It seems that on the basis of Frederick and Waddock's views, the concept of corporate social rectitude is synonymous with business ethics.

The concept of **Corporate Social Performance (CSP)** constitutes another stage in the development of the idea of corporate social responsibility (Waddock, 2004; Rybak, 2004) or its alternatives (Carroll, 1999). One of the first proposals for a CSP definition was suggested by A. Carroll (Wartick and Cochran, 1985), who developed a three-dimensional model of corporate social performance. According to this concept, CSP comprises the following components: the type of social responsibility, the subject of a social problem, and the type of corporate responsiveness (Carroll, 1979). Such an approach is a combination of the normative CSR approach, social needs, and corporate responsiveness.

Wartick and Cochran (1985) elaborate on the above model. They indicate that the idea of corporate social responsiveness is revealed in three dimensions: the principle of social responsibility; the process of responding to social and political problems; and the policy, understood as the method of operationalzing corporate responsiveness to social issues. The principles of corporate social responsibility and the ways of responding to social concerns are directly derived from Carroll's model. The third element, the social policy of a company, represents the authors' own contribution and comprises identification of problems, problem analysis, and corporate activities (Wartick and Cochran, 1985).

Another CSP model is a concept elaborated by Wood (1991a). The author defines CSP as a configuration of social principles of corporate social responsibility, processes of social responsiveness, policies, programs, and observable policy results that are connected to corporate social relations (Wood, 1991a). In this approach, the author distinguishes three key elements of CSP: the principle of social responsibility, the process of responsiveness, and the process results. At this point, it should be emphasized that the model of the principle of social responsibility is considered at three levels: the institutional level, referring to the respon-sibility of a company before the society as the whole; the organizational level, connected to corporate responsibility before stakeholders; and finally the individual level, referring to the moral responsibility of managers for their deeds (Wood, 1991a).

The process of corporate social responsiveness involves environmental assessment, man-agement of relations with stakeholders, and the subject of management. The third element of the model focuses on the results of corporate operation, including social influences, social programs, and the corporate social policy (Wood, 1991a). It was assumed that the model created by Wood would help answer the question about the way companies contribute to enhancement of the welfare of society (Wood, 1991c). This would be achieved through de-velopment of a model that could be used as a basis for scientific research and for more effec-tive management of social issues in a corporation (Wood, 1991b). Undoubtedly, this concept has made a significant contribution both to the theory and practice of management of corpo-rate social responsibility. However, it is not free of shortcomings. Swanson (1995) has pointed out some conflicts between the economic and the ethical approaches present in the model, which leads to a situation of 'something for something' and excludes the possibility of harmonious and simultaneous execution of economic and ethical responsibilities that extend far beyond sheer compliance with legal requirements and abstention from harmful practices. The second objection with respect to Wood's model concerns lack of clear norma-tive CSR principles that could be applied in the assessment of management of social issues within a company and its results (Swanson, 1995).

The practical implementation of corporate social responsibility is mainly concerned with undertaking definite social initiatives, defined as corporate activities aimed at supporting social issues and fulfilling commitments of social responsibility (Kotler and Lee, 2005). Corporate social initiatives have a long history. In their early stage, they were connected to the period of industrialization and took place as early as the 19th century. Smith (1994) ob-serves that one of the spectacular examples of pro-social activities was moving Sir Titus Salt's textile factory outside the town of Bradford, which at that time was the world capital of the textile industry and one of the most polluted places in England. Titus Salt set up 'an industrial community' with 850 employee homes, a park, a church, a school, a hospital, and a library. Nonetheless, such activities were rather individual; and there were not many people who followed Salt's lead (Zasuwa, 2009).

The idea of corporate social responsibility started to enjoy greater popularity in the 1960s and 1970s in the U.S. (Vogel, 2005). It was then that the so-called '5 percent clubs' were brought into being. They were made up of companies that donated 5 percent of their pre-tax profit to charities. These expenses were aimed at improving social welfare together with the welfare of the companies functioning within the clubs. In 1970 only one in eight managers recognized such activities as a source of gains for their companies. Such an approach to CSR has been defined in the literature as 'doing good to do good' (Vogel, 2005).

The practice of transferring money from companies to charities had many adversaries, in-cluding Friedman (1970), one of the most famous and fervent opponents of this form of social responsibility. He raised two arguments against CSR. First, he argued that managers are representatives of company owners, and as such are obliged to take care of the interests of the owners. Therefore, they should engage in activities that result in an increase of corporate profits. Donating corporate money for a noble cause is at odds with owners' interests, and managers are not entitled to do this. In Friedman's opinion, if corporate money is to be transferred for a cause, it should be the owners themselves who decide to do this, and not managers. Second, Friedman argues that managers do not have any special knowledge about which social goal is more or less important. In this way, transferring money by companies is not any better than donating by 'ordinary people' (Friedman, 1970). The contemporary approach to the idea of corporate social responsibility seems different from the idea of doing good to do good. According to the expert mentioned above from the London Business School, today a new paradigm of corporate social responsibility has come into existence (Smith, 1994). Based on this paradigm, companies try to do business in such a way as to serve their interests along with the common interests. In this approach, a strong emphasis is placed on the connection between corporate social initiatives and direct benefits (doing good to do well). These benefits include a smaller risk of consumer boycotts, a better reputation, more consumer loyalty, better employee morale, easier access to capital, and lower costs of capital (Vogel, 2005).

The case: Nokia mobile technology and 21st century learning

Nokia and the Pearson Foundation are working together to use the latest mobile and digital technologies to personalize learning and share the results. Using mobile devices and services in new ways is the cornerstone of this strategic partnership. In a rapidly changing world, with constantly developing technology, this kind of training can enable youth aged 11-18 to develop the academic, analytic, and life skills they need to succeed in the society. It does so in a way that encourages participants to think positively about their future and to examine their own life goals and aspirations. In the program students learn how to film, mix, and edit with their mobile devices, but they gain many more skills on top: they learn about collaboration, innovation, problem-solving, systems analysis, project planning, time management, and of course teamwork. In the past, the initiative has also brought this innovative mobile learning program to children with special needs through a residency at Green Chimneys, a world-renowned education centre for children with emotional, behavioral, social, and learning challenges. This initiative is implemented in partnership with The Pearson Foundation, which extends Pearson's commitment to education by partnering with leading nonprofit, civic, and business organizations to provide financial, organizational, and publishing assistance across the globe.

Source: Nokia (2010)

It is noteworthy that corporate involvement in social initiatives is not restricted to temporary provision of financial support or to setting up noble-cause foundations, a practice that used to be popular in the 1960s and 1970s. At present, companies that are leaders in CSR initiate long-term programs directed at solving definite social problems. In addition to financial support for social initiatives, corporations help nonprofit organizations through counseling services and technological or logistical assistance. Such long-term and complex involvement of companies entails engagement on the part of many corporate departments, including marketing, human resources, and finance. These integrated programs are implemented by international corporations such as Johnson & Johnson, Philip Morris, Merck, and Danone (Smith, 1994). Current literature and observation of corporate operations seem to imply that the evolving approach to CSR is similar to the concept of management, e.g., management through quality (Smith, 2003; Kotler and Lee, 2004; Vogel 2005; Cone et al., 2003). From this perspective, expenses for CSR are treated as investments that help improve the competitive position of a company.

Corporate social initiatives present very varied activities. The classification of social initiatives by the subject they refer to, is one of the most obvious typologies and is used by many institutions and included in many publications. One of the most significant typologies has been presented in the so-called Green Paper on CRS (European Commission, 2001). This typology distinguishes some potential areas of pro-social corporate activities. Activities presented in Figure 10 concern the internal structure of an organization and are, to some extent, regulated by law. It was the European Commission's intention to indicate the corporate areas within which companies can make 'pro-social' investments in addition to what is required by law (European Commission, 2001). It is noteworthy that initiatives directed towards the inside of a company are mostly targeted at employees.

subject	examples of activities
human resources	<ul><li>ensuring employee development</li><li>providing information about a company situation</li><li>ensuring proper conditions for reconciliation of work and family duties</li><li>opening career paths for women</li><li>giving fair remuneration</li><li>introducing solutions enabling employees' participation in corporate profits</li></ul>
health and work safety	<ul><li>introducing solutions designed to improve work safety and employee health, especially implementing certified management systems</li></ul>
adaptation to a change	<ul><li>taking into consideration the results of restructuring with respect to the subjects concerned, in particular assisting employees in finding new work after reductions, supporting local labor markets</li></ul>
influence over environment	<ul><li>reducing usable natural resources</li><li>reducing emission of pollutants</li><li>seeking 'win-win' solutions for the company and the environment</li><li>introducing special environmental management systems</li></ul>

Source: European Commission (2001), p. 10

Figure 10. Internal corporate pro-social initiatives

Initiatives concerning the company's environment concentrate on local communities, business partners, human rights, and globalization. Examples of activities within these areas are presented in Figure 11.

subject	examples of activities
involvement in support of a local community	• ensuring work for the local community • providing tax income to local governments • caring about the natural environment of a given local community • organizing charity events • supporting the process of retraining unemployed people • participating in financing local culture and local sport
business partners and consumers	• quoting fair prices in cooperation with business partners • 'equal' treatment of all business partners • ensuring that CSR principles are also observed by sub-contractors – refers mainly to big corporations, • conveying credible information about products to consumers
human rights	• maintaining cooperation exclusively with organizations respecting human rights • respecting human rights in countries where it is not required by law • promoting observation of human rights in third world countries • promoting international work standards
globalization	• promoting CSR ideas by international organizations worldwide • introducing CSR criteria to supply chain management by international organizations

Source: European Commission (2001), p. 11

Figure 11. External corporate pro-social initiatives

A similar classification of corporate social initiatives is used in the U.S. One of the most common typologies has been elaborated by KLD Research & Analytics Inc., an institution that conducts research into CSR issues mostly for institutional investors (Zasuwa, 2009) and is considered to provide the most complex and objective information (Simerly, 2003). In the typology of KLD Research & Analytics Inc., pro-social activities fall into seven categories: community support, corporate governance, diversity, employee relations, environment, human rights, and product. By juxtaposing the EC and KLD classification, one can observe some differences between them. The European typology attaches great importance to employee issues, mostly visible in 'Human resources', 'Health and safety', and 'Adaptation to changes'. In the American classification, the employee issue is dealt with only in one area. One should take note of the fact that employee issues in the KLD classification belong to the 'Diversity' area, and embrace activities concerned with counteracting different types of discrimination. Additionally, the American typology involves the issue of corporate governance, a problem ignored in the European concept.

Corporate social initiatives may take different forms. Kotler and Lee (2005) have elaborated a very interesting classification. The researchers distinguished the following corporate social initiatives: cause promotions, cause-related marketing, corporate social marketing, corporate philanthropy, community volunteering, and socially responsible business practices. Social promotion is an initiative in which a company provides financial means or other resources in order to extend knowledge about and attract public interest to certain social issues. Activities within this area may consist of supporting the process of fund accumulation or seeking volunteers who would be capable of solving specific social problems. The very essence of socially involved marketing is for a company to provide support for a selected social problem that is connected to transactions between consumers and the company that generates profits (Varadarajan and Menon, 1988). Corporate support in this initiative is usually financial and is frequently connected to a price for a concrete product (Kotler and Lee, 2005). In social marketing, companies initiate or run a campaign aimed at changing certain behavior. Such campaigns are designed to improve social health conditions, increase safety levels, improve the condition of the natural environment, or enhance welfare (Kotler and Lee, 2004). Corporate philanthropy is probably the most popular and the oldest social initiative. It consists of direct support to definite charity initiatives or social concerns. This support is most often demonstrated by donating an amount of money or other corporate resources (Kotler and Lee, 2005). Community volunteering is an initiative by which companies create conditions and encourage employees to take on some voluntary work in favor of a nonprofit organization or a local community. Corporate support is most frequently effected by giving time to activities and calculating the activity as part of corporate work time. In such cases, the company's contribution consists of the organization of project teams or the provision of necessary tools and equipment (Kotler and Lee, 2005). Socially responsible business practices involve initiatives where companies undertake voluntary (not required by law) activities aimed at solving certain social issues or at increasing the welfare of a social community or the environment (Kotler and Lee, 2005). Additionally, these initiatives can be directed at solving the problems of employees in a mother company.

Clearly, social initiatives undertaken by companies operating in the international market can be derived from various theories. Their implementation may be both a result of a corporate social responsibility concept and other related theories, such as the Stakeholder Theory (Freeman, 1984; Donaldson and Preston, 1995; Mitchell et al., 1997; Frooman, 1999; Dunham et al., 2006), Corporate Citizenship (Waddell, 2000; Logsdon and Wood, 2002; De Bekker et al., 2005), or Sustainable Development (Gladwin et al., 1995; Aguirre, 2002; Fergus and Rowney, 2005).

2.2 Corporate mission as the basis of CSR in international markets

The **mission statement** is a crucial element of corporate marketing activity in international markets. It is explicit in the formulation of what a company stands for. The corporate mission is the most general expression of a company's goals, intentions, and marketing business. It reveals the enterprise's purpose for existence (Stoner et al., 2001) by defining the current and future domains of business operation. These domains are represented by the company's market, which is approached from two perspectives: the product (object-based market) and the buyer/customer (subject-based market). In contemporary corporate missions, special attention is paid to the second aspect of the corporate activity: target customers, which refers to customers' needs and ways of satisfying those needs (Hirota et al., 2010).

The case: Mission statement of Airbus S.A.S. and Nestle S.A.

Airbus S.A.S.
'Our mission is to create the best and safest aircrafts. Our mission is to meet the needs of airlines and operators by producing the most modern and comprehensive aircraft family on the market, complemented by the highest standard of product support.'

Nestle S.A.
'Nestle's main objective is to provide its customers with long-term benefits through satisfying their needs with regard to food, well-being, and trustworthy quality. We tailor our products to our customers' needs and tastes in over 100 countries. We are willing to listen to our customers' voices (…) and to respect their preferences.'

Source: Airbus S.A.S. (2010); Nestle (2010)

The Western origin of the mission statement concept can be recognized in the definition by C. Bart (1998). A good mission statement captures an organization's unique and enduring reason for being, and energizes stakeholders to pursue common goals. It compels a firm to address questions like the following: 'What is our business? Why do we exist? What are we trying to accomplish?'(Freeman, 1984).

In the literature, some authors identify the mission statement with the corporate vision; others consider the development of the company's mission to be the realization of its vision. For some, the corporate mission is a broader concept than the vision itself (Johnson, 2010). The mission gives the company a general direction; the vision represents the company's future projection (Rossi, 2010). In other words, the company's vision states where the company wants to be sometime in the future. Some companies include a marketing intent in the vision. The vision and the mission should give focus to everyone who is involved with the company, be it directly (e.g., employees) or indirectly (e.g., shareholders).

The company's mission statement should incorporate common moral values. The mission specifies the exceptional sense and purpose for the company's being. Moreover, being of normative character, the mission statement provides a general sense and reason for the company's existence, and indicates the direction of its development. The company's mission defines those fields of corporate activity that a company is able and willing to be involved with. Thus, the mission statement epitomizes the company's aspirations, and endeavors to mark the range of corporate social responsibility, i.e., its social commitment (Skydel, 2010). The mission statements of Polish companies highlight the significance of corporate social responsibility.

company	mission oriented around business and product
Zaklady Azotowe Kedzierzyn SA	'We are a company oriented to a long-term and dynamic value growth through development in every sphere of our activity. Whatever the economic condition, we want our value-added ratio to be higher than that of our competitors. We intend to become a branch leader and the first-choice company for our customers.'
Ciech SA	'We bring value to those sectors of the market segment where we have competencies and where we enjoy a strong and enduring position. Goals: Our goal is to create value for our shareholders through developing a leading position in the regional chemical sector.'
	mission oriented around the customer
Black Red White SA	'Fifteen years ago, right at the beginning of our activity, we decided to produce furniture to meet our Polish customers' needs: good quality at a reasonable price. This motto has been with us until today. As a branch leader, we offer over 800 furniture models. We always keep in mind the most crucial concerns: our customers, their needs, and their financial resources.'
Stalprodukt SA	'Our mission is to satisfy the needs and expectations of all our customers, buyers of cold-steel processing products and of Staleprodukt services.'
	mission oriented on CSR
Arctic Paper Kostrzyn SA	'We are a paper manufacturer providing products that are tailored to our customer needs. Our customer needs are of primary importance; therefore, they determine the direction of our company's development. We want to achieve a strong and stable position among European paper manufacturers through maintaining

	partnership-based relations with our customers and suppliers. The effective management system, business diligence, and productivity ensure our company a competitive position in the market. We motivate our staff members by creating good and safe working conditions and by providing opportunities for personal development. In our endeavor to protect the natural environment, we pursue long-lasting solutions. We consider ourselves to be part of the local community, and we feel committed to providing support for it. Our conduct is based on ethical norms.'
Kronopol Sp. z o.o.	'The principal philosophy of Swiss Krono Group is based on the conviction that only environmentally safe and friendly products bring benefit to people. As conservation of the environment is the crucial element of our corporate policy, investments in production are accompanied by investments in environmental protection. We put special focus on proper handling of natural resources right at the beginning of the production chain; on exclusion of harmful gases; and on protection of air, water and soil.'
Arcelor Mittal Sp. z o.o.	'The business activity of Ironworks of Arcelor Mittal, is conducted in accordance with the principle of Balanced Development. We are committed to providing top-quality products and to producing them in light of our customers' best interest and in full respect for all subjects that can be influenced by our operation: our employees, social communities, and the natural world.

Source: ZAK (2010); Ciech (2010); Black Red White (2010); Stalprodukt (2010); Arctic Paper Kostrzyn (2010); Kronopol (2010); Arcelor Mittal (2010).

Figure 12. Types of mission statements

The mission statement occupies a special place in companies operating in international markets because, through its content, it determines, integrates, and verifies all activities of an international organization. However, in each case, special attention should be placed on the specific character of each local market and the culture represented by branch employees and local customers (Monye, 2000). For example, the mission statement of American companies is an abstract statement of what the company stands for, its identity. In collectivist, high-context cultures, where companies function like families, what the company stands for is not necessarily made explicit; and if it is made explicit, it expresses the philosophy and vision of the company's leaders (Czinkota and Ronkainen, 2007). It is noteworthy that generally the corporate mission or vision, both in form and content, reflects the world view of its management, which usually represents the values of the culture of origin of the company. The most famous examples of Japanese strategic intents were Canon's 'Beat Xerox' and Komatsu's 'Encircle Caterpillar' (Murphy, 2004). Japan is a competitive society, and each company points its arrows at one (bigger) competitor. An example of Asian form and content is formulating the company statement as a 'message from top management', as at Toyota. The subtitle of this message forms the content: 'Harmony with People, Society, and the Environment' (Burton, 2009). The corporate philosophy of Japanese Canon is 'all people, regardless of race, religion, or culture, harmoniously living and working together into the future' (Hollensen, 2007). Korean Samsung's management philosophy is 'we will devote our human resources and technology to create superior products and services, thereby contributing to a better global society' (de Mooij, 2010).

American statements reflect the need for performance, leadership, greatness, and growth. General Electric's mission is, 'being a reliable growth company requires consistent execution of strategic principles that drive performance every quarter and every year'. This includes building leading businesses, driving growth, and spreading ideas across great people and teams (General Electric, 2010). Microsoft's mission is 'to help people and businesses throughout the world to realize their full potential' (Microsoft, 2010). This mission reflects the Anglo-Saxon value of self-actualization. Dutch Philips reflects the feminine value of quality of life by stating its mission as a passion to 'improve the quality of people's lives through the timely introduction of meaningful innovations' (Philips, 2011). French L'Oreal says its mission is 'to help men and women around the world realize their aspirations and express their individual personalities to the full. This is what gives meaning and value to our business and to the working lives of our employees. We are proud of our work' (Loreal, 2011). Polish PKN Orlen S.A. (a fuel distribution company) stresses its social corporate responsibility, stating in its mission that as a transparent company, it follows its business activities in full preservation of corporate and social responsibility, and in full care of employee development and the natural environment (Szymura-Tyc, 2009).

From the vision and mission, a corporate identity can be distilled, which reflects the core values of the company. This is revealed in definitions of corporate identity that are based on the identity concept. N. Ind (1992) defines corporate identity as 'an organization's identifying its sense of self, much like our own individual sense of identity. Consequently, it is unique'. Uniqueness and consistency of corporate identity in individualistic cultures is opposed to a collectivist's identity, which can change according to varying social positions and situations. When international companies define their corporate identities, they might consider including variations for the different cultural contexts in which they operate.

Usually, the task of creating a corporate identity begins with the selection of an appropriate corporate name. Other factors that contribute to corporate identity include the logo of the organization and the marketing communications. All this, including language, lettering, and associations, is logically a reflection of the home country of the organization. Many Western companies prefer worldwide consistency for all these elements without realizing that this can be counterproductive, as not all elements are equally meaningful or understood in all countries. Some American companies in China have learned to adapt. Coca-Cola, for example, has changed its name to adapt to the visual orientation of the Chinese. The company renamed its brand Kokou Kole, which translates to 'happiness in the mouth' (de Mooij, 2010).

A well-developed corporate identity should be perceived universally, but in reality translate differently in different parts of the world. Perception of a corporate identity is also dependent on the use of the company name as a corporate brand. For example, Henkel and Procter & Gamble are very large companies but hardly known to the general public because historically they have mainly marketed product brands. Other companies, such as Nestle, Heineken, Philips, or Sony, are world players who use their corporate name on almost all products. Some of these companies, such as Heineken (Amstel, Tiger) and Nestle (Nescafe, Perrier, Nestea, KitKat), in addition to the corporate brand name, keep using the brand names of companies they acquire. East Asian companies tend to stick to one corporate brand name. The reason for using a company brand in collectivist cultures is the need for trust in the company. Many Japanese companies change their product models more frequently then Western-ers. The Japanese avoid the purchase of an unfamiliar brand. As a result, corporate image has a stronger influence on Japanese than on American consumers (Souiden et al., 2006).

Driven by the cultural specifics of collectivist cultures like Russia, Japan, and China, Unilev-er has chosen to include its corporate name on all its brands. The very least that should be added to product brands in Asian advertising is the company's name. For some time, P&G in China has done so by adding a P&G signature, for example, to Head & Shoulders in TV commercials. And Nippon Lever in Japan has done so for its Japanese products. Danone also uses the company name on its sweet biscuits (ACNielsen, 2004).

Brand values should fit the values in the overall company vision and mission. Brand vision should match corporate vision, and they should enhance each other. This is of equal impor-tance in individualistic and collectivist cultures. If the brand and company vision are aligned and clear, trust in the company will transfer trust to the brand and vice verse. This strategy is more difficult for companies that have many brands, such as Unilever or Procter & Gamble. If a brand portfolio includes brands with contradictory values, protests may arise in the Western world because consistency is expected. An example is the contradictory values of Unilever's Axe and Dove brands. Axe's message is that by using Axe, men can get lots of attractive women; whereas Dove's message is that beauty is inside. An example of a positive connection is Unilever's mission 'to add vitality to life and to do this in a sustainable way' and Unilever's intention to have all its palm oil certified as sustainable by 2015 (Unilever, 2010).

In order to develop a company and brand vision that is relevant to consumers in the interna-tional market, the company must first listen to its consumers in all markets. Rather than doing market research in general, leading companies use consumer insights as the basis for their product development and brand-building activities. Consumer needs should determine which products or product extensions to develop for which markets. When developing a brand positioning statement, the first thing to know is consumers' wants and needs.

2.3   Business ethics in international markets

In the contemporary market economy, economic management goals, manner of goods distribution, and forms of participation in consumption are becoming a common subject of moral assessment. In other words, on the local, regional, national, and global level, social communities are increasingly involved in evaluating business and economic activities in terms of good and evil. This means that individual and group participation in economic management becomes a form (next to technological and phraseological rules) of observing moral rules and norms. As a result, various types of human economic coexistence (cooperation, competition, rivalry) are gaining (or should gain) the status of either morally desirable or morally unacceptable human relations. Economic and business ethics represent a philosophical (and/or religious) reflection upon the moral aspects of production, distribution, and consumption of goods and services (Lin et al., 2001).

Although the terms 'economic ethics' and 'business ethics' are not identical, they have a certain relationship to each other. **Economic ethics** represents the most general form of an ethical reflection about the practice of economic management and is an important element of economic philosophy. **Business ethics**, or market economic ethics, constitutes a part of economic ethics (Pogonowska, 2004). Currently, as a consequence of globalization, the scope of global ethics has been extended and diversified, which is demonstrated in a dichotomy of ethical views and of attitudes towards the process itself and towards its economic and social repercussions (Caldwell et al., 2010). In view of world economic disparities, extreme poverty, famine, unemployment, lack of access to education and health care as well as devastation of the natural environment, participants in the global market have been undertaking various initiatives to develop morally acceptable economic standards. One such initiative, the UN Global Compact of July 20, 2000, proposed by the UN secretary general, Kofi Annan, commits private businesses, UN organizations, international labor associations, and non-governmental organizations to observe and to protect the nine fundamental principles with respect to human rights, labor standards, and the natural environment (Porter, 2010). It is worth mentioning that the purpose of the project is to turn globally active companies into fully accountable businesses or more precisely into 'corporate citizens in all areas of their activity'. Anti-global or alter-global views also represent part of global ethics.

Ethical considerations over economic management appeared as early as 2,600 BC. The first traces of economic ethics can be found in Egyptian writings known as Ptahhotep's Teachings. Their author, an Egyptian priest, included in his work the following advice: 'Be happy all your life, don't do anything beyond what you are supposed to do; don't shorten the time for joy as it is outrageous to reduce time for pleasure. Don't waste your time working more than is necessary for your household. Remember that riches can be gained when desired, but what benefit can be obtained from them when the desire has perished?' (Davis, 1991).

Although the history of this reflection is very interesting, it was only in the 1970s that economic ethics appeared as an independent thought of Western culture. Until then it had constituted an integral, yet a rather minor, element of general ethics (except for Protestant ethics), developed on the margin of political considerations and employed, among others, by A. Smith in his macroeconomic studies. A breakthrough moment in the history of economic ethics came in 1891, when Pope Leon XIII announced his encyclical Rerum Novarum. The document had been preceded by the statements and texts of religious thinkers (W. von Ketteler, H.Pesh), who tried to approach the issue of the ethical problems of capitalism (workers' right to decent working conditions and remuneration, work of women and children, growth of social pathologies). The 1970s can be regarded as the beginning of the development of business ethics. During this period, curricula of American universities started to raise the issue of the social role and responsibility of business and the economy (Pogonowska, 2004).

The increasing interest of business in ethical issues was derived from various sources. Due to uncontrolled industrial activities and the development of the first ecological organizations, people started to be more aware of the devastation of the natural environment. Moreover, after a period of post-war stabilization, there came a time of social unrest (youth movement, protests against the war in Vietnam) and the development of the consumer rights movement (Moutinho and Chien, 2008). The mass media began to publicize economic scandals and the connections between business and the world of politics. One could observe a progressive loss of confidence in contemporary economic structures and in socio-political institutions. All of this led to the formation of non-governmental organizations and to the creation of a civil society. Business ethics as an independent strand of philosophical and ethical thinking began to develop in academic circles in the 1970s (Zou et al., 2009).

The development of business ethics and the growth of interest in ethical issues among economists, who started to be aware of a connection between business and morality, appeared not only as a reaction to numerous economic scandals, negative consequences of economic management (increase in unemployment, middle-class economic struggles during the 'Thatcher era', 'Reaganomics'), and further devastation of the natural environment, but also as a reaction to discussions and controversies over biomedical research and practices (also financed by big business). Bioethics, which developed as a response to deficiencies in the existing medical codes of ethics and codes governing the ethics of scientific research, was analogous to the world of business. In other words, principles of merchant honor, craftsman honesty, and so on, which were the bases of the townsman's ethics, proved unsuitable for the cultural context of contemporary economic management. Interest in business ethics became a sign of authentic concern about the 'common welfare', and a form of legitimizing business activity in the social perception (Velasquez, 2006).

The case: Ethical aspects of neuromarketing

Neuromarketing is a controversial new field of marketing that uses medical technologies such as functional Magnetic Resonance Imaging (MRI) to sell products. However, there are at least three significant potential problems with neuromarketing:

1) increased incidence of marketing-related diseases – the use of neuromarketing by companies that produce for example tobacco, alcohol, junk food or fast food could be damaging to public health;

2) more effective political propaganda – the use of neuromarketing could make such propaganda more effective, potentially leading to new totalitarian regimes, civil strife, wars, genocide, and countless deaths; and

3) more effective promotion of degraded values – many international corporations regularly promote, especially to children and teenagers, degraded values and products including materialism, addiction, violence, gambling, pornography, anti-social behavior, etc. Any increase in the effectiveness of the marketing these values and products could impact the character of consumers.

Source: Commercial Alert (2010)

The problem of business ethics has enjoyed unabated popularity. Events connected to the 'decade of greed' during the 1980s, symbolized by the practices of predatory and cruel yuppies, only reinforced the importance of a deeper reflection on the moral aspect of individual participation in economic activities. Cases of bankruptcy of large American and European corporations at the turn of the 21st century, displayed, on the one hand, the social and ethical (not only microeconomic) consequences of managerial irresponsibility, but, on the other hand, contributed to the growth of interest in the issue of business ethics. As a result of economic globalization and the 1980 U.S. financial crisis, which took on a global dimension, new ethical dilemmas have increasingly emerged. These dilemmas concern both legal regulations of business operations and mutual relations between individual economic entities, customers, and consumers (Brown, 2003). They also refer to moral aspects of corporate internal functioning, ways of managing conflicts, and attitudes towards the natural environment (Des Jardins, 2007).

Competitiveness presents the greatest challenge for the world economy. The concept has become the principal aspect of organized social life. It appears as a driving force for innovation and productivity as well as a stimulus for human aspirations. Competitiveness is a basic goal of producers, trade, banking institutions, and so on. Enthusiasts of the idea of competitiveness point out that a competitive market economy is the only effective and morally desirable method of economic development (Lennick and Kiel, 2005). Market competition provides room, however, for many moral dilemmas. The central issue concerns questions about the boundary between morally doubtful behavior and acceptable or justifiable ways of vying for access to the market and for maintenance of a market position. Competition seen as rivalry, where free market players compete to buy or sell rare market products, implies avoiding losses and achieving profits. The general principle of economic competitiveness raises questions about the limits of economic activities and about the types of activities that can be regarded as honest or dishonest.

Communities participating in the market game make attempts at establishing the rules of fair competition by pointing at harmful and unacceptable ways of competing, both for competitors and broader populations. **Fair competition** is considered to be based on rivalry that adheres to established rules; unfair competition violates accepted norms (Beauchamp, 2004). Established rules are intended to foster competition that brings benefits to all market subjects and that does not turn into a destructive force. Today, when competition is regarded as one of the most significant factors of economic growth, people try to find areas for its development, mainly through numerous agreements that facilitate economic relations, especially in the field of free trade. Competition is protected by means of anti-trust legislation and legislation that prevents unfair competition (Cavusgil et al., 2008).

The main idea of fair competition is based on **principles of rivalry** that do not stand in the competitor's way (Rugman and Collinson, 2009). In the literature, this is referred to as positive competition, the principles of which have been formulated by L.S. Pain (Vernon et al., 1996):

- The **principle of an independent initiative** has competing companies appear as independent entities, acting exclusively on their own behalf and within their own responsibility. Companies should make independent decisions, focusing on buyers and their needs. Each competing party is expected to follow its own goals, without focusing attention and effort on fighting competitors.
- The **principle of constructive operation** commits companies to act in their best possible manner. Like the principle of independent initiative, the constructive principle is based on the postulate of entrepreneurship, innovation, and a creative approach to economic activities.
- The **principle of equality** assumes that every economic subject should have equal economic opportunities. Real chances for competition may vary due to disparities among individual economic subjects with respect to their business experience, the volume of production resources and production potential, as well as individual abilities and possibilities.
- The **principle of respect for external subjects** defines competitive activities that do not threaten customers' or competitors' dignity or violate their basic rights. This refers to regulations concerning orders, promotion, and advertising.
- The **principle of rule observance** says that activities pursued by economic subjects should conform to generally accepted norms and laws.

The issue of ethical competition relates to the role of suppliers, subcontractors, and cooperating agents in the company's environment. The rules of fair cooperation exclude imposition or coercion of contractual terms. In ethical competition, collaboration takes the form of agreement based on negotiations. Negotiating the rules of fair cooperation assumes shifting from confrontation to cooperation, with both parties being convinced that transparent cooperation produces better results (McEwan, 2001). Legal regulations of most European countries do not assume participation of administrative bodies in the management of fair competition and in the consideration of relevant issues. This does not mean, however, that state institutions have no say in the functioning of this part of the economic sphere (Velasquez, 2006). Some tasks are fulfilled by ministerial departments and customs offices. In this respect, a special role is played by corporate organizations, including economic chambers that develop and promote business ethics, elaborate and modify norms of good conduct in the economy, and voice opinions about business practices (these opinions may be used by courts of law).

State and local political institutions constitute an important element of the corporate environment, as they affect business entities by providing laws and regulations that either allow or prohibit certain business practices. The legal and political environment of a company consists of a set of regulations governing business conduct and economic relations between the state and the economy (Cox et al., 2005). Therefore, company managers cannot remain oblivious to the political and legal environment, as the legal system and political institutions may either stimulate or destroy development of a business activity through imposition of various tax barriers as well as regulations.

Changes can be observed in the scope of managerial independence in decision making, which today, more than ever before, is based on negotiations, consultations, and agreements with representatives of local governments, trade unions, state agencies, as well as economic associations and organizations (Li and Persons, 2010). As a result, companies struggle to influence governmental decisions through personal contact, lobbying, political committees, and exchange of favors. The relations between a company and its political environment are mainly determined by the activities of **interest groups**, currently referred to as **lobby groups**, which try to influence business and legislative processes. Activities of interest groups are aimed at determining and executing tasks that are consistent with broader interests. The groups, in an active and deliberate way, exert different forms of pressure on particular governmental entities. Interest groups represent small, medium, and large companies from different industrial and economic areas, agricultural associations, trade unions, professions, ethnic and religious groups, and so on.

The main goal of lobbies is to influence state and local policy at every stage of the political hierarchy: from local, to regional, to central. The groups exert influence and pressure on various political activists, local and state officials, and senators and representatives so as to induce them to make political and economic decisions that are aligned with the interests the lobbyists represent. Consequently, decision makers and political decisions are expected to cater to the interests of a particular group, and to support or reject certain regulations, laws, or decisions. To this end, lobbyists not only resort to negotiating techniques, but also to bribery, persuasion, or even blackmailing (Bear and Moldonado-Bear, 1994). Lobby groups, whatever their types and classifications, share some characteristic features. In their attempts to affect official decisions that could secure their own interests, lobby groups influence political decisions and are 'a part of a society's government'. In order to strengthen their position, they seek various allies, or else enter into alliances with groups with common interests. Groups that do not have any interest in some current issue may 'lend' their power as, for example, votes in return for support on issues that will be their own concern in the future. Winning one group as an active ally and neutralizing potential opponents is part of a general strategy (Kirkhaug, 2010).

The significance and effectiveness of pressure exerted on state authorities depends on many factors such as financial resources and the number of group members able to canvass new supporters. Other important factors include concern about the interests of group members, group organizational coherence assessed through management cohesion, opportunities for overcoming group conflicts, proper organizational structure, level of member discipline and member conformity, as well as group social prestige. Group prestige depends on the prestige and authority of outstanding individuals within the group (Cox et al., 2005). It is noteworthy that the interaction between the government and the lobby groups is based on the principle of give-and-take. Sometimes this policy can appear to be promoting the interests of groups that, at a given moment, are more powerful than others. Thus, lobbying serves as a tool for 'influencing' the future of companies and business representatives. Lobbying is used in politics to influence political decisions and to formulate laws and regulations through active participation in the process of creating, modifying, or repealing particular acts of law. In its basic form, lobbying appears as a sheer sell-buy transaction (Sayles and Smith, 2006).

In general, lobbying occurs on three major levels: political, economic, and legal. Representatives of these socio-economic spheres have great impact on the shape of state politics and the economy of the state, which is clearly reflected in the careers of business people and politicians. The latter, once their tenure is over, are particularly quick at taking hold of seats on corporate supervisory boards, the members of which they know from previous contacts.

According to representatives of home businesses, it is difficult to conduct business activity without proper contacts with leading political parties (e.g., through co-financing of election campaigns). Such connections yield mutual benefits, as politicians are guaranteed a 'secure' position after termination of their political career, whereas business people can use their own or ex-politicians' connections against competitors. Lobbyists like lawyers, for example, sell their services in the form of ideas and tips on how to convince officials, mass media representatives, various decision makers, and the public about the existence of some significant problem that needs to be prioritized. Moreover, this 'service' can be implied in the necessity of accepting or proposing certain solutions and in the criticism of old problem-solving methods. Thus, lobbying is intended to provide adequate information to decision makers engaged in developing policies, laws, and executive regulations that are consistent with the needs of definite interest groups (Bear and Moldonado-Bear, 1994). Thanks to lobbying, it is possible to optimize decisions, reduce red-tape, balance influences, and provide necessary information. Moreover, lobbying enables citizens and companies to participate in the formulation of government policy and to stand up for their rights and interests. From the governmental perspective, lobbying creates opportunities for an exchange of opinions on various issues. All citizens are entitled to express their views, whereas politicians are expected to assess them in terms of the benefits they bring to the whole state and society. Lobbying is thought to comply with democratic principles of openness.

The case: Lobbying in Central and Eastern European Countries

In post–communist countries from the CEE region, the concept of a lobby as a pressure group conjures up rather negative images of backstage private business deals or bribery and morally doubtful business-political connections. Unlike CEE countries, Western states perceive lobbying as a method of communication of business, economic interests, and citizens with political elites and state officials. In CEE countries, lobbying is relatively new, which may partly explain deficiencies in relevant regulations. Therefore, it is worth wondering to what extent it is socially acceptable for state officials and state officers to gain advantages from business people who offer them, for example, gifts, souvenirs, invitations to hunting events, financing of trips, cars, 'test' mobile phones, and other freebies.

Polish lobbying is mainly done by organizations such as the Business Center Club, Polish Business Council, Polish Industrial Lobby, Confederation of Polish Employers, as well as trade unions, local authorities, counseling agencies, and other social associations. Interestingly, though, lobbyists do not openly identify themselves as such; instead business cards use the term 'public adviser' or 'government relations adviser'.

Apart from politicians and authorities, the most important audience for international companies to communicate with is their clients. This communication calls for different forms of influence and requires activities that achieve desirable effects. In practice, communication between a company and its clients takes place through advertising, an instrument that ensures companies public acceptance for different forms of their operation. Advertising appears as the most crucial but, at the same time, the most controversial marketing tool. The main ethical issue here relates to the question of the permissibility of advertising. Its adversaries argue that advertising is contradictory to the consumer's right of free choice, as persuasion poses a threat to consumer freedom, promotes bad taste, destroys human sensitivity, and creates artificial needs (Spence et al., 2005). Supporters of the opposite view emphasize that the basic purpose of advertising is to inform consumers about a product, as they have every right to obtain reliable information about the market offer (White, 1993). Considering the reality of the market economy, it is not so much a question of the legitimacy of advertising as its ethical aspects.

It is commonly maintained that the major role of advertising is to inform potential consumers about available products and positive product features. Nonetheless, this informative function is dominated by the persuasive one, designed to persuade the consumer to buy one concrete item. At this point, an important ethical problem arises, as it becomes clear that the aim of the advertising market is to press consumers to buy a certain product and to make them develop the proper attitude towards a given product and its manufacturers. At the same time, less emphasis is put on the reliability of the information (Kim et al., 2010). The question about the moral aspect of advertising corresponds to the question of its availability, contents, and range of influence as well as its ethical or unethical dimensions.

It is generally accepted that **unethical advertising** is against the law or against the code of good conduct, as it violates the interests of other business people or customers. In order to counteract unethical advertising, legal bans have been formulated with respect to its application. Advertising law, as part of the Unfair Competition Law, comes both under the Industrial Property Law and the Competition Law, and as such must remain in conformity with the EU norms. According to these regulations, advertising is prohibited under these circumstances (Pogonowska, 2004):

- it violates human dignity and is contradictory to good manners; this prohibition refers to goods that are regarded as socially harmful (alcohol, gambling) and offensive, or to forms of advertising that are indecent and abusive (religious, patriotic, etc.);
- it is likely to address the wrong recipient;
- it is deceitful, misleading, indirect, oppressive, and unreliable;
- it infringes on human privacy;
- it is importunate (e.g., pestering in public places, sending unordered goods at the customer's cost); and
- it appeals to the consumer by evoking fear or superstition, or it takes advantage of a child's gullibility.

Concern for the interests of the consumer seems to be of major importance in considerations of market advertising. The consumer is entitled to reliable information about a particular product and similar products on the market. The consumer has every right to get sound knowledge about product ingredients (e.g., sweets, food), technical parameters, conditions governing its use, side effects, and, above all, safety and protection against the risks involved in product use and product consumption. A company that intends to sell its products is obliged to provide the consumer with exactly the same product that was presented in the product offer. Consequently, a company must thoroughly inform the consumer about product characteristics, hidden faults, and the risks involved in product use or after-sales maintenance service (Stanwick and Stanwick, 2009).

By assuming that the number of market ethical systems directly corresponds to the number of markets (commodity, capital, labor, information; global, regional, national, local; type of political system – 'free' or 'mixed'), one can arrive at the scope of competencies (including the moral ones) of particular professions in definite markets. This relates to the issue of establishing, implementing, and supervising sets or systems of norms and ethical regulations in all kinds of professions connected with a definite type of business activity.

Looking back on the history of ethical codes related to human professional activity, one can observe that there are three types of professions that have or are being provided with legal regulations. All of them fall within the category of activity based on the norm of high social confidence, and require special long-term and tedious preparations and competencies. Additionally, the professions are quite risky (high randomness and unpredictability of results of the professional activity, time lapse between actions and effects, and high anonymity of human relations) and are difficult to monitor (Roth, 2004). Moreover, they require discretion, confidence, or even belief (as in medicine) that a specialist acts in good faith and in full conformity with procedures (learned during the educational process) and that he or she makes every effort to duly complete his or her tasks regardless of remuneration (or at least with little regard to it). The professions involve (Sayles and Smith, 2006) jobs that are strictly connected to the protection of life, health, safety, and freedom of individual people or groups of people, (doctors, lawyers, soldiers, police officers), jobs that enjoy the dignity or, in a broader sense, the privilege of introducing new generations into particular areas of culture (all kinds of teachers, representatives of institutional religions), and finally jobs connected to managing someone's property (mainly bankers, stock brokers, financial advisers).

The case: Good practices code of financial institutions in Poland

The good practices code was developed by the Conference of Finance Companies in Poland in 2005. The conference wanted to develop a code that, as an integral part of modern management, could contribute to fulfillment of European ethical standards and development of social responsibility, and could foster perception of Poland as a reliable partner.

According to the code, financial institutions, among other things, should
- conduct business activities in conformity with relevant laws and ensure consumer protection at each stage of the relationship with the customer;
- cooperate with one another in order to reduce the risk connected to activities related to unfair and unreliable entities on the market;
- not sell the credit facility after determining that the customer will be unable to meet his or her commitments;
- offer a new schedule of debt repayment when a customer files an application; the schedule should be appropriate to the customer's current financial condition; and
- conduct all activities related to debtors in a manner that protects consumer rights and respects the law, good manners, and the relevant rights of debtors.

Source: Kiezel (2007)

An ethical code is adopted by international companies in an attempt to assist those in the company called upon to make a decision. Usually most, if not all, understand the difference between 'right' and 'wrong', and apply this understanding to their decision. The ethical code, therefore, generally implies documents at three levels: code of ethics, code of conduct, and code of practice (Klimczak, 1996). A **code of ethics** often focuses on social issues. It may set out general principles about a company's beliefs on matters such as mission, quality, privacy, or the environment. It may delineate proper procedures to determine whether a violation of the code of ethics has occurred and, if so, what remedies should be imposed. The effectiveness of such codes of ethics depends on the extent to which management supports them with sanctions and rewards. The code of ethics links to and gives rise to a code of conduct for employees. A **code of conduct** is a document designed to influence the behavior of employees. It sets out the procedures to be used in specific ethical situations, such as conflicts of interest or the acceptance of gifts, and delineates the procedures to determine whether a violation of the code of ethics occurred and, if so, what remedies should be imposed. Violations of a code of conduct may subject the violator to the company's remedies, which can under particular circumstances result in the termination of employment. A **code of practice** is adopted by a profession or by a governmental or non-governmental organization to regulate that profession. A code of practice may be styled as a code of professional responsibility, which will discuss difficult issues and difficult decisions that will often need to be made, and provide a clear account of what behavior is considered 'ethical' or 'correct' or 'right' in the circumstances. In a membership context, failure to comply with a code of practice can result in expulsion from the professional organization.

The case: Ethical code of the Institute of Internal Auditors (IIA)

The IIA is a guidance-setting body. Serving members in 165 countries, the IIA is the internal audit profession's global voice, chief advocate, recognized authority, and principal educator. The IIA has three levels of Professional Standards.

1) Standards and Code of Ethics

These guidelines are mandatory for IIA members and internal audit organizations claiming to complete audits to IIA standards around the world. The Standards are recorded in what is referred to as the 'Red Book'. The four main principles of the IIA's Code of Ethics are Independence, Objectivity, Competence, and Confidentiality.

2) Practice Advisories

Practice Advisories are not guidelines, but are strongly recommended. They help define and explain the IIA standards.

3) Development and Practice Aid

Includes a variety of materials that are developed and/or endorsed by the IIA, including research studies, books, seminars, conferences, and other products and services related to the professional practice of internal auditing. The Global Technology Audit Guide (GTAG) is written in straightforward business language to address a timely issue related to information technology (IT) management, control, and security. To date, the IIA has released GTAGs on the following topics.

GTAG 1: Information Technology Controls
GTAG 2: Change and Patch Management Controls: Critical for Organizational Success
GTAG 3: Continuous Auditing: Implications for Assurance, Monitoring, and Risk
          Assessment
GTAG 4: Management of IT Auditing
GTAG 5: Managing and Auditing Privacy Risks
GTAG 6: Managing and Auditing IT Vulnerabilities
GTAG 7: Information Technology Outsourcing
GTAG 8: Auditing Application Controls
GTAG 9: Identity and Access Management
GTAG 10: Business Continuity Management

Source: The Institute of Internal Auditors (2010)

2.4   Consumer protection standards – an international perspective

In a market economy, the consumer should have the possibility of selecting the right product, as well as the form, place, and time of its purchase, and should have proper conditions for making the right decision (Schiffman and Kanuk, 2010). Such goals are achieved by means of various methods. This is why the importance of marketing for consumers should be considered in terms of both advantages and threats. The threats to consumer interests are usually connected to the following (Niepokulczycka, 1998):

- lack of transparency in the market (many diverse products, introduction of new products, etc.);
- depersonalization of the market;
- selling products in large shopping facilities;
- using sophisticated methods to seduce buyers, e.g., by arousing emotional motives to purchase a product;
- artificially provoking needs, e.g., through promotional activity of enterprises;
- increasing prices through manipulating the assortment of goods and by means of a well-developed brokering network; and
- over use of packing, which often causes an increase in prices and has ecological consequences, etc.

Highly developed countries have to face problems connected with the standard and quality of living in the whole society, limiting of competition, threats to the natural environment, and overly careless use of non-renewable sources of raw materials and energy. These are associated with marketing activities perceived as contradicting the original philosophy (Davies and Pardey, 1994). The complaints usually refer to quality, price, or consumer service; and they may, for instance, be related to the abuse of certain techniques and marketing instruments (Kaleta, 2006). Since most of the time the decisions related to buying goods are subconscious, it is both advisable and necessary to protect consumer interests. Consumers do not have the possibility of carefully analyzing every purchase, and so there are many ways of provoking consumer behavior based on subconscious reflexes (Bishop, 2010).

Consumer interests are threatened in many ways. Four spheres of operation of such threats are axiological, economic, qualitative, and commercial. The axiological sphere involves such activities of the producers as creating excessive needs, wrong needs, and the need for restitution. The economic sphere refers to threats caused by the purchase of goods of reduced mass and/or at an increased price. The qualitative sphere refers to latent defects of goods, legal defects, and contents that are harmful substances and components. In the commercial sphere, the consumer may suffer losses due to mismanagement arising from style of living, habits, lack of planning, and so on (Vizer, 2010).

Some of the threats to consumer interests are observed throughout the whole country, while others refer only to certain social groups. The countrywide threats are caused by civilization processes, industrial and technological processes as well as organizational processes in the economy, and lack of appropriate laws for consumer protection. Threats to the interests of social groups are usually connected with solutions adopted in the economy to settle certain problems. The premises for consumer interest protection as well as the number of various types of threats justify the need for those interests to be protected.

The term consumer interest protection is a descriptive term and is used to characterize a set of activities directed at the protection of consumers when their rights and interests are being threatened (Blackwell et al., 2001). The descriptive nature of the term has, however, some significant consequences. The manner of perceiving that set of activities, which is crucial for consumer interests, varies depending on the field the author specializes in, on the perspective taken to observe phenomena, and on the current socio-economic situation. The idea of consumer protection emerged in the 19th century when the market economy was born. The first activities aimed at the protection of buyers against exploitation and unfair trade practices were undertaken by the developing cooperative movement (Malis-zewska-Nienartowicz, 2004). The consumer movement as well as other social movements originated in the period of rapid industrialization in the second part of the 19th century, mainly in the U.S. The key event for the process was John F. Kennedy's address to the Congress on March 15, 1962, when four basic consumer rights were pronounced: the right to safety, the right to be informed, the right to choose, and the right to be heard. These rights were later developed by Consumers International until they became the basis for the Guidelines of the General Assembly of the UNO on consumer protection (adopted in 1985). The issue of consumer protection was also discussed in European Communities. The formation of community consumer protection was a multi-stage process (Kiezel, 2007).

The case: Problems of consumers in CEE countries

The system transformation and membership of most CEE countries in the European Union gives a new perspective to the issue of consumer interest protection. It is worth noting that due to the inferior position of the consumer in the market, the threats to consumer interests do not diminish with the development of the CEE countries and the European and global market. What changes, though, is the scope and direction of threats. Some of the unfavorable phenomena caused by the communist system have been eliminated, such as lack of commodities, queues, profiteering, or unfair trading practices; but they have been replaced by other problems. Nowadays the consumer is bewildered by the variety of offers but at the same time has to face the challenge of making the right decision. He/she needs help. He/she needs objective, reliable information in order to choose correctly.

The process is very often disturbed by the variety and intensity of messages coming from many sources, which often contradict one another. Moreover, the consumer is also manipulated and deceived due to his/her ignorance. The process of political transformation in CEE countries led to a decrease in the sense of social safety. This was connected to unemployment and limited access to many commodities and services, in particular among the most indigent families.

In addition to creating a group of receivers who benefited from the changes in the market, transformation resulted in considerable polarization of the society and marginalization of many social groups, who then had to face basic existential problems. This is also the reason why CEE consumers look forward to activities that will protect their interests.

Source: Gasparski (2004)

What ought to be considered, then, is the scope of consumer interest protection. This protection covers the most precious things, such as life, health, material interest, and position in the market. The subjects of protection are the consumer and the institutions organizing activities in the area of consumer interest protection. The latter include the state, self-governing bodies, social organizations, and consumers themselves. The activity of all these groups of subjects acting in favor of consumer interest protection should form an overall system of protection.

An important term related to consumer protection is consumerism. It is an umbrella term for all the activities undertaken by state, social, and private institutions for the benefit of consumers. In a broader sense, consumerism is a movement designed to increase the rights of consumers in their relationship with producers and providers of goods and services (Raymond, 2003). It is a mixture of people, ideas, and organizations representing groups and needs that were not represented before, trying to induce some changes or a reform of the existing rules. The movement defends basic consumer rights and these include (Doole et al., 2005) the following.

- The right to protection against products and services that are dangerous for health and life. No such products and services should be present on the market. For this purpose, safety requirements need to be stipulated, and consumers need to be informed of the possible risks connected with the use of particular products or services. Consumers also need to be protected against accidents.
- The right to protection of economic interests. This ought to provide consumer protection against the producers, brokers, or retailers abusing their position. It involves a ban on unfair competition and on imposing unfavorable terms in contracts, the idea of improving the quality of goods and services and caring for environmental protection.
- The right to information and to consumer education. The consumer should have the actual possibility of making a conscious choice in the market. This requires reliable information on the characteristics of products and information on the prices of goods and the methods of their use. Another important issue is information on procedures of executing consumer rights.
- The right to an effective system of pursuing claims. In the case of a complaint, the consumer should have access to professional aid.
- The right to representation. Consumers have the right to present their opinion on all matters concerning their individual as well as collective interests, i.e., the interests of a consumer community. Voluntary consumer associations constitute such representation.

The basic objective of consumerism is to extend the rights and powers of buyers in their relationship with sellers of goods and service providers. Thus consumerism motivates all subjects participating in economic life to be active in educating and informing consumers as well as in protecting consumer rights (Harris, 2010). What needs to be considered are the forms of protection and their instruments. The multiplicity of threats to consumer interests makes it difficult to apply a single method of protection. The forms of consumer protection include pro-consumer legislation and institutional forms. Those legal and extra-legal forms of protection are closely related and they intermingle. In the countries where a market economy is well developed, the governments create a system of laws and institutions to protect consumer interests. These nicely supplement the basic and effective protection provided by the market mechanisms, competition, and business ethics.

The instruments of consumer protection can be divided into three groups: state instruments, individual instruments, and mixed (Sawyer, 2010). The state instruments are activities of the state that, either directly or indirectly, protect the consumer without his/her active participation, e.g., obligatory standards of quality and safety, labeling food, anti-trust law, etc. The state acts on behalf of the consumer. Individual instruments are types of consumer behavior that protect him/her. Whether a consumer uses them or not depends entirely on him/her. They include all kinds of decisions made by the consumers, such as where to buy, for what price, how to use the product, how to treat a trademark, and so on. Mixed instruments are the laws that vest in consumers the right to protect their interests, such as the part of the Civil Code that refers to warranty and others.

It is worth noting that it is the consumers who bear the greatest responsibility for their own protection. The state, on the other hand, should establish the proper conditions by providing legal norms and regulations, education, and broad access to information. Economic processes undergo globalization and thus become more and more complex, technology changes rapidly, and economic pathology spreads. All these factors make state intervention on behalf of a consumer practically indispensable (Keay, 2010). Thus, consumer actions to protect their interests ought to be supported by the state.

The **protection instruments** may also be divided into the following groups: legal, economic, psychological, and ethical. Legal instruments are the laws that objectively concern consumers, the goods they buy, or the entities offering those goods, and such enactments that do not directly refer to the consumer, but that provide the conditions for the proper functioning of the market (packages of laws protecting fair competition and anti-trust laws). Economic instruments are those that are used by the consumers themselves as well as those that are used by the producers and vendors. This group of instruments includes some that are related to quality protection, such as trade-marks, quality standards, certificates, and others. Psychological and ethical instruments may also be of considerable importance, though their practical significance in present conditions is rather small (Wells and Prensky, 1996).

Forming consumer rights sealed the development of institutional forms of consumer interest protection. Activities in this matter are conducted, apart from consumer organizations, by specialised state bodies, self-governing bodies, social organizations, and others. Consumer rights ought to be represented in every country by all economic entities and organizations. Institutional forms of consumer interest protection in European countries create a complex and coherent organizational system, which is gradually evolving along with economic development. What is characteristic of this system is the functioning of specialized institutions, situated high in the governmental hierarchy, that shape and execute consumer policy. The activities of such entities supplement those of regional and local governments; civil organizations, including consumer organizations; and cooperative organizations (Groom, 2010).

Four models of institutional consumer protection systems are present in the European Union (Kiezel, 2007).

- **ombudsman model** – in which the crucial role in consumer protection is that of a single-person institution, a consumer advocate or ombudsman. He/she is administration-independent and is appointed for a fixed term, usually by the Parliament. A consumer advocate is usually vested with specified powers.
- **administrative model** – in which it is the administration that exercises the consumer policy. Consumer protection is usually performed by a single, specialized administrative body (usually situated in economic ministries), which usually has a well-developed structure throughout the country.
- **court model** – based on a highly advanced operation of courts, where common access and short procedures (the so called courts of petty matters, courts of small claims) guarantee quick compensation. This model also assumes the functioning of various public institutions executing and coordinating the consumer protection policy. The most characteristic feature for this model, however, is the presence of fast-operating courts, which only deal with deciding consumer litigation.
- **German model** – in this model the consumer policy is executed by means of strong consumer organizations. Consumer organizations are state-independent citizen associations that deal with the protection of buyer rights. They are present on the local and national level, and they have a joint representation in community institutions, which allows them to act on particular issues arising between buyers and vendors. They also fight to bring about changes in legal regulations that favor producers and traders.

In the European Union, institutional systems of consumer protection are usually mixed, with one of the models prevailing. The ombudsman model, for instance, is dominant in Scandinavia; the administrative model, in France; and the court model is common in Anglo-Saxon countries. Apart from the model approach to institutional solutions in the field of consumer interest protection, there is also a model approach to consumer law in EU countries, which includes the following models (Rokicka, 1996).

- **consumer code model** – e.g., in France, where a consumer code was adopted in 1993. The code was a comprehensive normative act relating to the two main branches of the law, i.e., to civil law and administrative law. The advantage of this model is that it collects all legal regulations concerning consumer protection in a single, dominant act.
- **framework regulation model** – applied in the countries that have passed laws on consumer protection. It is based on a formal principle, namely the adoption of consumer protection law.
- **distributed regulation model** – characterized by the lack of a single consumer law, either in the form of a code or a detailed statute. Instead there exist numerous special acts

governing only parts of the consumer protection issue. This model is applied in countries with a long consumerism tradition, where the legal acts were being added one by one for dozens of years, e.g., in the United Kingdom.

In the European Union there are a number of institutions and organizations in which consumer protection is the basic activity. Special institutions protect consumer interests on the country level, but there are also some transnational ones.

Particularly countries in the European Union have developed their own institutional solutions within the framework of consumer protection. They provide a good reference point when discussing the situation in other countries, especially in less-developed countries. Institutional forms of consumer protection in highly developed countries create a complex and well-integrated organizational system that evolved gradually alongside economic development in those countries and adjusted itself to the needs of the market and its subjects. In this system, there is usually some specialized institution with enough power to shape and execute the state consumer policy (Kher et al., 2010). Some examples are the following:

- in France – the National Council for Consumption;
- in Germany – the Federal Ministry of Food, Agriculture and Consumer Protection;
- in Sweden – the minister for Consumer Policy;
- in Great Britain – the National Consumer Council (deals with the general problem of consumer policy and living conditions), the Office of Fair Trading (a supervisory institution), and the British Standards Institute (establishes the minimum standards for the quality of consumable products); and
- in Norway – the Ministry of Consumer Affairs. (In Sweden and in Norway, there are also Market Courts and Consumer Advocates. The role of regional and local governments as well as that of citizen and consumer organizations is also significant.)

The case: Finish institutional system of protecting consumers

In Finland, consumer interests are protected by the Consumer Agency, whose scope, under its articles, is to prepare and spread consumer information as well as to educate consumers. There are other organizations and economic entities that provide consumer information, but the agency is the main and coordinating party. Its principal objective is to furnish consumers with a sufficient number of basic informative materials, which are distributed among the citizens free of charge by municipal consumer advisors and other persons. The agency also focuses on providing information on current matters and on active collaboration with mass media. It also publishes the results of all sorts of comparative tests and examinations in its magazine, 'Kuluttaja – lehti', and on Internet websites. It supports schools in the formation of consumer awareness and furnishes entrepreneurs with information, which should add to greater consumer satisfaction with better services, more beneficial terms of contracts, and faster consideration of claims and complaints.

Since the mass media play a crucial part in the public debate, the agency cooperates with journalists and editorial staff. It also prepares didactic aids connected with current issues, provides expert knowledge during teacher training, and cooperates with organizations that arrange disputes on various topics in schools. Under the articles of the Finnish Consumer

Agency, its main objective is to prepare and spread consumer information and to educate consumers.

Another institution operating in Finland is the Office of Consumer Claims, which is an impartial and independent body. It is financed by the state. Its procedures partly resemble those of a court, though, in some respects, it is also similar to administrative bodies and has some features uniquely its own. As a countrywide body, it usually deals with all sorts of consumer-related disputes and is a part of the consumer protection system that was formed in Finland in the 70s. The office does not protect the consumer directly, in the manner that a Consumer Advocate does, but it provides indirect protection and conducts preventive activities. Its principal and original task is to propose solutions for disputes between consumers and traders concerning goods and services. However, since 1995 the office has broadened the scope of its operation, and now it deals with disputes arising from housing transactions. It also issues statements for courts on matters within its competence. It provides information for municipal consumer advisors and in effect also for traders. Using the mass media and publishing, it informs other consumer-related bodies and the general public of the decisions it has adopted. The office operates within the borders of the country. When international issues emerge, it acts in compliance with the provisions of the Lugano Convention and the Brussels Convention. If a trader's registered office is based in a different country, the office may only undertake action on an issue after having fulfilled particular conditions. If a contract was concluded in Finland, the office has jurisdiction in the matter even if the consumer's place of residence is outside the country. The members of the office are nominated by the government for a period of four years. They represent consumers and traders on equal terms due to their impartiality. The members are often affiliated with professional and agricultural consumer organizations and employer organizations. The membership in the office is a part-time job based on public confidence. The office has about sixty members.

Source: DG SANCO (2010)

Another interesting question is the development of **arbitration courts** in Europe. Their operation may greatly reduce the burden of the work of common courts. In EU countries, arbitration courts are of great renown. A very specific example of the importance of arbitration courts for issues of consumer protection is Spain, where consumer rights protection is provided for in the constitution. There is a public arbitration system organized by the central and local administrative bodies as well as many specialized arbitration systems that settle disputes between consumers and the entrepreneurs operating within a particular sector (Mak, 2010). In European countries, there also are the so called **Alternative Dispute Resolution (ADR)** systems. They operate outside the court structure and help to settle disputes between consumers and entrepreneurs who are unable to reach an understanding on their own. The experience of the EU Member States shows that such alternative extrajudicial systems of dispute settlement may be very beneficial both for consumers and for entrepreneurs. Their main advantages are the low costs of the proceedings and the short time for settling a dispute. In order to help consumers and entrepreneurs reach an understanding, a third party is usually involved – an arbiter, a mediator or an ombudsman (Kiezel, 2007). Extrajudicial procedures are usually an alternative to court proceedings. They may also function as preliminary or supplementary proceedings. As far as material jurisdiction is concerned, there are systems that deal with issues concerning only a single sector, e.g., telecommunications or insurance, and those that deal with all consumer matters. Extrajudicial systems of resolving disputes are usually formed under agreements between both entrepreneur and consumer organizations. In Scandinavian EU countries, disputes are resolved out of court by state institutions. The binding force of the decisions delivered by each system varies considerably. In some cases, the decisions are merely recommendations, e.g., the mediator or ombudsman model; while in other cases they are binding for the entrepreneur, e.g., arbitration, claims committee; and in still others they bind both parties, e.g., arbitration (DG SANCO, 2007).

The main types of alternative systems of extrajudicial resolution of consumer disputes (ADR) that function in the European Union countries are these.

- **Mediation and conciliation** – through mediation and conciliation, the parties try to reach a settlement through the agency of a third party. The task of the mediator is to help the parties find a satisfactory solution to the problem. He or she does not impose any solution, but only tries to guide the parties to reach compromise on their own. In the conciliation model, the third party first listens to the arguments of the disagreeing parties and then presents the best solution to their problem. This suggested solution does not have to be binding for both parties. In the mediation and conciliation proceedings, the parties are not limited by the regulations of material law and law of procedure. Thus, the resolution of the dispute does not have to be based on any particular legal norm, but may invoke the principles of honesty, righteousness, loyalty, and decency. A settlement reached in such a procedure usually requires an enforcement clause to be appended by the court (Kaleta, 2006).
- **Arbitration** – this method of extrajudicial resolution of disputes is the closest in nature to court proceedings. The most important legal instrument governing arbitration is the United Nations Convention on the Recognition and Enforcement of Foreign Arbitral Awards, dated June 10, 1958. In arbitration, the parties choose one or more neutral persons and present the problem to them. These persons then deliver a final and legally binding resolution. Arbitration may either be interim or institutionalized. In interim arbitration, each party appoints one or more arbiters who then, jointly, appoint one supreme arbiter. The elected panel resolves a dispute in accordance with previously stipulated rules. The operation of institutionalized arbitration is usually based on a professional arbitration organization. Some models of arbitration require additional enforcement proceedings before a common court (Rokicka, 1996).
- **Claims committee** – this may be formed by consumer organizations, associations of entrepreneurs, or economic institutions – jointly or independently. Their functionality is based on the common legal regulations or on the principle of 'autoregulation' (the so called soft-law). Claims committees are collective by nature and both groups – consumers and entrepreneurs – are equally represented in them. The resolutions of such committees are usually not binding, though in some systems they are binding for the entrepreneur. Some claims committees may conduct consumer cases without the consent of the entrepreneur. In that case, the final decision is not binding, but it does affect the entrepreneur's reputation (Groom, 2010).

- **Ombudsman** – namely a spokesperson, who is a single-person institution appointed for the purpose of resolving disputes between entrepreneurs and consumers. An ombudsman has to be a very well-qualified, highly respected person of impeccable character. This type of ADR is usually formed on the initiative of entrepreneurs from a particular sector and constitutes one of the instruments of 'autoregulation'. Even though an ombudsman is appointed by entrepreneurs, he/she is usually an independent body. An ombudsman is generally competent in a limited range of issues; and his/her decision is based on legal regulations, the principle of equality, or on guidelines accepted in a given sector. Ombudsman's decisions are usually binding for the entrepreneur or are not binding for either party (Kiezel, 2007).

Since extrajudicial systems of dispute resolution in the EU countries are so diverse, there are also differences as far as the binding force of their decisions is concerned. Moreover, the systems of dispute resolution exercised in Europe do not secure rights equally effectively. Bearing all this in mind, the European Commission has stipulated the minimum standards for solving extrajudicial consumer disputes. They are based on the principles of independence, transparency, effectiveness, and observance of the law; and their purpose is to help consumers in pursuing claims arising from international transactions within the framework of the single EU market (DG SANCO, 2007). The minimum standards for ARD are stipulated in

- the Commission Recommendation 98/257/EC of March 30, 1998, on the principles applicable to the bodies responsible for out-of-court settlement of consumer disputes – Official Journal of the European Communities L115 of April 17, 1998, and
- the Commission Recommendation 2001/310/EC of April 4, 2001, on the principles for out-of-court bodies involved in the consensual resolution of consumer disputes – Official Journal of the European Communities No. 109 of April 19, 2001.

The European Union Member States notify the European Commission of the national extra-judicial entities that meet the minimum requirements stipulated in the Commission Recommendations. The information on ADR is collected, updated, and made accessible by the European Commission through a database (link). This database is mainly used in trans-border disputes. It helps consumers, entrepreneurs and consumer organizations determine the most appropriate, available extrajudicial method of resolving disputes. It also allows a comparison of various models of ADR systems operating in the EU Member States and development of cooperation between the European ADR systems. The network of European Consumer Centers supports the EU Member States and the European Commission in the development and promotion of ADR systems as well as in updating the database. The ECC network provides information and assists consumers in pursuing claims by the agency of ADR systems in trans-border disputes.

List of References

Ackerman, R. W., 1973. How companies respond to social demands. *Harvard Business* Review, 1: 88-98.

ACNielsen, 2004. Global mega brand franchise: Extending brands within a global marketplace [online]. [cited 01.02.2011]. Available from World Wide Web: http://www.acnielsen.com/content/corporate/us/en/search.html/q=Global+brands+survey/.

Aguirre, B. E., 2002. Sustainable development as collective surge. *Social Science Quarterly*, 83: 101-118.

Airbus S.A.S., 2010. Corporate information [online]. [cited 18.12.2010]. Available from World Wide Web: http://www.airbus.com/en/corporate/ethics/mission-values/.

Arcelor Mittal Sp. z o.o., 2010. Arcelor Mittal in Poland [online]. [cited 18.12.2010]. Available from World Wide Web: http://www.arcelormittal.com/poland/default.aspx?docId=3323.

Arctic Paper Kostrzyn SA, 2010. Group [online]. [cited 16.12.2010]. Available from World Wide Web: http://www.arcticpaper.com/pl/PL-Local-Site/Grupa/Our-mills/Arctic-Paper-Kostrzyn-SA/O-nas/.

Bart, C., 1998. Mission matters. *CPA Journal*, 8: 56-57.

Bear, L. A. & Moldonado-Bear, R., 1994. *Free markets, finance, ethics, and law.* New York: Prentice Hall.

Beauchamp, T. M., 2004. *Case studies in business, society, and ethics.* London: Pearson Higher Education.

Bishop, G., 2010. EU waves flag for consumers. *Financial Word*, 9: 24-49.

Black Red White SA, 2010. O firmie [online]. [cited 16.12.2010]. Available from World Wide Web: http://brw.com.pl/pl/strona/21-o_firmie.

Blackwell, R. D., Miniard, P. W. & Engel, J. F., 2001. *Consumer behavior.* Fort Worth: Hardcourt College Publishers.

Brown, M. T., 2003. *Ethical process: an approach to disagreements and controversia issues.* London: Pearson Higher Education.

Burton, D., 2009. *Cross-cultural marketing: theory, practice and relevance.* New York: Routledge.

Caldwell, C., Hayes, L. A. & Long, D. T., 2010. Leadership, trustworthiness, and ethical stewardship. *Journal of Business Ethics*, 96 (4): 497-534.

Carroll, A. B., 1979. A three-dimensional conceptual model of corporate performance. *Academy of Management Review*, 4 (4): 497-505.

Carroll, A. B. & Schwartz, M. S., 2003. Corporate social responsibility: a three domain approach. *Business Ethics Quarterly*, 13 (4): 503-530.

Carroll, A. B., 1999. Corporate social responsibility. Evolution of a definitional construct. *Business & Society*, 38 (3): 268-295.

Cavusgil, T., Knight, G. & Reisenberger, J., 2008. *International business: strategy management, and the new realities.* London: Pearson Higher Education.

Ciech SA, 2010. Misja [online]. [cited 16.12.2010]. Available from World Wide Web: http://www.ciech.com/PL/PoznajCiech/Strony/FilozofiaBiznesowa.aspx.

Clarkson, M. B. E., 1995. A stakeholder framework for analyzing and evaluating corporate social performance. *Academy of Management Review*, 20 (1): 92-117.

Commercial Alert., 2010. Issues [online]. [cited 15.12.2010]. Available from World Wide Web: http://www.commercialalert.org/issues/culture/neuromarketing.

Cone, C., Feldman, M. A. & DaSilva, A. T., 2003. Causes and effects. *Harvard Business Review*, 81 (7): 95-101.

Cox, B. G., Hunt, R. W. & Hunt, M. B., 2005. *Ethics at work.* New Jersey: Prentice Hall.

Czinkota, M. R. & Ronkainen, A., 2007. *International marketing.* Mason: Thomson South-Western.

Davies, P. & Pardey, D., 1994. *Marketing w praktyce.* Warszawa: Kamsoft.

Davis, K., 1960. Can business afford to ignore social responsibilities. *California Management Review*, 2: 70-76.

Davis, K., 1967. Understanding the social responsibility puzzle. *Business Horizons*, 10 (4): 45-50.

Davis, K., 1973. The case for and against business assumption of social responsibility. *Academy of Management Journal*, 16 (2): 312-322.

Davis, K., 1991. *Human behavior at work. Organizational behavior*. New York: Routledge.

De Bekker, F. G. A., Groenewegen, P. & Den Hond, F., 2005, A bibliometrick analysis of 30 years of research and theory on corporate social responsibility and corporate social performance. *Business & Society*, 44 (3): 283-317.

De Mooij, M., 2010. *Global marketing and advertising. Understanding cultural paradoxes*. Los Angeles: SAGE.

Des Jardins, J., 2007. *Business, ethics, and the environment: imagining a sustainable future*. London: Pearson Higher Education.

DG SANCO, 2007. *Consumers in Europe. facts and figures on services of general interest*. Brussels.

DG SANCO, 2010. Consumers [online]. [cited 20.12.2010]. Available from World Wide Web: http://ec.europa.eu/dgs/health_consumer/index_en.htm.

Donaldson, T. & Preston, L. E., 1995. The stakeholder theory of the corporation: concepts, evidence, and implications. *Academy of Management Review*, 20 (1): 65-91.

Doole, I., Lancaster, P. & Lowe, R., 2005. *Understanding and managing customers*. New York: Financial Times Press.

Dunham, L., Freeman, E. R. & Liedtka, J., 2006. Enhancing stakeholder practice: a particularized exploration of community. *Business Ethics Quarterly*, 16 (1): 23-42.

Epstein, E. M., 1987. The corporate social policy process: Beyond business ethics, corporate social responsibility, and corporate social responsiveness. *California Management Review*, 29 (3): 99-114.

European Commission, 2001. *Green paper. Promoting a European framework for corporate social responsibility*. Luxembourg.

Fergus, A. H. T. & Rowney, J. I. A., 2005. Sustainable development: lost meaning and opportunity? *Journal of Business Ethics*, 60: 17-27.

Fitch, H. G., 1976. Achieving corporate social responsibility. *Academy of Management Review*, 1: 38-46.

Frederick, W. C, Post, J. & Davis, K., 1992. *Business and society. Corporate strategy, public policy, ethics*. New York: McGraw-Hill.

Frederick, W. C., 1986. Toward CSR3: Why ethical analysis is indispensable and unavoidable in corporate affairs. *California Management Review*, 28 (2): 126-141.

Frederick, W. C., 1994. From CSR1 to CRS2: the maturing of business-and-society thought. *Business & Society*, 33: 150-164.

Freeman, E., 1984. *Strategic management. A stakeholder approach*. Boston: MA Pitman.

Friedman, M., 1970. The social responsibility of business is to increase its profits. *The New York Magazine*, September 13: 32-33.

Frooman, J., 1999. Stakeholder influence strategies. *Academy of Management Review*, 24: 191-205.

Garriga, E. & Mele, D., 2004. Corporate social responsibility theories: mapping the territory. *Journal of Business Ethics*, 53 (1/2): 51-71.

Gasparski, W., 2004. *Wyklady z etyki biznesu*. Warszawa: WSPiZ.

General Electric, 2010. General Electric Mission Statement [online]. [cited 16.12.2010]. Available from World Wide Web: http://www.samples-help.org.uk/mission-statements/general-electric-mission-statement.htm.

Gladwin, T. N., Kennelly, J. J. & Krause, T., 1995. Shifting paradigms for sustainable development: implications for management theory and research. *Academy of Management Review*, 20: 874-907.

Groom, S., 2010. New unfair commercial practice "Guidance". *Journal of Direct, Data and Digital Marketing Practice*, 11 (4): 345-349.

Harris, E. K., 2010. *Customer service: A practical approach: international edition*. London: Pearson Higher Education.

Hirota, S., Kubo, K., Miyajima, H., Hong, P. & Park, Y. W., 2010. Corporate mission, corporate policies and business outcomes: evidence from Japan. *Management Decision*, 48 (7): 1134-1148.

Hollensen, S., 2007. *Global marketing: decision-oriented approach*. Harlow: Pearson Education.

Ind., N., 1992. *The corporate image: strategies for effective identity programs*. London: Kogan.

Johnson, H. L., 1971. *Business in contemporary society: framework and issues*. Belmont: Wadsworth.

Johnson, S., 2010. *I'm on a mission*. Chicago: American Printer.

Kaleta, K., 2006. Czy konsument myśli racjonalnie. *Marketing i Rynek*, 3: 9-13.

Keay, J., 2010. The price of stability. *Global Finance*, 24 (8): 18-22.

Kher, S. V., Frewer, L. J., de Jonge, J. & Wentholt, M., 2010. Experts' perspectives on the implementation of traceability in Europe. *British Food Journal*, 112 (3): 261-289.

Kiezel, E., (ed.), 2007. *Ochrona interesow konsumentow w Polsce w aspekcie integracji europejskiej*. Warszawa: DIFIN.

Kim, G. S., Lee, L. Y. & Park, K., 2010. A cross-national investigation on how ethical consumers build loyalty toward fair trade brands. *Journal of Business Ethics*, 96 (4): 589-602.

Kirkhaug, R., 2010. Charisma or group belonging as antecedents of employee work effort? *Journal of Business Ethics*, 96 (4): 647-673.

Klimczak, B., 1996. *Etyka gospodarcza*. Wroclaw: AE.

Kotler, P. & Lee, N., 2004. Best of breed. When it comes to gaining a market edge while supporting a social cause, corporate social marketing leads the pack. *Stanford Social Innovation Review*, 14-23.

Kotler, P. & Lee, N., 2005. *Corporate social responsibility. Doing the most good for your company and your cause*. New York: John Wiley & Sons, Inc.

Kronopol SA, 2010. Firma [online]. [cited 16.12.2010]. Available from World Wide Web: http://www.kronopol.com.pl/Firma/Kim-jestesmy.

Lennick, D. & Kiel, F., 2005. *Moral intelligence: enhancing business performance and leadership success*. London: Pearson Higher Education.

Li, S. F. & Persons, O. S., 2010. Cultural effect on business students' ethical decisions: a Chinese versus American comparison. *Journal of Education for Business*, 86 (1): 10-17.

Lin, N., Cook, K. & Burt, R. S., 2001. *Social capital: theory and research*. New York: Aldine De Gruyter.

Logsdon, J. M. & Wood, D. J., 2002. Business citizenship: from domestic to global level of analysis. *Business Ethic Quarterly*, 12: 155-187.

Loreal, 2011. Our mission [online]. [cited 23.02.2011]. Available from World Wide Web: http://www.loreal.pl/_pl/html/nasza-firma/mosja.aspx.

Mak, V., 2010. Two levels, one standard? The multi-level regulation of consumer protection in Europe. *SSRN Working Paper Series*: 4.

Maliszewska-Nienartowicz, J. 2004. *Ewolucja ochrony konsumenta w europejskim prawie wspólnotowym*, Torun: TNOiK.

McEwan, T., 2001. *Managing values and beliefs in organizations*. London: Financial Time Press.

McWilliams, A. & Siegel, D., 2001. Corporate social responsibility: a theory of the firm perspective. *Academy of Management Review*, 26: 117-127.

Microsoft, 2010. Accessibility, mission, strategy, and progress [online]. [cited 16.12.2010]. Available from World Wide Web: http://www.microsoft.com/enable/microsoft/mission.aspx.

Mitchell, R. K., Agle, B. R. & Wood, D. J., 1997. Toward a theory of stakeholder identification and salience: defining the principle of who and what really counts. *Academy of Management Review*, 24 (4): 853-886.

Monye, S. O., (ed.), 2000. *The handbook of international marketing communications*. Oxford: Blackwell Publishers Inc.

Moutinho, L. & Chien, C., 2008. *Problems in marketing: applying key concepts and techniques*. Los Angeles: Sage Publications.

Murphy, J.J., 2004. The concepts of vision and mission revisited. Negotiation Academy [online]. [cited 11.11.2010]. Available from World Wide Web: http://www.negotiationeurope.co.uk/articles.

Nestle S.A., 2010. Nestle in Poland [online]. [cited 18.12.2010]. Available from World Wide Web: http://www.nestle.pl/wiadomosci.aspx?ArticleID=18.

Niepokulczycka, M., 1998. *Polityka konsumencka a ochrona konsumentów*. Warszawa: The Polish Consumer Federation.

Nokia, 2010. Education [online]. [cited 18.12.2010]. Available from World Wide Web: http://www.nokia.com/corporate-responsibility/mobility-in-society/education.

Philips, 2011. Mission [online]. [cited 23.02.2011]. Available from World Wide Web: http://www.philips.pl/about/missionandvisionvaluesandstrategy/index.page.

Pogonowska, B., (ed.), 2004. *Elementy etyki gospodarki rynkowej*. Warszawa: PWE.

Porter, G., 2010. Work ethics and ethical work: distortions in the American Dream. *Journal of Business Ethics*, 96 (4): 535-542.

Raymond, M., 2003. *Tomorrow people: future consumers and how to read them*. New York: Financial Times Press.

Rokicka, G., (ed.), 1996. *Model prawnej ochrony konsumenta*. Warszawa: Dom Wydawniczy Elipsa.

Rossi, C. L., 2010. Compliance: an over-looked business strategy. *International Journal of Social Economics*, 37 (10): 816-836.

Roth, W. F., 2004. *Ethics in the workplace: a systems perspective*. London: Pearson Higher Education.

Rugman, A. M. & Collinson, S., 2009. *International business*, New York: Financial Times Press.

Rybak, M., 2004. *Etyka menadzera – społeczna odpowiedzialność przedsiębiorstwa*. Warszawa: PWN.

Sawyer, N., 2010. A clear choice? *Risk*, 23 (8): 28-30.

Sayles, L. R. & Smith, C. J., 2006. *Rise of the rogue executive, The: how good companies go bad and how to stop the destruction*. New Jersey: Prentice Hall.

Schiffman, L. & Kanuk, L., 2010. *Consumer behavior: global edition*. London: Pearson Higher Education.

Schwartz, M. S. & Carroll, A. B., 1995. Are there universal aspects and contents of human values? *Journal of Social Issues*, 50: 19-46.

Schwartz, M. S. & Carroll, A. B., 2003. Corporate social responsibility: a three domain approach. *Business Ethics Quarterly*, 13 (4): 503-530.

Sen, S & Bhattacharaya, C. B., 2001. Does doing good always lead to doing better? Consumer reaction to corporate social responsibility. *Journal of Marketing Research*, 38: 225-243.

Simerly, R. L., 2003. An empirical examination of the relationship between management and corporate social performance. *International Journal of Management*, 20 (3): 353-359.

Skydel, S., 2010. Customer commitments. *Fleet Equipment*, 36 (8): 34-37.

Smith, C., 1994. The new corporate philanthropy. *Harvard Business Review*, 72 (3): 105-116.

Smith, C., 2003. Corporate social responsibility: whether or how? *California Management Review*, 45 (4): 52-76.

Souiden, N., Kassim, N. M. & Hong, H. J., 2006. The effect of corporate branding dimensions on consumers' product evaluation, a cross-cultural analysis. *European Journal of Marketing*, 40 (7/8): 825-845.

Spence, E., Van Heekeren, B. & Boylan, M., 2005. *Advertising ethics*. London: Pearson Higher Education.

Stalprodukt SA, 2010. Mission [online]. [cited 16.12.2010]. Available from World Wide Web: http://www.stalprodukt.com.pl/misja.

Stanwick, P. & Stanwick, S., 2009. *Understanding business ethics: international edition*. London: Pearson Higher Education.

Stieb, J. A., 2001. Social responsibility within and without self-interest: emergent technologies and situations. *Business and Society Review*, 106 (3): 72-91.

Stoner, J. A. F., Frejman, R. E. & Gilbert, D. R., 2001. *Kierowanie*. Warszawa: PWE.

Swanson, D. L., 1995. Addressing a theoretical problem by reorienting the corporate social performance model. *Academy of Management Review*, 20 (1): 43-64.

Szymura-Tyc, M., (ed.), 2009. *International marketing and business in the CEE markets*. Katowice: AE.

The Institute of Internal Auditors, 2010. Governance [online]. [cited 15.12.2010]. Available from World Wide Web: http://www.theiia.org/guidance/standards-and-guidance/grc/.

Unilever, 2010. Our company [online]. [cited 17.12.2010]. Available from World Wide Web: http://www.unilever.com/ourcompany/newsandmedia/pressreleases.

Varadarajan, P. R. & Menon, A., 1988. Cause – related marketing: A coalignment of marketing strategy and corporate philanthropy. *Journal of Marketing*, 52: 58-74.

Velasquez, M. G., 2006. *Business ethics: concepts and cases*. London: Pearson Higher Education.

Vernon, R., Well, L T. & Rangan, S., 1996. *The manager in the international economy*. New Jersey: Prentice Hall.

Vizer, A., 2010. Legal protection. *Canadian Insurance*, 115 (7): 50-89.

Vogel, D. J., 2005. Is there a market for virtue? Business case for corporate social responsi-bility. *California Management Review*, 47 (4): 19-45.

Waddell, S., 2000. New institutions for the practice of corporate citizenship: historical, intersectoral, and developmental perspectives. *Business and Society Review*, 105: 107-126.

Waddock, S., 2004. Parallel universes: companies, academics, and the progress of corporate citizenship. *Business and Society Review*, 109: 5-42.

Wartick, S. L. & Cochran, P. L., 1985. The evolution of the corporate social performance model. *Academy of Management Review*, 10 (4): 758-769.

Wells, W. D & Prensky, D., 1996. *Consumer behavior*. New York: John Wiley & Sons, Inc.

White, T. I., 1993. Business ethics: a philosophical leader. London: Pearson Higher Education.

Windsor, D., 2001. The future of corporate social responsibility. *The International Journal of Organizational Analysis*, 3 (3): 229-267.

Wood, D. J., 1991a. Corporate social performance revised. *Academy of Management Review*, 16 (4): 691-718.

Wood, D. J., 1991b. Social Issue Management: theory and research in corporate social performance. *Journal of Management*, 17 (2): 383-406.

Wood, D. J., 1991c. Toward improving corporate social performance. *Business Horizons*, 34: 66-73.

Yoon, Y. & Gurhan-Canli, Z., 2003. The effects of corporate social responsibility on product quality evalua-tions. *Advances in Consumer Research*, 30 (1): 323-324.

Yoon, Y., 2003. *Negative consequences of doing good: the effect of inferred motives underlying corporate social responsibility*. Michigan: University of Michigan.

ZAK SA, 2010. O firmie [online]. [cited 16.12.2010]. Available from World Wide Web: http://www.zak.eu/o-firmie.

Zasuwa, G., 2009. *Uwarunkowania reakcji konsumentów na inicjatywy społeczne przedsiębiorstwa*. Katowice: AE.

Zenisek, T. J., 1979. Corporate social responsibility: conceptualization based on organizational Literature. *Academy of Management Review*, 4: 359-368.

Zou, S., Kim, D. & Cavusgil, S. T., 2009. *Export marketing strategy: tactic and skills that work*. New York: Business Expert Press.

3 Chapter: The international business environment

- Describe the process from the formulation of business objectives to strategy decisions.

- List the major elements of the three-step approach to an integrated market analysis.

- Identify the variables of a firm's macro environment.

- Describe the variables of the industry environment.

- Explain why analysis of the environment should be a continuous process.

- Describe the contents and tools of a micro analysis. Provide examples of portfolio analysis models.

3.1 Setting Business Objectives

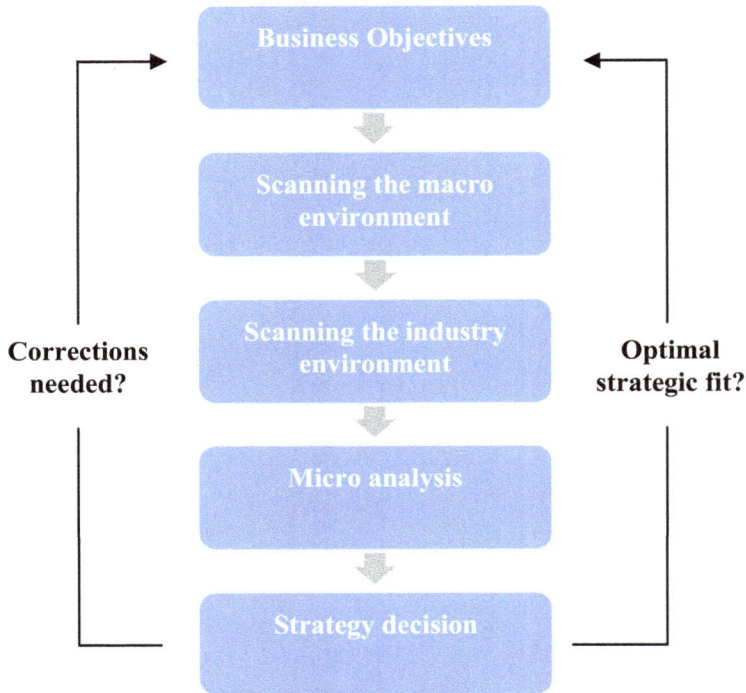

Figure 13. The process from the formulation of business objectives to strategy decision

A firm's management has to examine and formulate **business objectives** before alternative strategies are generated and evaluated. Business objectives include the goals and targets of a firm concerning turnover and net income, the development of brands and the firm's reputation, the product portfolio, and market and customer groups. Problems in performance can result from an inappropriate statement of objectives, which may be formulated too narrowly or too broadly. They can either focus too much on short-term operational goals or be so general that they provide little real guidance. Because the external environment of the firm is changing continuously, objectives should constantly be reviewed to ensure their usefulness (Wheelen and Hunger, 2010).

The case: Business objectives of Mueller Auto Komponenten GmbH, Otzenhausen, Saarland, Germany

Mueller Auto Komponenten GmbH (Mueller AK GmbH) a medium-sized auto component supplier with about 240 employees, located in the southwestern part of Germany, plans to expand its export business in Central and Eastern European (CEE) markets. The firm had not developed business contacts and did not have sales experience in the CEE regions until now.

On the other hand, the management can rely on a strong position as a niche supplier in the German home market, with a solid reputation among the German automotive manufacturers. Some automotive firms such as Kia, VW, and Audi have already established manufacturing facilities in the CEE regions. The image of Mueller AK GmbH has developed positively over several decades, particularly because of its innovative and high quality products.

The management is aware of the sales potential in the Eastern European markets, which are very promising, compared to the saturated Western European markets. Therefore, the management develops business objectives that target an export volume to the CEE markets of € 75 million. In the CEE region, the marketing executives of Mueller AK GmbH forecast that Romania, the Czech Republic, Slovakia, and Hungary are the most promising markets because of local automotive manufacturing clusters that have been established there since the 1990s, among other reasons.

Formulation of general business objectives of Mueller AK GmbH for CEE market entry 2012

- start CEE business in 2012 through growth strategy in the auto components industry
- secure overall leading ecological standards in manufactured products
- market entries in new CEE markets mainly through exports
- CEE export volume target: € 75 million p.a.
- secure profitability of a minimum of 6 percent
- potential target countries: Slovakia, the Czech Republic, Hungary, and Romania because of geographically established industry cluster
- evaluation and selection of suitable auto component customer in the new target markets
- indication and promotion of long-term relationships with potential customers, which is more important than spot business opportunities
- differentiation from competitors through leading technological products, reliable and flexible order management
- high quality and service contribute to the firm's brand reputation in the CEE markets
- holding several patents and continued R&D efforts (eight percent of turnover) secures technological leadership in the CEE markets in the near future

---

Figure 14. General business objectives of Mueller Auto Komponenten GmbH

As described in the case above, the firm's management first decides on the business aims and formulates corresponding objectives. After the definition of objectives, the firm's marketing executives procure the general (macro) analysis, followed by the scan of the industry environment, and the micro analysis. A consistent process is important in order to determine an optimum strategy for the firm as discussed in the following sections.

3.2   A three-step structured approach for an integrated market analysis

3.2.1   Scanning the elements of the macro environment

The correct interpretation of opportunities and threats in the firm's external environment is a critical function for the firm's marketing research; and, therefore, the interpretation should come from a systematic process. The steps of the process should be methodologically sound, well documented, and as much as possible, planned in advanced. Marketing research involves the identification, collection, analysis, dissemination, and use of information found in the external environment that will provide competitive advantages for the firm (Malhotra, 2009). Well performed, it enables the firm to connect with its environment and invest its resources wisely. In the best case, internal strengths are connected with external opportunities, thereby gaining competitive advantages. During 'sense making', the firm receives and interprets information about developments in the firm's external environment. This information is necessarily evaluated in light of individuals' and the overall organization's experience and knowledge. In essence, the marketing management interprets global forces that have an impact on competition. Interpretative activity is basically a form of theorizing about the market and firm behavior (Teece, 2000). The scanning is a permanent process applied by the marketing executives and contains the following elements: first, the general firm environment; second, the characteristics of industries where the firm is embedded; and third, the firm's micro environment (customers and the firm's resources and capabilities). The environmental scan basically contains three parts and is carried out starting first, with the general macro environment; second, with the industry environment; and third, with the micro analysis (the firm and the customer). A suitable strategy decision can be made only when the review process is completed. The three-step process is illustrated below.

Process step	Analysis focus	Elements	Analysis methods
1. step Macro Level	The firm's general (macro) environment	▪ Natural environment ▪ Natural resources ▪ Climate conditions ▪ Natural events ▪ Societal environment ▪ Society [S] ▪ Ecology [E] ▪ Economy [E] ▪ Law [L] ▪ Expertise [E]	▪ Focus on the 'external part' of *SWOT* (opportunities and threats)
2. step Industry Level	Characteristics of the firm's industry	▪ Industry environment ▪ Market attractiveness ▪ Competition ▪ Technology life cycles and product life cycles ▪ Customer life style ▪ Market entry barriers ▪ Market exit barriers ▪ Suppliers ▪ Customers ▪ Shareholders ▪ Stakeholders	▪ Country risk analysis ▪ Evaluation of market attractiveness
3. step Micro Level	The firm's (micro) environment and its interface with the markets	▪ Internal firm environment ▪ Resource availability ▪ Organization efficiency ▪ Product portfolio	▪ Focus on the 'internal part' of *SWOT* (strenghts and weaknesses) and its combination with the external part ▪ Portfolio analysis

Figure 15. A three-step structured approach for an integrated market analysis

Environmental scanning is multifaceted and complex. It starts with the evaluation of major variables of the firm's general (macro) environment. The firm's **macro environment** consists of the **natural environment** and the **societal environment** (Wheelen and Hunger, 2010).

Elements of the natural environment:

- Natural resources: access, quantity, quality, and portfolio of raw materials, agricultural land, and animal and plant varieties; and access to drinking water, lakes, rivers, and the ocean.
- Climate conditions: temperature variations, periods of drought and rainy seasons, seasonal lengths of daylight and darkness.
- Natural events: earthquakes, thunderstorms, hurricanes, floods, and tsunami.

The case: A global dimension

Europe is currently consuming twice what its land and seas can produce. There is mounting evidence that the status of many ecosystems is reaching or has already reached the point of no return. In the same way that a 2 degree rise in global temperature above pre-industrial levels would lead to catastrophic climatic change, the loss of biodiversity beyond certain limits would have far-reaching consequences for the very functioning of the planet. Between 12 percent and 55 percent of selected vertebrate, invertebrate, and plant groups are threatened with extinction at the global level; the decline of wild vertebrate species between 1970 and 2006 is especially severe in the tropics (59 percent) and in freshwater ecosystems (41 percent). Currently, only 0.7 percent of oceans are protected.

Up to 25 percent of European animal species, including mammals, amphibians, reptiles, birds, and butterflies, face the risk of extinction and are therefore included in the EU Regional Red List. The rate of tropical deforestation decreased nearly 20 percent between 2000 and 2010 but is still very high: 13 million hectares are lost each year (equivalent to the area of Greece). 70 percent of species are threatened by the loss of their habitat. Farmland birds declined by 20–25 percent between 1990 and 2007. 30 percent of species are threatened by overexploitation. For instance, 88 percent of stocks are being fished beyond maximum sustainable yields and 46 percent outside safe biological limits, which means that stocks may not be replenished. Despite improvements in some areas, 26 percent of species are threatened by pesticides and fertilizers like nitrates and phosphates. 22 percent of species are threatened by invasive alien species. Exploiting natural resources at current rates is steadily reducing biodiversity and degrading ecosystems.

Simply designating protected areas is not enough to halt this decline. Biodiversity must be further integrated into other relevant policies (agriculture, fisheries, energy, transport, structural policies, and development). To monitor progress and measure trends beyond 2010, the European Environment Agency and the European Commission have developed a 'baseline' – a snapshot of the current state of biodiversity to establish the evidence base necessary for stepping up EU action to address the global biodiversity crisis.

Source: European Environment Agency (2010)

In the second step, after analyzing the natural environment, the firm must evaluate major characteristics of the societal environment in the target market (Wheelen and Hunger, 2010). This evaluation contains five elements (S.E.E.L.E).

- **Society (S)**: overall acceptance of equal human rights in the society, freedom of religion and diversity of religions, family life attitudes. Furthermore, the nature of a society is determined by the number of single households; marriage and divorce rates; attitudes towards handicapped people; embedding of children (e.g., kindergarten network) and pensioners (e.g., elderly care); materialistic versus non-materialistic priorities in life and corresponding symbols; attitudes towards technology (e.g., nuclear power generation versus wind generation of energy); life expectancies, birth and death rates; age distribution of the population; the quality of health care and the pension system; work ethic; eating behavior (quality and average time spent); rate of saving versus consumption; preferences in leisure time (e.g., participating in sports, use of the Internet, gaming, and television); national concern with and budgeting for museums, theater, opera, libraries, public sports facilities, etc.; integration of immigrants; and openness of the society to speaking foreign languages and learning about and understanding other cultures. A vital part of each society is connected to education and research. Appropriate goals of education consist of equal access to education for all people; life-long learning systems; and quality elementary schools, higher education, and universities. Indicators of a country's education efforts are the literacy level of the population and the average spending on education in relation to the gross domestic product. Research includes industry product development activities and new technological inventions, mirrored in the number of patents registered per year. There is no doubt that the crime rate and tendency toward corruption reflect the educational level of a society.
- **Ecology (E)**: attitudes of the society regarding exhausting/protecting the environment, quality of life/health, quality of air and water, level of noise disturbance, industry emission standards, environmental standards for traffic, acceptance/refusal of chemical or genetically manipulated animals and plants for food consumption, influence of industry lobbying on politics, mass media in favor/against environmental protection, and acceptance or rejection of certain manufacturing procedures (e.g., electricity generation in nuclear power plants, solar, wind, and water power energy).
- **Economy (E)**: liberalized market economy versus planned economy, gross domestic product trends, stability of banking and finance system, availability and cost of capital, currency policy and exchange system, unemployment rates, inflation and deflation rates, national state surplus/deficit rates, national trade balances (imports vs. exports), average wage and salary levels, saving rates and purchasing power, profit and nonprofit aims in business and society.
- **Law (L)**: overall protection of human rights; free election and multi-political party system; private property rights; demonstration rights; freedom of opinion; non-censored mass media; and freedom for authors, writers, and correspondents.
- **Expertise (E)**: specific knowledge utilized in industries, plant utilization and industry efficiency, quality consciousness, innovative potential, technological affinity of population and willingness to make use of new and often complex techniques, and national infrastructure and logistics (road, air, rail, and water system).

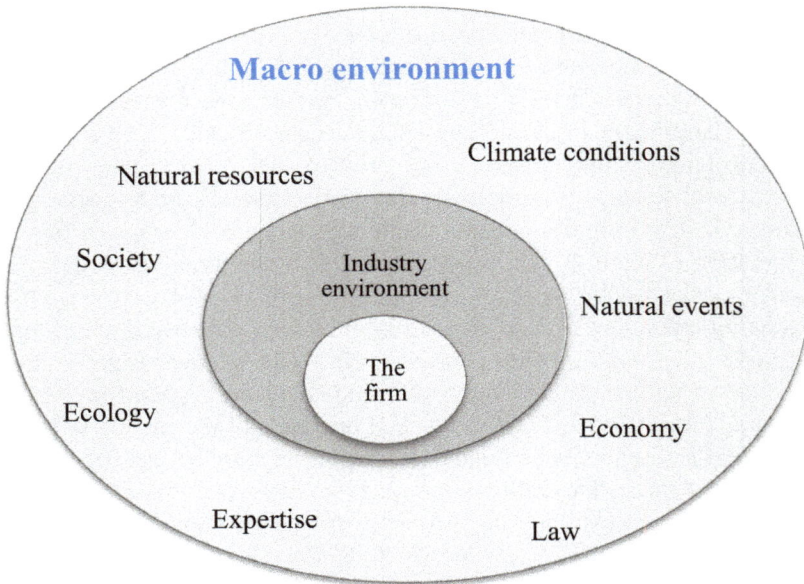

Figure 16. Important elements of the macro environment of a firm

The case: The impact of education on national prosperity

On average across OECD countries, 35 percent of 25-34 year-olds have completed higher education (e.g., college, university), compared with 20 percent of 55-64 year-olds. South Korea, Canada, and Japan are in the lead, along with the Russian Federation, which is a candidate for OECD membership, all with over 50 percent of 25-34 year olds with tertiary qualifications.

Unemployment rates among people with a tertiary level of education have stayed at or below 4 percent on average across OECD countries during the recession. For people who failed to complete upper secondary education, by contrast, unemployment rates have consistently exceeded 9 percent.

Methods of financing tertiary education vary considerably between countries, with more than 60 percent of costs covered from private sources in Chile, Japan, Korea, the U.K., and the U.S., compared with less than 10 percent in Belgium, Denmark, Finland, Iceland, and Norway. As more and more people look beyond their home countries' borders for a university education, both academic and commercial benefits accrue from attracting foreign students. In 2008, the latest year for which complete figures are available, over 3.3 million tertiary students were enrolled outside their country of citizenship, an increase of 10.7 percent over 2007.

New players are emerging in an increasingly competitive market for international education. The Russian Federation expanded its market share by two percentage points over the
past decade and Australia, South Korea, and New Zealand each by one percentage point.
Over the same period, the share of the U.S. dropped from 26 percent to 19 percent, and
Germany, the United Kingdom, and Belgium also lost ground.

The largest numbers of international students are from China and India. China accounts for
17 percent of all international students enrolled in OECD countries (not including an additional 1 percent from Hong Kong, China), with 21.6 percent of international students from
China going to the U.S. and 15.3 percent to Japan.

Women in most countries and at most education levels still earn much less than men,
potentially discouraging women from making full use of the skills they have acquired and
hampering economic growth. On average in OECD countries, a woman between the ages
of 35 and 44 with upper secondary and post-secondary non-tertiary education can expect to
earn 76 percent of male earnings. This ratio falls to 74 percent for those who have not
completed an upper secondary education and to 71 percent for those who have completed a
tertiary education.

Source: OECD (2010)

The mix and significance of the elements in the firm's macro environment contribute to the
country-specific market uncertainty. Market risk consists of factors that are common to and
uncontrollable for the entire firm. Foreign markets vary in their level of uncertainty and unpredictability, and firms' fortunes vary considerably within those markets (Beckman et al.,
2004). The characteristics of political, economic, and legal factors determine the cost of
doing business in a country. Generally, the costs and risks associated with foreign business
activities are lower in economically advanced and politically stable democratic nations and
greater in economically less developed nations, which often have politically unstable environments and the risk of corruption. Nevertheless, the potential long-run benefits are dependent not only on a nation's current stage of economic development or political stability but
also on likely future economic growth rates. This leads one to conclude that, other things
being equal, the benefit-cost-risk trade-off is likely to be most favorable in politically stable,
developed countries with high education standards and competitive markets, lower rates of
inflation, and relatively low public and private sector debts. Foreign business is likely to be
least favorable in politically unstable countries and/or nations where speculative financial
bubbles have led to excess borrowing, resulting in public deficits (and a risk of inflation) and
high debt in private households, which limits the purchasing power of consumers (Hill,
2009).

In times of crisis, some politicians raise the subject of 'unfair trade' behavior by foreign
firms, often initiated and protected by their local governments. Politicians claim that discri-
minatory trade attitudes damage home industries and provoke the loss of jobs (among potential voters). As a result of GATT and WTO mechanisms, raising (traditional) import duties or
quotas has become difficult. Moreover, import tariffs are relatively transparent, thus easy to
prove if charged. Instead, governments may install non-tariff barriers, such as hygiene,

safety, functionality, and industry standard tests or bureaucratic requirements (e.g., approval procedures for product certificates) to constrain foreign competitors from gaining access to local markets. Antidumping laws are a common instrument used to protect local industries from foreign competition. Dumping occurs when a company sells its products on the foreign market at lower price levels than in the home market. Alternatively, if a firm is accused of selling its products abroad 'at prices below cost', local competitors and as a result of lobbying activities, their governments, usually claim 'dumping practices'. Nevertheless, for outsiders it is difficult, and subject to speculation, to correctly calculate the costs of foreign products and services. In some situations, the imported product is not sold or offered with the same product features or service packages (e.g., duration of guarantee) as in the home country. In these cases, there is no common basis for comparing the prices offered in the local and the foreign markets. Overall, whether a firm has set unfair pricing policies or not is the subject of ongoing and controversial discussion. Because of the nebulous interpretation of dumping behavior, it is safe to conclude that antidumping activities by governments will continue in the future (Kotabe and Helsen, 2008).

The outcomes of the global financial and economic crisis in 2010 indicate an increasing threat of protectionism. The engagement of local governments in some industries, such as the finance industry (e.g., acquisition of shares or even bank takeovers by local governments) and the automotive industry (e.g., subsidies and support through debt guarantees), result in a move away from market economy mechanisms to increasing governmental influence. Because politicians have to prove wise investment of public money (in other words, the people's tax payments), the risk of national egoism may increase.

The case: Sweden's traditional brand Volvo sold to China's Geely

Chinese car maker Zhejiang Geely Holding has signed a deal to buy Sweden's Volvo Cars from U.S. auto maker Ford. 'I can confirm that a final agreement on the sale of Volvo to Geely was signed at 2:40 p.m.', Volvo Cars spokesman Per-Åke Fröberg told AFP ahead of a news conference scheduled at around 3.30 p.m. The deal was signed at Volvo headquarters in Gothenburg by Ford's financial director, Lewis Booth, and Geely's president, Li Shufu, Froeberg said. Booth confirmed that the sale was for USD 1.8 billion, less than a third of the USD 6.4 billion Ford paid for Volvo Cars in 1999. Volvo has 22,000 employees worldwide, including 16,000 in Sweden.

Ford Motor Company announced in December that it had agreed on the main terms of the sale of its money-losing Swedish subsidiary, Volvo Cars, to Geely, one of China's largest private automakers. The deal will bring an end to Ford's decade-long association with the premium Swedish brand, known for its sturdy, family-friendly cars. Volvo unions had earlier voiced opposition to the deal on the grounds that it was vague about expansion plans and possible layoffs. Three Volvo unions this week pressed for details 'on the capital that will finance Volvo's daily activities, investment in future projects, and the production target of 600,000 vehicles by 2015'. But on Saturday, they pronounced themselves satisfied. Ford had said it anticipated 'a definitive sale agreement will be signed in the first quarter of 2010, subject to appropriate regulatory approvals'. Geely reportedly secured the financing needed for the purchase earlier this month, which the Financial Times valued at about USD 1.8 billion.

The newspaper said more than a billion would be loaned by the European Investment Bank and the Swedish and Belgian governments.The Swedish media had questioned the ability of Geely, a relatively young player, to finance the takeover. The deal was a 'leap in the dark' said the Dagens Nyheter newspaper the day after the accord was announced. But Svenska Dagbladet said on Saturday that Geely's chairman had given guarantees that all research and development activities would remain in Sweden and that production would first be assured for plants in Sweden.

Geely chairman, Li Shufu, had previously told Chinese news agency Xinhua that nothing will change for Volvo except the boss. 'Volvo and Geely will be two independently managed brands', he said.

Source: AFP The Local Sweden (2010)

In addition to antidumping procedures against foreign competitors and tax incentives and subsidies provided for local industries, governments also influence national currencies; and this is another tool for favoring local firms in international business. Assuming monetary policy is the responsibility of the national central banks, how does the government influence currency exchange rates? First of all, in centrally planned economies such as China, the government takes direct control of the local currency exchange rates. The lower the value of the home currency when exchanged with other currencies, the cheaper the exported products in foreign markets. At the same time, imported products from abroad become more expensive. Assuming a country depends on commodity imports (e.g., oil and gas), depreciating home currencies makes these raw materials more expensive, which may cause 'import inflation'.

The United States, due to its huge trade and state deficit ('twin deficit problem') in combination with accumulated debts of private households and continued relatively high unemployment rates (9.6 percent in October 2010), favors an expansive monetary policy (United_States_Labor_Department, 2010). Pumping money liquidity into the markets may stimulate the national economy in the short run, which is, instead of securing monetary stability, another important aim of the Federal Reserve (FED), the central bank of the United States. The exchange rate of the U.S. dollar against other currencies continues to depreciate, which makes U.S. products abroad cheaper and imports (e.g., from China and the EU) more expensive. Without using the instrument of aggressive monetary policy, Germany, rather indirectly, gains currency exchange advantages due to its membership in the Euro currency union. Countries such as Greece, Ireland, and Portugal run relatively high state deficits, which generally weakens the Euro currency, but, simultaneously, stimulates German export-oriented industries. (These industries additionally benefit from the decreasing real income of the labor force since the 1990s in Germany.)

The case: IMF call to work together for growth, jobs, financial sector reform

IMF Managing Director Dominique Strauss-Kahn called on the 187 members of the IMF and World Bank to work together to restore confidence in an uncertain world. Addressing the opening session of the 2010 IMF-World Bank Annual Meetings in Washington DC, Strauss-Kahn said countries also need to focus on restoring fiscal sustainability, promoting job-creating growth, and completing reform of the financial sector. 'If you want to restore confidence in an uncertain world, you need to work together. If you want to put people back to work, you need to work together. If you want to build a better and safer world for our children and grandchildren, you need to work together. And this Annual Meeting is certainly the place to do so', Strauss-Kahn declared. Amid the much more extensive linkages among the world's economies, working together is a win-win process in which, with the right policies, everyone can be better off, Strauss-Kahn stated. At the global level, recovery has arrived; but it is fragile because it is uneven, he noted. Recovery is going well in Asia and South America, and growth is rising in the countries of sub-Saharan Africa faster than in past recoveries. But in Europe and the United States, recovery is sluggish and subdued.

Strauss-Kahn said the IMF did not expect a 'double-dip' return to world recession. But he specified four downside risks to the recovery.

Public debt
Countries should aim to return to fiscal sustainability over the medium term, while using available fiscal space to boost growth in the short term.
Jobless recovery
Growth may not be enough if it is growth without jobs. Countries should promote sustainable growth that creates jobs.
Change in the financial sector
Financial regulation needs to be supplemented by better supervision and a crisis-resolution mechanism. The best rules, if not supervised, will achieve nothing.
Diminishing commitment to cooperation
The world avoided a crisis as big as the Great Depression by working together, but now the commitment to cooperation needs to be invigorated.

Source: The International Monetary Fund (2010)

3.2.2 Scanning elements of the industry environment

A firm's direct environment is characterized by its industry surroundings and contains factors that have a fundamental impact on the firm's immediate business performance. The firm's business naturally is driven by its market potential. **Market attractiveness** is a result of the competitive rivalry that varies among industries. New upcoming service industries such as health care; alternative energy generation (e.g., solar); and ground, water, and air cleaning technologies indicate promising market potential. Innovative firms often enjoy favorable market conditions, and realize, for a certain time until competition intensifies, attractive market surroundings. The higher the market demand, relative to the supply capacities, the more attractive the market and industry (micro) environment of the firm. Nevertheless, attention should be paid to running industry overcapacities, which creates nebulous and, therefore, misleading forecasts about the market demand. A potential mistake of the firm's marketing management, because of cognitive dissonance (positive information tends to be overvalued and negative information tends to be neglected by the marketing management), is to forecast market volumes that are too promising.

How is market attractiveness indicated? Management executives make forecasts of market demand, usually on short-term (twelve months), medium (twelve months to three years), and long-term perspectives (three years and longer). Depending on the physical condition of the (tangible) product, the market demand (volume) is expressed in quantities (e.g., piece, barrel, and liter) and/or weights (e.g., kilogram, tons) and/or currency units. Markets of (intangible) services are usually recorded in currency units. Market volumes accumulate and, thus, attractiveness increases if, for example, the foreign target country is a member of an economic and monetary union (the EU) or a free trade association – e.g., the North American Free Trade Association (NAFTA) or the Association of Southeast Asian Nations (AFTA). Favorable market conditions (e.g., as recorded in turnover growth and profit margins) attract new market entrants, which, in the course of time, balances the demand/supply ratio and increases competition. Less market attractiveness causes new competitors to hesitate to enter the market, and finally causes firms to exit the market.

The dynamics of technological life cycles and product life cycles serve as additional important elements of the micro environment of the firm. Product and technology changes accelerate the threat of substitution and provide another influencing factor for the competitive rivalry in the industry.

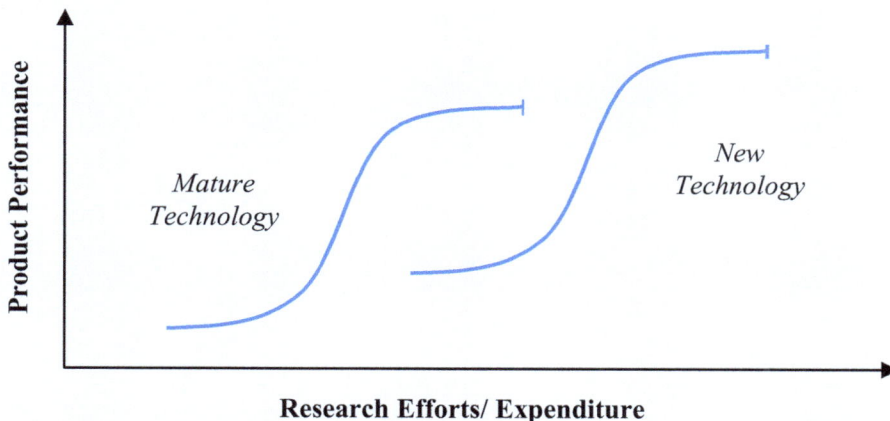

Source: Pascarella (1983), in: Wheelen and Hunger (2010), p. 122

Figure 17. Mature vs. new technology R&D related efforts

The faster the products and technologies change in the industry, the less time firms have available to realize a return on R&D, manufacturing, and marketing mix investments. There are several examples of product modifications due to new technological inventions, such as the substitution of digital cameras for photo cameras and the replacement of the typewriter by the computer and printer.

Changes in **customer life styles** create potential risks for competition not only in one industry sector but also in industries that are not obviously related. For example, information sources in the World Wide Web might cause shrinking sales of encyclopedias as printed books. For health reasons, some people increase bicycle use (instead of their car). Thus, the attractiveness of the bicycle industry increases. Additionally, cycling consumers feel healthier, which could cause pharmaceutical firms to realize a declining market demand for some of their medicine (e.g., to control blood pressure) and so on. (The authors are aware that the current reality in many European countries is rather opposite but The Netherlands and Denmark may serve as promsining benchmarks.)

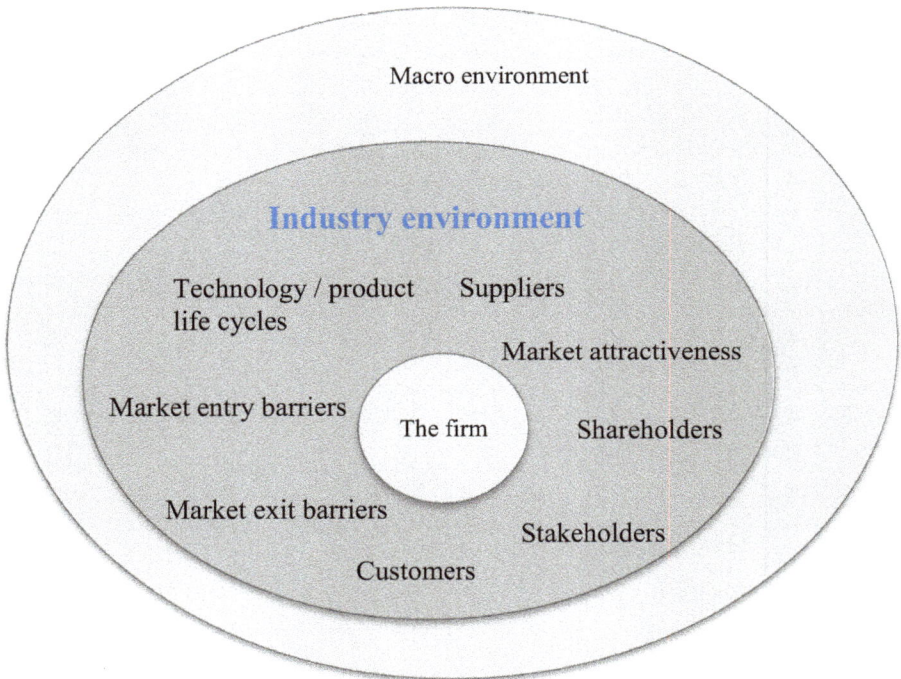

Figure 18. Important elements of the firm's industry environment

Shorter technological and product life cycles combined with large industry-specific investments, for example in R&D, in order to maintain technological survival serve as **market entry barriers** for industry outsiders. Telecommunications is an industry with a comparatively rapidly changing technological micro environment. The introduction of cell phones has caused a shrinking market for fixed-line telecommunication networks.

Among others, R&D and marketing efforts as well as national licenses such as for mobile phone broadcasting standards are costly. Of necessity, resource cushions have to be available for new industry entrants in order to overcome these market entry barriers. As a result, potential competitors may decide not to enter a country-specific telecommunications market. Thus, on the one hand, market entry barriers increase the market attractiveness, at least in the short run, for industry insiders. On the other hand, perceived safety leads to shrinking efficiency efforts and technological and managerial innovativeness. Large investments made in the past often cause the phenomenon that a firm, instead of leaving the market, stays for too long a time in unattractive industries. The management, often for career and promotion reasons, delays acknowledging that previous decisions to procure large investments, such as for acquisitions or R&D, were wrong. Instead of repositioning the enterprise and restructuring the firm's organization, the management keeps trying as long as possible to realize a minimum return on investments. Behavioral aspects in management present one of the most important market exit barriers for a firm.

Shareholders and stakeholders serve as additional important elements in the firm's industry environment. Institutional and private investors along with banks and national governments are important capital shareholders. A firm's stakeholders are individuals or groups that have particular interests in the firm's ethics and business performance. They can be divided into internal and external stakeholders. Internal stakeholders are individuals or groups who work for or own the business. They include all employees, the board of directors, entrepreneurs, and stockholders. Typical external stakeholders are unions, associations for consumer protection and quality standards, Greenpeace, Human Rights Watch, and local communities, thus the public in general (Hill, 2009). Naturally, customers and suppliers also have interests in the firm, and thus are stakeholders. Due to their importance in the firm's environment, they will be discussed in greater depth in the following pages. Suppliers and corresponding industry networks represent a driving force in the firm's industry environment. The value of supplier relationships is associated with access to the resources (e.g., know-how) they provide. When firms develop relationships with their supplier, both parties also learn about each other's needs, competences, and capabilities. Mutual knowledge transfer and learning is an important element in technological development in general and product and process development specifically (Forsgren et al., 2005). The negotiation power of a supplier is not only a result of its technological know-how and R&D expertise. A supplier's regional availability, reputation, product quality, order flexibility, delivery reliability, size, and alternative procurement sources contribute to its bargaining power (Porter, 1999).

The characteristics and attitudes of intended customer groups are as important as suppliers' influences on product adaptation decisions. Even when the benefits sought are quite similar, the physical and cultural characteristics of the customer have an impact on product and service adaptation. Marketers, depending on the target market, differ on quality, design, service packages, pricing, and product positioning. The pricing policy is influenced by the customers' purchasing power in the foreign target country. Product positioning refers to consumers' perception of a brand compared to that of the competitors' brands (Czinkota and Ronkainen, 2007).

The demands of customers in a market produce a competitive pressure for local manufacturers. Enterprises are forced to be innovative, which positively influences the development of the whole industry. The expectations and wishes of customers often lead to new technological trends in the future (Porter, 1990). The mutual negotiation power of supplier and customers depends on the **supply and demand exchange conditions**. In the case of a monopoly (one supplier faces many buyers in the market), the supplier may dictate the contract conditions. A firm, at least temporarily, may obtain a monopoly position, for example in the case of a leading invention such as a medicine to cure cancer. Conversely, a monopsony is present if only one buyer faces many suppliers (e.g., the government calls for vendors of military equipment). Supply oligopoly markets are characterized by a small number of suppliers who face many buyers. In these markets, due to the limited number of suppliers, communication and control mechanisms tend to be less complex; thus the risk of collusive pricing increases. In polypoly markets, a high number of suppliers face a corresponding high number of buyers (Theisen, 1970). These markets come as close as possible to the ideal economic intent of a market economy ('perfect competition'). The World Wide Web (WWW), due to its transparency and a concentrated supply and demand 'in one place', is close to the ideal of 'perfect competition'. Paradoxically the WWW simultaneously involves enormous risks because of its virtual product and service offering characteristics; for example, a party making offers can give incorrect information about its location, which usually causes legal challenges in the case of delivery, product, and service quality problems. The dependency on electronic systems with regard to product offerings and payment procedures without personal contact frequently results in attempts of fraud by criminals from various locations around the world.

The perceived value of a product's status influences the product's positioning in a foreign market. For example, in Germany a car can be a status symbol. Car manufacturers make use of characteristic German customer attitudes when they calculate the average prices of their cars, which may be sold at comparatively higher levels in Germany than, for example, in the U.S. The process of identifying, attracting, differentiating, and retaining customers when firms focus their efforts disproportionately on their most lucrative clients is defined as **customer relations management (CRM)**. The initial difference between traditional and relationship marketing is based in the entire approach. The traditional concept concentrates on the effective combination of the seller's marketing mix instruments that target a purchase decision by the customer. Relationship marketing is seen as a series of interdependent purchase episodes. These purchase episodes, therefore, become the basis for a firm-customer relationship that is beneficial for both sides. Marketing executives emphasize the firm's overall technological and managerial competence. As a result, a customer's uncertainty about a purchase decision is reduced when the customer is convinced that the partner is stable and competent, which improves the customer's competitive power now and in the future. Relationship marketing reduces marketing inefficiencies created through generating on-off transactions, each of which requires a greater amount of effort and resources than is needed for encouraging repeat business and long-term retention. Marketing performance through relationships is gained through better understanding of the customer, better knowledge of the customer's needs and expectations, and increased individual service and communication. The firm's business is positively enhanced through customer satisfaction and word-of-mouth recommendations (Hoffman et al., 2009).

Instead of further developing competitive forces in free markets, resource-rich multinationals and their globalized investment flows help to provide capital for merger and acquisitions, which have caused an increasing industry concentration in recent decades. In other words, it has been observed in several industries that smaller firms disappear while fewer but larger firms survive. Ultimately, this trend leads to increased market dominance by the remaining firms, limited competitive forces, or quasi-monopoly positions. The European pharmaceutical industry is illustrative of relatively intensive industry concentration as the following description indicates. Synthélabo acquired Henning Berlin in 1996. Synthélabo merged with Sanofi in 1999. In 1999, Rhône-Poulenc merged with Hoechst and created Aventis. A couple of years later, in 2004, Aventis merged with Sanofi-Synthélabo and Sanofi-Aventis was established (Hoffmann et al., 2003). Today, Sanofi-Aventis together with Pfizer, GlaxoSmithKline, Novartis, Boehringer, Bayer, and Merck dominate the worldwide markets and, because of their size, have acquired corresponding lobbying power with their local governments. In other industries, such as the automotive industry, car assemblers attempt to get increasingly involved in the after-sales business. The increasing complexity of automobiles, because of such features as passive crash safety systems and various electronic components and because of changing manufacturing methods (gluing instead of welding), cause, for example, independent car repair shops to be pushed out of the market.

The case: Fuerk Karosseriebau, Berlin, Germany

The company Fuerk Karosseriebau was established in 1965 in Berlin. The small firm, which consists of three employees and the owner, deals with auto maintenance and body repair, for example after an accident. Concerning the increasingly dominant role of the leading car manufacturers in the industry, the firm owner, Mr. Fuerk, comments: 'The complexity of cars, particularly because of their electronic components has increased in recent years. In the past, for example, after an accident, one could repair certain parts of the car by replacing a part or by repairing the part. This is no longer possible. Nowadays, following an accident, instead of single parts such as a car fender or a door, several integrated auto components must be replaced, which definitely leads to increasing repair costs for consumers. Of course, the auto manufacturers point to improved passive security standards, which result from chassis-integrated car bodies.

On the other hand, auto manufacturers like Daimler, BMW, or Volkswagen do not have an interest in seeing that small firms like us are able to make a repair using traditional skilled craftsmanship. Manufacturer-specific tools and electronic testing instruments have multiplied, simultaneously with the variety of auto models, and are now so expensive that a relatively small firm like us cannot acquire all of them for our business. It simply becomes unprofitable. Thus, we are gradually pushed out of the industry. Our business, traditional auto body repair, will probably soon disappear. After accidents, vehicles then must be taken for repair to the workshops of the big car manufacturers, which can determine the price for repair or recommend buying a new car instead. I noticed that altogether the value of vehicles declines more rapidly'. After running a car for 36 months or approximately 15,000 kilometers (around 10,000 miles) a year, the car is valued only at about 35 percent of the purchase price. According to a BMW car dealer in Berlin (who preferred to remain anonymous), a maximum of 1/3 of the cars currently sold to private

consumers are paid for in cash and 2/3 are financed with loans. The ratio of private customers who need to finance a car is increasing, and auto companies tend to finance or lease
their cars themselves.

Mr. Fuerk further commented, 'From my point of view, these days, a car should keep
running no more than eight years'. So the continuous flow of auto manufacturing, sales,
and financing all contribute to safeguarding the profits of the big players in the auto industry.

Source: Interview with the firm owner, Walter Fuerk (2010, September 27th)

Not only small firms, but also large multinationals facing a reduction of resources as a result
of competitive pressures can easily become a target for (friendly or hostile) acquisition
through the process of industry concentration, as the case of the purchase of Volvo by Gely
in 2010 illustrates. Because the industry environment is continuously changing, the frequent
collection and analysis of up-to-date market information regarding the movements of customers and suppliers, stakeholders, and competitors' capabilities and intentions are of vital
importance if the firm is to survive in the global marketplace. Traditionally, marketing researchers were responsible for assessing market information, whereas marketing decisions
were made by product sales and marketing managers. However, these traditional roles are
changing. Marketing researchers are becoming more involved in decision making, whereas
marketing managers are becoming more involved with research (Malhotra, 2009).

In **country (market) attractiveness analysis,** macro and industry variables are explored and
rated based on management's evaluation of whether these variables indicate an opportunity
or a threat to realizing the firm's business objectives (Meissner, 1995). Macro indicators are
elements of the natural and societal environment (S.E.E.L.E.). Important variables of the
industry environment are market attractiveness (e.g., expected turnover and net income),
dynamics of competition, market entry and market exit barriers, momentum of changes in
product and technology life cycles, supplier and customer characteristics as well as the influencing power of shareholder and stakeholder. As illustrated in Figure 19 below, alternative
target countries (markets) can be compared and their potential for the firm explored, which
supports the management in the process of making a market decision.

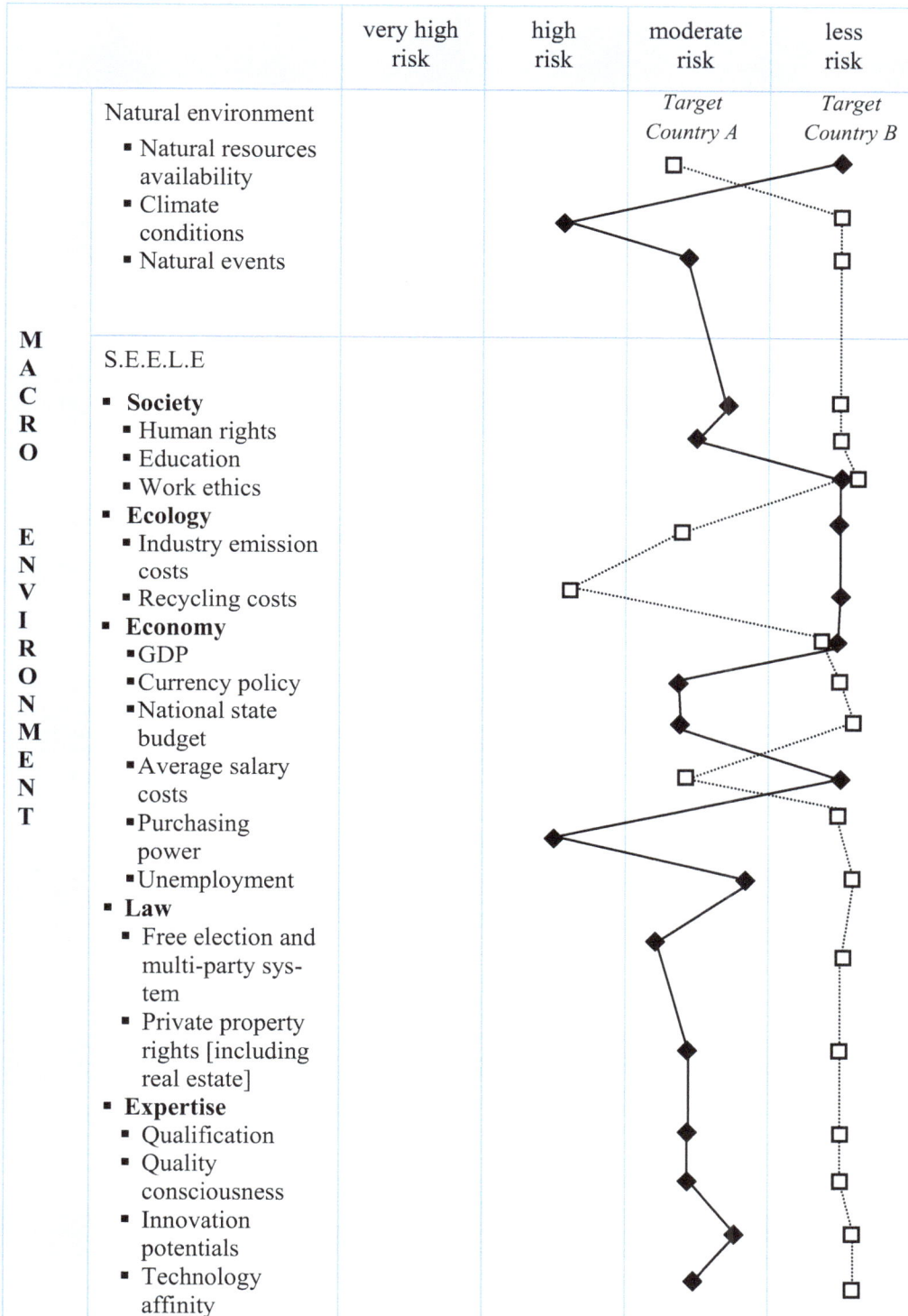

		very high risk	high risk	moderate risk	less risk
M A C R O **E N V I R O N M E N T**	Natural environment • Natural resources availability • Climate conditions • Natural events			*Target Country A*	*Target Country B*

	S.E.E.L.E
	• **Society**
	  • Human rights
	  • Education
	  • Work ethics
	• **Ecology**
	  • Industry emission costs
	  • Recycling costs
	• **Economy**
	  • GDP
	  • Currency policy
	  • National state budget
	  • Average salary costs
	  • Purchasing power
	  • Unemployment
	• **Law**
	  • Free election and multi-party sys-tem
	  • Private property rights [including real estate]
	• **Expertise**
	  • Qualification
	  • Quality consciousness
	  • Innovation potentials
	  • Technology affinity				

		very high risk	high risk	moderate risk	less risk
I N D U S T R Y E N V I R O N M E N T	▪ Market attractiveness ▪ Industry competition ▪ Market entry barriers ▪ Market exit barriers ▪ Momentum of changes in the product life cycles ▪ Supplier availability and bargaining power ▪ Customer characteristics and bargaining power				

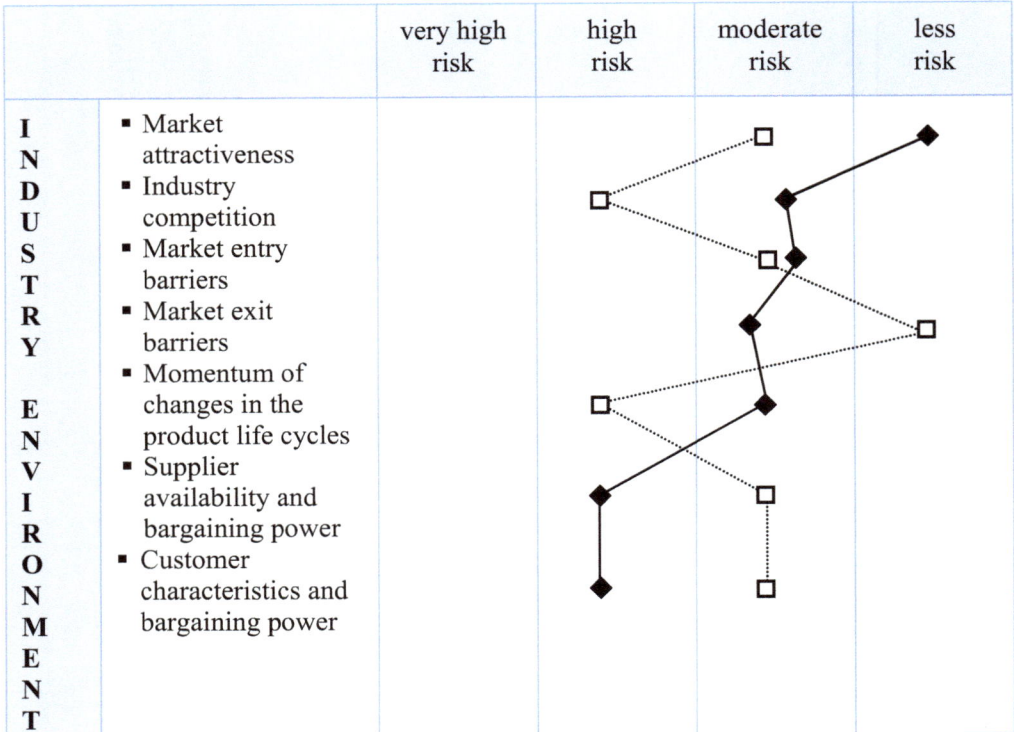

□ Target Country A = VW Germany

◆ Target Country B = VW do Brasil

Figure 19. An example of a country risk analysis

3.2.3   The micro analyses

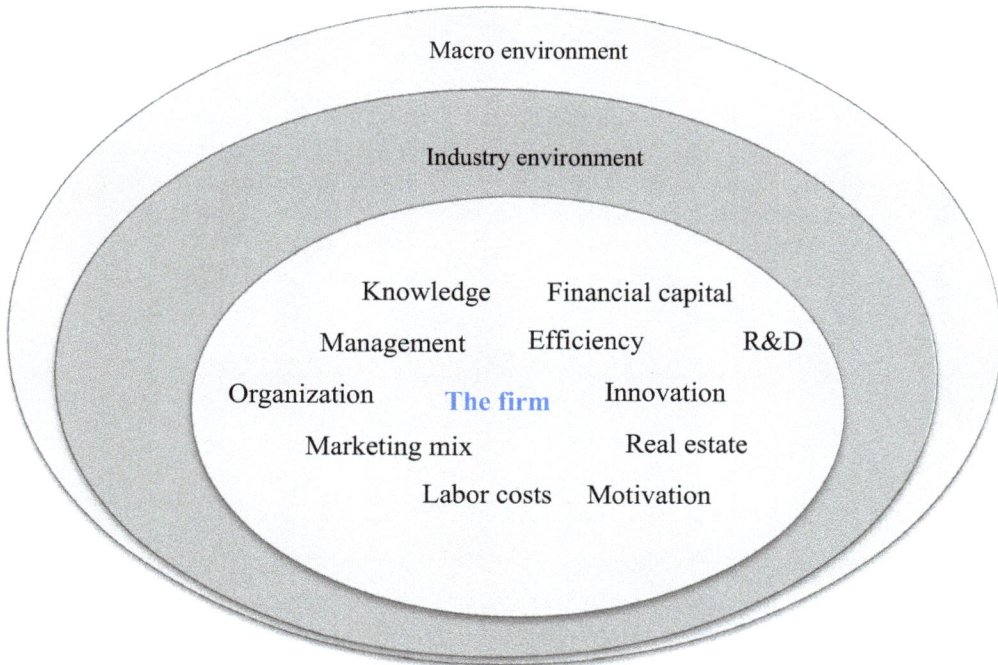

Macro environment

Industry environment

Knowledge   Financial capital

Management   Efficiency   R&D

Organization   **The firm**   Innovation

Marketing mix   Real estate

Labor costs   Motivation

Figure 20. Important elements of a micro analysis

After the elements of the macro and industry environment are explored and evaluated as described in the sections above, the next step is to contrast the characteristics of potential target markets with the firm's internal strengths and weaknesses. The **SWOT analysis** is a tool to list and contrast external opportunities and threats with internal strengths and weaknesses (Kotler et al., 2007). The **resource-based view (RBV)** holds that a firm's competitive advantages are particularly derived from its 'inner resources' (micro environment), such as managerial, organizational, technological and knowledge resources, which serve as firm strengths and/or weaknesses (Barney, 1991; Fahy, 2002; Wernerfelt, 1984). The RBV perceives the firm as a unique bundle of idiosyncratic resources and capabilities developed over time, where the primary task of management is to maximize value through the optimal deployment of existing resources and capabilities. In light of accelerated technological and product life cycles and against the background of globalized trade patterns, fostering and developing knowledge resources is of vital importance if the firm is to gain a competitive advantage. Assets include tangible resources, real estate, labor costs, and financial capital. Intangible resources include the firm's potential for generating ideas, research and development capabilities, innovation, and fast time to market responses, all of which are fundamental resource properties and, consequently, important strengths for a firm in the modern service and product driven economy. During the course of evaluating the firm's internal resources, the management is able to deduce strengths and weaknesses. Finally, the marketing manager's task is to develop competitive advantages through a favorable selection of promising target markets that harmonize best with the internal firm resource assets.

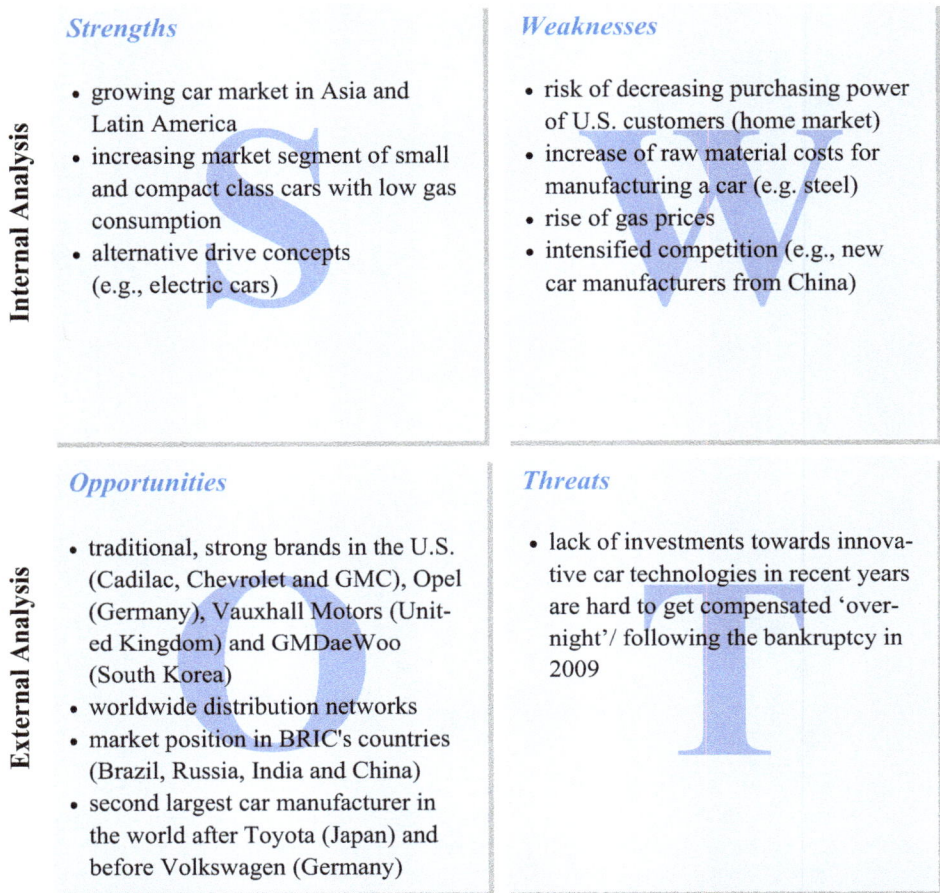

Internal Analysis	**Strengths**	**Weaknesses**
	• growing car market in Asia and Latin America • increasing market segment of small and compact class cars with low gas consumption • alternative drive concepts (e.g., electric cars)	• risk of decreasing purchasing power of U.S. customers (home market) • increase of raw material costs for manufacturing a car (e.g. steel) • rise of gas prices • intensified competition (e.g., new car manufacturers from China)
External Analysis	**Opportunities**	**Threats**
	• traditional, strong brands in the U.S. (Cadilac, Chevrolet and GMC), Opel (Germany), Vauxhall Motors (United Kingdom) and GMDaeWoo (South Korea) • worldwide distribution networks • market position in BRIC's countries (Brazil, Russia, India and China) • second largest car manufacturer in the world after Toyota (Japan) and before Volkswagen (Germany)	• lack of investments towards innovative car technologies in recent years are hard to get compensated 'overnight'/ following the bankruptcy in 2009

Figure 21. SWOT analysis of the 'New General Motors Company' (status 2010)

The macro environment (natural resources and the elements of S.E.E.L.E.), the industry environment, and the micro environment where the operating firm and the customers are embedded resemble a circular process of mutually influencing variables. The momentum of change can be initiated in any part, which means in the macro environment (e.g., change of laws), the industry environment (e.g., new competitor), the customer (e.g., changing lifestyle), or the firm itself (e.g., pioneering inventions). The management's responsibility is to explore opportunities in the firm's general environment that potentially have an influence on the industry and to develop corresponding internal resources in the firm's organization. Through that process, the firm better serves the needs and expectations of its customers and thus better realizes the firm's business objectives. Because international markets are complex, competitive dynamics may easily become a threat to the firm's business. In a negative case, the firm management cannot adequately respond because of internal (resource) weaknesses that had not been identified or that had been neglected for too long a time by the management. This situation significantly worsens the competitive position of the firm in the future. In order to avoid such drawbacks, a continual scanning of the firm's macro and micro environment is of vital importance. The dynamics of the environment/firm circle might be explained best against the background of the following example. Assuming that raw material prices such as oil prices are increasing in the worldwide market (refer to macro environment: natural re-courses, ecology), customers may hesitate or refuse to buy cars with high gas consumption. For some car producers (industry environment) that sell cars with high gas consumption, increasing prices surely constitute a threat. For other firms that assemble cars with alternative and/or energy-saving technologies, rising oil prices provide a chance to improve their com-petitive position in the markets. As a result of market forces, non-innovative car assemblers, producing autos with high emissions and high gas consumption, are pushed out of the market, which helps to create a healthier life for the population because of a cleaner environment.

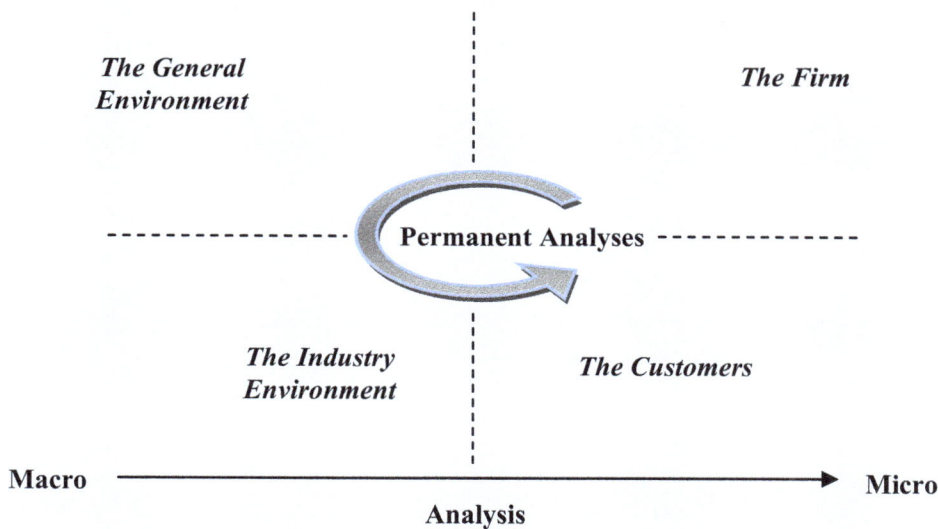

Figure 22. Mutual influencing elements of a firm's macro and micro environment

Portfolio models serve as an instrument for contrasting external market attractiveness with the firm's competitive position (Czinkota and Ronkainen, 2007). One of the best known portfolio analyses is the 'market growth – market share' matrix as introduced by the **Boston Consulting Group (BCG)**. The BCG matrix helps to segment the firm's products and ser-vices in its markets according to their relative market share and the attractiveness of the mar-ket as indicated by market growth rates (Henderson, 1971). Market attractiveness represents one vital element of the firm's industry environment, and the relative market share indicates the competitive position of the firm (as a result of internal resource strengths or weaknesses). According to the BSG matrix, question marks are products where market growth rates are promising, but the firm's relative market share remains rather low. **Question marks** are usually newly developed products in new markets, where the firm needs to bind financial resources for activities such as promoting the product and investing in order to expand the manufacturing capacity. Assuming there is a market for these products in the future, internal firm resources are efficiently applied, and continued product development is managed well; question marks can become the firm's cash cows in the future.

Cash cows are products located in saturated markets, where the firm holds a relatively high market share. Due to an advanced experience curve and economies of scale effects, the products are manufactured at efficient costs; thus sales of cash cow products contribute the highest liquidity incomes of the firm. Nevertheless, cash cow markets normally are saturated; and the product life cycle indicates a rather declining stage. As a result, a firm's cash cow market today may downsize in the future because product substitutions are likely. According to the BCG portfolio matrix, stars are products in markets where the firm holds a relatively strong market share, and the market has substantial expected growth rates. A new and innovative product invention, difficult to assimilate by the firm's competitors, provides the best preconditions for a firm's star product. The 'stars' of today's business should be continuously developed, improved, and, depending on changing demand conditions, if necessary, modified, in order to become the cash cows of the firm's future business.

Finally, products categorized as poor dogs are not located in attractive growth markets; and the firm does not hold a satisfactory market share. Previous failures in market research or poor management decisions in the past contribute to the undesirable outcome of poor dog products. Because poor dogs generate losses, the firm's management should terminate the corresponding businesses. Self-assessment by the management and acceptance that a decision in the past led to the poor dogs and therefore obviously was wrong usually serves as the most critical issue. For egoistical reasons combined with the risk of obstructing one's own career opportunities, management executives often hesitate and delay essential decisions to give up business segments. Ideally, the product portfolio of a firm ensures that the net income generated by cash cows and stars balances the losses caused by the poor dogs and, moreover, provides a financial cushion for development of the question marks (Hedley, 1977; Müller-Stewens and Lechner, 2005).

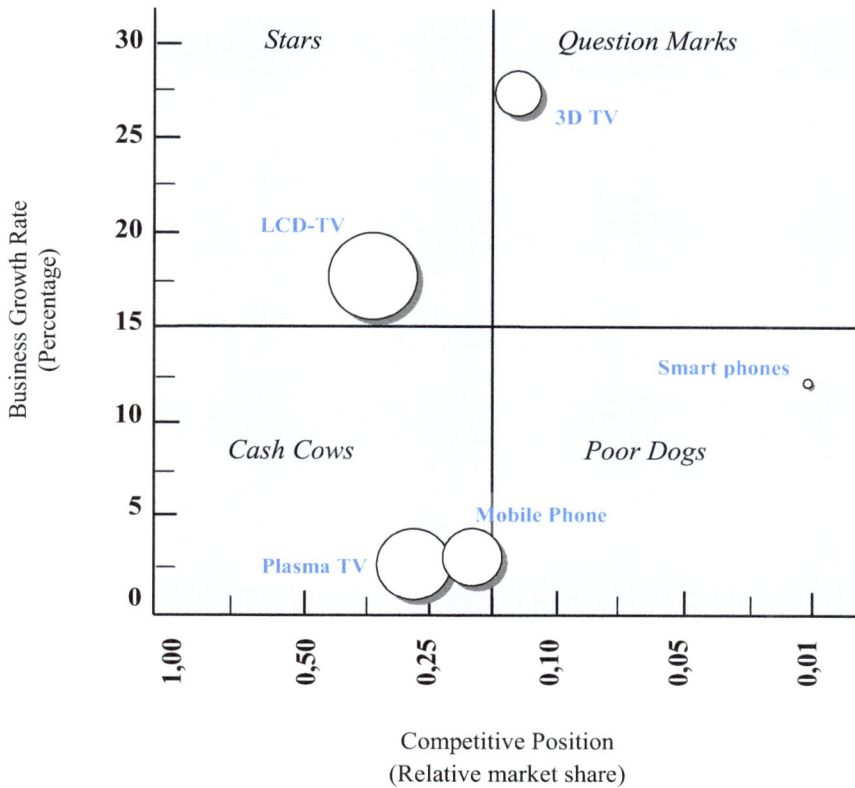

Figure 23. Portfolio analysis of Samsung Electronics in its European markets (status 2011)

Question marks and stars are located in promising markets at the beginning stage of their product life cycles, whereas cash cows and dogs are positioned in saturated and declining markets. Due to experience curve effects and relatively high market shares, cash cows generate the highest net income for the firm. Poor dogs are products usually positioned at the end of the product life cycle with relatively high unit costs, mainly due to limited sales volumes in unattractive markets. Overall these products cause losses. Stars, because of their strong position in growth markets and corresponding high sales volumes, have reasonable unit costs and therefore are the net income generators of the firm.

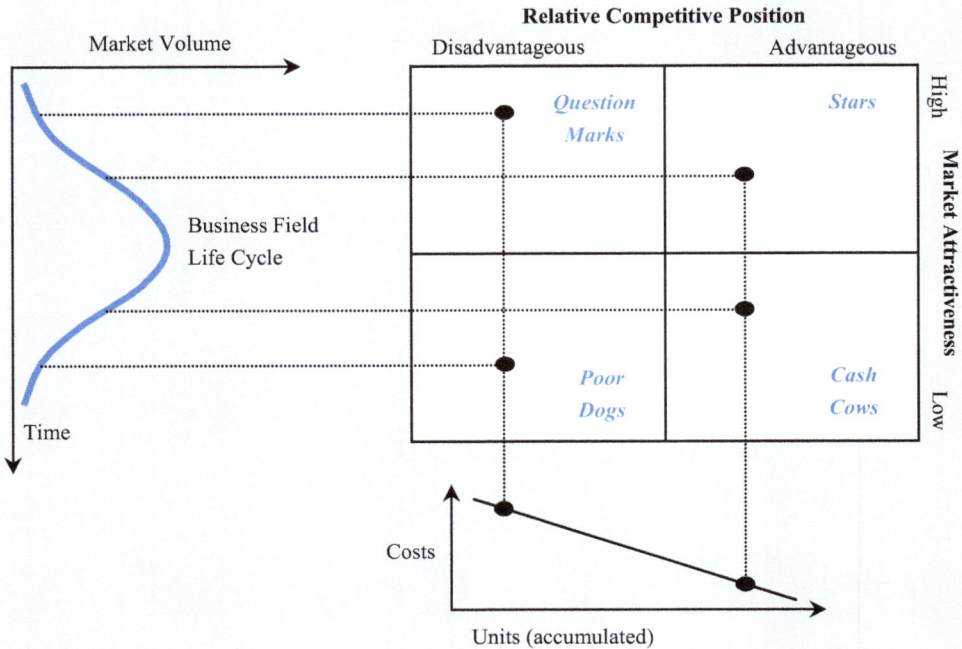

Source: Müller-Stewens and Lechner (2005), p. 305

Figure 24. BCG, product life cycle and cost regression

Strategic marketing decisions, despite the overall efforts of marketing executives, can never be based on 'perfect' market information. Moreover, from the perspective of the firm's management, there are controllable, hybrid, and uncontrollable variables that have an impact on the decision process (compare Figure 25). **Uncontrollable environmental variables** in the external macro environment are first, variables of the natural environment (natural resources, climate conditions, and natural events) and second, the S.E.E.L.E variables, such as society, ecology, economy, law, and expertise. Generally, external factors of the macro environment are out of the control of the firm's management. **Hybrid controllable environmental variables** are elements of the industry environment, such as suppliers, customers, shareholders, and other stakeholders. Firms can take an active part in developing their industry environments, thus having, at least to some extent, an influence on the stakeholders (e.g., industry associations, suppliers, and customers). The hybrid variables, depending on the firm's negotiation power, reputation in the society, and direct communication policies, are influenced by but definitively not under the control of the firm's marketing management. **Controllable variables** by the marketing management are primarily decisions on strategies based on the firm's internal resources. Firm resources – such as organizational efficiency and qualifications and motivation of employees, access to procurement sources, marketing skills, and others – belong to the firm's internal environment and simultaneously represent firm-specific strengths and weaknesses. Depending on the resources of the firm, the marketing management designs the corresponding marketing mix of instruments (product and pricing policy, promotion, and selection of distribution channels) and supervises their implementation and control.

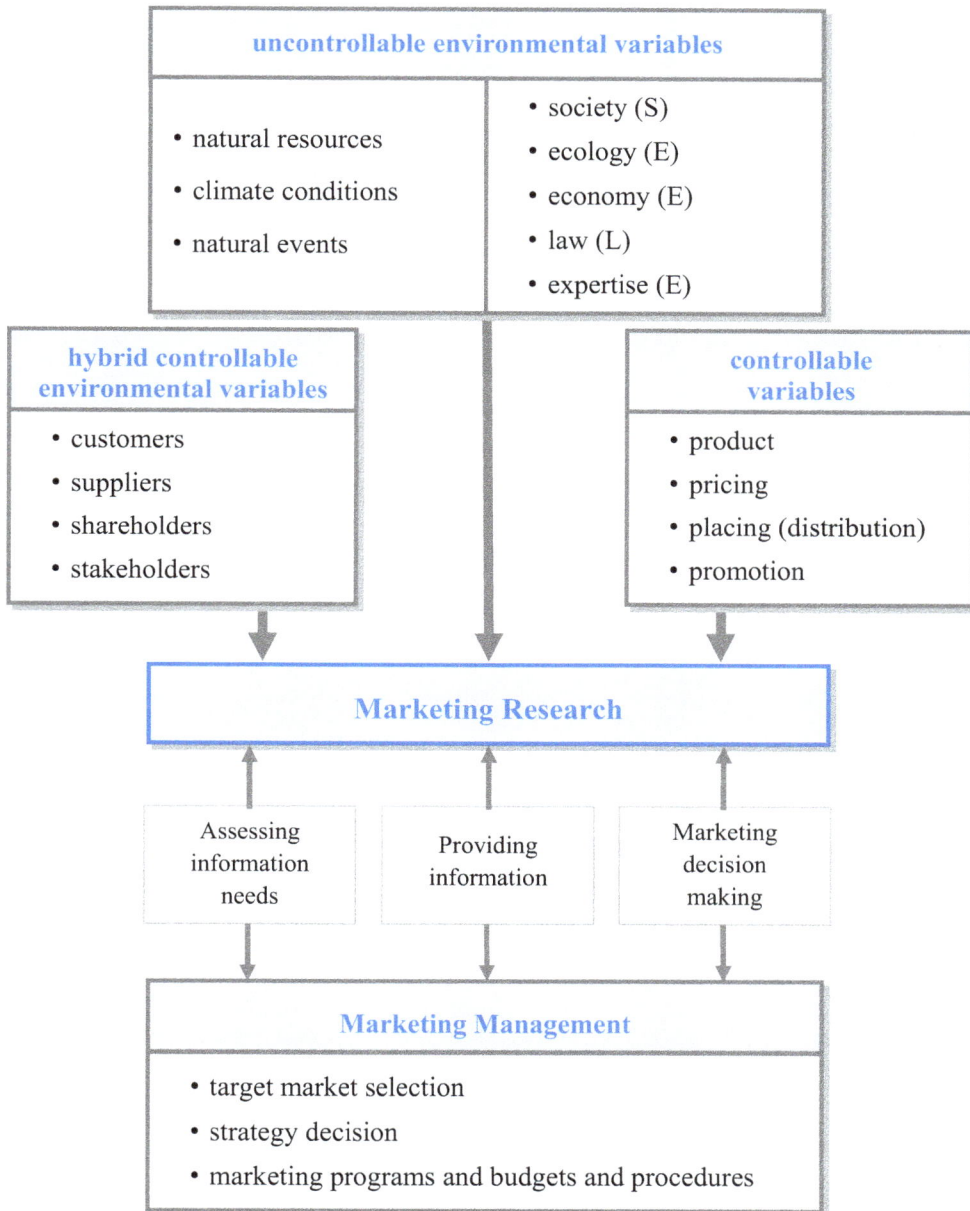

uncontrollable environmental variables	
• natural resources • climate conditions • natural events	• society (S) • ecology (E) • economy (E) • law (L) • expertise (E)

hybrid controllable environmental variables	controllable variables
• customers • suppliers • shareholders • stakeholders	• product • pricing • placing (distribution) • promotion

Marketing Research

Assessing information needs	Providing information	Marketing decision making

Marketing Management

- target market selection
- strategy decision
- marketing programs and budgets and procedures

Source: modified from Malhotra (2009), p. 12

Figure 25. The role of marketing research

Management executives are responsible for leading the firm towards an effective combination of internal firm strengths and external environmental opportunities in order to realize the firm's overall business objectives. Based on the information gained from the macro, industry, and micro analysis, which is aimed at realizing the firm's goal of determining the best business practices, the management, at the end of the process, is able to develop successful strategies. The concept of 'building a firm strategy' is introduced and described in the next chapter.

List of References

Afp_the_Local_Sweden, 2010. Volvo sold to China's Geely [online]. [cited 20.10.2010]. Available from World Wide Web:<URL:http://www.thelocal.se/25784/20100328>.

Albaum, G., Duerr, E. & Strandskov, J., 2008. *International marketing and export management*. Essex: Pearson Education Limited.

Barney, J., 1991. Firm resources and sustained competitive advantage. *Journal of Management*, 17: 99-120.

Bartlett, C. A. & Ghoshal, S., 1990. *Internationale Unternehmensführung. Innovation, globale Effizienz, differenziertes Marketing*. Frankfurt: Campus.

Bartlett, C. A. & Ghoshal, S., 1998. *Managing across borders: the transnational solution*. Harvard: Harvard Press.

Beckman, C. M., Haunschild, P. R. & Phillips, D. J., 2004. Friends or strangers? Firm-specific uncertainty, market uncertainty, and network partner selection. *Organization Science*, 15 (3).

Cateora, P. R., Gilly, M. C. & Graham, J. L., 2009. *International Marketing*. Boston: McGraw-Hill Irwin.

Chidlow, A., Salciuviene, L. & Young, S., 2009. Regional determinants of inward FDI distribution in Poland. *International Business Review*, 18: 119-133.

Czinkota, M. R. & Kotabe, M., 2005. *Marketing management*. Cincinnati: Atomic Dog Publishing.

Czinkota, M. R. & Ronkainen, I. A., 2007. *International marketing*. Mason, OH: Thomson Higher Education.

Doole, I. & Lowe, R., 2008. *International marketing strategy. Analysis, development and implementation*. London: South-Western Cengage Learning.

Drori, G. S., Meyer, J. W. & Hwang, H., 2006. *Globalization and Organization*. Oxford: Oxford University Press.

Dunning, J. H., 2000. The eclectic paradigm as an envelope for economic and business theories of MNE activity. *International Business Review*, 9 (2): 163-190.

Eu_Commission, 2010. The Doha round [online]. [cited 04.10.2010]. Available from World Wide Web:<URL:http://ec.europa.eu/trade/creating-opportunities/eu-and-wto/doha/>.

European_Environment_Agency, 2010. European_Environment_Agency. Where does Europe stand in 2010? [online]. [cited 23.08.2010]. Available form World Wide Web:<URL:http://www.eea.europa.eu/publications/eu-2010-biodiversity-baseline/flyer-european-biodiversity-baseline-2014>.

Fahy, J., 2002. A resource-based analysis of sustainable competitive advantage in a global environment. *International Business Review*, 11: 57-78.

Forsgren, M., Holm, U. & Johanson, J., 2005. *Managing the embedded multinational. A business network view*. Cheltenham: Edward Elgar Publishing Limited.

Forssbaek, J. & Oxelheim, L., 2008. Finance-specific factors as drivers of cross-border investment. An empirical investigation. *International Business Review*, 17: 630-641.

Ghoshal, S., 1987. Global strategy: an organizing framework. *Strategic Management Journal*, 8: 425-440.

Hedley, B., 1977. Strategy and the business portfolio. *Long Range Planning*, 10 (1): 9-15.

Henderson, B. D., 1971. *Construction of a business strategy. The Boston Consulting Group. Series on corporate strategies.* Boston.

Hill, C. W. L., 2009. *International business: competing in the global marketplace.* Boston: McGraw-Hill/Irwin.

Hoffman, K. D., Bateson, J. E. G., Wood, E. H. & Kenyon, A. K., 2009. *Services marketing. Concepts, strategies and cases.* London: South-Western Cengage Learning.

Hoffmann, W., Roventa, P. & Weichsel, D., 2003. *Marktveränderungen und Konsolidierungswelle in der Pharma-Industrie: Kommt der Mittelstand unter die Räder?* Ludwigshafen.

Holtbrügge, D. & Welge, M. K., 2010. *Internationales Management. Theorien, Funktionen, Fallstudien.* Stuttgart: Schäffer-Poeschel.

Homburg, C. & Krohmer, H., 2009. *Marketingmanagement: Strategie – Instrumente – Umsetzung – Unternehmensführung.* Wiesbaden: Gabler.

Imf, 2010. Time series data on international reserves and foreign currency liquidity official reserve assets and other foreign currency assets [online].[cited 07.11.2010]. Available from World Wide Web: <http://www.imf.org/external/np/sta/ir/IRProcessWeb/data/802P816.pdf>.

International_Monetary_Fund, 2010. IMFsurvey magazine: In the news. IMF call to work together for growth, jobs, financial sector reform [online]. [cited 14.10.2010]. Available from World Wide Web:<http://www.imf.org/external/pubs/ft/survey/so/2010/NEW100810A.htm>.

Johanson, J. & Mattsson, L.-G., 1988. Internationalization in industrial systems – a network approach. In Hood, N. & Vahlne, J.-E. (Eds.) *Strategies in global competition:* 468-486. New York: Croom Helm.

Johanson, J. & Vahlne, J.-E., 1977. The internationalization process of the firm – a model of knowledge development and increasing foreign market commitments. *Journal of International Business Studies,* 8 (1): 23-32.

Keillor, B., Davila, V. & Hult, T. G., 2001. Market entry strategies and influencing factors: a multi-industry/multi product investigation *The Marketing Management Journal,* 11: 1-11.

Kotabe, M. & Helsen, K., 2008. *Global marketing management.* Hoboken, NJ: John Wiley & Sons.

Kotler, P., Keller, K. L. & Bliemel, F., 2007. *Marketing Management. Strategien für wertschaffendes Handeln.* München: Pearson Education.

Luostarinen, R., 1980. *Internationalization of the firm. An empirical study of the internationalization of firms with small and open domestic markets with special emphasis on lateral rigidity as a behavioral characteristic in strategic decision-making.* Helsinki: The Helsinki School of Economics.

Malhotra, N. K., 2009. *Marketing research. An applied orientation.* New Jersey: Pearson Education International.

Meissner, H. G., 1995. *Strategisches Internationales Marketing.* München: Oldenbourg Wissenschaftsverlag.

Müller-Stewens, G. & Lechner, C., 2005. *Strategisches Management. Wie strategische Initiativen zum Wandel führen.* Stuttgart: Schäffer-Poeschel.

Nokia, 2008. Nokia to refocus its Japanese operations [online]. [cited 15.07.2010]. *Nokia Press Services.* Available from World Wide Web:URL:http://pressbulletinboard.nokia.com/tag/japan/.

Oecd, 2010. *Education: Governments should expand tertiary studies to boost jobs and tax revenues.* Paris: OECD.

Özsomer, A. & Simonin, B., 1999. Antecedents and consequences of market orientation in a subsidiary context. Enhancing knowledge development in marketing. *American marketing association educators proceedings, Summer 1999.*

Penrose, E., 1995. *The theory of the growth of the firm.* New York [first published 1959]: Oxford University Press.

Perlmutter, H. V., 1969. The tortuous evolution of the multinational corporation. *Columbia Journal of World Business*, 4: 9-18.

Perreault, W. & Mccarthy, E. J., 2005. *Basic marketing. A global marketing approach.* Burr Ridge McGraw-Hill.

Porter, M. E., 1990. *The competitive advantage of nations.* New York: The Free Press.

Repetzki, B., 2010. Germany Trade and Invest. Polen kaufen mehr Haus-, Audio- und Videogeräte [online]. [cited 18.07.2010]. Available from World Wide Web:<URL:http://www.gtai.de/fdb-SE,MKT200710238001,MSN.html>.

Ritter, T., Wilkinson, I. F. & Johnston, W. J., 2004. Managing in complex business networks. *Industrial Marketing Management*, 33: 175-183.

Rugman, A. M. & Collinson, S., 2009. *International business.* Essex: Pearson Education Limited.

Samiee, S., 2006. Supplier and customer exchange in international industrial markets: an integrative perspective. *Industrial Marketing Management*, 35: 589-599.

Teece, D. J., 2000. *Managing intellectual capital.* New York: Oxford University Press.

Theisen, P., 1970. *Grundzüge einer Theorie der Beschaffungspolitik.* Berlin: Duncker & Humblot.

Unctad, 2009. United Nations Conference on Trade and Development - Statistics [online]. [cited 17.8.2009]. Available from World Wide Web:<URL:http://www.unctad.org/sections/dite_fdistat/docs/wid_cp_hu_en.pdf>.

Unctad, 2010. Inward and outward foreign direct investment stock, annual, 1980-2009 [online]. [cited 12.12.2010]. Available from World Wide Web: <www.http://unctadstat.unctad.org>.

Union, A. E., 2010. Automotive Cluster - West Slovakia [online]. [cited 18.07.2010]. Available from World Wide Web:<URL:http://www.autoclusters.eu/index.php/partner/127-automotive-cluster-west-slovakia>.

United_States_Labor_Department, 2010. Bureau of Labor Statistics. Employment situation summary [online]. [cited 15.10.2010]. Available from World Wide Web:<URL:http://www.bls.gov/news.release/empsit.nr0.htm>.

Welge, K. M. & Holtbrügge, D., 2010. *Internationales Management.* Stuttgart: Schäffer-Poeschel Verlag.

Wernerfelt, B., 1984. A resource based view of the firm. *Strategic Management Journal*, 5 (2): 171-180.

Wheelen, T. L. & Hunger, J. D., 2010. *Strategic management and business policy.* New Jersey: Pearson Education Ltd.

Wind, Y., Douglas, S. P. & Perlmuttter, H. V., 1973. Guidelines for developing international marketing strategies. *Journal of Marketing*, 37 (2): 38-46.

Wto, 2010a. Understanding the WTO: The GATT years from Havana to Marrakesh [online]. [cited: 05.10.2010]. Available from World Wide Web:<URL:http://www.wto.org/english/thewto_e/whatis_e/tif_e/fact4_e.htm>.

Wto, 2010b. *World trade report.* Geneva.

4   Chapter: Strategy Building

- Describe the alternative directional strategies.

- Explain the strategy hierarchy levels of top, middle, and operating management.

- Describe international market entry strategies.

- Explain the pros and cons of concentration strategies.

- Explain the pros and cons of diversification strategies.

- Identify strategy variants on the functional (department) level.

- Differentiation versus cost leadership: Identify suitable strategy equivalents on the functional level.

- Explain the important contents of strategy implementation and control.

4.1 Corporate Strategy

4.1.1 Market entry and retrenchment

The strategy of a firm is developed by answering these questions: where does the firm compete, and how does it compete? The first question concerns the external scope of the firm's activities: in which products, markets, and businesses should the firm be involved? The second question is concerned with how the firm plans to establish a competitive advantage over its rivals within the markets that it serves. The organizational capabilities that form the foundation of **corporate strategies** are dependent on organizational structures and processes (internal scope) (Grant, 2002).

According to Chandler (1962: 23), strategy is to be understood 'as the determination of basic long-term goals and objectives of an enterprise and the adoption of courses of action and the allocation of resources necessary for carrying out these goals'. A firm's strategy forms a comprehensive master plan that states how the management will achieve its business objectives based on existing internal resources. Strategy formulation is the development of long-range plans for the effective management of environmental opportunities and threats in light of corporate strengths and weaknesses. Corporate strategy describes a company's overall direction in terms of its general attitude toward the business and the management of its markets and corresponding product lines. Firm **policies** serve as a link between strategy formulation and its implementation. Companies develop policies to make sure employees throughout the firm demonstrate working behaviors that support the realization of the firm's objectives (Wheelen and Hunger, 2010). Adequate firm policies ensure that customers are well served. For example, 'sense and simplicity' encourages Philips' engineers to develop products that are easy for their customers to install and use. Airlines usually design a timetable that suggests that flights will be longer than they actually are, allowing them to give the impression that their scheduling is good as most flights will arrive earlier than the stated arrival time (Wilson et al., 2008).

How does the management proceed in the process of integral corporate strategy building? By reviewing business objectives in light of the environmental analysis, management executives decide the basic route of the firm's business. Thus, at first, the firm's **directional strategies** are formulated at the top management level. There are three alternative directional strategies: **growth, stability,** and **retrenchment strategies** (Wheelen and Hunger, 2010). Among these strategy variants, the growth strategy is the most attractive strategic alternative since it targets the expansion of the firm's business. Essential characteristics of a growth strategy are an increase in the firm's sales volume, reflected by an increase of market share and net income margins. Stability strategies, among others, often follow recent acquisition(s) of the firm, and usually target harmonizing internal organization structures and increasing overall efficiency. The management decides on retrenchment strategies when the competitive position (indicated in turnover and profit margins) of operating business units is performing below expectations or even generating losses. As a result of retrenchment strategies, business units are either outsourced to contract manufacturers or to a joint venture; or, as another alternative, stakes of these operating units are completely sold to other firms.

In the second step of the process of developing directional strategies, the decision must be made as to whether business activities in existing markets or new markets should be procured. Third, the management has to make up its mind as to whether it wants to expand, stabilize, or draw back its activities in the domestic (home) market or in foreign markets. Fourth, the firm's executive management needs to evaluate and make the decision of whether to concentrate on internal resources, for example expanding manufacturing capacities or increasing asset efficiency in existing plants or to pursue the external path (e.g., capital participation). Assuming the firm's management is considering the internal path, the fundamental question is: Do we have the corresponding resources? Alternatively, if the firm is considering the external path, the basic question is: Are there synergy effects (for example, when establishing a joint venture)?

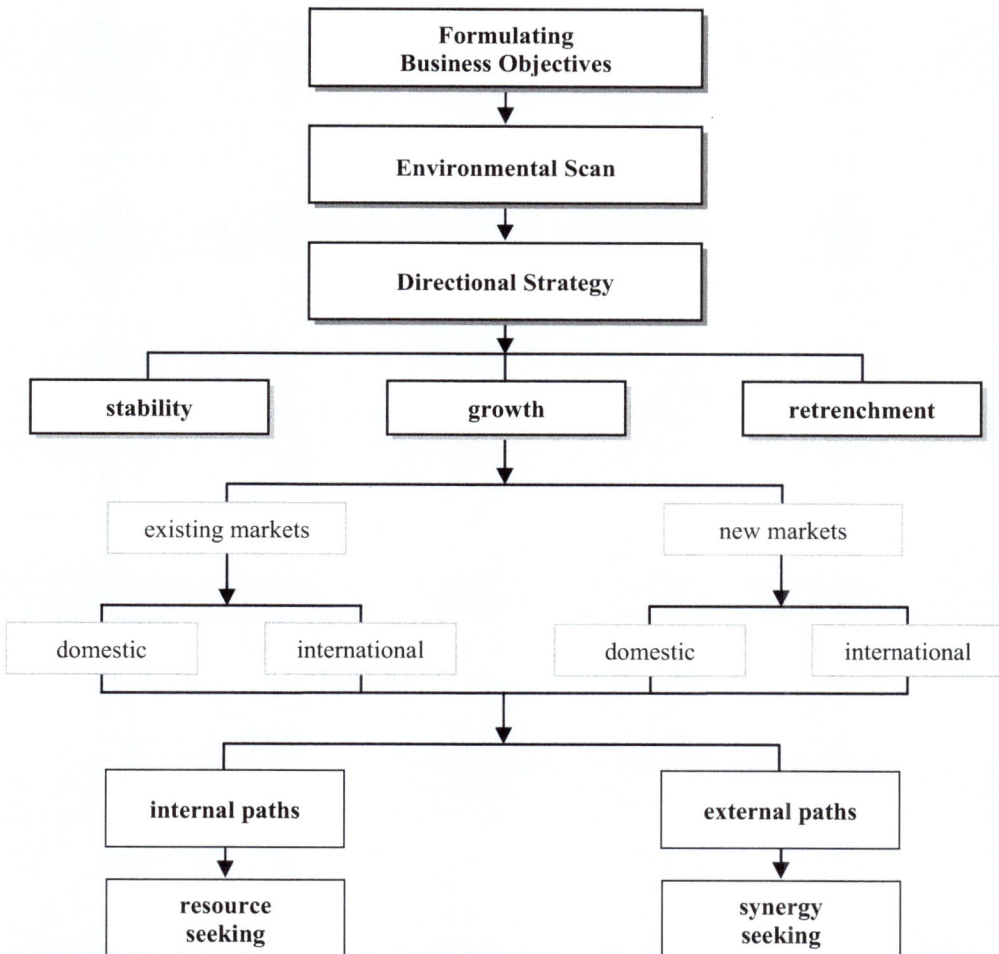

Figure 26. Strategy building

In case the firm seeks to expand abroad, the management decisions involve choosing suitable market entry strategies in foreign markets. International market entry strategies, following the transaction costs theory (Williamson, 1975; Williamson, 1985), can be divided into contractual modes (market transaction), cooperative (hybrid) forms, and foreign direct investments (hierarchy) as briefly introduced below.

Contractual modes (market transactions):

- **Indirect export**: the firm delivers products and/or services to a domestic exporting company or to a firm located in a foreign country. The business is initiated and arranged by an intermediate (middleman), who usually receives a commission calculated as a percentage of the gross-border business.
- **Direct exports**: the firm undertakes direct business relations with the customer abroad and arranges the market research, negotiations, and contracting and delivery management by themselves (Hill, 2009).
- **Original equipment manufacture (OEM)**: firms expand their value added activities in lower-cost locations (increase of production capacities) or outsource component assembly (part assembly) or transfer the complete manufacturing process (full assembly) to lower-cost producers (Morschett, 2005).
- **Licensing**: means a contractual transaction in which the owner of knowledge assets (intellectual or industrial property) grants, for payment of a fee, another firm the right to use these assets for a defined purpose (Luostarinen and Welch, 1997).
- **Franchising**: is a term used to describe a business concept in which the franchisor sells to the franchisees, which are typically small business owners, the right to commercialize goods or services under its established brand name (market goodwill) and a proven business concept for the payment of fees (Combs et al., 2004).
- **Turnkey operation:** refers to a practice in which a company designs, constructs, and starts-up a project in a foreign country (i.e., building of a power plant), qualifies local personnel, and then 'turns the key over' to the local government in return for an agreed upon payment of use fee (Deresky, 2002).
- **Management contracts**: offer a means through which a firm may use some of its personnel to assist a firm in a host county for a specified fee and period of time. This allows a firm to continue to earn some income from its investment and keep the operations going until local management is trained (Wheelen and Hunger, 2010).

Cooperative forms of market entry (hybrid forms):

- **Strategic alliances**: are agreements between two or more participating organizations to strengthen their mutual competitive position (e.g., joint introduction of new technological standards) and to fulfill business objectives that are rather long term. The formal difference compared to a joint venture is that a strategic alliance is typically a non-equity cooperation, meaning that the partners do not commit equity into or invest in the alliance (Hollensen, 2004).
- A **joint venture**: is formed when two or more legally distinct organizations decide to undertake a common business, e.g., manufacturing and sales of a particular product, and

create a new enterprise as a legal entity in order to pursue a set of agreed upon goals. The parties agree to contribute equity and share the revenue and expenses of the joint venture (Zentes et al., 2007).

Foreign direct investment (FDI) (hierarchy):

FDI describes a mode of market entry through capital investment in manufacturing, sales, and service facilities in a foreign country. The firm secures the partial or full ownership of firm-related activities, such as for example, plants, R&D laboratories, and sales representative offices or assets in distribution chains in the target market abroad. When a greenfield investment (internal path) is procured, the firm sets up its own manufacturing and administrative facilities. Labor forces are recruited and trained and organization structures are established. Unlike a merger, major internal management challenges linked with the process of bringing together separate, often culturally diverse management and labor teams are avoided, since the firm builds the entire operation abroad from scratch. Greenfield investments tend to be costly and firms are often faced with infrastructure challenges as well the challenge of finding qualified personnel in the target region (Kotabe and Helsen, 2008).

Therefore, the firm's management favors other alternatives to FDI, such as merger and acquisition and capital participation (external path). A merger entails two or more legally independent enterprises exchanging their capital and as a result, establishing a new firm. Mergers usually occur between firms of similar size and are usually friendly. Through an acquisition, a firm is completely purchased by another corporation. Acquisitions usually occur between firms of different sizes (Wheelen and Hunger, 2010). Instead of a complete purchase, capital participation is another FDI market entry mode. Common business objectives are agreed upon by the alliance partners, such as, for example, market entry in either one or the other partner's home market or joint R&D, manufacturing, and sales activities through capital participation of one firm in the other (partner) firm. Business practitioners, when promoting reasons for capital participation because of 'joint business objectives', synergies in marketing, and R&D often use the term 'strategic partnership' or 'strategic alliance'.

The main intention of mergers and acquisitions and capital participation (strategic partnership) is to increase competitive positions in the global markets, particularly because of joint resources. According to Albaum et al. (2008), there are potential risks and costs attached to cross-border acquisitions and mergers, which apply also to partial capital investments depending on the financial investment (share in capital).

- Foreign acquirers tend to pay more than a domestic buyer would, often with unrealistic hopes in gaining (illusive) synergies.
- Differences in language and national and corporate cultures aggravate integration of two management teams and possibly headquarters.
- Misperceptions about the home market of the acquired firm can lead to marketing mistakes.
- Employees tend to be even more frightened of management executives when they come from abroad.

- It is often difficult to integrate practices and operating methods of the acquired company into the overall management structure and philosophy.
- Integrating management styles or patterns of decision making is particularly challenging in cross-border mergers and acquisitions.

The case: The merger of Air France and KLM

In May 2004, two of the largest European airlines, Air France and KLM, merged their business activities and became Air France – KLM. One holding (Air France - KLM) listed at the European stock exchange markets was established with two separate operating companies and three strategic business units (passenger, cargo, and maintenance). Each operating airline remains responsible for its own commercial and operational management (e.g., human resources, safety, flight and ground operations, etc.).

The chairman and CEO of Air France – KLM was the former Air France chairman and CEO. The previous president and CEO of KLM became vice-chairman of the board of directors of the newly established airline holding. KLM appointed four directors to the Air France Board of Directors. Air France appointed four directors to sit on the KLM Supervisory Board. In 2007, Air France appointed five of the nine members of the KLM Supervisory Board. A strategic management committee (SMC) was established, responsible for the overall group strategy such as coordination of networks and hubs, budgets and mid-term planning, fleet and investment strategy, and alliance strategy.The SMC consists of eight members (four representatives from each airline), each of whom have a vote for the nomination of the Air France - KLM chairman and CEO. The new holding organization of Air France-KLM (status 2009) is illustrated below.

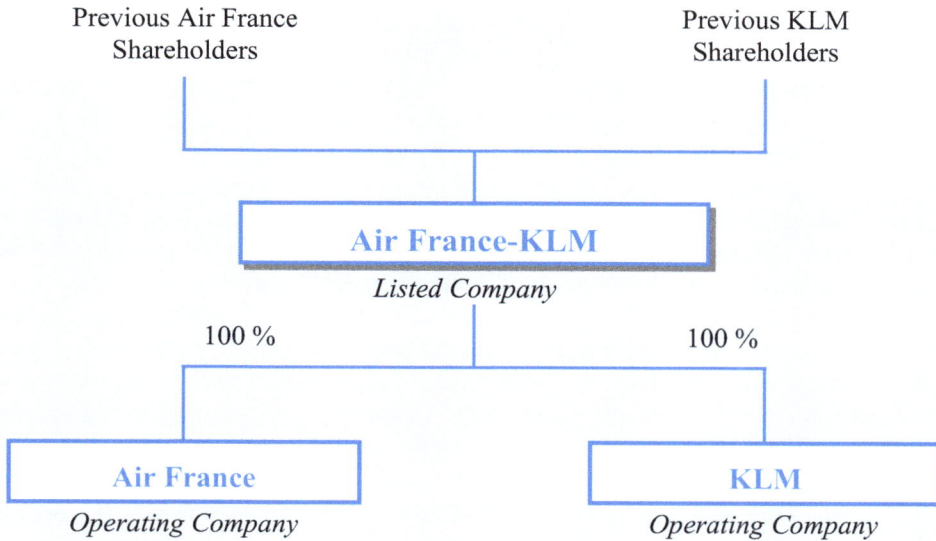

Source: Kartman (2009)

Figure 27. The Air France – KLM holding (status 2009)

Air France – KLM = 1 Group, 2 Airlines, 3 Businesses

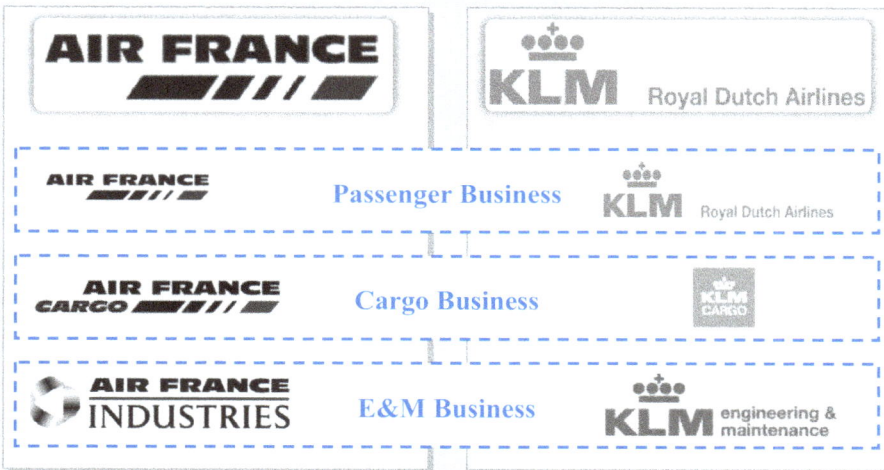

Source: Kartman (2009)

Figure 28. Air France – KLM business segments

When a firm has a comparatively weak competitive position in one or more business segments, which usually occurs with decreasing sales and when profits become losses, the management may decide to procure a **retrenchment** strategy. Alternatives of retrenchment strategies range from turnaround, to divestment, sell-out, and liquidation of the relevant business activities. **Turnaround strategy** emphasizes the improvement of overall operational efficiency, which is often combined with the (re-)focus on the firm's entire (core) business segments or the development of business concepts, products, and services for promising alternative markets. When the firm has several operating business lines and the management chooses to sell off a division with rather low growth potential to another firm, this strategy is named **divestment** (Wheelen and Hunger, 2010). Instead of selling the entire business unit, the firm may sell a part of its capital stake to another investor and remains as a minority or majority shareholder of the business unit. Divestment strategies are also used after the firm acquires a multi-business unit enterprise in order to shed some of the operating units that do not fit with the firm's overall strategic orientation. **Sell-out** strategy is used if the whole firm is sold to another firm. The strategic alternative of sell-out is desirable if the management is able to obtain a reasonable price for its shareholders, and the employees are able to keep their jobs. This alternative is often linked with the expectation that the acquiring firm will have the necessary resources and determination to return the company to profitability. Bankruptcy and liquidation strategies represent the worst strategic alternatives in the portfolio of business retrenchment alternatives. These alternatives, however, are often simply not avoidable if the firm's competitive position is worsening; and losses are continuously accumulating. **Bankruptcy** involves giving up the management of the firm to the courts in return for some settlement of the firm's obligations. As a result of the bankruptcy process, the management hopes that once the court decides the claims on the company, the remaining, reorganized enterprise will be stronger and better able to compete in its markets. In comparison to bankruptcy, which seeks to perpetuate the enterprise following its repositioning in the markets and internal restructuring, the liquidation strategy targets the overall termination of the firm. When the industry is unattractive and the firm's competitive position so weak it cannot be sold as an entire organization, the management has no other alternative than to select as many saleable firm assets as possible to cash, which is then distributed to the shareholders after all obligations are paid, such as, for example, bank loans, suppliers' invoices, and employees' salaries (Wheelen and Hunger, 2010).

4.1.2   Concentration and diversification strategies

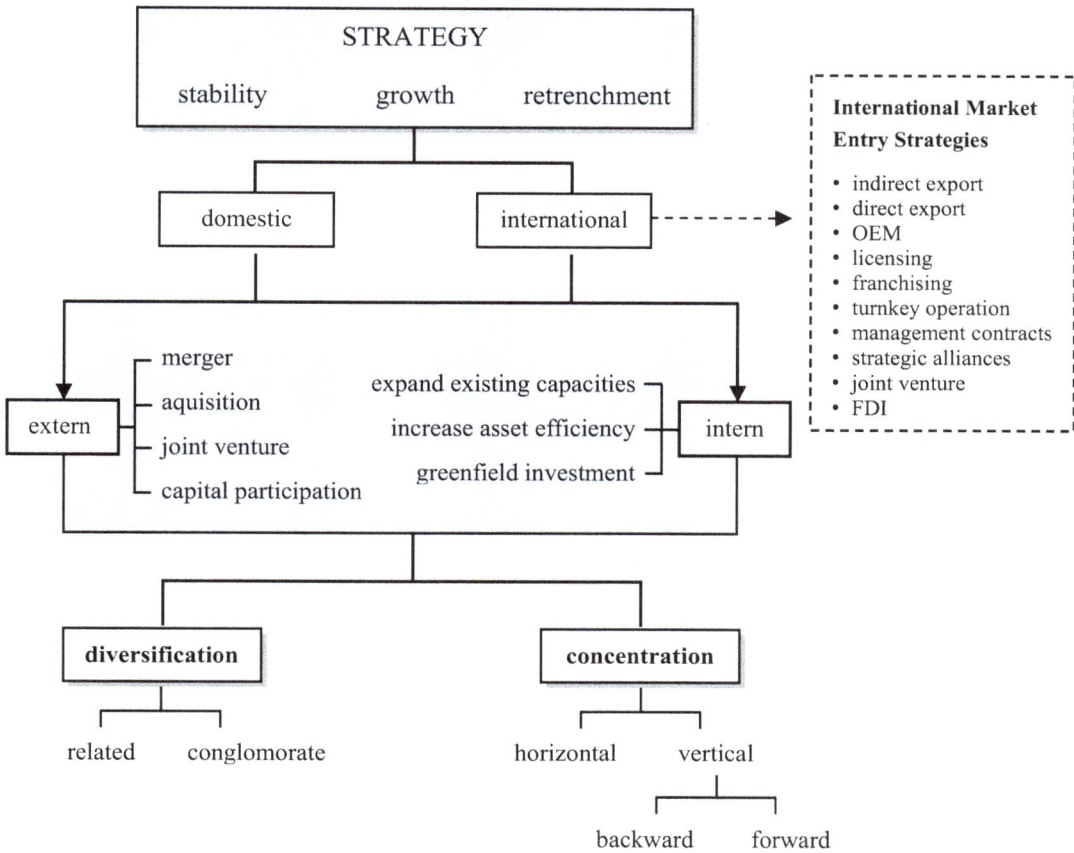

Figure 29. Positioning of diversification and concentration strategies

In the next step of the process, the management decides whether the enterprise will concentrate on its value added activities in its current industry, in familiar, or even in unfamiliar industries. A **horizontal concentration strategy** occurs when the firm focuses its entire resources in the same line of business in current or new markets (domestic or abroad), for example, increasing the product and service portfolio, making organization and manufacturing efficiency improvements, and initiating new product and technology developments. For companies that procure domestic and international businesses but have little product differentiation, a functional organizational structure is desirable, as illustrated below (Perlitz, 2004).

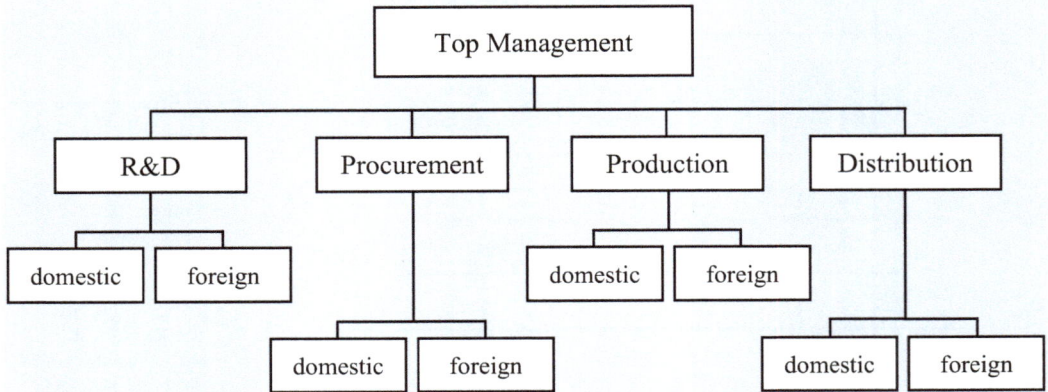

Source: modified from Perlitz (2004), p. 603

Figure 30. The integrated functional structure

Concentration strategy through vertical integration is utilized when the firm operates in multiple locations in an industry's value chain, such as extracting raw materials to manufacturing to distribution. **Vertical backward integration** occurs when the firm is doing value added activities in-house that were previously provided by its supplier(s). **Vertical forward integration** involves the firm getting actively engaged in value creation previously done by its distributor. Concentration strategies are desirable in attractive markets with potent growth rates and margins, where the firm holds a strong competitive position (Wheelen and Hunger, 2010). The more specific and strategically important the value added activities, the more advisable to integrate them in the firm's own hierarchy (Williamson, 1975). However, vertical integration usually is accompanied by various risks, such as industry dependency and an increase in fixed costs, which simultaneously reduce the firm's operating flexibility. The pros and cons of vertical integration are contrasted in the figure below.

Concentration strategy through vertical integration	
Pros	Cons
▪ Access to rare raw resources, e.g., material and/or components (backward integration) ▪ Direct customer contact through own distribution chains (forward integration) ▪ Delivery punctuality ▪ Overall process quality control ▪ Economies of scale ▪ Experience curve effects ▪ Specialization	▪ Increase of fixed costs ▪ Industry dependency ▪ Increase of firm-internal communication needs ▪ Increase of complexity ▪ Less organizational flexibility ▪ Risk of running overcapacities ▪ Limited innovation potentials

Figure 31. Pros and cons of vertical concentration strategy

Assuming the firm's market environment becomes unattractive or mature, it can be desirable to diversify the firm's business into different industries that indicate more promising market potentials in the future. Diversity refers to the extent to which a system consists of uniquely different elements, the frequency distribution of these elements, and the degree of difference among the elements (Stirling, 2007). The term diversity affects the relative novelty of knowledge available and the ease with which the firm can recognize, assimilate, and utilize this knowledge in its business networks (Phelps, 2010). If a firm, in the domestic and foreign markets, offers distinctive products, for example targeting different customer segments (e.g., contrasting brands) and/or applies distinctive manufacturing technologies (e.g., special stainless steel and iron steel), the integrated divisional organization is desirable. In this firm structure, the products are separate; and individual business areas are assigned (Perlitz, 2004).

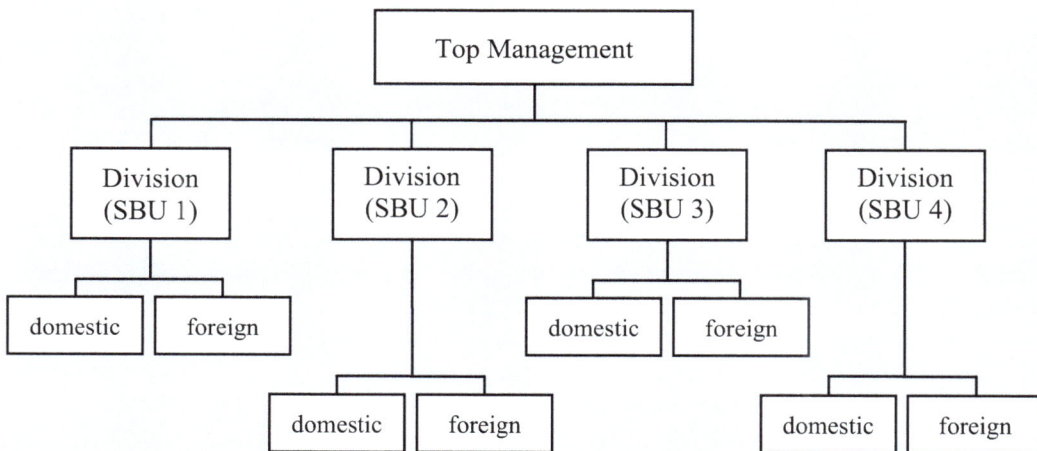

Source: modified from Perlitz (2004), p. 604

Figure 32. The integrated divisional organization

Related diversification strategies occur when the firm's value added activities of current and new lines of business are somehow familiar. For example, 'Daimler AG', Germany, manufactures passenger cars of different sizes (e.g., Maybach, E-Class, and Smart) but also assembles trucks and busses. The traditional German automotive manufacturer is able to use its industry-specific expertise in several vehicle segments.

The case: Strategic Focus Areas of Daimler AG

'In order to achieve our strategic targets, we have laid down four focal areas for strategic action:

Operational excellence and a high performance culture

Our goal is to develop, produce, and sell superior products using highly efficient processes. We create clear structures and lean processes, and use the opportunities of standardization and modularization for further productivity enhancements in all our business operations. Clear structures, efficient processes, and a culture of excellence are essential for staying competitive in the future. This is why operational excellence will continue to be one of our strategic focuses in the years to come as well.

Expansion of core business in traditional market segments and utilization of new opportunities on a regional basis

Unique products and customer services are crucial prerequisites for profitable growth. We are on the right track with our strategies for products, services, and markets. In the medium term, we will significantly increase unit sales at Mercedes-Benz Cars. Daimler Trucks will further expand its leading position in trucks above six tons gross vehicle weight with first-class products and services. Mercedes-Benz Vans intends to consolidate its leading position in Europe and to penetrate new markets. Daimler Buses will maintain its market leadership in buses over eight tons and continue to grow in established and new markets.

Daimler Financial Services intends to strengthen its position as one of the leading captive financial services providers for cars and further consolidate its position as the largest financer of commercial vehicles in the world.

With regionally adapted products and – if and when required – with the support of local partners, we intend to expand our position in the future markets of China, India, and Russia.

Further development of innovative and customer-oriented services and technologies

We are working intensively on the development of innovative, customer-oriented technologies along the entire automotive value chain.

Because the demands placed on mobility will become increasingly varied, in the future we will have various drive systems for our vehicles. In the context of our 'Road to Emission-free Mobility' strategy, we are working in parallel on several propulsion technologies, including the further optimization of the combustion engine, hybrid, battery-powered engines, and fuel-cell driven vehicles. We also support the development, production, and distribution of clean fuels for combustion engines as well as alternative energy sources for emission-free driving.

Traffic safety will be a key element of sustainable mobility in the future. As part of our 'Vision of Accident-free Driving', substantial investments have been planned for traffic safety in the coming years. With our pioneering safety innovations we intend to remain the benchmark for the competition in the future as well.

We apply the results of our research and development in a wide range of very different vehicles, because through the close networking of our R&D activities, we can ensure that the entire Group benefits from new technologies. For example, through the modularization of electronic drive components, we utilize synergies across all vehicles and segments and thus enhance the efficiency of all our business operations.

Parallel to the further technological development of our products, we will also expand the range of services we provide in connection with these products.

Development and implementation of new businesses activities in related areas

We will make targeted use of the results of the work done by our research and development departments, our attractive customer base, and our strong brands to utilize new business potential in related areas. An important prerequisite for this is that the new business ideas are related to our core business and contribute to profitable growth. One of the first major business ideas of this kind is car2go, a completely new mobility concept that enables simple and flexible mobility for all'.

Source: Daimler Aktiengesellschaft (2010)

A conglomerate diversification occurs when the new business field does not have value added activities in common with the original one (Müller-Stewens and Lechner, 2005). Conglomerate diversification strategies make sense if the current business segments of the firm indicate less satisfying margins and/or the firm's market is shrinking and price competition is intensified. For firms that procure business activites in domestic and foreign markets with highly diversified products, a international matrix organization is indicated.

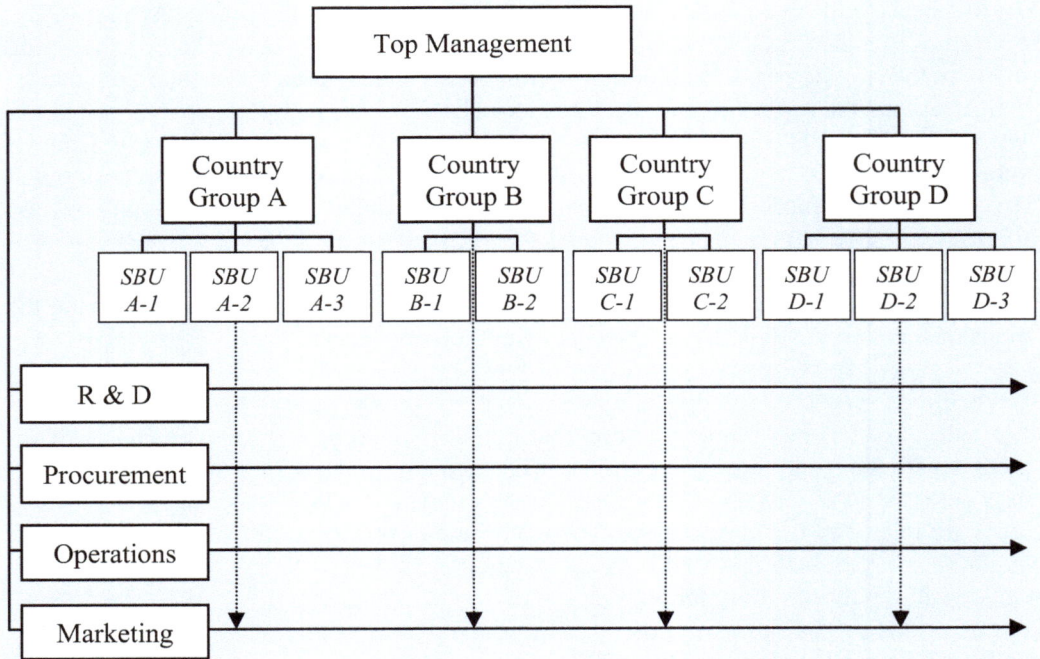

Source: modified from Perlitz (2004), p. 605

Figure 33. International matrix organization

The firm's executive management is better able to develop a risk portfolio through the firm's engagement in diversified business segments, which results in a reduced dependency on one industry. Another reasonable argument for non-related diversification strategies is to provide package offerings that help to improve the firm's competitive position. For example, car sales offerings often contain financing tools, such as a loan to private customers providing them the opportunity to purchase a new car. Enterprises often make use of car leasing. This has led to diversified strategy building among various car manufacturers. They integrated financial services into their organization in addition to their core competency, which is auto assembly. For example, various automotive firms, such as Volkswagen and BMW, established their own banks and have started selling financial products.

Diversification Strategy	
Pros	Cons
■ Moving to more attractive markets than current industries (e.g., mature or declining market characteristics) ■ Brand loyalty transferred to other business ■ Less dependency on one industry supports better risk portfolio ■ Balancing seasonal sales in different business segments ■ Overall capacity utilization ■ Package offers	■ Increase in organization and communication complexity ■ Risk of relocating firm internal resources away from core competencies ■ Possible risk of overestimation of market potentials ■ Limited industry experience

Figure 34. Pros and cons of diversification strategies

Along with the important pros and cons of diversification strategies listed and contrasted above, diversification strategies are usually accompanied by various challenges that tend to be more complex than concentration (horizontal/vertical integration) strategies. In general, the tendency is that the more unfamiliar the new businesses are with the current core competencies of the firm, the higher the probability that market opportunities and corresponding synergies are overestimated and risks ignored.

4.2   Competitive Strategies of the Strategic Business Units

Marketing executives are engaged in strategic planning to match the market environment with the internal resource assets of the firm in an efficient manner. The major strategic planning target is to contribute to financial performance and nonfinancial objectives in order to strengthen the overall competitive position in the markets. Strategic Business Units (SBUs) are groupings in the firm's internal organization that implement the company's overall strategy direction on the operational level. Therefore, SBUs are usually designed based on product-market similarities or customer target groups (Czinkota and Ronkainen, 2007). The firm's marketing management has three different choices available, (1) cost leadership, (2) differentiation, or (3) focus strategy, in order to carry out what is decided in earlier stages on directional strategy (growth, stability, or retrenchment) (Porter, 1999). A leading competitive position goes to those firms that can generate superior value, and the way to create superior value is to drive down the cost structure of the business activities and/or differentiate the product in some way so that customers value it more and are prepared to pay a higher price than the average market price (Hill, 2009).

In pursuing cost leadership, the firm offers an identical product or service at lower costs than its competitors. This often means investments in scale economies and strict cost control in administration, material procurement, manufacturing, marketing, and sales (Czinkota and Ronkainen, 2007). The management's overall aim is to conduct its value added activities in a most efficient manner. Experience curve effects particularly realized in large mass production contribute to decreasing unit costs. The higher the firm's market share, the more units are sold and, as a result, the higher the experience curve effects and corresponding efficiency and profitability. Highly standardized commodity products in price competitive markets (e.g., mobile phones, laptops) lead to an increasing elasticity of demand driven by price, which recommends cost leadership strategies (Müller-Stewens and Lechner, 2005).

A firm utilizes a differentiation strategy, thus distinguishing itself from its main competitors, for example through ongoing technological innovations or an outstanding product quality and/or design and/or services. The effective management of the physical evidence (e.g., number of service counters of an airline in an airport) can also be a source of differentiation. The appearance of personnel and facilities often has a direct impact on how consumers perceive the firm will handle the service aspects of its business and, therefore, has a significant impact on the firm's differentiation efforts (Hoffman et al., 2009). Overall, corporate social responsibility standards, transparent business compliance procedures, and the entire firm's responsibility towards the society and ecology are increasingly important elements for building a successful differentiation strategy (Gugler and Shi, 2009).

The third type of competitive strategy, according to Porter (1980, 1999), is called focus (or niche) strategy (Porter, 1999). Particularly for small and medium-sized firms, with comparatively fewer resource assets than multinationals, the concentration of market niches often provide promising competitive positions. Smaller firms specialize in particular supply components and/or services. They have, for example, unique knowledge in R&D and manufacturing, which helps to develop innovation and efficiency. For firms with inimitable products and/or specialized service not available in the general market, it is advisable to use differentiation focus strategies. In comparison to multinationals, manufacturers that utilize differentiation focus strategies emphasize specific product and service designs with rather low sales volumes, for instance when only one or a few machineries are specifically developed according to the customer's manufacturing requirements (Müller-Stewens and Lechner, 2005). Successful differentiation focus strategies usually involve personalized customer treatment and flexible order handling and delivery service. Differentiation focus strategies do not necessarily imply a significant market share. Successful firms can operate with rather low market shares because the product/service meets the individual wishes of segmented customer groups, which simultaneously comes along with the chance that the price elasticity of the demand tends to be low. Consequently, the firm is able to realize higher prices in its niche segment than average market price levels. Alternatively, when the firm has cost advantages in a particular market segment, cost focus strategies make sense. Cost advantages are derived from a unique access to valuable resources or specific skills of engineers and employees and a relatively high market share in the particular market niche. As long as the smaller firm remains in its niche, it is better protected against potential attacks by large, financially rich enterprises, which from their perspective, lack the specified resources requested by a particular customer segment.

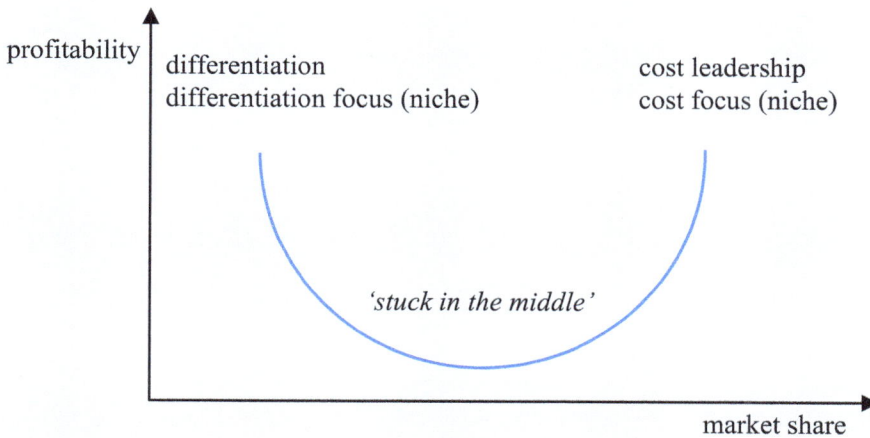

Source: modified from Müller-Stewens and Lechner (2005), p. 269; based on Porter (1980)

Figure 35. Correlation of competitive strategy, market share and profitability

When the firm utilizes neither cost leadership nor differentiation strategies, the executive management faces the risk that the business does not perform as expected because of the competitive strategy concept 'stuck in the middle'. Here, the customer is unable to recognize the firm among its competitors because the products and services neither provide a cost advantage (e.g., attractive price) nor a differentiation advantage (e.g., innovative technology, guarantee package, etc.). As a result of failing to develop a differentiation, cost leadership, or focus strategy concept, the profitability of the firm remains low or even becomes a loss, which causes the firm to leave the market sooner or later (Müller-Stewens and Lechner, 2005; Porter, 1980).

4.3   Functional Strategies

The firm owner/top management make the decision about the future business direction of the firm (where do we compete?). Following the decision on the upper level of the firm hierarchy, the middle management has to decide and thus has to find the answer to the question of how to compete in the SBUs, e.g., through differentiation, cost leadership, or niche strategies (How do we compete?) (Porter, 1990). The firms' departments (functions) have to realize and implement the strategy concepts as decided at the top and middle management levels. Thus, the activities are driven by the question: How do we implement?

Hierarchy	Strategy Decision	Questions to the Management
firm owner/top management (CEO, executive board)	*Directional Strategy*	Where do we compete?
middle management (SBUs)	*Competitive Strategy*	How do we compete?
operating management (departments/functions)	*Functional Strategy*	How do we implement?

HRM	Finance	Procurement	R & D	Operations	Marketing

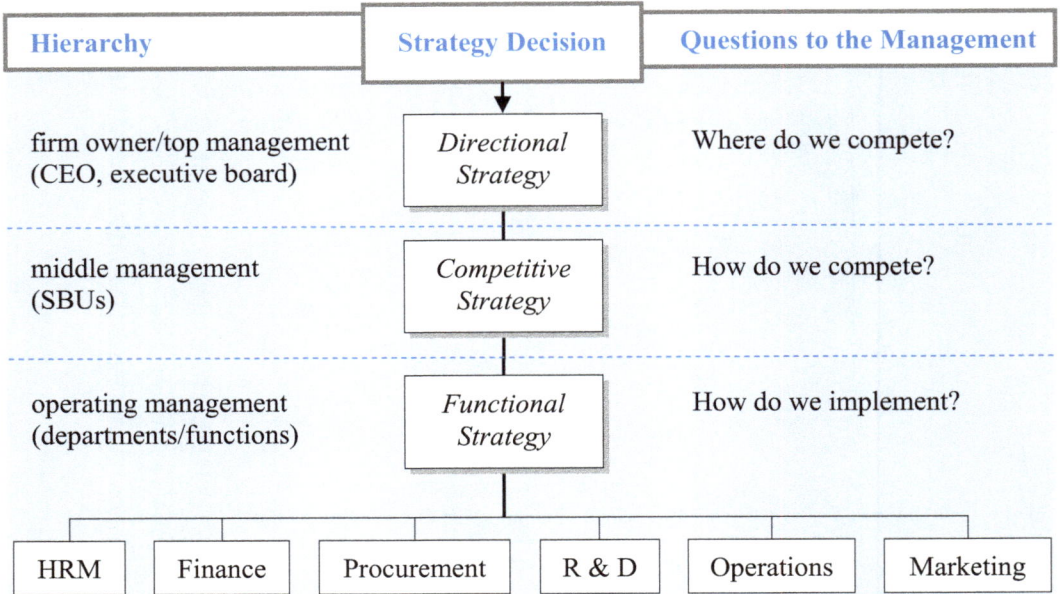

Figure 36. Hierarchy-strategy decision-questions for the management

Functional strategies implement strategic decisions made on the corporate and competitive strategy level into the corresponding firm departments (functions) in order to realize the overall firm objectives by maximizing profitability. The marketing, R&D, human resource management (HRM), finance/controlling, procurement, and operations departments have to adjust their strategic options in their individual units according to prior strategy decisions made at upper levels of the firm.

4.3.1   Marketing

Products and places
In order to realize the directional strategy route as decided on the top management level, the marketing department basically has two alternative choices. First, the marketing manager can decide to use a **market development strategy**, which means seeking larger market shares with current products in existing markets, for example through intensified market penetration activities. As an alternative, the marketing efforts are routed towards new markets with current products and service concepts. When the firm procures a **product development strategy**, new products in existing markets or, alternatively, new products in new markets are launched (Kotler et al., 2007).

Marketing Strategy

market development strategy

product development strategy

current products in existing markets

current products in new markets

new products in existing markets

new products in new markets

market penetration

market entry

market penetration

market entry

risk

margin

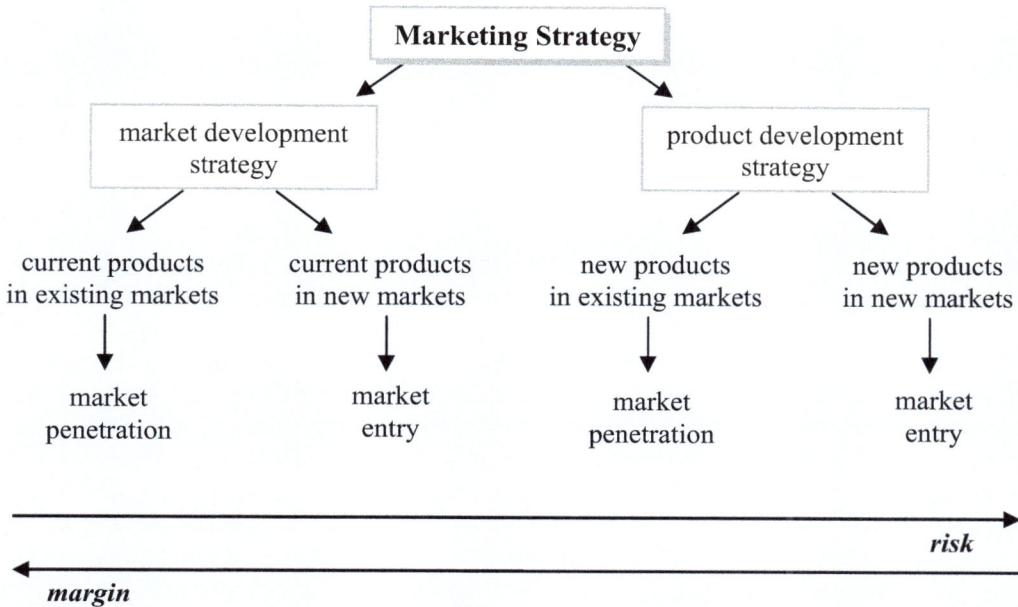

Source: modified from Kotler et al., 2007, p. 105

Figure 37. Alternative marketing strategies

In the case of a **domestic market extension orientation,** the domestic business of the firm has priority and foreign sales are seen as an attractive extension of domestic operations (Cateora et al., 2009). Minimal efforts are made to adapt the marketing mix to foreign markets. Nevertheless, the marketing department's orientation is to market its customers abroad in the same manner in which the firm markets its domestic customers. The marketing manager mainly approaches foreign markets where the product demand characteristics, such as communication policy, pricing, product quality, design, and functions, are similar to the home market. Firms having the domestic market extension orientation are classified as ethnocentric firms (Perlmutter, 1969).

Once marketing managers recognize the market differences in individual countries, their sense of direction shifts towards a **multi-domestic marketing orientation**. A firm guided by this concept is convinced that foreign markets have different environments relative to home; and, therefore, business success requires specific marketing mix modifications for each separate market abroad. Products are adapted for each market and advertising campaigns are localized as are the pricing and distribution policies. Firms with a multi-domestic market orientation are classified as polycentric (Perlmutter, 1969).

A firm with a **global marketing orientation** markets its products and services worldwide, targeting efficiency advantages through developing a standardized marketing mix policy. The global marketing approach views an entire set of country markets as a unit, identifying groups of prospective buyers with similar needs as a global market segment (e.g., purchasing power) and develops corresponding marketing plans that strive for standardization wherever it is cost and culturally effective. That means, for example, the marketing manager has a standardized product but country-specific advertisement campaigns, or the firm makes use of a brand logo (corporate design) but adapts products and services to meet specific demand requirements. The global marketing orientation conforms to the regiocentric or geocentric marketing and management philosophy (Cateora et al., 2009; Wind et al., 1973).

Pricing

Skimming pricing belongs to a marketing strategy concept on the functional level, where a new and often technologically leading product/service is introduced at a relatively high price level in the markets. The firm mainly targets innovative customers who have a preference for 'state of the art' products and/or particular services. This customer segment, in return, is willing to pay a higher price than the average mass market is ready to pay. A special form of skimming is prestige pricing applied by marketing managers who offer high-quality or status products and services. For example, some airline enterprises (e.g., 'First Class' by Lufthansa), hotels ('Premium Membership'), and financial institutions ('Gold Card') apply upper pricing strategies not only during the market launch of a new product. Products and services are continuously offered at higher price levels for selected customer groups. These offerings come along with more differentiated and upgraded services packages. Customers who use this approach may actually value the high price because it represents prestige or a quality image.

The strategy of penetration pricing is applied when new products and services are introduced to stimulate trial purchases by potential customers, and their widespread use in the markets is desired. Penetration pricing for a firm's product and service is desirable when (1) economies of scale effects are important and possible with large sales volumes, (2) potential competition is expected immediately after introduction in the markets, and (3) there is no forecast of a customer segment willing to pay a higher price even in the early stages of introduction in the market (Wilson et al., 2008).

Communication

In the context of advertising and control, there are basically two strategic choices called 'pull' and 'push' strategies. Factors that determine the marketer's decision on pull or push strategies are industry competiveness, degree of product standardization, customer target groups, and corresponding branding concepts. A push strategy is characterized by spending a large amount of money on trade promotions in order to protect or gain further market share. Trade promotions include discounts, in store special-offers, and other incentives developed to gain market penetration for the product – pushing it through the distribution channels (Wheelen and Hunger, 2010). Highly standardized products (e.g., laptops, mobile phones) allow better prerequisites for the customer to compare different offerings. Finally, assuming the features of the product offered by the competing firms are almost equal, the customer makes a buying decision based more or less on the purchase price. Transparent markets with standardized products contribute to industry competition. Intense industry competition in saturated markets sometimes leaves no chance for the firm other than to approach a push strategy of the product into the markets. Cost leadership provides the best precondition to using push strategies successfully.

A firm utilizes a **pull strategy** when advertising campaigns are designed in order to build and/or to develop 'brand awareness'. The main intention is to raise 'attention' among existing and potential customers who, in the ideal case, desire the product and start investigating where to buy it in the markets. Strong brands provide customer loyalty, which protects the firm from intense price competition. A pull strategy ideally fits with the firm's differentiation strategy. On the other hand, brand building is time consuming and costly. While it takes years to develop a powerful brand in the markets, quality problems or service constraints can destroy the firm's reputation 'overnight'. Discounts or price reductions, eventually launched in order to boost sales, have significant negative impacts on the brand. Customers may feel cheated when they recognize that the price has been cut sharply; thus the true 'value' of the brand is questioned. Extensive price allowances are always costly for the firm but potentially cause brand damage and, therefore, compromise the overall differentiation strategy concepts.

4.3.2   Research and development

Technological leadership strategy is a synonym for technological inventions the firm aims to launch earlier than its competitors. Innovative products and services provide promising potentials to drive the firm's business in the future. An innovator has certain technological knowledge about how to do things better than the existing state of the art. Leading technological knowledge is reflected in an improved product performance and efficiency, design, ecological, and health protection (e.g., emission, noise, recycling opportunities). In order to generate advantages from a unique, often only temporarily leading know-how, the marketing management needs to concentrate first on communicating the advantages of the new invention. In almost all cases, the successful commercialization of a product innovation requires that the know-how in question be launched in conjunction with additional service offerings. Important services segments are product training, product installation, and after sales service packages. Before the dominant technology emerges, manufacturing volumes are low; thus economies of scale are rare. In the beginning stage of the technology life cycle, the price is not a principal competitive factor. Later, when the technology begins to penetrate the markets, manufacturing volumes increase and opportunities for economies of scale induce firms to begin gearing up for mass production by acquiring specialized tooling and equipment, and possibly distribution as well (Teece, 2000).

Imitation and adaptation (without infringing on intellectual property rights) of leading innovative products is referred to as a **technological followership** strategy. The major advantage of followership strategies is lower risk that a new invention or technology will fail in the market and corresponding R&D costs are lost. Moreover, the firm can 'learn from the other's mistakes', which provides the opportunity to launch a product with an improved performance that often better suits customer demand. In many cases, assuming the competitor's invention is not protected by a patent, research activities concentrate more on product adaptation than on basic research; and, consequently, costs are saved. Thus, the firm is better able to offer its products at lower prices than the inventing firm. Subsequent product standardization supports fast adaptation to market changes and contributes to the technological followership strategy. Disadvantages of the technological followership strategy arise because of an 'imitators' image and a delayed market entry. Thus, the overall firm reputation tends to be weak and building a unique brand is difficult. A firm that uses a followership strategy usually starts its sales activities when the markets have already reached a mature phase, and industry competition has accelerated. The faster the firm pushes its products into the market, thus realizing economies of scale, the higher the probability of a successful strategy.

4.3.3 Human resource management

Essential tasks of the **human resource (HR)** department are to find appropriate employees on the labor market and to acquire them for the enterprise in time and at reasonable costs. In the context of recruitment activities, the HR department is responsible for the determination of manpower requirements and for the corresponding vacancy announcements. The HR department usually makes pre-selections of suitable candidates during the recruitment process and organizes initial skill adaptation trainings for newly hired employees. Personnel managers and department staff have different instruments at their disposal to carry out their tasks (Müller-Stewens and Lechner, 2005). Typically they arrange the firm's participation in recruitment fairs, and they design suitable selection procedures on the basis of pre-defined qualification profiles and necessary certificates for potential candidates. Furthermore, HR schedules interviews with candidates with the personnel department and with representatives of the specialty department, and so on. Another important task of the HR department is to evaluate the potential of the employees and to organize appropriate training and qualification enhancements. Ideally, there is a compliance desired that harmonizes the objectives of the company and its employees. A firm that manufactures standardized products in mass production – following a cost leadership strategy – mainly utilizes monetary incentives to motivate employees. Monitoring and control procedures based on quantitative indicators, such as material input and production output, administrative and manufacturing costs, and yield rates, serve as appropriate indicators for performance evaluation. In accordance with the cost leadership strategy, management by objective (MBO) goals focuses on quantitative measurable outcomes, such as for example sales volumes and/or number of customers (marketing managers), manufacturing yield rates (production managers), and purchasing price reductions negotiated by the procurement managers.

In the case that the enterprise pursues, for example, a niche strategy, such as high-quality luxury products based on individual customer orders, other indicators than quantitative measures of achievement are applied. Here, for example, information about customer satisfaction and the achievement of superior quality standards are utilized for the employee's assessment. In addition, it is assumed that the company does not apply standardized recruitment procedures. When looking for professionals with individual skills, more flexible personnel selection procedures are used, depending on the job description and/or the project to be undertaken. Marketing managers are valued, for example, from the point of view of whether they have improved the brand image or overall firm reputation or whether they have successfully launched products in new and attractive market segments with customers with a relatively high purchasing power.

4.3.4   Operations

A firm engaged in the **manufacturing industry** generally can choose, depending on their market environment and internal resources, between individual order manufacturing, series production, and mass production strategies. A small and medium-sized firm, for example an **individual order manufacturer** of a piece of furniture assembled according to individual customer specifications, ideally pursues a niche strategy. Hence, the manufacturing processes are designed in order to be able to adequately meet the particular customer requests (e.g., raw materials, design, furniture surface, etc.,) and the corresponding quality and punctuality of delivery standards. Altogether the manufacturing processes of an individual order assembler are less standardized due to the specific customer requests. Economies of scale effects have virtually no meaning. Therefore, qualitative aims (e.g., special design) are more important than quantitative goals (e.g., production output) as performance measure indicators. The most important target is to maximize customer satisfaction.

In many industries, such as consumer electronics, continuous activities to lower manufacturing unit costs are of vital importance to secure competitive survival; and these require largely automated production processes. The application of advanced manufacturing technologies simultaneously amplifies the complexity of the production processes, which necessarily leads to increased standardization of manufacturing. **Series production** allows model-specific product variations compared to **mass production**, which mainly is recommended for uniform products, manufactured in larger numbers. In firms with series production and mass production, a clear definition of duties and areas of management responsibility and operating staff responsibility are apparent within the context of strongly formalized organization structures. Conversely, a rather decentralized decision-making process and employee participation in management decision processes are found in the individual-order manufacturing firms. In the case of series and mass production, (tangible) products can be produced for stock, which is an advantage compared to individual order manufacturing. However, this is only possible if the marketing department delivers reliable sales planning figures.

Some firms engaged in the **services industry**, to a limited extent, are able to 'produce to stock' (e.g., standard computer software). These products are sold by the marketing and sales people at the time the customer places an order. Most services firms (e.g., consulting, advertising, and media design) are not in a position to 'produce to stock' because of the intangible characteristic of the product. Knowledge-based firms utilize an open communication atmosphere inside the organization, which emphasizes idea generation and implementation in management decision processes. Thus, the borders blur between decision making and implementation in a knowledge-based service firm. The 'value added activities philosophy' and the corresponding management culture of companies engaged in knowledge-based services resemble individual order manufacturing firms located in manufacturing industries. The philosophy of the latter two is different to a large extent from the philosophy of manufacturing firms involved in series assembly and mass production.

4.3.5   Procurement

Procurement strategies deal with obtaining the raw materials, components, and supplies needed to perform the operation function at the right time. Basically, there are three procurement strategy choices available: sole, parallel, and multiple sourcing. **Sole sourcing** strategies rely on only one supplier for a particular part, which entails long-term business relationships. The selection of one supplier makes sense, if for example the firm needs a specific component that is not generally available in the markets. Thus, supplier involvement from the beginning allows better prerequisites for product specific developments in order to meet the purchasing firm's individual technical needs. Sole sourcing is often used by highly specialized firms procuring a niche or differentiation strategy. Sole sourcing increases mutual dependency, which can foster the risk of opportunistic behavior either on the supplier or customer side. Additionally, if the supplier is unable to deliver a necessary part or component, the purchaser has no other alternative than to stop production and delay delivery to its own customer, which damages the firm's reputation (Samiee, 2006; Wheelen and Hunger, 2010). The risks of sole sourcing are minimized through the procurement strategy of **parallel sourcing**. In parallel sourcing, two vendors are the selected suppliers of two different parts or components; but, usually, they are also backup suppliers for each other's materials. If one firm is not in a position to supply the cargo at the time agreed upon or in case of quality constraints, the other firm is asked to fill the delivery balance (Richardson, 1993).

In **multiple sourcing,** the purchasing firm orders a particular part from several suppliers. Multiple sourcing provides several advantages. First, it forces vendors to compete for the orders; thus it helps reduce the costs from the perspective of the purchasing firm and may serve as a vital precondition for a cost leadership strategy. Second, if one firm cannot deliver, another firm usually can fill the gap; thus the punctual arrival of the materials to the purchasing firm is secured (Wheelen and Hunger, 2010). From sole to parallel to multiple sourcing, the planning, forecasting, and communication complexity increases accordingly. Furthermore, if the total manufacturing volume of a particular material or component of the procuring firm is divided between several vendors, the supplying volume of each firm is reduced; and thus the bargaining power of the purchaser concerning the price is limited.

The requirements of the purchaser's planning accuracy and the vendors' delivery reliability are enhanced by **just in time (JIT) strategies** for procurement. The JIT system was originally developed by Toyota Motor Company but is now used worldwide, and has been very effective in reducing costs and improving quality and productivity. The system, if fully developed, is based on five major elements (Albaum et al., 2008).

- The extensive use of warehouse inventories creates large amounts of fixed costs. It is expensive for the firm because of costs tied up in materials, the cost of warehouse space to store the inventories, and corresponding insurance. Defective parts are not discovered until they have been input in the manufacturing process. JIT allows direct and timely quality control of the incoming materials by the vendor firms.
- At every stage in the production process, the parts required should arrive at the work station just in time to be installed.

- Flexibility can be built into the production system to allow more than one product or product design to be made on one production line.
- The highest level of quality is attained if each individual worker is responsible for assuring that the incoming component arriving at his or her work station is of proper quality, that the job is done properly, and that the outgoing component leaving the work station is of proper quality. In order for the individual worker to really be responsible, he or she must be able to control his or her machinery and corresponding processes ('my machinery principle').
- Relationships with suppliers must be stable and provide for small shipments at frequent intervals, and shipments must be received just in time with the necessary quality in order to be used.

During the last years, some supplier-purchasers have intensified JIT so that a representative of the vendor, e.g., technical service staff, engineer, etc., has a desk next to the purchasing firm's plant floor. In case of quality limitations, this arrangement opens direct communication channels between the firm and the supplier's engineer, who knows about the vendor's own internal manufacturing processes and the materials used. Thus, the time spent on finding quality problems caused by the vendor is shorter, and countermeasures can be initiated immediately. Overall JIT places an enormous amount of responsibility on purchasing managers. Sourcing from foreign suppliers requires greater procurement know-how and is riskier (e.g., currency risk, foreign law, transportation risk, etc.,) than using local sources. Purchasing managers have to be confident about their international know-how in order to seek long-term procurement engagements (Kotabe and Murray, 2003).

4.3.6   Financing

Finance strategies examine the firm's financial demands and secure the capital requirements necessary to run the business. This can provide competitive advantage through lowering the costs of borrowing money or increasing the revenues from investment of the firm's own financial resources. Overall, the **financial strategy** attempts to maximize the financial value of the firm (Wheelen and Hunger, 2010).

In comparison to small and medium-sized companies, large-scale enterprises tend to have broader possibilities for their capital procurement. For example, through listing at the stock exchange markets, large corporations have greater opportunity to attract financial investors. Multinational corporations make use of differing costs for capital borrowing depending on a country's overall economic condition and national capital markets. Firms with a cost leadership strategy tend to invest a lot of capital in the construction of manufacturing capacities. These serve, primarily, to realize economies of scale effects. The implementation of cost leadership is supported by standardized planning procedures and strict monitoring of costs and outputs.

Firms procuring a differentiation strategy, for example in the services industry, spend a large amount of money in customer relations management systems. Firms with innovative and technologically leading products located in pharmaceutics or alternative energy generation industries (e.g., solar energy) invest a major part of their financial capital in R&D. Thus, the management applies less standardized financial planning criteria.

There are several successful medium-sized companies, such as in Germany, The Netherlands, Austria, and Switzerland, that run a relatively low debt ratio. These firms pursue a rather conservative financial strategy. Their positioning in niche markets with differentiated products protects against intense price competition. For that reason, the implementation of economies of scale is not always the primary goal. For small and medium-sized businesses, therefore, a stabilization strategy often is far better than, as usually advocated, an ultimate growth strategy. The financial strategy in the context of a stabilization strategy focuses, for example, on an effective dunning of debt recovery and consequent use of supplier discounts, which helps to contribute to the overall firm's financial performance. Investments are made only when a sufficient equity ratio is guaranteed. A conservative financial strategy as part of a stabilization strategy seeks independence from external donors, thus leading to a reasonable level of borrowing costs.

4.3.7   Timing

Once the strategy decision has been decided on a directional, competitive, and functional level, the **timing of the market** entry and the ensuing penetration stages have to be undertaken. The management needs to decide whether to enter/penetrate its markets successively ('**waterfall strategy**') or to enter/penetrate simultaneously ('**shower strategy**'). Following the waterfall strategy, after an introductory stage in which the firm collects experiences with the product/service in its domestic market, comes a second stage in which the product/service is sold in a foreign country. The first target market abroad should be geographically and culturally similar to the firm's home market. The number of foreign markets is increased incrementally in later stages of international business. Thus, the waterfall strategy resembles the Uppsala internationalization theory, which describes a stepwise international entry, starting in markets that are geographically close to the home market and indicate a lower 'psychic distance' (e.g., expressed in language, values, norms, and ethics) (Johanson and Vahlne, 1977). The waterfall strategy provides the following advantages (Backhaus et al., 2005; Kalish et al., 1995).

- Through utilizing the waterfall strategy, the management reduces the business risk. The firm tests the foreign target markets incrementally, so the marketing executives can terminate their efforts at any stage if it becomes obvious that sales of the product are unlikely to be as successful as originally expected.
- Especially smaller firms frequently do not have sufficient resources at the beginning of the internationalization process to operate in parallel in a large number of markets. Using the waterfall strategy allows the management to expand internationally with its available resources.
- Incremental introduction offers the advantage that products that have been tested and improved in the domestic markets have better prerequisites for successful launching in foreign markets.

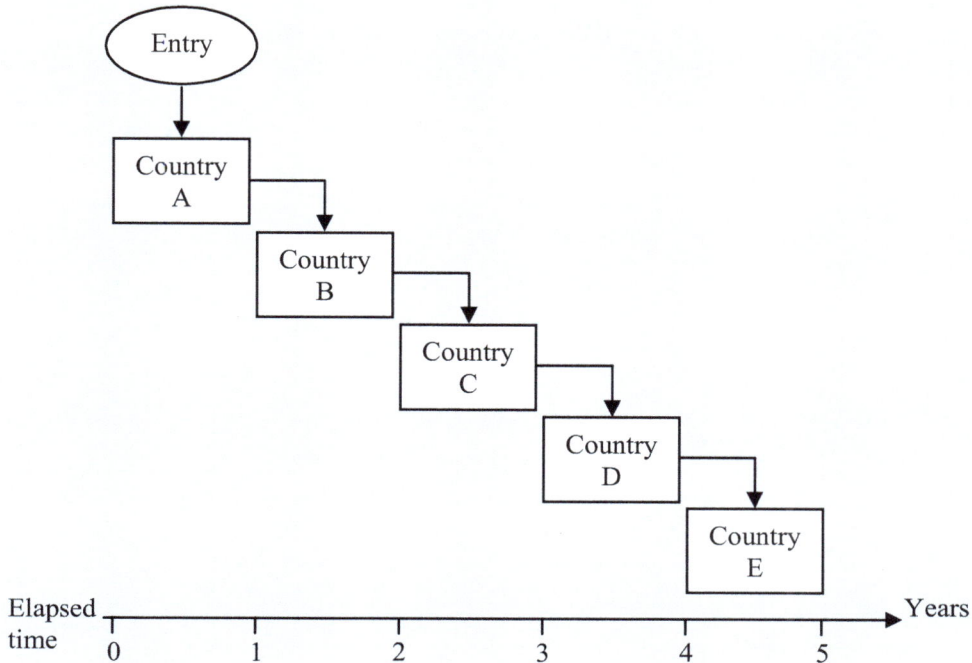

Source: modified from Backhaus et al. (2005), p. 111.

Figure 38. 'The waterfall strategy'

There is a potential risk that, assuming the firm fails to initiate successful sales activities in market A, the management may decide not to enter market B, which is, for example, geographically more distant and has a (theoretically according to the model) higher perceived market uncertainty. Nevertheless, market B, though located far away from the firm's home market, can be far more attractive, e.g., because of the market size, infrastructure, and local purchasing power. Thus, if the management strictly follows the waterfall strategy, it may miss these promising sales chances in more distant markets because of its business failure and consequent termination in the geographically closer markets that were entered earlier (Backhaus et al., 2005).

In contrast to the 'waterfall strategy' in which the markets of individual countries are entered successively, the 'shower strategy' is a simultaneous market entry in selected countries within a relatively short period of time. The shower strategy has the following advantages.

- Due to worldwide competitive forces and developments in sciences and global communication systems, there is a tendency towards shorter product and technology life cycles. In some industries, such as mobile phone devices and computer hardware and software, firms are compelled to launch their products simultaneously in all target markets because a new product generation can be expected so soon that it is impossible to enter foreign markets successively. Parallel entry in selected markets worldwide avoids the risk that advanced technologies and products will be launched by competitors in these markets before the firm has completed its market entry and penetration activities.

• Through a simultaneous international market entry, the firm creates market entry barriers for potential competitors that plan to introduce their products at a later time. An early and parallel market entry in selected target countries worldwide contributes to an innovator's image (first mover advantage), which hinders the market entry of rival firms in the future (Backhaus et al., 2005).

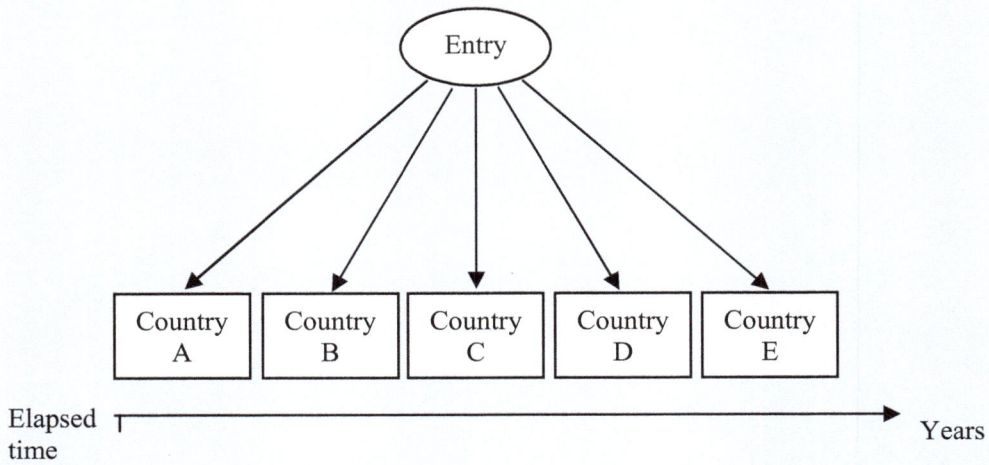

Source: modified from Backhaus et al. (2005), p. 119

Figure 39. 'The shower strategy'

Challenges for the executive management in the 'shower strategy' include greater planning and communication complexity due to the parallel market launch of the products and services. Moreover, the firm needs to relocate resource assets in order to secure its global sales activities. In particular, after-sales service activities (e.g., investigation of quality failures, spare-part component supply, and eventually, recycling or return of defective products) bind financial and administrative resources. Small and medium-sized firms may prefer an incremental market entry in order to avoid too much risk burden.

4.4   Strategy implementation and control

In light of globalized trade and value added activities patterns, many industries are confronted with rapidly changing technology and product life cycles, which provokes permanently changing efforts of the operating staff on the functional level. Firms gain competitive advantage, which requires timely responsiveness and flexible product innovation coupled with management's **dynamic capability** to effectively coordinate and redeploy internal and external competencies (Teece et al., 1997). The term 'dynamic' refers to the firm's capability of renewing competencies that meet the changing business environment. Innovative responses are of particular importance when the rate of technological change is rapid, such as in the consumer electronics industry, so that immediate 'time-to-market' reactions are required (Eisenhardt and Martin, 2000). The term 'capability' emphasizes the key role of marketing executives in appropriately adapting, integrating, and reconfiguring internal and external skills, resources, and functional competencies to match the requirements of the changing environment (Erramilli et al., 2002). 'Dynamic capabilities are the capacity to sense opportunities and to reconfigure knowledge assets, competencies, and complementary assets so as to achieve sustainable competitive advantage' (Teece, 2000).

Strategy implementation of divergent strategy approaches accelerates negative developments and finally results in business failure. Thus, the key challenge for the executive management is to select and combine strategic alternatives on the corporate, competitive, and functional level and harmonize them in a way that effectively combines external business opportunities with internal resource assets to gain competitive advantages. Which implementing strategies ideally complement each other? Assuming the case where a firm's management decides to pursue a directional growth strategy through a cost leadership strategy on the SBU level, the strategies on the functional level must be adjusted accordingly. In the case of cost leadership, for example, the marketing department had better develop mass markets worldwide rather than niche markets in selected countries. A penetration and push strategy combined with a shower strategy help to increase the turnover globally within a relatively short time. Due to the cost leadership strategy, not only marketing but other functional departments such as HRM, finance/controlling, procurement, R&D, and manufacturing follow an overall philosophy that concentrates on standardization, centralized decision making, efficiency, cost monitoring, and economies of scale effects. In order to efficiently implement the strategies, functional departments necessarily have to coordinate their activities instead of seeking individual department aims. The ideal strategy counterparts on the functional level for a growth strategy through cost leadership are illustrated below.

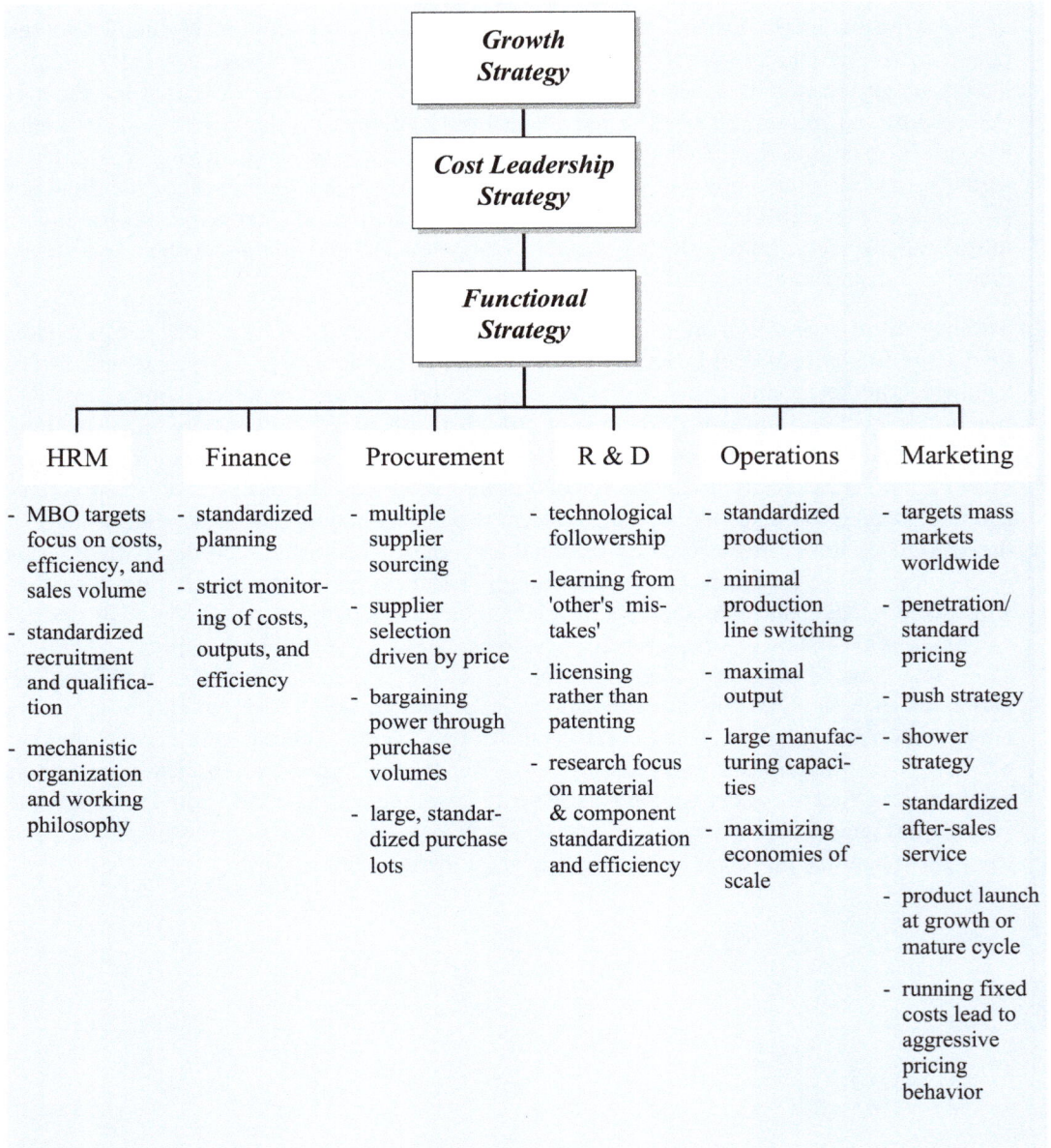

HRM	Finance	Procurement	R & D	Operations	Marketing
- MBO targets focus on costs, efficiency, and sales volume - standardized recruitment and qualification - mechanistic organization and working philosophy	- standardized planning - strict monitoring of costs, outputs, and efficiency	- multiple supplier sourcing - supplier selection driven by price - bargaining power through purchase volumes - large, standardized purchase lots	- technological followership - learning from 'other's mistakes' - licensing rather than patenting - research focus on material & component standardization and efficiency	- standardized production - minimal production line switching - maximal output - large manufacturing capacities - maximizing economies of scale	- targets mass markets worldwide - penetration/ standard pricing - push strategy - shower strategy - standardized after-sales service - product launch at growth or mature cycle - running fixed costs lead to aggressive pricing behavior

Figure 40. Growth strategy through cost leadership – functional strategy alternatives

Conversely, in the case of a differentiation strategy, functional departments have to install divergent strategies in order to guarantee an overall strategic fit. Assuming the firm pursues differentiation through innovative, quality, and design-leading products, the marketing department ideally utilizeses a skim strategy. Brand development and individual pricing for selected customer segments (e.g., brand loyal customers with high incomes) through a skim pricing strategy are combined with the waterfall strategy (e.g., development of markets/countries with a high per capita income first and after a time delay, entry, and penetration of lower income markets/countries). The overall firm philosophy as shared among all functional departments is characterized by service, customer satisfaction, decentralized decision making, flexibility, and market leading technologies. Strategic combinations on the functional level vary depending on the firm's industry and products. A growth strategy through differentiation and corresponding strategy variations on the functional level are illustrated in the figure below.

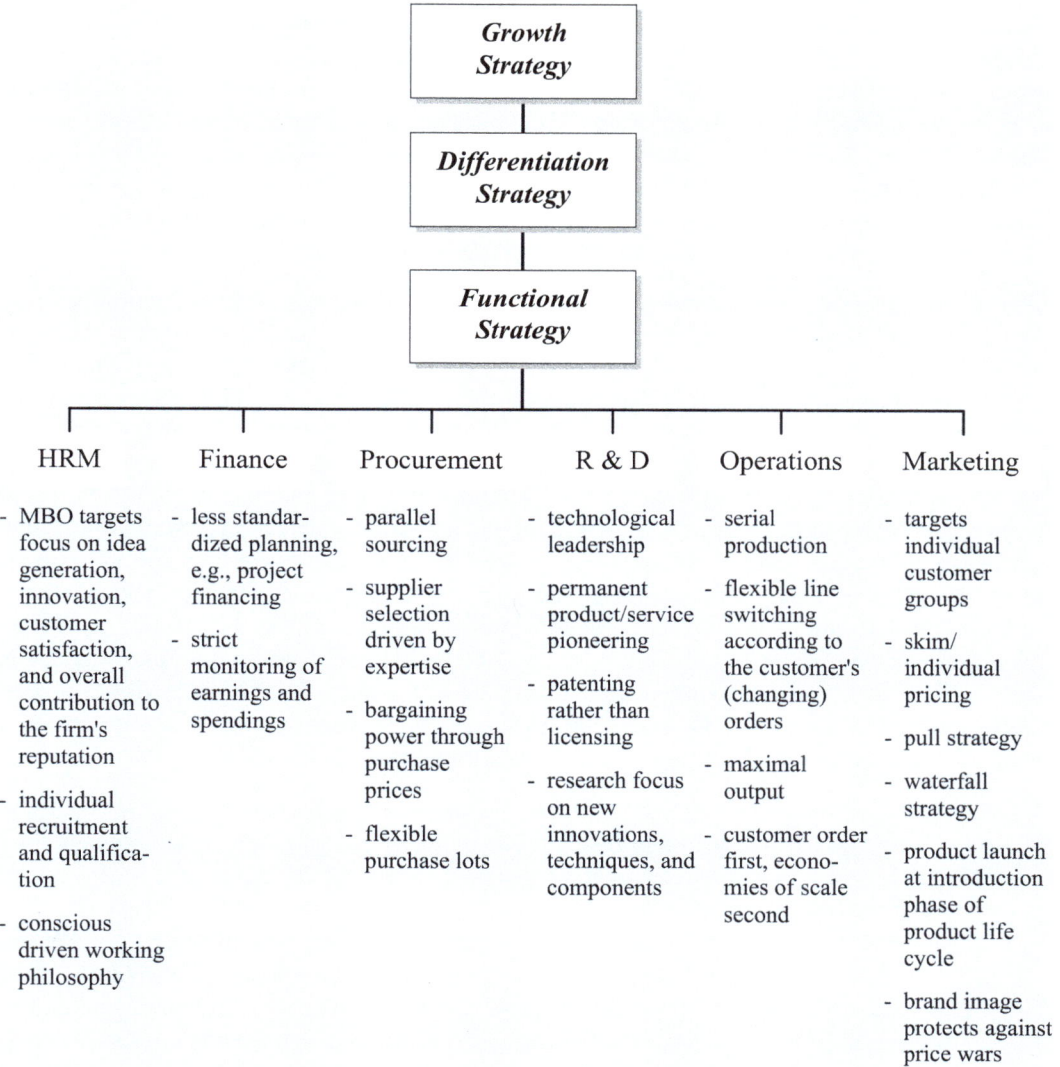

| **Growth Strategy** |
| **Differentiation Strategy** |
| **Functional Strategy** |

HRM	Finance	Procurement	R & D	Operations	Marketing
- MBO targets focus on idea generation, innovation, customer satisfaction, and overall contribution to the firm's reputation - individual recruitment and qualification - conscious driven working philosophy	- less standardized planning, e.g., project financing - strict monitoring of earnings and spendings	- parallel sourcing - supplier selection driven by expertise - bargaining power through purchase prices - flexible purchase lots	- technological leadership - permanent product/service pioneering - patenting rather than licensing - research focus on new innovations, techniques, and components	- serial production - flexible line switching according to the customer's (changing) orders - maximal output - customer order first, economies of scale second	- targets individual customer groups - skim/ individual pricing - pull strategy - waterfall strategy - product launch at introduction phase of product life cycle - brand image protects against price wars

Figure 41. Growth strategy through differentiation - functional strategy alternatives

Control is a fundamental function of management that involves developing plans for the firm and its divisions and then deciding what to do when actual operational results differ from those planned (Rugman and Collinson, 2009). Management executives have several instruments as choices for controlling whether the strategies selected on the upper management level are properly implemented in the firm's organization. Widely used instruments to monitor **strategy implementation** are administrative control systems and output measurement control methods. Their relative emphasis varies with the strategy of the firm. Generally, in their daily job, supervisors control their subordinates through personal communication. Moreover, each company philosophy provides invisible **rules and procedures** to help implement the strategy concepts. For example, a service driven firm pursuing a differentiation strategy may include in their firm philosophy 'that the customer is always served best'. **Administrative control** systems are applied through a system of rules and procedures that direct the actions of the operating staff in the subunits. The most common tool of administrative control is the **budget**. Budgets set the financial resources strategic business units and departments on the functional level have available during a certain period of time (e.g., a weekly, monthly, and yearly basis). Most budgets are negotiated between the top management (directional strategy level), SBU management, and management on the functional level (e.g., marketing and procurement department) (Hill, 2009).

Output controls involve setting quantitative targets to achieve in terms of manufacturing output, quality performance (e.g., defects counted in ppm – parts per million), turnover growth, market shares, and so on. Using management by objectives (MBO), the performance of the managers on the SBU and department level is judged by their ability to achieve the MBO goals (Hill et al., 1992; Vollmann et al., 2005). If goals for strategy implementation are met or exceeded, subunit managers will be rewarded. In case the goals set are not met, the top management will normally intervene to evaluate the reasons for failure and select appropriate countermeasures. Control of strategic implementation is achieved by comparing actual performance against targets and intervening selectively to take corrective action. Departments on the functional level are more likely to be given goals related to their particular activity, for example R&D will be given product development goals; manufacturing will be given output/productivity and quality goals; and the marketing department's performance is measured by the number of new customers, sales per customer, market share development, prices negotiated, and so forth (Hill, 2009). According to Wheelen and Hunger (2010), a firm's management should consider the following guidelines for effective control.

- Control should involve only the minimum amount of information needed. Extensive control reduces effectiveness and results in de-motivation of staff. Focus on strategic factors by following the 80/20 rule: monitor those 20 percent of the factors that determine 80 percent of the results.
- Control should monitor only meaningful activities and results, regardless of measurement difficulty. If cooperation between divisions is important to corporate performance, some form of qualitative and quantitative measure should be established to monitor cooperation.
- Control should be timely so that corrective action can be taken before it is too late. Steering controls, controls that monitor or measure the factors influencing performance, should be stressed so that advance notice of problems is given and adequate countermeasures for problem solving are launched.

List of References

Afp_the_Local_Sweden, 2010. Volvo sold to China's Geely [online]. [cited 20.10.2010]. Available from World Wide Web:<URL:http://www.thelocal.se/25784/20100328>.

Albaum, G., Duerr, E. & Strandskov, J., 2008. *International marketing and export management*. Essex: Pearson Education Limited.

Backhaus, K., Büschken, J. & Voeth, M., 2005. *Internationales Marketing*. Stuttgart: Schäffer-Poeschel.

Barney, J., 1991. Firm resources and sustained competitive advantage. *Journal of Management*, 17: 99-120.

Bartlett, C. A. & Ghoshal, S., 1990. *Internationale Unternehmensführung. Innovation, globale Effizienz, differenziertes Marketing*. Frankfurt: Campus.

Bartlett, C. A. & Ghoshal, S., 1998. *Managing across borders: the transnational solution*. Harvard: Harvard Press.

Beckman, C. M., Haunschild, P. R. & Phillips, D. J., 2004. Friends or strangers? Firm-specific uncertainty, market uncertainty, and network partner selection. *Organization Science*, 15 (3).

Cateora, P. R., Gilly, M. C. & Graham, J. L., 2009. *International Marketing*. Boston: McGraw-Hill Irwin.

Chandler, A. D., 1962. *Strategy and structure. Chapters in the history of industrial enterprise*. Cambridge: MA.

Chidlow, A., Salciuviene, L. & Young, S., 2009. Regional determinants of inward FDI distribution in Poland. *International Business Review*, 18: 119-133.

Combs, J. G., Michael, S. C. & G.J., C., 2004. Franchising: a review and avenues to greater theoretical diversity. *Journal of Management,* 30 (6): 907-931.

Czinkota, M. R. & Kotabe, M., 2005. *Marketing management*. Cincinnati: Atomic Dog Publishing.

Czinkota, M. R. & Ronkainen, I. A., 2007. *International marketing*. Mason, OH: Thomson Higher Education.

Daimler_Aktiengesellschaft, 2010. Strategic focus areas [online]. [cited 26.11.2010]. Available from World Wide Web: <URL:http://www.daimler.com/dccom/0-5-1314146-1-1315590-1-0-0-0-0-0-8-7145-0-0-0-0-0-0-0.html>.

Deresky, H., 2002. *Global management, strategic and interpersonal*. New Jersey: Prentice Hall.

Doole, I. & Lowe, R., 2008. *International marketing strategy. Analysis, development and implementation*. London: South-Western Cengage Learning.

Drori, G. S., Meyer, J. W. & Hwang, H., 2006. *Globalization and organization*. Oxford: Oxford University Press.

Dunning, J. H., 2000. The eclectic paradigm as an envelope for economic and business theories of MNE activity. *International Business Review*, 9 (2): 163-190.

Eisenhardt, K. M. & Martin, J., 2000. Dynamic capabilities: What are they? *Strategic Management Journal*, 21 (10-11), Special Issue: 1105-1121.

Erramilli, M. K., Agarwal, S. & Dev, C., 2002. Choice between non-equity entry modes: an organizational capability perspective. *Journal of International Business Studies*, 33 (2): 223-242.

Eu_Commission, 2010. The Doha round [online]. [cited 04.10.2010]. Available from World Wide Web:<URL:http://ec.europa.eu/trade/creating-opportunities/eu-and-wto/doha/>.

European_Environment_Agency, 2010. European_Environment_Agency. Where does Europe stand in 2010? [online]. [cited 23.08.2010]. Available form World Wide Web:<URL:http://www.eea.europa.eu/publications/eu-2010-biodiversity-baseline/flyer-european-biodiversity-baseline-2014>.

Fahy, J., 2002. A resource-based analysis of sustainable competitive advantage in a global environment. *International Business Review*, 11: 57-78.

Forsgren, M., Holm, U. & Johanson, J., 2005. *Managing the embedded multinational. A business network view*. Cheltenham: Edward Elgar Publishing Limited

Forssbaek, J. & Oxelheim, L., 2008. Finance-specific factors as drivers of cross-border investment. An empirical investigation. *International Business Review*, 17: 630-641.

Ghoshal, S., 1987. Global strategy: an organizing framework. *Strategic Management Journal*, 8: 425-440.

Grant, R. M., 2002. Corporate strategy: managing scope and strategy content. In Pettigrew, A., Thomas, H. & Whittington, R. (Eds.) *Handbook of strategy and management*. London: Sage Publications.

Gugler, P. & Shi, J. Y. J., 2009. Corporate social responsibility for developing country multinational corporations: lost war in pertaining global competitiveness? *Journal of Business Ethics*, 87: 3-24.

Hedley, B., 1977. Strategy and the business portfolio. *Long Range Planning*, 10 (1): 9-15.

Henderson, B. D., 1971. *Construction of a business strategy. The Boston Consulting Group. Series on corporate strategies*. Boston.

Hill, C. W. L., 2009. *International business: competing in the global marketplace*. Boston: McGraw-Hill/Irwin.

Hill, C. W. L., Hitt, M. E. & Hoskisson, R. E., 1992. Cooperative versus competitive structures structures in related and unrelated diversified firms. *Organization Science*, 3: 501-21.

Hoffman, K. D., Bateson, J. E. G., Wood, E. H. & Kenyon, A. K., 2009. *Services marketing. Concepts, strategies and cases*. London: South-Western Cengage Learning.

Hoffmann, W., Roventa, P. & Weichsel, D., 2003. *Marktveränderungen und Konsolidierungswelle in der Pharma-Industrie: Kommt der Mittelstand unter die Räder?* Ludwigshafen.

Hollensen, S., 2004. *Global marketing. A decision-oriented approach*. Essex: Pearson Education Limited.

Holtbrügge, D. & Welge, M. K., 2010. *Internationales Management. Theorien, Funktionen, Fallstudien*. Stuttgart: Schäffer-Poeschel.

Homburg, C. & Krohmer, H., 2009. *Marketingmanagement: Strategie - Instrumente - Umsetzung - Unternehmensführung*. Wiesbaden: Gabler.

Imf, 2010. Time series data on international reserves and foreign currency liquidity official reserve assets and other foreign currency assets [online].[cited 07.11.2010]. Available from World Wide Web: <http://www.imf.org/external/np/sta/ir/IRProcessWeb/data/802P816.pdf>.

International_Monetary_Fund, 2010. IMFsurvey magazine: In the news. IMF call to work together for growth, jobs, financial sector reform [online]. [cited 14.10.2010]. Available from World Wide Web:<http://www.imf.org/external/pubs/ft/survey/so/2010/NEW100810A.htm>.

Johanson, J. & Mattsson, L.-G., 1988. Internationalization in industrial systems - a network approach. In Hood, N. & Vahlne, J.-E. (Eds.) *Strategies in global competition,*. 468-486. New York: Croom Helm.

Johanson, J. & Vahlne, J.-E., 1977. The internationalization process of the firm - a model of knowledge development and increasing foreign market commitments. *Journal of International Business Studies*, 8 (1): 23-32.

Kalish, S., Mahajan, V. & Muller, E., 1995. Waterfall and sprinkler: new product strategies in competitive global markets. *International Journal of Research in Marketing*, 12 (2): 105-119.

Kartman, M., 2009. Merger AirFrance - KLM [online]. [cited 16.11.2010]. Available from World Wide Web:<URL:http://ec.europa.eu/transport/air/events/doc/eu_us_labour_forum/miriam_kartman.pdf>.

Keillor, B., Davila, V. & Hult, T. G., 2001. Market entry strategies and influencing factors: a multi-industry/multi product investigation *The Marketing Management Journal*, 11: 1-11.

Kotabe, M. & Helsen, K., 2008. *Global marketing management*. Hoboken, NJ: John Wiley & Sons.

Kotabe, M. & Murray, J. Y., 2003. Global sourcing strategy and sustainable competitive advantage. *Industrial Marketing Management*, 33: 7-14.

Kotler, P., Keller, K. L. & Bliemel, F., 2007. *Marketing Management. Strategien für wertschaffendes Handeln*. München: Pearson Education.

Luostarinen, R., 1980. *Internationalization of the firm. An empirical study of the internationalization of firms with small and open domestic markets with special emphasis on lateral rigidity as a behavioral characteristic in strategic decision-making*. Helsinki: The Helsinki School of Economics.

Luostarinen, R. & Welch, L., 1997. *International business operations*. Helsinki: Kyriiri Oy.

Malhotra, N. K., 2009. *Marketing research. An applied orientation*. New Jersey: Pearson Education International.

Meissner, H. G., 1995. *Strategisches Internationales Marketing*. München: Oldenbourg Wissenschaftsverlag.

Morschett, D., 2005. Contract manufacturing. In Zentes, J., Swoboda, B. & Morschett, D. (Eds.) *Kooperationen, Allianzen und Netzwerke. Grundlagen-Ansätze-Perspektiven*. Wiesbaden: Gabler Verlag.

Müller-Stewens, G. & Lechner, C., 2005. *Strategisches Management. Wie strategische Initiativen zum Wandel führen*. Stuttgart: Schäffer-Poeschel.

Nokia, 2008. Nokia to refocus its Japanese operations [online]. [cited 15.07.2010]. *Nokia Press Services*. Available from World Wide Web:URL:http://pressbulletinboard.nokia.com/tag/japan/.

Oecd, 2010. *Education: Governments should expand tertiary studies to boost jobs and tax revenues*. Paris: OECD.

Özsomer, A. & Simonin, B., 1999. Antecedents and consequences of market orientation in a subsidiary context. Enhancing knowledge development in marketing. *American marketing association educators proceedings, Summer 1999*.

Penrose, E., 1995. *The theory of the growth of the firm*. New York [first published 1959]: Oxford University Press.

Perlitz, M., 2004. *Internationales Management*. Stuttgart: Lucius & Lucius.

Perlmutter, H. V., 1969. The tortuous evolution of the multinational corporation. *Columbia Journal of World Business*, 4: 9-18.

Perreault, W. & Mccarthy, E. J., 2005. *Basic marketing. A global marketing approach*. Burr Ridge McGraw-Hill.

Phelps, C. C., 2010. A longitudinal study of the influence of alliance network structure and composition on firm exploratory innovation. *The Academy of Management Journal*, 53 (4): 890-913.

Porter, M. E., 1980. *Competitive strategy*. New York: Free Press.

Porter, M. E., 1990. *The competitive advantage of nations*. New York: The Free Press.

Porter, M. E., 1999. *Wettbewerbsstrategie. Methoden zur Analyse von Branchen und Konkurrenten*. Frankfurt/M.: Campus Verlag.

Repetzki, B., 2010. Germany Trade and Invest. Polen kaufen mehr Haus-, Audio- und Videogeräte [online]. [cited 18.07.2010]. Available from World Wide Web:<URL:http://www.gtai.de/fdb-SE,MKT200710238001,MSN.html>.

Richardson, J., 1993. Parallel sourcing and supplier performance in the Japanese automobile industry. *Strategic Management Journal*, 14 (5): 339-350.

Ritter, T., Wilkinson, I. F. & Johnston, W. J., 2004. Managing in complex business networks. *Industrial Marketing Management*, 33: 175-183.

Rugman, A. M. & Collinson, S., 2009. *International business*. Essex: Pearson Education Limited.

Samiee, S., 2006. Supplier and customer exchange in international industrial markets: an integrative perspective. *Industrial Marketing Management*, 35: 589-599.

Stirling, A., 2007. A general framework for analysing diversity in science, technology and society. *Journal of the Royal Society Interface*, 4: 707-719.

Teece, D. J., 2000. *Managing intellectual capital*. New York: Oxford University Press.

Teece, D. J., Pisano, G. & Shuen, A., 1997. Dynamic capabilities and strategic management. *Strategic Management Journal*, 18 (7): 509-533.

Theisen, P., 1970. *Grundzüge einer Theorie der Beschaffungspolitik*. Berlin: Duncker & Humblot

Unctad, 2009. United Nations Conference on Trade and Development - Statistics [online]. [cited 17.8.2009]. Available from World Wide Web:<URL:http://www.unctad.org/sections/dite_fdistat/docs/wid_cp_hu_en.pdf>.

Unctad, 2010. Inward and outward foreign direct investment stock, annual, 1980-2009 [online]. [cited 12.12.2010]. Available from World Wide Web: <www.http://unctadstat.unctad.org>.

Union, A. E., 2010. Automotive Cluster - West Slovakia [online]. [cited 18.07.2010]. Available from World Wide Web:<URL:http://www.autoclusters.eu/index.php/partner/127-automotive-cluster-west-slovakia>.

United_States_Labor_Department, 2010. Bureau of Labor Statistics. Employment situation summary [online]. [cited 15.10.2010]. Available from World Wide Web:<URL:http://www.bls.gov/news.release/empsit.nr0.htm>.

Vollmann, T. E., Berry, W. L., Whybark, D. C. & Jacobs, F. R., 2005. *Manufacturing planning and control for supply chain management*. New York: McGraw-Hill/Irwin.

Welge, K. M. & Holtbrügge, D., 2010. *Internationales Management*. Stuttgart: Schäffer-Poeschel Verlag.

Wernerfelt, B., 1984. A resource based view of the firm. *Strategic Management Journal*, 5 (2): 171-180.

Wheelen, T. L. & Hunger, J. D., 2010. *Strategic management and business policy*. New Jersey: Pearson Education Ltd.

Williamson, O. E., 1975. *Markets and hierarchies - analysis and antitrust implications*. New York: The Free Press

Williamson, O. E., 1985. *The economic institutions of capitalism. Firms, markets, relational contracting*. New York: The Free Press.

Wilson, A., Zeithaml, V. A., Bitner, M. J. & Gremler, D. D., 2008. *Services marketing. Integrating customer focus across the firm*. London: McGraw-Hill.

Wind, Y., Douglas, S. P. & Perlmuttter, H. V., 1973. Guidelines for developing international marketing strategies. *Journal of Marketing*, 37 (2): 38-46.

Wto, 2010a. Understanding the WTO: The GATT years from Havana to Marrakesh [online]. [cited: 05.10.2010]. Available from World Wide Web:<URL:http://www.wto.org/english/thewto_e/whatis_e/tif_e/fact4_e.htm>.

Wto, 2010b. *World trade report*. Geneva.

Zentes, J., Morschett, D. & Schramm-Klein, 2007. *Strategic retail management*. Wiesbaden: Gabler Verlag.

5   Chapter: International marketing research

- Describe the notion of international marketing research.

- List the types of marketing research in an international environment.

- Describe the methods and techniques used in international marketing research.

- Identify limitations in the use of secondary data in international marketing research.

- Present the methodological problems concerning international marketing research.

- List the possibilities for using the Internet in research on global markets.

- Create measurement tools to identify consumer preferences in the EU.

5.1   Marketing research in an international environment

Globalization processes provide the basis for developing marketing research to inform decisions made by companies operating in the international market. One can venture a thesis that
international marketing studies are gaining more importance as international and global marketing concepts develop. The research studies comprise both business entities and individual
consumers. The expansion of business operations beyond the domestic market entails making decisions that carry a greater risk compared to routine decisions in the home market. The
decision-making environment of international marketing can be extremely different from the
one in the domestic market. Hence, international decisions need to be supported with much
more information. Primary as well as external secondary sources of information appear to be
insufficient, as they provide only background to the direct international research that is
needed. This research cannot be regarded as a simple extension of research conducted in the
home market.

International marketing research can be defined as a regular and objective process of
gathering, processing, and presenting information necessary for making marketing decisions
in the international market (Churchill and Iacobucci, 2009). In traditional terms, international
marketing research is considered to be a study designed to support decisions with respect to
more than one country (Burns and Bush, 2008; McGivern, 2009; Malhotra et al., 2008). On a
basic level, such research can refer to only one market outside the domestic one. Generally,
however, this research is carried out simultaneously or sequentially on several foreign markets. Following this approach, international marketing research does not constitute a set of
national studies. Instead, it has a comparative character and is used in the process of decision
making on an international scale – e.g., allocation of resources on a global scale (Craig and
Douglas, 2001).

In the contemporary economy, an increasing number of companies focus their activity on
gaining a competitive edge in various markets (transnational, international). Consequently,
marketing research should be of a similar character. Such research is not simply an extension
of a domestic study in a target foreign market, but presents a new and specific skill-based
and knowledge-supported form of gaining information in order to solve international marketing problems (Rialp and Rialp, 2006). On the other hand, the process is not entirely different
from research on a national market. In terms of methodology, it shares more similarities than
differences. The basic differences arise from the existence of various macro and microeconomic conditions of the countries under study, and even more importantly, from the necessity of assuming these differences are bound to pose problems with comparability of research
results (Skaates and Cova, 2005; Steenkamp, 2001). This suggests that international marketing research should be treated as an isolated part of marketing research and should be given
special attention at the stages of research development, implementation, and interpretation.

International marketing research can be divided according to the following criteria:

- the scope of the research subject,
- the type of information sources used in the research,
- the character of the research goal and the information to be obtained,

- the types of international marketing decisions that are to be based on the research results,
- the geographical range and sequence of the research,
- the type of international research project, and
- the research orientation.

The criteria are neither entirely distinguishable nor sufficient, yet they have been proposed to somehow classify various **types of international marketing research**. The first three criteria are used to introduce the typology of all sorts of marketing research, whereas the remaining ones are used to provide a classification of international studies.

division criterion	type of research
scope of the research subject	▪ research into conditions of business operation ▪ research into operation of instruments ▪ research into performance results
sources of information	▪ desk research (indirect, secondary) ▪ field research (direct, primary)
character of the research goal and the information to be obtained	▪ exploratory and explanatory research ▪ qualitative and quantitative research
types of marketing decisions	▪ research concerning the commencement of foreign expansion and its directions ▪ research into forms and ways of entering overseas markets ▪ research into development of marketing activity programs ▪ research into management of an international marketing activity
geographical range and sequence of the research	▪ research into a concrete oversees market ▪ independent multinational research ▪ sequential multinational research ▪ simultaneous multinational research
type of research project	▪ comparative research ▪ interactive research
research orientation	▪ ethnocentric research ▪ polycentric research ▪ comparative research ▪ geocentric research ▪ culture-synergy research

Figure 42. Division criteria and types of international marketing research

With respect to the subject matter of the research, the basic areas under international marketing research are

- research into international conditions of business operations (international macroeconomic and competitive environment),

- research into corporate instruments and their effect on the international market, and
- research into business performance results in the international market (Karcz, 2004).

The scope of this type of research greatly depends on the stage of internationalization of the company that intends to use the research results.

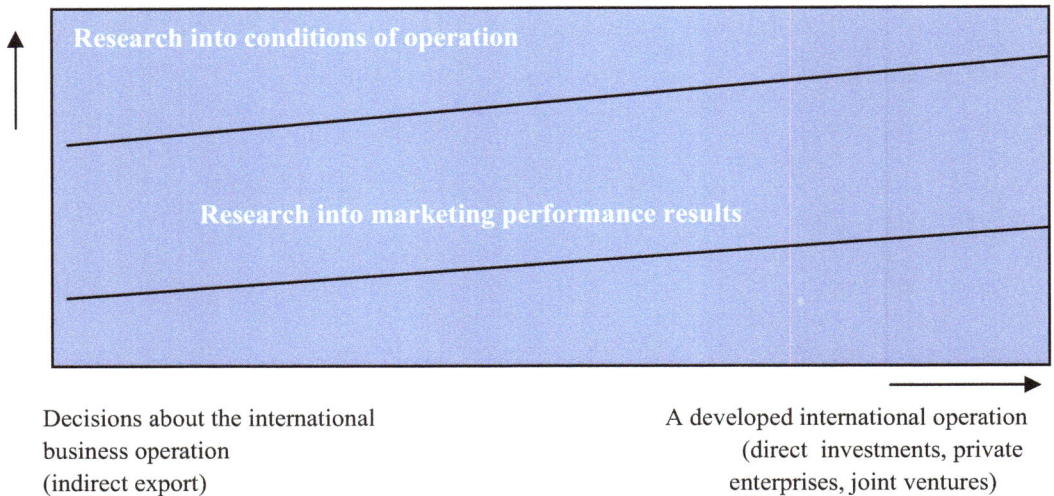

Source: Karcz (2004), p. 93

Figure 43. Significance of marketing research at different internationalization stages

It can be assumed that the study of corporate performance results is of equal significance for a company exporting (directly and indirectly) its products to certain countries, as well as for a production company with a large capital share running a manufacturing business in an overseas market (joint ventures, private enterprises). The role of research into operation instruments depends on the degree of the corporate involvement in an international market-ing activity and necessitates application of a wide assortment of marketing instruments. Thanks to marketing research, it is possible for a company not only to properly define its marketing mix, but also to make decisions about standardization of a product, price, distribu-tion, and promotion strategy, as well as about necessary adaptation to foreign market needs (Thuy and Hau, 2010).

The growing engagement of companies in international operations enhances managerial knowledge about the macro and microeconomic conditions behind certain decisions (as a result of current contacts with the market), and makes them more aware of cultural, social, political, and economic differences. At the same time, one can observe a relative drop in the significance of research into the conditions of business operation. Such research is mainly used by companies that are on the threshold of the internationalization process and face deci-sions about exporting products into definite markets (Churchill and Iacobucci, 2009). Re-search into business operation conditions comprises the whole spectrum of factors determining access to foreign markets as well as factors related to economic, social, cultural, technological, and organizational infrastructure. Taking into account all types of information sources, marketing research can be divided into

- desk research, in other words, indirect secondary research and
- field research, in other words, direct primary research.

Desk research consists of using all available internal and external (domestic and foreign) secondary sources of information (Proctor, 2005; Wright and Crimp, 2000). The whole research process can be managed from behind a desk, with a computer and the Internet at hand. Undoubtedly, such research constitutes a basis for extended international research projects. The principle "secondary sources come first, primary ones come second" is even more appropriate with respect to research conducted in a home country, as it helps researchers quickly and relatively cheaply become familiar with the specific character of a foreign market and prepares them for developing field research. Field research, in turn, comprises information gathered from primary sources. This information is adequate to a research problem. Field research requires application of special research tools that correspond to direct research methods and techniques selected for a research goal (Moutinho and Evans, 1992; Schmidt and Hollensen, 2006).

criterion	exploratory research	causal research
research goal	general situation recognition	detailed verification of conjectures or support in selection of a problem solution variant
scope of indispensable information	unclear	strictly defined
source	vaguely defined	clearly defined
form of gathering information	simple perfunctory superficial	systematized
manner of gathering information	flexible without defined techniques and procedures	fixed with designed techniques and procedures
information analysis	informal usually a qualitative analysis	formal usually a quantitative analysis
conclusions and recommendations	suggestions	final decisions

Source: Kedzior and Karcz (2001), p. 42

Figure 44. Characteristics of exploratory and causal research

In many cases, when designing international field research, managers are unable to precisely define research problems and hypotheses, or even potential information sources. At this juncture, it is necessary to carry out so-called exploratory research, which can be helpful in problem identification and in determining directions for future analysis. Exploratory research is useful when it is indispensable for comprehending the international specificity of studied phenomena and determining the scope of information to be gathered. This research is an introduction to causal research (descriptive and cause-and-effect research) conducted on the basis of clearly defined information sources pooled in an orderly and systematic manner (Kedzior and Karcz, 2001; Schmidt and Hollensen, 2006). The principal characteristics of exploratory and causal research are shown in Figure 44.

In terms of the character of the obtained information, one can distinguish qualitative and quantitative research. Qualitative research focuses on collecting information about the quality of studied phenomena and processes (motives, attitudes, preferences, cultural conditions, etc.). It is usually conducted on small samples or consists in observing a small number of cases, thus allowing for an in-depth analysis of studied phenomena; yet it cannot be used to form general opinions and do statistical analysis (Malhotra and Birks, 2007; Burns and Bush, 2008). Quantitative research is designed to gather data reflecting quantitative aspects of studied phenomena. This research uses standardized research methods and techniques and is carried out on numerous samples. After statistical processing, the research results are standardized over the whole population under study. It should be emphasized that the two types of research are not substitutable, but should be considered complementary to each other (Malhotra and Birks, 2007; Burns and Bush, 2008). International marketing research underlying the corporate decision-making process refers to (Malhotra et al., 2008)

- the commencement of a business operation abroad and selection of countries (a country) and markets (a market) to be targeted;
- selection of forms and manners of entering the international market;
- development of marketing operation programs (product, price, distribution, promotion); and
- organization, management, and monitoring of an international business operation.

The first group of decisions relates to the demand for information about corporate development perspectives in the home market in the context of the international market potential (benefits and threats connected with developing the business operation abroad). Next, it is necessary to answer the question about the number of targeted markets (one or several), and about the sequence of entering markets, taking into account their current and future potential, costs and profits forecast, risk, and competitiveness assessment. While choosing the manner of entering a given market, a company needs information about current and predicted effectiveness, as well as about the risk involved in export (managed individually or through agents), and in licensing, franchising, joint venture, or direct investments. With regard to the choice of marketing strategies, the most important issue is to determine whether a strategy can be standardized or whether there is a need for adaption of marketing-mix elements to the specifics of a definite market or markets. The fourth group of decisions requires information about the company's performance results in terms of the effectiveness of applied organizational solutions (structure, competence distribution, decentralization, centralization of specific marketing functions, development of branches, etc.)

With respect to a space criterion (geographical), apart from research into one foreign market, when it is necessary to formulate an operation strategy for a single foreign market (regarded as vital in terms of the corporate global strategy), one can distinguish research conducted within three broader criteria (Kumar, 2000).

*   **Independent multinational research** (international) is research conducted independently across many countries, often by branches of one corporation (company) and budgeted locally. This research is not coordinated; and frequently, in spite of being related to the same problem, it is carried out by means of other research methods and techniques, which excludes the possibility of comparing results on an international scale.
*   **Sequential multinational research** (international) is research conducted sequentially in many countries. The research is introduced into one market, and then gradually extended into other markets. By learning from mistakes, it is possible to modify various elements of a research project. Another positive aspect of the research is the possibility of extending costs over a longer time period and reducing costs due to application of the same research tools (common costs at the preparatory stage of the research in all countries that are studied).
*   **Simultaneous multinational research** (international) is research that can be conducted simultaneously across all markets. This type of research represents one of the most complicated research forms as it requires simultaneous engagement of considerable resources and excellent research coordination. Nonetheless, it provides comparable information that can be used in building operation strategies and in developing business operations in international markets with respect to the synergy effect and proper allocation of resources.

In terms of a basic type of a research project, international research can be classified as follows (Churchill and Iacobucci, 2009).

*   **Comparative research** consists in comparing studied phenomena and processes, as well as the conditions of their occurrence, across many countries so as to be able to identify differences and similarities among them. Differentiation of markets may result either from existence of various political, economic, physical, social, cultural, and technological conditions or from inherent characteristics of consumers and organizations. Such research may be of a synchronic character, i.e., concerning the same time moment, or diachronic, i.e., referring to two or more time periods.
*   **Interactive research** focuses on studying interactions between individual as well as group subjects from different countries (cultures). This research is concerned with typical interactions that exist between people, organizations, buyers and sellers, and workers and managers across various countries and cultures.

It is also possible to distinguish different types of international research on the basis of the approach taken by researchers. Consequently, the research can be described as follows (Adler, 1983).

- In ethnocentric research, researchers choose to work on the basis of theories, patterns, and methods typical of a home country. (In the case of countries with rich research traditions, i.e., the USA, some researchers refer to this approach, a bit humorously, as 'parochial research' – conducted from the perspective of one's own parish.)
- Polycentric research is concerned with description, explanation, and interpretation of the behavior of market subjects in different countries, both at the stage of designing and conducting the research and when analyzing and interpreting research results, with each country approached as a separate research object.
- Comparative research focuses on identification of similarities and differences between countries, and unlike polycentric research, ensures comparability of results.
- Geocentric research is conducted from the perspective of transnational companies and is intended to identify similarities existing between countries, thus allowing for standardization of a marketing strategy on a global scale.
- Culture-synergy is concerned with cross-cultural interactions and focuses on examination of both similarities and differences in order to bring out effective global, yet locally-tailored strategies (culture-sensitive).

There exists the possibility of combining different types of research (e.g., international comparative sequential quantitative research or qualitative polycentric exploratory research), but some combinations occur extremely rarely.

5.2   International marketing research based on secondary data

It is assumed that any researcher who is to design some research has sufficient theoretical foundations and knowledge to properly formulate a research problem by relating it to the existing state of affairs. The researcher is also very familiar with all available secondary sources that should be used while conducting the international research (an example of a list of publications of institutions that disclose international market data in Poland can be found in Kedzior and Karcz (2001); Kaczmarczyk (2002); Mruk (2003).

5.2.1   Secondary sources in international marketing research

Secondary sources of information in international marketing research can be divided into the following (Reece, 2010):

- secondary internal sources – available in a company that, during its operation in the international market, has gathered information about different aspects of a business activity in definite time, space, and subject-object sections (by customer segments and product segments);
- secondary external domestic sources – deposited with various administrative and economic institutions, associations, institutes, and research-and-scientific centers, as well as

institutions of public statistical information (such as GUS in Poland or INSFE in France); and

- secondary external foreign sources.

In the course of international comparative research, it is necessary to ensure access to foreign data (see Figure 45), which can be grouped in the following ways:

- official statistics and international documentation (publications of international statistical organizations and institutions);
- official statistics and national documentation;
- foreign information materials published by specialist national institutions (e.g., chambers of commerce, trade associations and trade institutions, institutes of price and economic research, research agencies); and
- other publications (e.g., market monographs, all-economy press, specialist and trade press).

International marketing research draws its basic information from official statistical data issued by international organizations (mainly the United Nations, the European Union, and the Organization of Economic Cooperation and Development). International statistical institutions do not produce their publications by sheer replication of data provided by member states, but they usually standardize and process them in order to facilitate international comparison (e.g., assurance of sequence continuity, expression of data in comparable units) (Ember and Oterbein, 1991). Examples of publications of the most significant international organizations are shown in Figure 46.

governmental sources	type of data sources
official statistics and international documentation (publications of international statistical institutions and organizations)	statistical yearbooks, data reviews and reports, including key economic and market data, e.g., the food market (FAO), the tourist market (WTO), and financial markets (e.g., World Bank publications)
official statistics and national documentation	official information of state statistical offices or industrial statistical offices (e.g., British Business" published by The Office of Industrial Statistics)
other publications	national censuses; other publications of statistical as well as economic and political character
nongovernmental economic organization sources	**type of data sources**
economic nongovernmental organizations	foreign information materials issued by specialist national institutions (chambers of commerce, trade associations and institutions, institutes of economic and price research, etc.)
periodical press	**type of data sources**
specialist press	all-economy press; specialist press
catalogs, guides, directories, indexes	general guides; address books
sources of different companies and institutions	**type of data sources**
banks	bank publications
research firms	methodological materials and thematic research results
other companies	business stock market publications, market research associations (e.g., ESOMAR based in Brussels, or London Market Research Society)

Source: Karcz and Kedzior (2001), p. 51

Figure 45. Foreign data sources for international marketing research

name of organization	examples of secondary data sources (titles)
United Nations (UN)	<ul><li>Statistical Yearbook</li><li>Demographic Yearbook</li><li>Population and Vital Statistics Report</li><li>World Population Prospects</li><li>Compendium of Human Settlements Statistics</li><li>Industrial Commodity Statistics Yearbook</li><li>Energy Statistics Yearbook</li><li>International Trade Statistics Yearbook</li></ul>
United Nations Industrial Development Organization (UNIDO)	<ul><li>International Yearbook of Industrial Statistics</li></ul>
Food and Agriculture Organization (FAO)	<ul><li>FAO Yearbook. Production</li><li>FAO Yearbook. Fishery Statistics</li><li>FAO Yearbook. Trade</li></ul>
UNESCO	<ul><li>UNESCO Statistical Yearbook</li></ul>
International Monetary Fund (IMF)	<ul><li>World Economic Outlook</li><li>International Financial Statistics Yearbook</li><li>Balance of Payments Statistics Yearbook</li></ul>
The World Bank	<ul><li>World Tables</li><li>World Development Report 1996. From Plan to Market</li><li>The World Bank Atlas</li></ul>
Organization for Economic Cooperation and Development (OECD)	<ul><li>Main Economic Indicators</li><li>OECD. Environmental Data</li><li>National Accounts</li><li>Monthly Statistics of Foreign Trade</li><li>Short-term Economic Indicators, Transition Economies</li><li>OECD in Figures. Statistics on the Member Countries</li></ul>
World Health Organization (WHO)	<ul><li>World Health Statistics</li></ul>
International Labor Organization (LO)	<ul><li>Yearbook of Labor Statistics</li><li>Statistics on Occupational Wages and Hours of Work and on Food Prices</li></ul>
European Union	<ul><li>Official Journal of the European Community</li><li>L (Legislation) and C (Information and Notices) series</li><li>Bulletin of the European Union</li><li>Panorama of EU Industry, Employment in Europe</li><li>Vocational Training European Journal: the Production of competences in the company</li><li>'EUROPE INFO', Eurostat Yearbook</li></ul>

Source: Karcz and Kedzior (2001), p. 52

Figure 46. Publications of selected international organizations

In the case of more in-depth analysis, it is necessary to refer to national statistics of the countries under comparison, as they include more detailed and more relevant data compared to collective international statistics. It should be borne in mind, however, that the advantages of national statistics are overshadowed by difficulties in data comparability, a lower level of transparency, greater inconvenience of the presentation form as well as reduced processing capacity (Malhotra and Birks, 2007). In the course of the research, one also refers to publications of nongovernmental institutions (publications of economic organizations, all-economy and specialist press, publications of marketing research companies and institutions).

The so-called syndicated data sources represent another interesting source of information. They are gathered in joint information sets so they can be used by other users who are in need of obtaining similar information. These data are derived from panel research conducted on samples of consumers, households, companies of different trades, retailers, wholesalers, and others in regular time intervals. The sources are publicly available and partly free of charge; therefore, they can be used by decision makers before they choose to conduct indirect research (Wilson, 2006).

Information about syndicated data sources can be accessed on many Internet websites, including the most popular ones such as AC Nielsen and Information Resources, which deal with the American market, and ESOMAR, relating to the EU market. The most important international databases comprise the following (Karcz, 2004).

- Global Scan collects detailed information about sales of over 1,000 products according to brands and categories.
- Research International (RI) provides information from panel research conducted in forty countries. The data concern products such as food, beverages, domestic appliances, and services (financial, tourist, etc.). RI Automotive offers, in turn, continuous monitoring of buyer behavior in the motor car market (including data from panel registers on a sample of 40,000 car owners).
- Euro MOSAIC gathers information about consumers according to the layout of demographic and special features (place of residence). The system has classified 310 mln consumers in terms of their place of residence, thus making it possible to identify 300 segments of consumers living in the European Union and representing different lifestyles.

Managers who are planning to carry out direct research are also in search of information about local research agencies that, without much risk, could be commissioned to do the field research. World Opinion sponsored by Survey Sampling INC is an available auxiliary tool of information collection and is entirely dedicated to marketing research. The periodical press also provides an abundance of secondary information sources relating to international issues. The most prestigious press articles dealing with marketing research in the international environment fall into two categories: general and marketing press.

General press

American Sociological Review, Cross-Cultural Research, International Journal of Psychology, International Journal of Intercultural Relations, Journal of Applied Psychology, Journal of Cross-Cultural Psychology, Mind and Language

Marketing press

Dentsu Japan Marketing Advertising, European Journal of Marketing, International Journal of Advertising, International Journal of Research in Marketing, International Marketing Review, Journal of Advertising, Journal of Advertising Research, Journal of Consumer Policy, Journal of Consumer Research, Journal of International Consumer Marketing, Journal of the Academy of Marketing Science, Journal of the Market Research Society, Journal of Marketing, Journal of Marketing Research, Marketing and Research Today (previously European Research), Marketing Science, Marketing – Zeitschrift fur Forschung and Praxis, Psychology and Marketing, Recherche et applications en marketing.

5.2.2   Limitations in the use of secondary data sources

International research into the behavior of market subjects starts with an examination of available secondary data sources, which enables the researcher to become more familiar with a problem and to construct hypotheses. In some cases, after being properly processed, data obtained from secondary sources may prove sufficient for marketing decisions. Nevertheless, the abundance of data from secondary sources may be only apparent, and that is why it is necessary to carefully evaluate the sources in terms of their reliability, validity, accuracy, precision, comparability, and availability.

The use of secondary data sources in international marketing research poses problems connected with the following limitations (Schroeder, 1996; Craig and Douglas, 2001; Wilson, 2006):

- limited availability or lack of some types of information, especially with respect to developing countries where obtaining information about people's income level, retail prices, commercial infrastructure, etc. may be problematic;
- limited comparability as a result of various methodologies of data collection, aggregation, and classification, as well as diverse frequencies of conducting definite research types (e.g., census data, which is organized in developed countries every 10 years, and in developing countries every 20-25 years or is not conducted at all);
- limited data precision as a result of measurement difficulties and the specific cultural or economic character of various countries (e.g., problems with the estimation of the so-called black zone);
- limited data accuracy due to the fact that information is gathered for other purposes and does not suit the research goals and research problems formulated from the perspective of the decision needs of a particular company;
- limited validity as a result of a lapse of time between data collection and data publication (this particularly refers to international and national statistics); and

- limited information reliability, especially information published by the general and specialist press, as well as by companies operating in a definite market whose aim is to create a positive corporate image.

There is no doubt that much of the comparative research can be conducted on the basis of available secondary sources, with the provision that they are methodologically disciplined. Such research can provide an excellent foundation for the development of a direct research project. Secondary data sources are used to create a database for international comparative research.

5.2.3 Goals and application of international comparative research

Research into the behavior of market subjects serves two basic purposes (Churchill and Iacobucci, 2009):

- completion, systematization, and verification of knowledge about the behavior of companies, institutions, households, and household members (consumers) and
- collection of information that can be transferred into the language of economic decisions made by subjects of macro and mesoeconomic (regional) levels and by manufacturing, trading, and service providing companies.

From a model perspective, international comparisons find a complex application in all stages of the research process (diagnosis, forecast, model), across all sections (subject, object, space, and time), as well as on the macro and microeconomic scale. The usefulness of international comparisons at each of the distinct stages, sections, and scales varies depending on the goals to be achieved by international comparative research, as well as on research assumptions and hypotheses. A skillful exploitation of international comparative research enhances the decision-making process by providing an international context, ensuring information that is otherwise inaccessible.

The application of international comparisons may be considered in two ways (Schmidt and Hollensen, 2006):

- from the perspective of employing international comparative research in the process of studying corporate and individual consumer behavior on a macro and micro scale – information processes – and
- from the perspective of employing international comparisons in the definition of the goals of a socio-economic policy, in the selection and construction of policy tools (macro scale), and in the development of corporate marketing strategies (micro scale).

The main goal of the complex exploitation of international comparisons is to harmoniously combine both approaches so that the cognitive aspects (information processes) can be associated with the practical ones (decision processes). Thanks to **international comparative research**, which is designed to describe market and consumption phenomena, it is possible to (Karcz, 2004)

- on a macro scale:
  - determine the degree of disturbance of proper balance between various elements of consumption, production, and exchange systems and
  - provide grounds for development of tools that could restore proper balance and relations;
- on a micro scale:
  - formulate some hypotheses about changes in consumer and corporate behavior by analogy to countries with a developed market economy and
  - provide grounds for assessment of development opportunities of manufacturing and trading companies active in the international market of goods and services.

One should emphasize the importance of the methodology of international comparative research, as it may be useful in the corporate decision-making process in international markets. The **process of international comparative research** is presented in Figure 47.

The selection of comparative attributes constitutes one of the most crucial stages of the analysis since it guarantees either success or failure in the production of research results. These attributes are used to define the units to be studied. These units are often referred to as multi-attribute objects and are represented, for example, by particular states, regions, cities, and the like. The accuracy of attribute selection determines the essential correctness of the analysis. The grouping itself is already a technical practice. The diagnostic attributes can be divided into the following (Reece, 2010; Proctor, 2005):

- stimulants – attributes in a direct relation: the higher the level of a given attribute, the higher the level of a studied phenomenon (a synthetic variable) (e.g., the higher GDP per capita, the higher the standard of living);
- destimulants – attributes in an inverse proportion, i.e., the higher the attribute level, the lower the level of a studied phenomenon (e.g., the higher the level of infant mortality rate, the lower the level of the standard of living); and
- nominants – attributes of the so-called normal values (e.g., inflation rate, interest rates).

Determination of aggregated (synthetic) variables is conditioned by normalization of diagnostic variables, ensuring (Hair et al., 2010)

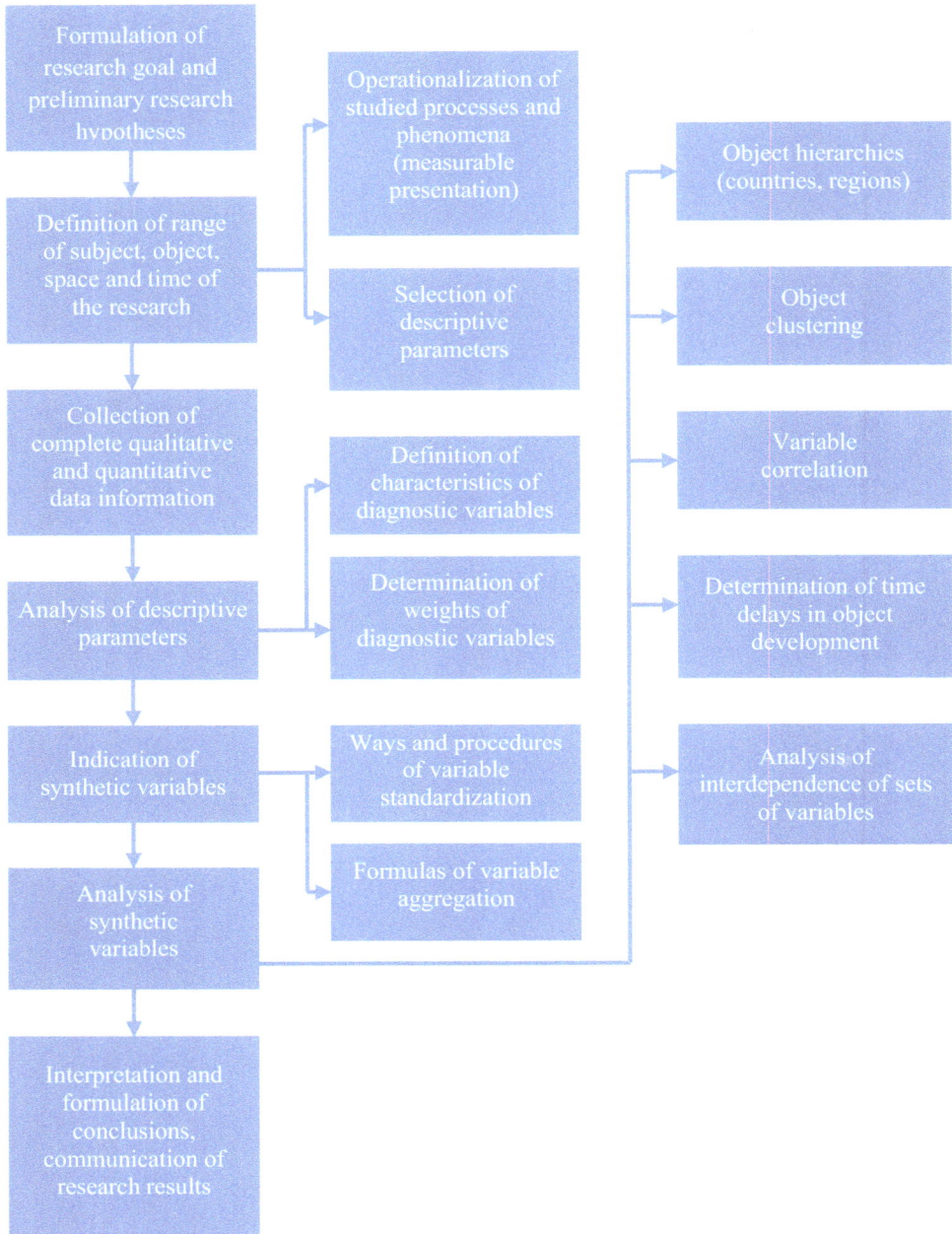

Source: Zelias (1998), p. 237

Figure 47. Stages and methodology of international comparative research

Simple international comparative research is based on volume indices and methods of attribute normalization. More complicated research is conducted by means of taxonomic methods (Glowacki et al., 1980; Mruk, 2003; Churchill and Iacobucci, 2009). Intensity ratios are commonly applied in international comparative research as they make it possible to easily establish the relation of quantities of one particular set to quantities of another set. Despite denoting two different phenomena, the quantities should be logically combined with each other. They define the volume (intensity) of the phenomenon occurrence. By means of relative numbers, the researchers determine the relation of studied phenomena to a particular set from which they are derived or in which they occur. Examples of such quantities can be seen in population density per 1 km² (number of residents divided by surface unit size in km²), consumption rate per capita (volume of consumption of a given product divided by the number of residents), or work effectiveness (production volume divided by the number of employees or the number of labor time units) in particular countries under comparison (Schiffman and Kanuk, 1994).

In order to obtain a simple spatial measurement of differentiation in market phenomena, one can refer to the method of attribute standardization. Although the method may lack some precision, it serves its purpose by defining the scale of differentiations with the provision that the subjectivity of certain decisions be supported by the researcher's experience and expertise. Thanks to the transformation methods of secondary source data used in international comparisons presented above, it is possible to get information that is useful in the marketing decision-making process. Such research can be treated as complementary to direct research based on primary sources.

5.3 International marketing research based on primary sources

When setting out on international marketing research, it is important to take into consideration three dimensions (sections) of a research project, described by Usunier (1998), as the depth, height, and width of a project (Figure 48).

When defining the depth of a project, researchers should answer questions concerning whether they want to do the research, what elements of the behavior of market subjects to be studied are different in compared countries (what?), in what ways they differ (how?), why they differ (why?). Depending on the question type, the research may become more complex due to an increase in the number of explanatory variables. Consequently, operationalizing such variables in a complex international setting may pose solution problems, which mainly refers to a situation where the researcher intends to identify the influence of some hidden cultural values over market and consumption behavior. Another difficulty relates to the distinction between economic and socio-cultural variables. In addition, in many cases, there is a lack of a proper theoretical basis for correct conceptualization and formulation of research hypotheses (Blackwell et al., 2001).

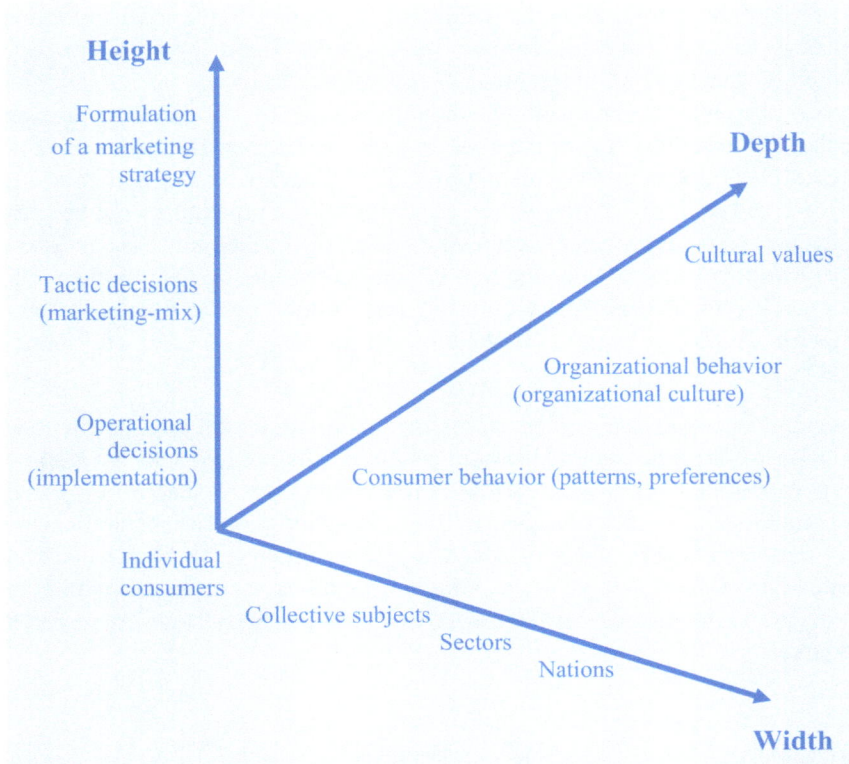

Source: Usunier (1998), p. 81

Figure 48. Dimensions of international research projects

The width dimension relates to the selection of analysis units (research subjects), ranging from individual subjects; to grouped subjects; to mega-groups such as nations, geographical regions, and integration groups. The research can be conducted on large country and respondent groups in each separate country, as well as on small (in terms of number), comparative samples of two countries, or even on one company in many countries, and so on. The height dimension is concerned with the level of aggregation of the marketing decision problems that are to become the object of the research as well as the subject of the analysis of results. Atop the axis are placed issues connected with strategic decisions, since they are of key importance for a company, whereas issues such as the degree of product standardization, the choice of a marketing campaign, or motivation of sales reps come second. The dimensions of research projects open up room for an infinite number of possible combinations. Each single research project can be visualized as a point in space, which, through the process of mapping onto the dimension axes, can be defined with respect to the type and level of aggregation of research subjects (width); strategic, tactical, or operational application of research results (height); as well as complexity of studied phenomena and conditions of their occurrence (depth).

5.3.1 Methodological problems at the preparatory stage

Each marketing research project follows a certain definite procedure, in other words, a certain manner of research organization, from the application of definite research methods and techniques constituting groups of research tasks and activities. The research takes place in four stages (Kedzior and Karcz, 2001):

- research preparation,
- research performance,
- result analysis, and
- communication of results.

The formulation of a research problem together with an indication of research goals and definition of hypotheses constitute the so-called conceptual phase (definition phase) of a research design. While constructing the research, it is vital to establish the scope of the research (subject, object, space, and time), point out the basic methods of collecting and processing information, and define the research costs and research schedule. The process of research design requires decisions about

- the manner of defining and understanding the problems to be studied with respect to international conditions (definition of concepts and scopes) and
- algorithm (rules) of conduct, which allows for collection and analysis of indispensable information by observing general principles of correctness and objectivity at the lowest possible cost (a pracseological principle of cost minimization with simultaneous achievement of an assumed goal). In the case of a limited budget, it is possible to apply the principle of effect maximization (obtaining the greatest amount of information in order to be able to solve a decision problem) at definite costs.

A research design and its scientific assumptions ought to be tested during the trial research (pilot research), which is an integral part of the research process. The analysis of the pilot research results provides for definition of final versions of a research problem, hypotheses, and research tools. Methodological problems, a result of research conducted in a cross-cultural environment, arise at the very first stage of the research process.

research tasks and activities	methodological problems
definition of a research problem and a research goal; determination of a research scope	▪ comparability of phenomena, processes and behavior of market subjects ▪ universal and specific values ▪ isolation of a self-reference criterion
research approach	▪ multi- and interdisciplinary approach ▪ *emi* vs. *etic* approach
formulation of research hypotheses	▪ application of universal or specific theories and models ▪ search for similarities or differences
selection of a method of direct and indirect information collection	▪ assessment of credibility, reliability, validity, and usefulness of secondary-source data ▪ application of qualitative research ▪ selection of methods and techniques of direct research ▪ guarantee of data comparability ▪ development of research tools (problems, measurement problems, and proper translation problems)
definition of a sample selection procedure	▪ sample group comparability (number, features, selection methods)
preliminary decisions about directions and methods of analysis of gathered information	▪ selection of quantitative data processing methods and application of statistical packages ▪ task distribution with respect to qualitative data processing (participation of local researchers)
testing and evaluation of research assumptions (pilot research)	▪ setting up of the international team responsible for assessment of project correctness ▪ participation of experts
definition of the final version of a research problem, research hypotheses and research tools	▪ competence distribution with respect to final decisions about the formal, merithoric, and organizational aspect of research

Source: Malhotra et al., (1996), p. 9

Figure 49. Methodological problems at the preparatory stage

5.3.2   Problem of equivalence in international marketing research

Marketing research that is to be conducted in a multicultural environment should be based on the prior assurance that the processes and phenomena to be studied are equivalent (in nature) and that the obtained results will be comparable. The main difference between various equivalence categories results from the fact that some of them may be noticed *ex ante*, and some only *ex post*. It is assumed that even with great researchers' knowledge of cultural characteristics of the countries to be studied, one should recommend checking the equivalence after completion of direct research.

The problem of **equivalence in international marketing research** can be approached with respect to four issue groups (Cavusgi and Das, 1997; Holzmuller, 1995):

- equivalence of a research object,
- measurement equivalence,
- research sample equivalence, and
- equivalence of a direct research process.

categories	types
equivalence of a research object	▪ conceptual equivalence ▪ functional equivalence ▪ categorization equivalence
measurement equivalence	▪ calibration equivalence ▪ metric equivalence ▪ translational equivalence
research sample equivalence	▪ sample unit equivalence ▪ equivalence of a sampling frame of a studied population ▪ equivalence of sample selection method
equivalence of a direct research process	▪ equivalence of data collection procedure ▪ contextual equivalence ▪ time (temporal) equivalence

Figure 50. Equivalence categories of marketing research in a multicultural environment

The first problem that needs resolving concerns conceptual equivalence. This refers to the question of whether a given concept or an object refers to the same thing in all studied cultures and whether it is expressed through the same attitudes and behavior. Once the conceptual equivalence is ensured, another problem may relate to functional equivalence, which means determining whether a certain concept, behavior, or product has the same function across different cultures. Another difficulty may be encountered while assuring equivalence of categorization, a way of clustering (categorizing) such research objects as consumer reactions and behavior, products, and brands. In some cases, the criteria for categorizing certain products may differ considerably, and thus pose difficulties in comparisons of certain types of behavior with respect to cross-cultural categories. A proper definition of a research object that takes cultural specificity into account constitutes a basis for designing the measuring process. This measuring consists in assigning numbers to certain objects (phenomena, processes) so that the numbers can reflect, in a reliable way, a measured feature of an object. The accuracy of the measurement, i.e., its precision, depends on proper selection of the so-called observable indices of studied objects, and in the case of international research, also on the country specific character (Schmidt and Hollensen, 2006; Karcz, 2004).

At this research stage, it is advisable to guarantee the calibration equivalence (equivalence of measurement units), so that the measurement is expressed in the same units of money, weight, distance, quantity, and the like. The measurement also needs to take into consideration perceptual differences (e.g., the number of colors recognized by members of a given community and the symbolic interpretation of colors, as well as perception of space, shape, materials, and smells in one's own culture) (Rzepinska, 1983; Steenkamp, 2001).

The measuring process uses different measuring scales. International research requires metric equivalence with respect to verbal measuring scales, since distances between certain points (in verbal descriptions) are not equivalent across various languages. This problem is strictly connected with the assurance of translational equivalence, i.e., with a translation of measuring scales applied in research tools such as interview questionnaires, questionnaire forms, projective tests, and so on. Here, the difficulties go far beyond grammatical and lexical issues as language represents one of the elements of culture that determines the perception, denotation of, and interaction with the external world (Ryan et al., 1999). The approach to linguistic issues may affect the whole research procedure and is related to basic research paradigms.

One of the key tasks at this stage of marketing research in a cross-cultural environment is to properly select research samples that can be used as a basis for producing results generalizable to the study populations. The **process of sample selection** consists of five stages (Schiffman and Kanuk, 1994):

- definition of a study population,
- establishment of a list (sampling frame) of a study population,
- determination of sample size,
- choice of a sample selection method, and
- sampling.

The researcher tries to define as closely as possible a study population by distinguishing in the operating definition such components as a subject (element) of research, a sample unit, as well as a time and place at which the samples are subject to the research. In the case of individual subjects (e.g., individual consumers), the sample element becomes the sample unit, whereas in the case of group subjects, it is necessary to decide who will speak on behalf of such a subject. For example, when a household is a research subject, the sample unit can be represented by the head of a household, whereas in the case of a company, such a role can be assigned to the chief accountant or manager of a supply unit.

The achievement of sample comparability constitutes the main problem of the sample selection method when marketing research is conducted in a multinational environment. Many authors claim that it is practically impossible to obtain full comparability. The main problem to be dealt with by the researcher concerns a proper definition of a sample on two levels:

- the sample level of countries and cultures and
- the sample level of defined individual and group subjects within countries and cultures.

Hofstede (2000) clearly states that despite the fact that data are collected from individual respondents, for the sake of the analysis, they are compared on the country level. In his research, the mean values of respondent questions were subject to calculation in each country. However, the studies compared not the individuals, but a dominant tendency of respondents' questions for a particular country. The author warns against using such results in construction of stereotypes referring to concrete individuals. National indices are not used to describe an individual, but to characterize social systems that can be developed by these individuals. Based on research results, no one should say that Suzuki is a Japanese company, and consequently is characterized by collective values, or that Ms. Smith is an American, so she believes in individualistic values. Nonetheless, if one intends to collaborate with Suzuki Corporation, one can follow the assumption that the corporation is managed by collective values, whereas if one wants to enter into cooperation with Smith Company, it will be safer to assume that the company is founded on individualistic values. In international studies, it is indispensable to ensure sample unit equivalence by a proper sample definition and by selection of respondents that can enable achievement of comparability on an international scale. This does not necessitate the selection of respondents who share the same demographic-social-economic features, but ones that represent the same target group (buyer segment). It should be borne in mind that depending on the culture, different individuals play definite roles in the purchasing process.

The problem of guaranteeing the equivalence of a sampling frame for a study population in international research relates to difficulties in obtaining proper lists (frame) of defined research populations across various countries. In many countries, such frames can be represented by general population lists, voter lists, or telephone directories; but in some states, it is impossible to make use of them (frames) since, as in Saudi Arabia, such lists do not exist and directories are incomplete (Wells and Prensky, 1996). This poses a problem, particularly when the research is to be conducted by means of a random sampling method.

In international research, it is extremely difficult to achieve the equivalence of a sample selection method, i.e., the choice of a selection method that is feasible in all countries to be compared. In order to choose a proper sample selection method, it is necessary to choose a method guaranteeing sample representativeness in each country and one that provides data that can facilitate international comparisons (Malhotra and Birks, 2007). In practice, researchers – despite numerous methodological reservations – often employ non-random sampling methods, although such a selection excludes the application of statistical methods to estimate unknown population parameters. The possibility of achieving international comparability calls for using a selection method that is not based on a probability calculus. Additionally, such data can be obtained at a relatively low cost and in a manner concurrent with the research goals.

In the course of direct research, the equivalence of data collection procedures should be guaranteed and efforts should be made to adopt the same research techniques in all countries under comparison. It is absolutely necessary to ensure equivalence, at least within the framework of definite research types.

The studies must also take into account contextual equivalence (the situation in which information is gathered), which is connected to respondents' cultural reluctance to talk about taboo issues. Researchers should be aware of the fact that in certain situations some answers may not reflect the real state of affairs and respondents' genuine attitudes, but may only express respondents' opinions about socially acceptable views.

International research should also be conducted with respect to time (temporal) equivalence, which takes into account the process of relative data aging. One cannot ignore the fact that income or price data become outdated much later in countries with a low inflation rate than in countries with a multi-digit inflation rate. The equivalence of time can also be considered with respect to differences in the economic and technological development of various countries. A certain definite situation in one country may be 'an equivalent' of a similar situation in another country twenty years ago. The distance estimation in years can be used to make forecasts by way of analogy to a model country.

5.3.3   Selection methods and techniques in international marketing research

Before carrying out field research, it is indispensable to make a decision about selection of adequate methods of gathering information from primary sources. Such information can be obtained through observation of certain people, objects, or events or through communication (direct or indirect) with the right people. International marketing research employs various **methods** and **techniques** of pooling information from primary sources including (Churchill, 2002)

- observations,
- interviews,
- questionnaires,
- projective methods,
- experiments, and
- heuristic methods (creative thinking).

measure methods	measure techniques
observation	<ul><li>disguised and undisguised</li><li>direct and indirect</li><li>participative and non-participative</li></ul>
interview	<ul><li>direct (personal, individual)</li><li>telephone</li><li>depth</li><li>focused</li></ul>
questionnaire	<ul><li>mail (sent-out)</li><li>press</li><li>auditorium testing</li><li>packaging</li><li>computer</li></ul>
projective methods	<ul><li>word associations</li><li>sentence completion</li><li>storytelling</li><li>product acceptance test</li><li>price acceptance test</li><li>economic situation acceptance test</li></ul>
experiments	<ul><li>field (market)</li><li>artificial (laboratory, simulated)</li></ul>
heuristic methods (creative thinking methods)	<ul><li>expert assessment method</li><li>Delphi method</li><li>Brainstorming</li></ul>

Figure 51. Selected methods and techniques of international direct research

In international studies, the methods enumerated above are usually combined and selected with respect to the goal and subject of the research.

The case: Some facts about primary research in Europe

- 75% of expenditures for marketing research are focused on consumers – mostly on FMCGs.
- Marketing research in institutional markets mostly focuses on government sectors and pharmaceutical markets.
- 55% of research companies' income in Europe is generated by individual projects (ad hoc research); the following 45% is generated mostly by panel studies.
- 80% of research in European research agencies has a quantitative character, 15% qualitative, and 5% desk research.
- Qualitative research is the most popular in France, Austria, and Ireland.
- Direct interview is the most popular method (60-70%).

Source: Karcz (2004)

Before choosing a data collection method, researchers must first consider whether the information they are in search of is of a qualitative or quantitative character. Most marketing studies conducted in a cross-cultural environment are of a quantitative character and are based on research samples. However, a prevailing view holds that studies should more frequently take advantage of qualitative research (idiographic studies), as qualitative research conducts in-depth field research on a smaller number of companies or consumers. Each case (a sample unit) is described separately, and the researcher tries to comprehend reasons behind the observed differences and similarities. If managers or researchers are not fully familiar with the cultural specifics of foreign markets, it is recommended that they begin the project with qualitative exploratory research. At the introductory stage, such research provides indispensable information and helps generate proper hypotheses and models to be verified by quantitative research (McGivern, 2009). At the same time, qualitative research allows for reduction of the psychological distance between the researcher and respondents from various cultural backgrounds.

The most useful research methods and techniques comprise group focus interviews, depth interviews, and projective techniques. The focus interview is conducted in the form of a discussion, which is led by a moderator on the basis of some scenario (Proctor, 2005). The discussion involves 8-12 preselected participants and is recorded (dictaphone, video camera), observed indirectly ('two-way mirror'), or observed directly. The depth interview is held on the basis of some thematic scenario where questions are not predetermined; instead the respondents can express their own opinions without being confined by a questionnaire framework (Wright and Crimp, 2000). In projective techniques questions and stimuli are provided indirectly. Respondents are expected to assess certain attitudes, motives, and behavior, thus unconsciously attributing their own features to them (subconscious projection) (Mikulowski, 1999).

The first two methods make it possible to obtain both verbal and nonverbal information (such as intonation, gestures, facial expressions, and the like). This is important especially in the comparison of high- and low-context cultures. According to the concept proposed by Hall (1995), only a small part of communication takes place on the level of conscious and direct speech acts, whereas most of the communication process comprises nonverbal behavior and is greatly influenced by situational factors. Thus, communication is not confined to a simple exchange of signals between interlocutors; instead its content is determined by a general cultural context. The context is about the referential function of communication, i.e., it relates to what the communication is referring to. Hall (1995) distinguished two types of culture:

- high-context culture, where communication context is encoded in group customs and habits, where there exists a clear-cut distinction between insiders and outsiders, and where superiors are accountable for their subordinates; representatives of a definite culture have responsibility for their closest relatives, so communication is mostly based on intuition and the embarrassing situation of 'losing face' is tantamount to embarrassing the whole group; and
- low-context cultures where communication content is expressed individually; representatives of culture rely only on themselves and communication takes place by means of

words and unambiguous gestures; this eliminates the possibility of projecting 'loss of face' onto the whole group.

With regard to this typology, high-context cultures are represented by the countries of Latin America, Eastern and Western Africa, Saudi Arabia, and Greece; low-context cultures, in turn, can be observed in Scandinavian countries, Switzerland, Great Britain, the USA, Australia, and Israel. Any research to be conducted in a high-context culture should take account of the fact that only a part of information is conveyed *explicite*. Hence, it is necessary to ensure the use of research techniques that allow for observation of studied individuals without making them express statements that could expose them to the risk of 'losing face'. In spite of the problems connected with designing and conducting qualitative research, its usefulness must be admitted in identifying and comprehending cultural phenomena. In more advanced projects, qualitative research constitutes only an introduction to quantitative research. Apart form observation, the most common quantitative research techniques comprise personal and telephone interviews, as well as mail questionnaires. Figure 52 presents a comparison of basic quantitative data collection techniques in terms of their usefulness in marketing research conducted in a cross-cultural setting.

criteria	personal interview	telephone interview	mail questionnaire
research sample	+	+	-
difficulties in reaching respondents at home	-	+	+
shortage of adequate interviewers in a studied country	-	+	+
high rate of rural residents	+	-	+
lack of valid phone directories	+	-	+
lack of address lists	+	+	-
low rate of telephone penetration	+	-	+
lack of an effective post system	+	+	-
high illiteracy rate	+	+	-
'face to face' communication culture	+	-	-

+ stands for recommendation to conduct the research by means of a definite technique;

- stands for lack of possibility of conducting the research with the use of a definite technique.

Source: Malhotra et al., (1996), p. 17

Figure 52. Comparison of usefulness of research techniques

It is obvious that in a situation where the research is to be carried out in a country with a high illiteracy rate and a low telephone penetration rate, the personal interview is the only applicable technique, even if it means hiring and coaching interviewers. A mail questionnaire is recommended as a research technique in the case of an effective domestic post system and respondents' reluctance to accept interviewers' visits at home or at work.

In many countries, a telephone survey presents an excellent solution provided it is supported by proper technical infrastructure. This technique is advisable particularly with respect to institutional buyers, as even in countries with a low level of telephone penetration, a majority of companies do have telephone access. This research can be managed from one head call center and conducted in many countries. It draws on time differences between time zones: late night interviews in the country where the center is based reduce the costs of international telephone conversations. The only prerequisite for a successful application of this technique is finding interviewers who are fluent speakers of the target language of the country under study. In many countries, there exist many specialized companies that provide services by adopting the telephone survey technique on an international scale. The research based on the CATI system (Computer-Assisted Telephone Interview) allows for very efficiently and simultaneously entering the obtained data into the computer system. However, the questionnaire-based studies conducted on a sample of eighty-three leading research agencies in seventeen countries demonstrate great discrepancies both on the international and national levels with respect to the way the interviews are conducted. The biggest differences lay in the sample selection (random phone number selection or nonrandom selection), which confirms the thesis that reconciliation of the ways of carrying out research with respect to theoretical correctness, low-cost engagement, and marketing aptitude is still not feasible (Taylor, 1997).

The **experiment** as an international research method is considered to be exceptionally complicated. Nonetheless, among many theoreticians as well as pragmatists the opinion prevails that this method is likely to grow in significance (Kwarciak, 2000). Experimental projects are based on the principle of manipulating explanatory variables and observing changes in the explained variable. Therefore, it is necessary to determine which factors can be regarded as a cause and which as an effect; in addition, the whole experiment should be monitored. Another factor to be taken into account is time, since effects of certain activities may emerge only after a longer period of time.

It is extremely difficult to develop an experimental project that can be conducted in international studies without having to be altered. One such experiment, which was carried out in a natural environment, took place in the USA, the UK, and Japan. The experiment was designed to demonstrate the effect of fruit juice displays on the purchase volume in supermarkets. In the USA, juices are usually arranged on shelves in four rows. In the experiment, the arrangement of juices was changed by placing them in three or five rows. After making sure that there was no other competitive promotional campaign in progress and that the price of the juice was stable, changes in the juice sales volume were observed. The same procedure was followed in the other countries. During the research it turned out, however, that in the UK, juices were arranged in three columns and in Japan in two. This made the researcher change the principles behind the experiment in order to adapt to the specific character of the studied markets (Karcz, 2004).

Unlike the experimental method, the observational one does not pose so many technical, organizational, and cultural problems. **Observation** is a method of data gathering in a deliberate, planned, and systematic way in order to obtain an answer to a clearly defined question (Wilson, 2006). The observation may comprise people and their behavior as well as objects. The gathered data are pooled and registered in the form of special observation questionnaires (registers), cameras, or recorders. This method is popular with Japanese managers who prefer to use participative or disguised observation techniques rather than interviews or questionnaires. To provide an example, Toyota used the technique of a disguised observation while working on some improvements for a Corolla model that was very popular among women. The observation was made on a group of women whose behavior was being viewed while getting into or out of the car and while operating it. The research revealed that many women had problems with opening the car and with operating the controls. Armed with this knowledge, Toyota engineers streamlined the facilities and did some redesigning in order to eliminate any difficulties.

5.3.4   International direct research on the Internet

The Internet has opened up new opportunities for conducting direct research, as it 'has introduced' the consumer to the company, and the company to the consumer's home or workplace. By visiting the WWW website of a definite organization or by shopping online, the consumer leaves behind many traces that the computer can secure, and if necessary, find and present to the organization in a meaningful and comprehensible manner.

The Internet enables organizations to send questions to customers that help identify consumer needs, preferences, and opinions in a much shorter time and at much lower costs than traditional marketing studies. By crossing the time, space, and cost boarders, the Internet is revolutionizing marketing research (Strzyzewska, 2002). What was within the reach of a very few companies only recently, today has become accessible to almost everyone. Due to high costs, traditional marketing research was available only to very large and very wealthy companies, but even they could not afford to make use of services provided by research agencies very frequently. The Internet allows for cost reduction, which means availability of services to all companies and an increased motivation to use them. Nonetheless, such cooperation is not always necessary, as the Internet gives companies the possibility of conducting marketing studies on their own. The Internet constitutes a fully accessible and an abundant source of data that can be used both by large and small organizations. Due to its low participation costs, easy access, and simple operation, the Internet creates equal opportunities in terms of information availability (Burns and Bush, 2010).

The possibility of ensuring regular and cheap marketing data results in the emergence of a tendency for switching from individual projects to whole marketing research systems managed over the Internet. Such research can be carried out (McGivern, 2009)

- without the respondent's engagement (consisting in observation of the Internet user's behavior by means of special software) or
- with the respondent's engagement.

The Internet has all the makings for being a medium of conducting questionnaire studies. The Internet survey resembles a mail questionnaire, though in some cases it is similar to a general questionnaire, where the respondent individually downloads the questionnaire from some broadly accessible Internet location such as the WWW website of the organization involved in the research.

The advantage of an e-mail questionnaire over a traditional one is unquestionable. The positives of electronically sent-out questionnaires include (Unold, 2001; Sznajder, 2000) the following:

- the possibility of conducting the research on a global scale;
- the possibility of reaching a large group of respondents quickly and simultaneously;
- easier access to the least available groups of respondents;
- a short waiting time for return of completed questionnaires (it is observed that a large number of questionnaires are returned within 24 hours);
- a higher rate of return of completed questionnaires;
- lower costs of conducting research;
- the possibility of equipping the questionnaire forms with multimedia elements (graphics, animation, sound);
- no participation of agents (the questionnaire is usually received only by the respondent, which means more control over the data-collection process);
- asynchronous communication;
- provides for better answer quality (fewer omitted questions, no legibility problems with handwritten answers, presents the questionnaire in the form of a pop-up sequence with one question per box preventing the respondent from returning to previous questions and changing answers based on the perspective of later questions, closer to the direct interview as a result of this solution, allows for further examination of spontaneous or list-assisted knowledge of product brands, for example, which is not feasible in the case of a traditional questionnaire);
- lower costs and a shorter time of encoding answers (database creation);
- the possibility of altering the questionnaire during the research; this affects the result interpretation, but in the case of the Internet questionnaire, the approval of a definite questionnaire shape is not irreversible;
- greater convenience for the researcher (no need to print questionnaires, assemble and send letters, or enter answers into the computer);
- greater convenience for the respondent (possibility of completing and sending filled-in questionnaires at any time);
- lesser probability of errors connected with questionnaire processing; and
- the possibility of real-time data processing.

The Internet questionnaire is not a universal tool, and as such has the following downsides:

- restricts the research to e-mail users who, in most cases, cannot be considered to be representative of a population, especially a population of individual consumers (Karcz, 2004);
- in some cases, allows respondent's to create alterations to the questionnaire;

- does not ensure absolute confidentiality (this research form does not guarantee anonymity if the researcher does not include a procedure to protect the respondent's privacy);
- involves topographic and technical problems (certain characters cannot be used in e-mail correspondence; some words can be illegible so it is necessary to be disciplined with text width; some e-mail boxes are not equipped to handle lengthy questionnaires, so they have to be split into smaller parts); and
- absence of world e-mail address lists, which would be needed in the research (Bajdak, 2003).

The Internet is a perfect tool for conducting omnibus research. Research agencies that possess the e-mail address base are able to carry out fast questionnaire surveys at the request of several independent clients. Omnibus research can be done both among individual and institutional consumers (Kiezel, 2010).

The Internet also gives a possibility of conducting observatory research by means of the so-called cookies, text files sent by the server and placed in the WWW visitor software. Cookies allow for counting the number of visits to a website by specific users, following users' web navigation, and developing their profile. Additionally, cookies enable a researcher to analyze the information sought by a user, and thus to identify a user's preferences with respect to presented information. Nonetheless, cookies violate privacy, which makes them very unpopular with Internet users; therefore, they should be applied with great care. Another disadvantage of cookies as a source of research information relates to their being computer-based, which means that in the case of several users, they are distinguished only when the browser uses individual user profiles (Bajdak, 2003).

On top of that, attempts are being made to use the Internet in qualitative research, especially research based on focus group interviews, which can be organized on so-called chats, i.e., during a simultaneous discussion held by Internet users. However, some researchers are skeptical about the quality of information obtained in this way. In an Internet focus group interview, neither the moderator nor the respondents can see one another, which rules out the possibility of reading so-called body language. Moreover, opinions expressed online are not spontaneous since the discourse is limited only to written statements, which are shorter and more balanced.

5.3.5   Construction of measurement tools

The survey or interview questionnaire constitutes a basic instrument employed in direct research. A properly constructed **questionnaire** determines the adequacy of the research results. When considering the problem of questionnaire development for marketing research in foreign markets, it is necessary to focus mainly on the following issues (Blythe, 2009):

- formulating questions,
- scaling answers, and
- translating the questionnaire into target languages.

The length of a questionnaire is not measured by the number of questions, but by the duration time of interview or questionnaire completion. In different countries, respondents have a different perception of the amount of time they are willing to spend answering questions, even if they give their consent to participate in the research. If a German respondent is informed that the interview lasts thirty minutes, it is expected that the respondent himself will ask to stop the interview after the time is over. French and Italian respondents are more flexible in this respect. Scandinavian respondents, in turn, are much more willing to participate in studies; and the refusal rate in these countries is lower compared to the Mediterranean region.

Questionnaires use open, closed, and semi-open (semi-closed) questions. However, depending on the culture, respondents make different use of semi-open questions, which enable them to add their own opinions to the proposed ones. Only 3% of Americans and as many as 20% of South Asians usually provide extra answers in semi-open questions (Karcz, 2004). International marketing research based on the questionnaire method should not be provided with open questions, or, at least, open questions should be reduced to a bare minimum, not only due to the risk of answer default, but also due to the possibility of problems with categorizing answers during data processing.

In the course of answer formulation, it is important to take account of cultural differences among the countries under study. For example, research into ethical and social accountability issues employs the 33-point Marlow scale (Social Desirability Scale). One of the items reads as follows: 'I never make a long trip without checking the safety of my car'. Using such an item to compare respondents' behavior in for example, the USA or Hong Kong, is not adequate for this reason: because of Hong Kong's geographic position and area size, long car journeys are not possible for Hong Kong residents (McDonald, 2000).

Formulation of questions is based on measurement scales that measure the attributes, attitudes, opinions, and behavior of studied objects. The development of scales starts with a definition of a logical or a mathematical system on which a given scale is based. There are four basic measurement scales (Sagan, 1998; Zaborski, 2001):

- a nominal scale, which makes it possible to determine whether measured attributes are equal or different; it consists in 'labeling' the attributes, but numbers assigned to them are only of a symbolic character (they can be exemplified by dichotomous, multi-category, or positional scales);
- an ordinal scale, which helps order attributes and determine the relation of magnitude between them (ordinal scales include rank-order scales, the Likert scale, the semantic differential scale, grading scales, paired comparison scales);
- an interval scale, thanks to which it is possible to determine the magnitude relation between the attributes and the distance between intervals; this scale is of a metric character and has an arbitrarily established zero point (e.g., Thurston scale); and
- a ratio scale, which allows for the top level of measurement thanks to the existence of a natural zero or a natural measurement unit (e.g., constant sum scale).

At this point, the question arises as to whether these scales can be adopted in international research. Here, during the studies, the researcher may face problems connected with respondents' level of education, as well as with cultural differences, which can lead to serious errors in the course of the research. It is generally assumed that verbal scales are more comprehensible, and thus more effective, even in studies carried out among less educated people as illiterates also express their opinions by means of words. In developing countries, research is sometimes based on graphic rating scales such as 'sad-to-happy' faces. The scale consists of five face drawings with various eye and mouth expressions depicting a state of mind from 'very happy' to 'very unhappy'. Respondents are read a question (statement), and then asked to express their degree of interest or compliance by indicating a proper drawing on the scale (e.g., strong interest corresponds to a 'very happy face'). It should be remembered that application of such a scale may induce some negative reactions in people who consider themselves too educated and too intelligent to be presented with such a scale. At this juncture, it is advisable to prepare another answer scale.

Semantic differential is regarded as a pan-cultural scale. It consists of a sequence of simple bipolar sub-scales; most frequently bipolar adjectives such as: good-bad, strong-weak, fast-slow, etc. that need to be properly translated (i.e., taking account of cultural differences). The use of the Likert scale, in turn, evokes many controversies (Yu et al., 1992). Americans tend to use five- or seven-point scales, and so do Poles. French people often use twenty-point scales, which they find familiar given their experience with the scales used for progress assessment at school.

Also different school experiences may cause problems connected with the use of numeric scales in a global dimension. In some countries (e.g., Germany, Slovakia), the grade 1 at school stands for very good, whereas in others (e.g., Poland), for very bad. Even if instructions were provided with respect to answers about assessing a product, an attribute, or an event, and even if it were clearly stated that the answer should be given in a 1-5 scale (with 1 denoting the lowest grade and 5 the highest grade), respondents could have problems when choosing the answer due to their previous experience with a reversed scale order. This problem is illustrated in Figure 53, which presents school grade scales across various countries.

country	fail	unsatisfactory	satisfactory	good	very good	excellent
Belgium	0-9	10	12-13	14-15	16-17	18
Denmark	0-5	6	7	8-9	10-11	12-13
Germany	5	4	4	3	2	1
Greece	1-4	5	5	6	7-8	9-10
Holland	0-5	6	6-7	7-8	8-9	10
Italy	1-18	19-23	24-26	27-28	29	30
Poland	1	2	3	4	5	6

Source: Schroeder (1996), p. 63

Figure 53. Qualitative grades and their numeric equivalents

5.3.6   Procedures of research tool translation

Proper translation of a questionnaire into foreign languages determines whether questions are correctly understood, which is of key importance to the credibility and usefulness of obtained answers. The simplest direct translation rendered by one translator may include errors due to, for example, lack of absolute language competence or incomplete knowledge of idiomatic expressions. Based on practice, several translation techniques have been developed. Their advantages and disadvantages are presented in Figure 54.

translation techniques	process	positives	negatives
direct translation	$A \rightarrow B$	easy to conduct, cheap, less time-consuming	leads to serious mistakes and differences between A and B, which are difficult to be noticed instantly
back translation	$A \rightarrow B$; $B \rightarrow A'$, comparing A with $A' \rightarrow$ the final version B_f	helps discover most differences and ambiguities connected with translation; relatively cheap	requires availability of two translators: one from A country, another from B (both native speakers)
parallel translation	$A \rightarrow B$, $A \rightarrow B'$ comparing B with $B' \rightarrow$ final version B_f	easier to be rendered in A country with B country translators; relatively less time-consuming	allows for a proper translation into B, but does not secure concept equivalence; a possibility of one dominant translator; relatively high costs
decentering translation	$A \rightarrow B$, $A \rightarrow B'$, $B \rightarrow A'$, $B' \rightarrow A''$, comparing A' with A'' and further iterations up to the final version B_f	allows for the best suitability of both versions and the highest credibility of the translation; makes it possible to change (modify) the original version and to tailor it to a cultural specificity	very expensive; difficulties with finding translators; requires readiness for changing the original version

A – the original language, B – the target language

Source: Usunier (1998), p. 5

Figure 54. Positive and negative aspects of selected translation techniques

With the goal of ensuring methodological correctness while taking account of cultural differences, it is possible to formulate some recommendations for procedures to follow in translating the research tools used in marketing research. It is important to

- employ combinations of translation methods with a special focus on the decentering translation,
- involve two independent translators in the translation process,
- ensure the translator's presence during data collection (when the researcher does not have sufficient knowledge of the target language),
- analyze several small random subgroups of a studied sample in order to identify possible problems with respondents' understanding of questions or to find default on answers, and
- conduct a simple introductory statistical analysis (correlations, distributions) for data processing before applying more advanced methods (Kotler et al., 2009).

On the one hand, these recommendations call for increased research costs at the preparatory stage of studies and for a longer research time. On the other hand, if researchers attempt to save, the result may be lack of translation equivalence. In extreme cases, this can result in inability to compare the international research, and thus in failure with respect to the research goal and application of research results.

5.4 Methodological problems at different stages of research

Methodological problems that are typical of research conducted in a multicultural environment arise at the level of field research, data analysis, and data interpretation, as well as communication of research results (see Figure 55).

activities and tasks	methodological problems
field research	<ul><li>standardization versus adaptation of field research to local market conditions</li><li>research organization</li><li>participation of research agencies</li><li>organization of field research teams</li><li>interviewer selection and interviewer coaching</li><li>relations between the interviewer and respondents</li><li>field work monitoring</li></ul>
data processing	<ul><li>data standardization</li><li>sections of the analysis</li><li>methods of data processing (analysis of qualitative data)</li></ul>
research result communication	<ul><li>data interpretation</li><li>the form of a written presentation, visualization techniques</li><li>oral presentation</li></ul>

Source: Malhotra et al., (1996), p. 9

Figure 55. Methodological problems at different stages of research

5.4.1   Standardization of international marketing research

At the beginning of international marketing research, an organization about to conduct a study is faced with a decision problem concerning the purpose and the possibility of standardization of a research procedure. Literally, standardization of the research on an international scale means conducting it by virtue of identical sets of methods, techniques, and instruments, on identical sample groups in terms of their size and selection methods, and with application of identical data analysis and data processing as well as communication of results (Schmidt and Hollensen, 2006).

This concept of total standardization is counterbalanced by another approach, according to which marketing studies conducted across different countries have nothing in common (Craig and Douglas, 2001). Practically, decisions concerning research standardization, as in the case of standardization of a marketing strategy, are not dichotomous, i.e., they are not based either on selection of total standardization or total adaptation to specifics of the countries to be studied.

From the perspective of an organization, the principal advantages of research standardization are the possibility of comparing research information and results across countries, the possibility of reducing costs (joint costs at the designing stage), and improving implementation and supervision of the research on a global scale (Howard, 2003). In addition to potential benefits, research standardization has serious drawbacks related to the specific character of domestic markets (economic, social, cultural conditions, etc.); to conditions of the 'research infrastructure'; and, in some cases, to legal issues. The degree of standardization of international marketing research depends on various factors, including (Karcz, 2004)

- characteristics of research subjects,
- a macroeconomic and competitive environment,
- the nature of studied local (domestic) markets, and
- corporate organizational factors.

Generally speaking, standardization is possible when the markets to be researched share many similarities (in subject, space, and object sections). Decisions about the degree of standardization in international studies affect the selection of the organizational forms in which the research is conducted and coordinated.

5.4.2 Organization of international marketing research

The level of monitoring of research efforts is determined by a company's internal organizational structure. Organization of international research varies according to the management style, the range of research, and the importance of studied countries and markets to the company itself. In multinational corporations operating in the international market, one can distinguish three principal approaches to marketing research (Figure 56):

- centralized activity,
- coordinated activity, and
- decentralized activity.

specification	personnel of company's head office	database in head office	research agencies in the head office country	subsidiary (branch) personnel	local agencies (national)
centralized activity model	research design processing and analysis	data gathering			field research
coordinated activity model	identification of research problems research results		research design processing and analyzing		field research
decentralized activity model	general research goals research results			research design result review	field research, analysis, and presentation

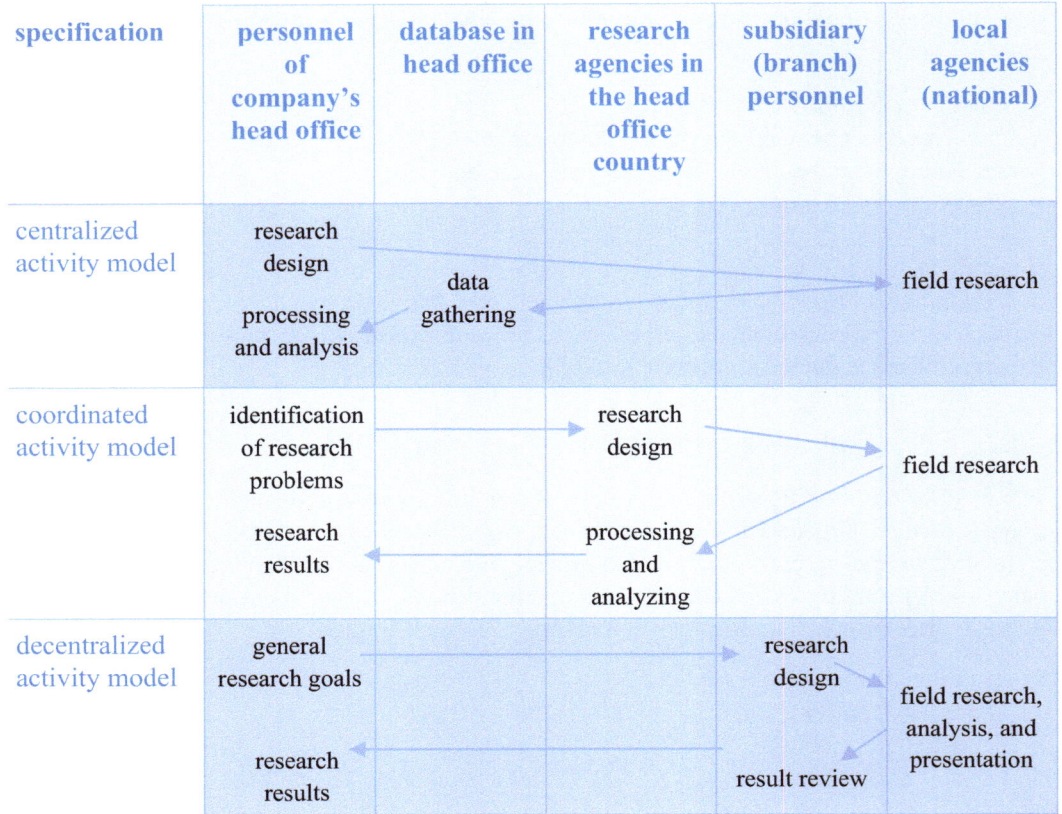

Source: Czinkota and Ronkainen (1993), p. 347

Figure 56. Alternative models of organization and coordination of research

5.4.3   Analysis and interpretation of international marketing research results

The choice of a statistical method to be used in the analysis of international research data is determined by the same factors as in the case of research conducted in one country. The most important factors include

- research goals and research hypotheses,
- measurement scale application, and
- assumptions underlying statistical tests.

When selecting the method, the marketer has to determine whether the analysis is concerned with one variable, and, if so, whether this variable reflects either metric or non-metric measurement, or whether the analysis is concerned with many variables. If one of these variables is treated as explained (dependent), while others need to explain the former variable (independent), then one can talk about dependence analysis. If, on the other hand, the marketer is interested in relations between variables, then one can refer to it as interdependence analysis. It should be borne in mind that international marketing research comprises more than one sample, which means that when selecting a statistical test, it is necessary to consider issues concerning the relationship between these samples (Pauwels and de Ruyter, 2005). Possible statistical methods are presented in Figure 57. Methodological problems arise not only at the stage of conducting the research, but also at the level of result analysis and interpretation. This mainly refers to projects that employ experimental methods, qualitative methods, and depth as well as face-to-face interviews.

specification	scales		
	nominal	**ordinal**	**interval or ratio-based**
	one-factor analysis		
independent tests	Chi-square test	Mann-Whitney test	test $_z$ test $_t$ variance analysis
dependent tests	Mc Nemar test	Wilcoxon test bilateral Friedmann test	test $_t$
	multi-factor analysis		
dependence analysis	contingency coefficient	correlation coefficient	regression analysis discriminatory analysis
interdependence analysis	factor analysis	Kendall coefficient	factor analysis cluster analysis

Source: Churchill (2002), p. 670

Figure 57. Statistical methods adopted in data analysis

In these types of studies, data are screened by the researcher's perception. Information from qualitative research should not be subject to classic statistical processing, as this could evoke in less knowledgeable recipients the impression that the research is representative of a broader population in qualitative terms. Reports on qualitative research are characterized by many quotations from respondents', whereby it is possible to find out how they express their views and what language they use to that end (Kitzmiller and Miller, 2003). The analysis of information in qualitative research, like the research itself, is of a subjective character, where much depends on the experience and skills of the people in charge of the research.

In terms of interpretation of results, questionnaire surveys and research focused solely on quantitative data collection carry a lower risk of cultural errors. Widespread use of information technology has enabled researchers to apply the same standard programs of statistical data analysis almost everywhere. Although many methodological issues still remain unsolved, it should be acknowledged that all available programs offer marketers enough possibilities to carry out in-depth qualitative data analysis.

5.4.4   Preparation of report on international marketing research

Preparation of an **international marketing research report** is based on the general principles applicable to presentation of results of marketing research conducted within one country (one culture) (Kumar, 2000; Churchill, 2002). The most significant principle of report
preparation is to adapt its content to the recipient. Generally, managers who order the research are not so much interested in methodological and technical details of the research.
What they care about the most are results and conclusions presented in a form that facilitates
the decision-making process. Consequently, such a report needs to include terminology that
is aligned with the recipient's knowledge. Additionally, it should use a comprehensible style
and employ graphic presentation methods.

The entire report is usually divided into three parts (Skaates and Cova, 2005; Rialp and
Rialp, 2006):

- the introduction, with precisely defined goals, ranges, methods, manners, and conditions
  of conducting the research, as well as the main directions of result application;
- the analysis, including a systematic presentation of the obtained results divided into
  smaller parts in order to streamline the report analysis; and
- the conclusion, with cognitive, practical, and key conclusions as well as recommendations on possible marketing activities and their consequences.

The source appendix constitutes an integral part of the report; and it contains working tables,
methodological details, patterns of measurement instruments, and the like. The report should
also include an abridged version, the so-called managerial summary, containing the most
vital information. The report can be complemented with an oral presentation delivered to a
group of the most interested recipients. The presentation makes it possible to clarify any
existing doubts as well as to make certain conclusions and recommendations precise. Additionally, it has all the advantages of a 'face-to-face' communication, especially in high-
context cultures where it is needed as the final element of the research process. In the case of
international research, results frequently need to be presented in several languages to different types of audiences with diverse decision needs (Wright and Crimp, 2000). It is generally
assumed that reports should be comparable despite differences in their layout, which depend
on a country's specific rules about report preparation.

With respect to oral presentations, there is a general principle that the speaker should be
'culture-conscious', which means familiar with the formal polite language typical of various
cultures, with accepted and understood forms of result visualization, and with the business
code of formal meetings. On top of that, such a person is expected to know when to use col-
loquialisms and jokes. Identification and understanding of the cultural differences of market
subjects are possible thanks to properly designed and conducted international marketing
research that takes the cultural perspective into account. Results of research may provide
sound grounds for decisions made by corporations operating in international markets unless
they are squandered at the stage of result communication. Hence, it is extremely vital to take
into consideration the basic communication rules of a multicultural environment and to possess indispensable knowledge about the dynamics of cross-cultural meetings.

List of References

Adler, N., 1983. A typology of management studies involving culture. *Journal of International Business Studies*, 14: 31-32.

Bajdak, A. (ed.), 2003. *Internet w marketingu*. Warszawa: PWE.

Blackwell, R. D., Miniard, P. W. & Engel, J. F., 2001. *Consumer behavior*. Fort Worth: Harcourt College Publishers.

Blythe, J., 2009. *Essentials of marketing*. London: Financial Times Press.

Burns, A. C. & Bush, R. F., 2008. *Basic marketing research using Microsoft Excel data analysis: international edition*. London: Pearson Education.

Burns, A. C. & Bush, R. F., 2010. *Marketing research: global edition*. London: Pearson Higher Education.

Cavusgi, S. T. & Das, A., 1997. Methodological issues in empirical cross-cultural research: a survey of the management literature and a framework. *Management International Review*, 37: 71-96.

Churchill, G. A. & Iacobucci, D., 2009. *Marketing research: methodological foundations*, South Western: Educational Publishing.

Churchill, G. A., 2002. *Badania marketingowe. Podstawy metodologiczne*. Warszawa: PWN.

Craig, C. S. & Douglas, S. P., 2001. Conducting international marketing research in the twenty-first century. *International Marketing Review*, 18 (1): 80-90.

Czinkota, M. R. & Ronkainen, J. A., 1993. *International marketing*. Fort Worth: Dryden Press.

Ember, M. & Oterbein, K. F., 1991. Sampling in cross-cultural research. *Behavior Science Research*, 32: 129-139.

Glowacki, R., Kramer, J. & Żabiński, L., 1980. *Analiza rynku*. Warszawa: PWE.

Green, P. E., Carmone, F. J. & Smith, S. M., 1989. *Multidimensional scaling. Concepts and applications*. Needham Heights: Allyn & Bacon.

Hair, J. F., Black, W. C., Babin, B. J. & Anderson, R. E., 2010. *Multivariate data analysis*. London: Pearson Education.

Hall, E., 1995. *Managing cultures*. London: John Wiley & Sons.

Hofstede, G., 2000. *Kultury i organizacje – zaprogramowanie umysłu*. Warszawa: PWE.

Holzmuller, H. H., 1995. *Konzeptionelle und methodische Probleme in der interkulturellen Management- und Marketingforschung*. Stuttgart: Schäffer-Poeschel Verlag.

Howard, C. A., 2003. The internationalization of marketing discipline. *Research in Global Strategic Management*, 8: 27-41.

Kaczmarczyk, S., 2002. *Badania marketingowe. Metody i techniki*. Warszawa: PWE.

Karcz, K. 2004. *Miedzynarodowe badania marketingowe*. Warszawa: PWE.

Karcz, K. & Kędzior, Z., 2001. *Zachowania podmiotów rynkowych w Polsce a proces integracji europejskiej*. Katowice: CBiE AE.

Kedzior, Z. & Karcz, K., 2001. *Badania marketingowe w praktyce*. Warszawa: PWE.

Kiezel, E. (ed.), 2010. *Konsument i jego zachowania na rynku europejskim*. Warszawa: PWE.

Kitzmiller, G. & Miller, J., 2003. International marketing research. *Research in global strategic management*, 8: 84-101.

Kotler, Ph., Keller, K., Brady, M., Goodman, M. & Hansen, T., 2009, *Marketing management: first European edition*. London: Prentice Hall.

Kumar, V., 2000. *International marketing research*. New Jersey: Prentice Hall.

Kwarciak, B., 2000. Obiektywnie, indywidualnie, podłużnie, synchronicznie i eksperymentalnie. *Modern Marketing,* 12: 22-25.

Malhotra, N. & Birks, D., 2007. *Marketing research: an applied approach*. New York: Financial Times Press.

Malhotra, N., Hall, J., Shaw, M. & Oppenheim, P., 2008. *Essentials of marketing research:an applied orientation*. New York: Prentice Hall.

Malhotra, N. K., Agarwal, J. & Peterson, M., 1996. Methodological issues in cross-cultural marketing research. A state-of-art review. *International Marketing Review*, 13: 9-21

McDonald, G., 2000. Cross-cultural methodological issues in ethical research. *Journal of Business Ethics*, 27: 89-104.

McGivern, Y., 2009. *The practice of market research: an introduction*. London: Pearson Education.

Mikulowski, J., 1999. *Komunikacja międzykulturowa. Wprowadzenie*. Krakow: AE.

Moutinho, L. & Evans, M., 1992. *Applied marketing research*. London: Addison-Wesley.

Mruk, H., 2003. *Analiza rynku*. Warszawa: PWE.

Pauwels, P. & de Ruyter, K., 2005. Research on international service marketing: enrichment and challenges. *Advance in International Marketing*, 15: 95-112.

Proctor, T., 2005. *Essentials of marketing research*. New York: Financial Times Press.

Reece, M., 2010. *Real-time marketing for business growth: how to use social media,measure marketing, and create a culture of execution*. London: Pearson Education.

Rialp, A. & Rialp, J., 2006. International marketing research: opportunities and challenges in the 21st century. *Advance in International Marketing*, 17: 64-81.

Ryan, A., Chan, D., Ployhart, R. E. & Slade, L. A., 1999. Employee attitude survey in a multinational organization: considering language and culture in assessing measurement equivalence. *Personnel Psychology*, 53: 37-58.

Rzepinska, M., 1983. *Historia koloru w dziejach malarstwa europejskiego*. Warszawa: Wydawnictwo Literatów.

Sagan, A., 1998. *Badania marketingowe. Podstawowe kierunki*. Krakow: AE.

Schiffman, L. G. & Kanuk, L. L., 1994. *Consumer behavior*. New Jersey: Prentice Hall.

Schmidt, M. & Hollensen, S., 2006. *Marketing research: An international approach*. New York: Financial Times Press.

Schroeder, J., 1996. *Badania marketingowe rynków zagranicznych*. Poznan: AE.

Skaates, M. A. & Cova, B., 2005. Marketing industrial project-related services internationally: A multilingual literature review. *Advance in international marketing*, 15: 72-94.

Steenkamp, J-B. E. M., 2001. The role of national culture in international marketing research. *International Marketing Review*, 18 (1): 30-44.

Strzyzewska, M., 2002. *Marketingowe zastosowanie Internetu w Polsce*. Warszawa: IFGN SGH.

Sznajder, A., 2000. *Marketing wirtualny*. Krakow: Dom Wydawniczy ABC.

Taylor, H., 1997. The very different methods used to conduct telephone surveys of the public. *Journal of the Market Research Society*, 39: 421-433.

Thuy, P. N. & Hau, L. N., 2010. Service personal values and consumer loyalty. A study of banking services in a transitional economy. *International Journal of Bank Marketing*, 28 (6): 46-58.

Unold, J., 2001. *Systemy informacyjne marketingu*. Wrocław: AE.

Usunier, J. C., 1998. *International and cross-cultural management research*. London: Sage Publications.

Wells, W. D. & Prensky, D., 1996. *Consumer behavior*. New York: John Wiley & Sons, Inc.

Wilson, A., 2006. *Marketing research: an integrated approach*. New York: Financial Times Press.

Wright, L. T. & Crimp, M., 2000. *The marketing research process*. New York: Financial Times Press.

Yu, J. H., Keown, C. H. & Jacobs, L., 1992. Attitude scale methodology: cross-cultural implications. *Journal of International Marketing,* 3: 320-327.

Zaborski, A., 2001. *Skalowanie wielowymiarowe w badaniach marketingowych.* Wrocław: AE.

Zelias, A., 1998. *Metody statystyki międzynarodowej.* Warszawa: PWN.

6   Chapter: Relationship marketing

Chapter learning objectives

- Describe the meaning of relationship marketing.

- Explain the important elements of marketing knowledge needed to explore opportunities in international business.

- Describe the process of developing business relationships.

- Explain the contents of the cultural dimension models.

- Describe the methodological weaknesses of cross-cultural research.

6.1   Marketing as relationships

Those engaged in marketing, whether employed in a market research institute or in the marketing department of a firm, mainly are concerned with **knowledge** exploration. Detailed and continuously updated information about the firm's macro and industry environment, its suppliers, customers, and stakeholders, is of vital importance to gaining competitive advantages. Marketers seek relevant market information from secondary sources and their own field research. Representative data collected through field research consumes resources (e.g., manpower, time) and is, therefore, costly. Since firms are normally confronted with internal resource limitations, the alternative for gaining relevant knowledge about markets and their participants is **relationship marketing**. Marketing practitioners and entrepreneurs should realize that strategic business networks can provide firms with tangible and intangible rare resource assets that provide competitive advantages (Capaldo, 2007).

According to Johanson and Vahlne (2009: 1411), 'markets are networks of relationships in which firms are linked to each other in various, complex and, to a considerable extent, invisible patterns'. **Business networks** are seen as market structures in which an internationalizing firm is embedded. The concept of 'network position' focuses on the location of the firm within the complex set of interacting relations in which the firm is embedded (Johanson and Mattsson, 1992). Network position refers to the role a firm plays in the network and how it is linked directly (e.g., joint ventures, strategic alliances) or indirectly (e.g., competitors) to other firms in the network (Wilkinson and Young, 2002). Conversely, 'market position' focuses on how a firm's products and services are positioned in relation to competing offers in the minds of potential customers.

A lack of **institutional market knowledge** means having limited information about the foreign target environment, such as the society, ecology, economy, laws, and expertise (S.E.E.L.E). Limitations in market knowledge are related to a firm's direct business environment. According to the business network view, the environment consists of firms with which a particular firm procures business relationships or tries to do business, and the relationships between firms and their environments. Therefore, a firm's success requires that it is well established in one or more networks. Anything that happens occurs within the context of relationships, and a firm that is well established in a relevant network or networks is an 'insider', whereas a firm that does not have a position in a relevant network is an 'outsider' (Johanson and Vahlne, 2009).

Relationship marketing takes into account that a firm is frequently connected in a set of diverse relationships with its suppliers, customers, and stakeholders; and these networks usually are constructed over the long-term. The term 'connected' means that exchanges in one relationship are linked to exchanges in another network (a firm's supplier may also maintain business relationships with the firm's major competitor). These webs of connected relationships are called business networks (Anderson et al., 1994; Hakansson and Ford, 2002). The firm is able to create market knowledge through exchanges in its network of interconnected relationships. Relationships are basically socially constructed, for example by the executive management, market research employees, and service and after sales staff. Marketing people are able to acquire knowledge about a firm's relationship partners, such as for example knowledge about

- customer needs and expectations,
- competitors' movements,
- intensity of industry competitiveness,
- suppliers' capacities,
- market forecasts,
- customers' expectations and quality consciousness,
- technological innovations,
- threat of product substitutions, and
- foreign target country risks.

Successful internationalization requires a reciprocal commitment between the firm and its counterparts (e.g., suppliers, customers, stakeholders, etc.). A working relationship is the result of considerable investment in the past and represents an important and valuable firm resource today and for the future. A firm's sophisticated relationship marketing provides a privileged access to information about its relationship partners and their business networks (Agndal and Chetty, 2007). As a result, marketing people explore new business opportunities and are sensitive to environmental threats. The process may be unilateral, with a particular firm learning about another firm's needs, capabilities, markets, and networks, thereby identifying opportunities and threats. Alternatively it may be bilateral when two firms in interaction identify an opportunity (Johanson and Vahlne, 2009). It may even be multilateral, with several firms interacting and increasing their commitment towards new business opportunities (e.g., alliance in order to launch common technological standards). In the context of upcoming threats such as the ongoing increase in oil and gas prices, firms intensify their network engagement (e.g., automotive manufacturers cooperate in the development of alternative energy concepts).

Business relationships are not set once and for all. They are created, developed, modified and, eventually, broken by those who manage them. A firm may discover that the needs and capabilities of a new partner (e.g., supplier, logistics firm) link up usefully with its own needs and capabilities, which in turn are based on its business relationships with other business partners; thus a business network is created. Business relationships may be connected with relationships that involve governmental regulatory units, e.g., in order to get an investment approval. Coordination with government agencies is of the same nature, in principle, as coordination across business relationships. With regards to knowledge, the combination of knowledge from the set of a firm's relationships is what gives the firm its specific competitive ability. Through its market exchanges in a set of interrelated business relationships, the firm creates new knowledge. The knowledge-creating processes of the firm with its partners are developed through its business relationships, and this coordination may well extend far beyond the horizon of a specific firm (Forsgren et al., 2005).

A firm's strategic planning is not just about changing the future course of events to achieve desired goals but also is a means of acquiring and developing knowledge about the opportunities and limitations of action in relations and networks. Relationships assume substantial investments in time, money, and effort. As a result, knowledge or other strategically important resources are accessed and created by marketers. For that reason, coordination between and within the relationships becomes a central managerial concern. The larger the network size, the greater the complexity and, thus, the more intensive are the corresponding coordination efforts (Wilkinson and Young, 2002).

Because relationships are connected to each other, companies are not free to act according to their own aims. They do not operate in isolation from others. Instead, each company's considerations and actions can only be understood within the context of its network counterparts. For marketing managers, several important consequences follow from this. **Relationship diversity** gives all marketing managers myriad opportunities, but the ability to act and the effect of their actions is constrained by the existing structure of the network. Changes within firms occur through changes in the structure of the business network and the participants (e.g., suppliers, competitors, and customers). The existence of the structure and its inertia makes activities within the network more difficult, and simultaneously more important. The firm can initiate changes, such as internal (e.g., product portfolio) and external (e.g., foreign market entry) only through changes in its networks. Thus, the management should display persistence in convincing other network participants of the benefits of that change and managing their expectations within the network. The acting firm's management must give its relationship counterparts a picture of the intended direction of a change and find ways to combine changes in its internal resources and connections that properly relate them to the network partners' own motivations and resources. Because any change in a network is initially dependent on existing structure and resources, it is difficult for a company to achieve change by seeking new network counterparts. The firm's management first has to find a potential network counterpart with applicable resources (Granovetter, 2004; Hakansson and Ford, 2002). When relationship partners are found, the firm learns about its network partners and from its network partners and creates knowledge together with the network partners. As strategy is concerned with positioning the firm for an unknown future, the 'relating', which implies joint learning and commitment building, helps decrease the level of uncertainty. As a consequence of the network view, it is reasonable to regard markets as networks (Johanson and Vahlne, 2010).

6.2   The impact of culture in relationships

Culture has often served simply as a synonym for nation without any further conceptual grounding. A person is not born with a given culture: rather, she or he acquires it through the socialization process that begins at birth. National differences found in the characteristics of organizations or their members have been interpreted as cultural differences. The primary causes of failure in multinational enterprises, international joint ventures, and so on, stem from a lack of understanding of essential differences in managing human resources. Certain management philosophies and techniques have proved successful in the domestic environment. However, their unrestrained application in a foreign environment can lead to frustration, failure, and underachievement in international business activities (Dowling and Welch, 2004).

Within the '**international business (IB)**' literature, mainly Western scientists categorized human behavior and its impact on management as segmented in 'cultural dimensions'. Hall and Hall (2000) based their cultural dimension on the degree of directness of communication between people. A **high context communication** is one in which most of the information is in the person while very little is in the coded, explicit, transmitted part of the message. A **low context communication** is just the opposite. The informational content of the message is expressed in the explicit code.

6.2.1 Cultural dimensions according to Trompenaars

Based on Parsons and Shils (1951) and Kluckhohn and Strodtbeck (1961), Trompenaars (1993) developed categories of behavioral management as a reflection of national cultural roots. These are introduced and segmented in the table below (Deresky, 2002; Trompenaars, 1993).

Cultural Characteristic	Cultural Dimensions	
	Universalism	**Particularism**
Society values, legal rules or, alternatively, interpersonal relationships	Importance of rules, legal systems, and contracts	Personal relationships and interpersonal trust
	Objectivity, 'one right way'	Importance of family and friends
		Relativity, 'many ways'
	Individualism	**Collectivism**
Potential dissonances between individual and group interests	Focus on interests, expectations, and wishes of the individual	Group interests, expectations, and wishes to be considered first and the individual's destiny second
	Achievement	**Ascription**
Higher status in the society is given or, alternatively, achievable through one's own activity	Status based on competency and achievement	Status and respect based on position, age, family, or other 'given' criteria
	Heterogeneous workforce	Homogenous workforce, primarily male
	Newcomers, younger people, and outsiders respected if they prove themselves	

	Specific	**Diffuse**
Separation versus mutual penetration of private and public life	Direct communication style Criticism expressed directly Separation of work and private life	Indirect communication style Direct criticism avoided Private and work life linked
	Neutral	**Affective**
Emotions in culture	Communication with less emotion Physical contact reserved for close friends and family members Subtle communication Emotions 'difficult to read from the lines of the face'	Emotional communication and strong 'body language' Physical contact possible depending on situation Expressive communication Emotions 'easy to read from the lines of the face'
	Sequential	**Synchronic**
Perceived feeling of time	Do we do things one after another?	Do we do things simultaneously?
	Internal control	**External control**
Environment	Are we able to control our environment? Every human being has control over her/his own destiny	Does the external environment control us? Personal destiny is determined from outside

Figure 58. Culture dimensions according to Trompenaars (1993)

6.2.2   Hofstede's cultural dimensions

Hofstede developed '**cultural dimensions**' based on a survey at IBM between 1967 and 1973 in more than seventy countries. The results indicate the country (culture) specific behavioral patterns of people and help firms to improve the communication effectiveness of their management in global business. Cultural dimensions according to Hofstede are described as follows (Hofstede, 2001).

Power Distance Index (PDI) is the extent to which the less powerful members of organizations and institutions (like the family) accept and expect that power is distributed unequally. This index represents inequality (more versus less), defined from below, not from above. It suggests that a society's level of inequality is endorsed by the followers as much as by the leaders. Power and inequality, of course, are extremely fundamental facts of any society and anybody with international experience will be aware that all societies are unequal, but some are more unequal than others.

Individualism (IDV) on the one side versus its opposite, collectivism, is the degree to which individuals are integrated into groups. On the individualist side, we find societies in which the ties between individuals are loose: everyone is expected to look after him/herself and his/her immediate family. On the collectivist side, we find societies in which people from birth onwards are integrated into strong, cohesive in-groups, often extended families, which continue to protect them in exchange for unquestioning loyalty. The word 'collectivism' in this sense has no political meaning: it refers to the group, not to the state. Again, the issue addressed by this dimension is an extremely fundamental one, regarding all societies in the world.

Masculinity (MAS) versus its opposite, femininity, refers to the distribution of roles between the genders, which is another fundamental issue for any society in which a range of solutions are found. The IBM studies revealed that (a) women's values differ less among societies than men's values; (b) men's values from one country to another contain a dimension from very assertive, competitive, and maximally different from women's values on the one side, to modest and caring and similar to women's values on the other. The assertive pole has been called 'masculine' and the modest, caring pole 'feminine'. The women in feminine countries have the same modest, caring values as the men; in the masculine countries, they are somewhat assertive and competitive, but not as much as men, so these countries show a gap between men's values and women's values.

Uncertainty Avoidance Index (UAI) deals with a society's tolerance for uncertainty and ambiguity; it ultimately refers to man's search for truth. It indicates to what extent a culture programs its members to feel either uncomfortable or comfortable in unstructured situations. Unstructured situations are novel, unknown, surprising, and different from the usual. Uncertainty avoiding cultures try to minimize the possibility of such situations by strict laws and rules; safety and security measures; and on the philosophical and religious level, by a belief in absolute truth. The opposite type, uncertainty accepting cultures, are more tolerant of opinions different from what they are used to; they try to have as few rules as possible; and on the philosophical and religious level, they are relativist and allow many currents to flow side by side (Hofstede, 2011).

Long-Term Orientation (LTO) versus short-term orientation: this fifth dimension was found in a study among students in twenty-three countries around the world, using a questionnaire designed by Chinese scholars. It can be said to deal with virtue regardless of truth. Values associated with long-term orientation are thrift and perseverance; values associated with short-term orientation are respect for tradition and fulfillment of social obligations.

The table below contrasts and summarizes differences between societies according to Hofstede's five cultural dimensions (2009).

Cultural Dimension

Power Distance	Low	High
	Inequality among people should be as low as possible	Less powerful people depend on powerful people
	Parents treat their children equal to their peers	Children treat their parents with respect
	Teachers expect their students to show initiative	Teachers are gurus and always right
	Criticism of teacher, superiors possible to some extent, reasonable arguments assumed	Criticism of superior is taboo
	Predominant political ideologies emphasize and practice separation of powers	Predominant political ideologies emphasize and practice power struggle

Individualism vs. Collectivism	Individualism	Collectivism
	Focus on individual and immediate family and friends	Humans are born into extended families or other 'we groups', which protect them later on and receive unrestrained loyalty in return
	Children learn to think in terms of self-awareness	
	Identity resides in the individual	Identity comes from the social network one belongs to
	To express one's opinion is a characteristic of an honest person	Children learn to think in 'we' terms
	Low-context communication	High-context communication
	Relationship between employer and employee is a contract, based on mutual benefit	Relationship between employer and employee is measured in ethical terms, similar to a familiar relationship
	Decisions about employment and promotion ideally based on individual skills and rules only	Decisions about employment and promotion focus on the employee's contribution to the group
	Self-realization of each individual represents the most important aim	Harmony and consensus in society are the most important aims

Masculinity vs. Femininity	**Masculinity**	**Femininity**
	Predominant principles are material achievement expressed in status symbols and professional advancement	Predominant principles in a society are looking after the other's feelings and keeping the values
	Emphasis is on fairness and competition between colleagues and performance	Interacting and personal relationships are important
		Emphasis is on equality, solidarity, and quality of the work life
Uncertainty Avoidance	**Low**	**High**
	Incertitude (uncertainty) is a normal phenomenon in life and is accepted as it comes	Life's incertitude is seen as a permanent threat that has to be resisted
	Unclear situations with unknown risks are accepted	Lots of stress; subjective feeling of fear
	Low stress; subjective feeling of well-being	Acceptance of known risks; fear of unclear situations and unknown risks
	Tolerant towards different and innovative thoughts and attitudes	Suppression of different thoughts and attitudes; resistance to innovation
Short-term vs. long-term Orientation	**Short-term**	**Long-term**
	Assertiveness, performance, and spending	Thrift, loyalty, humility
	An individual event is evaluated based on its short-term impact	An individual event must be evaluated within the overall time context

Figure 59. Cultural dimension by Hofstede (2009)

Based on the survey, Hofstede measured and ranked countries according to their indices, which are illustrated below for Germany, Poland, France, United Kingdom and Italy.

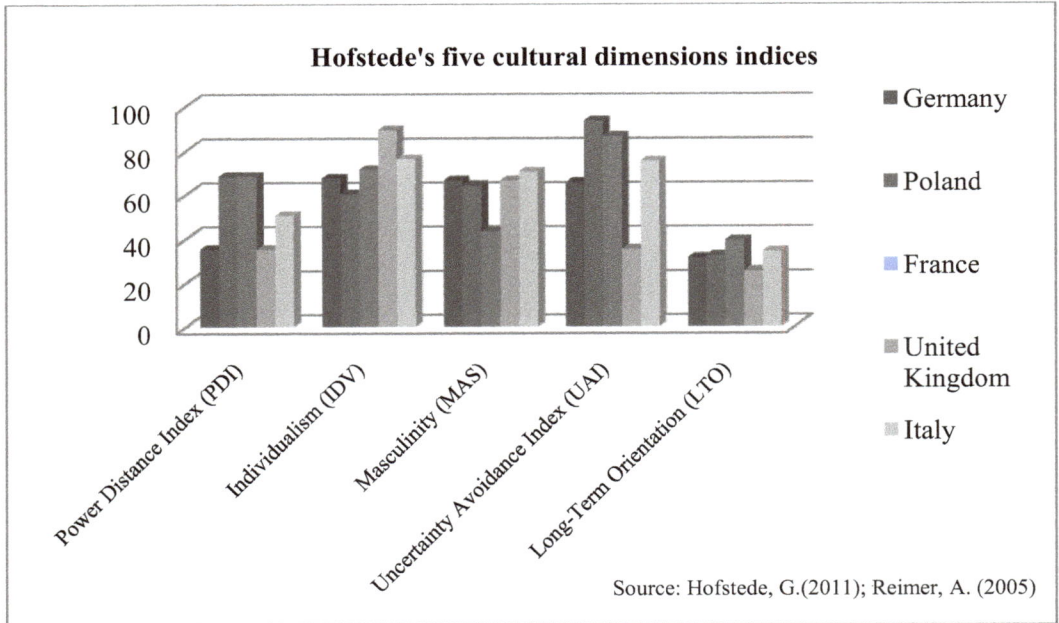

Figure 60. Cultural dimension indices according to Hofstede

6.2.3   The model of Schwartz

A cultural dimensions model that goes beyond Hofstede's has been developed by Schwartz and includes the following seven categories (Schwartz, 1994; Yolles, 2007).

- Conservatism: Embedding of the individual in group relations. Security, conformity, and tradition are priorities, as well as maintaining the established order of things.
- Hierarchy: Legitimacy of ascription of roles and fixed resources like social power, authority, humility, and wealth.
- Intellectual Autonomy: Values that stimulate autonomy to pursue goals and intellectual interests, including curiosity, open mindedness, and creativity.
- Affective Autonomy: Promotion and protection of attainment in positive affective experiences like pleasure, excitement, and variety.
- Mastery: The active and dedicated management of goals and challenges, and affirmation through risk, ambition, and success.
- Egalitarian compromise: Deferral of selfish interests in favor of the deserving poor in the society, which includes national concepts like equality, social justice, and sharing responsibility.
- Harmony: Concepts related to the integration of the individual in the social environment and living in unity with nature, including the protection of the environment.

6.2.4 Critics on cultural dimensions

In the literature, there is an opposing group of scholars who criticize the attempts to 'categorize human beings' through the construction of 'cultural dimensions'. According to Alon (2003), the literature on international management aspects has been heavily influenced by the United States over the last four decades. As a 'home paradigm', Western research is a product of centuries of the Aristotelian binary logic of 'functionalism', a way of seeing, an ideology or worldview that consistently distinguishes between right and wrong, black and white, and so on, which, moreover, is imposed on other studies of management and human behavior, such as Asian, African, and South American studies (Alon, 2003).

In contrast to the rational, linear Western worldview, which consolidates 'either-or antinomies', the Eastern (Asian) archetype is dialectic and emerges from an acceptance of the simultaneous multiple realities of a non-linear worldview, which sees contradiction and paradox as a normal, experiential, valuable, and coherent common sense. As a consequence, nothing is 'black and white', as everything is in a process of change from 'one shade of gray to another'. Fuzzy thinking emphasizes that structure is temporary and the process of change is imminent (Alon, 2003; Kosko, 1994). Western management thought is criticized because of its narrowed focus on individuality instead of collective responsibility. Individuality is expressed in firms' related business performance indicators, such as shareholder value and short-term oriented returns on investment. However, less attention is paid to ethical aspects, such as human relations as embodied in culture, which forms the basis of sustainable and commonly accepted business development internationally (Lessem and Palsule, 1997).

The Western attention on financial performance indicators is somehow proven against the background of literature related to 'corporate governance', which tends to emphasize aspects such as debt and agency costs, return on investments, internal control, and transparency mechanisms for stakeholders (Gillan and Starks, 1998; Gillan and Starks, 2003; Zingales, 1995). Recent literature contributions within the field of corporate governance outline, in addition to financial and shareholder transparency issues, the importance of corporate social responsibility and business ethics within the framework of corporate governance (Gugler and Shi, 2009; Wu, 2006). The worldwide financial and economic crisis beginning in 2008 as well as accelerated ongoing climate change may further move the discussion in the literature towards business ethics and environmental and social responsibility. Despite the methodological concerns about cross-cultural research, it is generally recognized that culturally insensitive attitudes and behaviors of management, stemming from ignorance or misguided beliefs like 'my way is best' or 'what works at home will work here too' not only are inappropriate but usually cause international business failure (Dowling and Welch, 2004).

List of References

Afp_the_Local_Sweden, 2010. Volvo sold to China's Geely [online]. [cited 20.10.2010]. Available from World Wide Web:<URL:http://www.thelocal.se/25784/20100328>.

Agndal, H. & Chetty, S., 2007. The impact of relationships on changes in internationalization strategies of SME's. *European Journal of Marketing*, 41 (11/12): 1449-1474.

Albaum, G., Duerr, E. & Strandskov, J., 2008. *International marketing and export management.* Essex: Pearson Education Limited.

Alon, I., 2003. *Chinese culture, organizational behavior, and international business management.* Westport: Praeger Publishers.

Anderson, J. C., Hakansson, H. & Johanson, J., 1994. Dyadic business relationships within a business network context. *Journal of Marketing,* 58 (4): 1-15.

Backhaus, K., Büschken, J. & Voeth, M., 2005. *Internationales Marketing.* Stuttgart: Schäffer-Poeschel.

Barney, J., 1991. Firm resources and sustained competitive advantage. *Journal of Management,* 17: 99-120.

Bartlett, C. A. & Ghoshal, S., 1990. *Internationale Unternehmensführung. Innovation, globale Effizienz, differenziertes Marketing.* Frankfurt: Campus.

Bartlett, C. A. & Ghoshal, S., 1998. *Managing across borders: the transnational solution.* Boston: Harvard Press.

Beckman, C. M., Haunschild, P. R. & Phillips, D. J., 2004. Friends or strangers? Firm-specific uncertainty, market uncertainty, and network partner selection. *Organization Science,* 15 (3): 259-275.

Capaldo, A., 2007. Network structure and innovation: the leveraging of a dual network as a distinctive relational capability. *Strategic Management Journal:* 28, 585-608.

Cateora, P. R., Gilly, M. C. & Graham, J. L., 2009. *International Marketing.* Boston: McGraw-Hill Irwin.

Chandler, A. D., 1962. *Strategy and structure. Chapters in the history of industrial enterprise.* Cambridge: MA.

Chidlow, A., Salciuviene, L. & Young, S., 2009. Regional determinants of inward FDI distribution in Poland. *International Business Review,* 18: 119-133.

Combs, J. G., Michael, S. C. & G.J., C., 2004. Franchising: a review and avenues to greater theoretical diversity. *Journal of Management,* 30 (6): 907-931.

Czinkota, M. R. & Kotabe, M., 2005. *Marketing management.* Cincinnati: Atomic Dog Publishing.

Czinkota, M. R. & Ronkainen, I. A., 2007. *International marketing.* Mason, OH: Thomson Higher Education.

Daimler_Aktiengesellschaft, 2010. Strategic focus areas [online]. [cited 26.11.2010]. Available from World Wide Web: <URL:http://www.daimler.com/dccom/0-5-1314146-1-1315590-1-0-0-0-0-0-8-7145-0-0-0-0-0-0-0.html>.

Deresky, H., 2002. *Global management, strategic and interpersonal.* New Jersey: Prentice Hall.

Doole, I. & Lowe, R., 2008. *International marketing strategy. Analysis, development and implementation.* London: South-Western Cengage Learning.

Dowling, P. J. & Welch, D. E., 2004. *International Human Resource Management. Managing people in a multinational context.* London: Thomson.

Drori, G. S., Meyer, J. W. & Hwang, H., 2006. *Globalization and organization.* Oxford: Oxford University Press.

Dunning, J. H., 2000. The eclectic paradigm as an envelope for economic and business theories of MNE activity. *International Business Review,* 9 (2): 163-190.

Eisenhardt, K. M. & Martin, J., 2000. Dynamic capabilities: What are they? *Strategic Management Journal,* 21 (10-11): 1105-1121.

Erramilli, M. K., Agarwal, S. & Dev, C., 2002. Choice between non-equity entry modes: an organizational capability perspective. *Journal of International Business Studies,* 33 (2): 223-242.

Eu_Commission, 2010. The Doha round [online]. [cited 04.10.2010]. Available from World Wide Web:<URL:http://ec.europa.eu/trade/creating-opportunities/eu-and-wto/doha/>.

European_Environment_Agency, 2010. European_Environment_Agency. Where does Europe stand in 2010? [online]. [cited 23.08.2010]. Available form World Wide Web:<URL:http://www.eea.europa.eu/publications/eu-2010-biodiversity-baseline/flyer-european-biodiversity-baseline-2014>.

Fahy, J., 2002. A resource-based analysis of sustainable competitive advantage in a global environment. *International Business Review*, 11: 57-78.

Forsgren, M., Holm, U. & Johanson, J., 2005. *Managing the embedded multinational. A business network view*. Cheltenham: Edward Elgar Publishing Limited

Forssbaek, J. & Oxelheim, L., 2008. Finance-specific factors as drivers of cross-border investment. An empirical investigation. *International Business Review*, 17: 630-641.

Fung, K. T., 2004. *Leading court cases on letters of credit*. Paris: International Chamber of Commerce.

Ghoshal, S., 1987. Global strategy: an organizing framework. *Strategic Management Journal*, 8: 425-440.

Gillan, S. L. & Starks, L. T., 1998. A survey of shareholder activism: motivation and empirical evidence. *Contemporary Finance Digest*, 2 (3): 10-34.

Gillan, S. L. & Starks, L. T., 2003. Corporate governance, corporate ownership, and the role of institutional investors: a global perspective. *Journal of Applied Finance*, 13 (2): 4-22.

Granovetter, M., 2004. The impact of social structure on economic outcomes. *Journal of Economic Perspectives*, 19 (1): 33-50.

Grant, R. M., 2002. Corporate strategy: managing scope and strategy content. In Pettigrew, A., Thomas, H. & Whittington, R. (Eds.) *Handbook of strategy and management*. London: Sage Publications.

Gugler, P. & Shi, J. Y. J., 2009. Corporate social responsibility for developing country multinational corporations: lost war in pertaining global competitiveness? *Journal of Business Ethics*, 87: 3-24.

Hakansson, H. & Ford, D., 2002. How should companies interact in business networks? *Journal of Business Research*, 55: 133-139.

Hall, E. T. & Hall, M. R., 2000. *Understanding cultural differences. Germans, French and Americans*. Yarmouth, ME: Intercultural Press.

Hedley, B., 1977. Strategy and the business portfolio. *Long Range Planning*, 10 (1): 9-15.

Henderson, B. D., 1971. *Construction of a business strategy. The Boston Consulting Group. Series on corporate strategies*. Boston.

Hill, C. W. L., 2009. *International business: competing in the global marketplace*. Boston: McGraw-Hill/Irwin.

Hill, C. W. L., Hitt, M. E. & Hoskisson, R. E., 1992. Cooperative versus competitive structures structures in related and unrelated diversified firms. *Organization Science*, 3: 501-21.

Hoffman, K. D., Bateson, J. E. G., Wood, E. H. & Kenyon, A. K., 2009. *Services marketing. Concepts, strategies and cases*. London: South-Western Cengage Learning.

Hoffmann, W., Roventa, P. & Weichsel, D., 2003. *Marktveränderungen und Konsolidierungswelle in der Pharma-Industrie: Kommt der Mittelstand unter die Räder?* Ludwigshafen.

Hofstede, G., 2001. *Culture's consequences - comparing values, behaviours, institutions and organization across nations*. California: Sage Publications Inc.

Hofstede, G., 2009. *Lokales Denken, globales Handeln*. München: Beck.

Hollensen, S., 2004. *Global marketing. A decision-oriented approach*. Essex: Pearson Education Limited.

Holtbrügge, D. & Welge, M. K., 2010. *Internationales Management. Theorien, Funktionen, Fallstudien*. Stuttgart: Schäffer-Poeschel.

Homburg, C. & Krohmer, H., 2009. *Marketingmanagement: Strategie - Instrumente - Umsetzung - Unternehmensführung*. Wiesbaden: Gabler.

Icc, 2010. About ICC [online]. [cited: 04.01.2011]. Available from World Wide
     Web:<URL:http://www.iccwbo.org/id93/index.html>.

Imf, 2010. Time series data on international reserves and foreign currency liquidity official reserve assets and
     other foreign currency assets [online].[cited 07.11.2010]. Available from World Wide Web:
     <http://www.imf.org/external/np/sta/ir/IRProcessWeb/data/802P816.pdf>.

Incoterms, 2010. *Revised trade rules for an inter-connected world*. Paris: International Chamber of Com-
     merce.

International_Monetary_Fund, 2010. IMFsurvey magazine: In the news. IMF call to work together for
     growth, jobs, financial sector reform [online]. [cited 14.10.2010]. Available from World Wide
     Web:<http://www.imf.org/external/pubs/ft/survey/so/2010/NEW100810A.htm>.

Johanson, J. & Mattsson, L.-G., 1988. Internationalization in industrial systems - a network approach. In
     Hood, N. & Vahlne, J.-E. (Eds.) *Strategies in global competition*. 468-486, New York: Croom
     Helm.

Johanson, J. & Mattsson, L.-G., 1992. Network positions and strategic action - an analytical framework. In
     Axelsson, B. & Easton, G. (Eds.) *Industrial networks: a new view of reality*. London: Routledge.

Johanson, J. & Vahlne, J.-E., 1977. The internationalization process of the firm - a model of knowledge
     development and increasing foreign market commitments. *Journal of International Business Stu-
     dies*, 8 (1): 23-32.

Johanson, J. & Vahlne, J.-E., 2009. The Uppsala internationalization process model revisited: from liability
     of foreignness to liability of outsidership. *Journal of International Business Studies*, 40 (9): 1411-
     1431.

Johanson, J. & Vahlne, J.-E., 2010. Markets as networks: implications for strategy-making. *Journal of the
     Academy of Marketing Science*: Online First 22. November 2010.

Kalish, S., Mahajan, V. & Muller, E., 1995. Waterfall and sprinkler: new product strategies in competitive
     global markets. *International Journal of Research in Marketing*, 12 (2): 105-119.

Kartman, M., 2009. Merger AirFrance - KLM [online]. [cited 16.11.2010]. Available from World Wide
     Web:<URL:http://ec.europa.eu/transport/air/events/doc/eu_us_labour_forum/miriam_
     kartman.pdf>.

Keillor, B., Davila, V. & Hult, T. G., 2001. Market entry strategies and influencing factors: a multi-
     industry/multi product investigation. *The Marketing Management Journal*, 11: 1-11.

Kluckhohn, F. R. & Strodtbeck, F. L., 1961. *Variations in value orientations*. Evanston/IL: Row, Peterson.

Kosko, B., 1994. *Fuzzy thinking*. London: Flamingo.

Kotabe, M. & Helsen, K., 2008. *Global marketing management*. Hoboken, NJ: John Wiley & Sons.

Kotabe, M. & Murray, J. Y., 2003. Global sourcing strategy and sustainable competitive advantage. *Industri-
     al Marketing Management*, 33: 7-14.

Kotler, P., Keller, K. L. & Bliemel, F., 2007. *Marketing Management. Strategien für wertschaffendes Han-
     deln*. München: Pearson Education.

Lessem, R. & Palsule, S., 1997. *Managing in four worlds: From competition to co-creation*. Oxford: Black-
     well Publishers.

Luostarinen, R., 1980. *Internationalization of the firm. An empirical study of the internationalization of firms
     with small and open domestic markets with special emphasis on lateral rigidity as a behavioral
     characteristic in strategic decision-making*. Helsinki: The Helsinki School of Economics.

Luostarinen, R. & Welch, L., 1997. *International business operations*. Helsinki: Kyriiri Oy.

Malhotra, N. K., 2009. *Marketing research. An applied orientation*. New Jersey: Pearson Education Interna-
     tional.

Meissner, H. G., 1995. *Strategisches Internationales Marketing.* München: Oldenbourg Wissenschaftsverlag.

Morschett, D., 2005. Contract manufacturing. In Zentes, J., Swoboda, B. & Morschett, D. (Eds.) *Kooperationen, Allianzen und Netzwerke. Grundlagen-Ansätze-Perspektiven.* Wiesbaden: Gabler Verlag.

Müller-Stewens, G. & Lechner, C., 2005. *Strategisches Management. Wie strategische Initiativen zum Wandel führen.* Stuttgart: Schäffer-Poeschel.

Nokia, 2008. Nokia to refocus its Japanese operations [online]. [cited 15.07.2010]. *Nokia Press Services.* Available from World Wide Web:URL:http://pressbulletinboard.nokia.com/tag/japan/.

Oecd, 2010. *Education: Governments should expand tertiary studies to boost jobs and tax revenues.* Paris: OECD.

Özsomer, A. & Simonin, B., 1999. Antecedents and consequences of market orientation in a subsidiary context. Enhancing knowledge development in marketing. *American marketing association educators proceedings, summer 1999.*

Parsons, T. & Shils, E., 1951. *Toward a general theory of action.* Cambridge/MA.

Penrose, E., 1995. *The theory of the growth of the firm.* New York [first published 1959]: Oxford University Press.

Perlitz, M., 2004. *Internationales Management.* Stuttgart: Lucius & Lucius.

Perlmutter, H. V., 1969. The tortuous evolution of the multinational corporation. *Columbia Journal of World Business,* 4: 9-18.

Perreault, W. & Mccarthy, E. J., 2005. *Basic marketing. A global marketing approach.* Burr Ridge McGraw-Hill.

Phelps, C. C., 2010. A longitudinal study of the influence of alliance network structure and composition on firm exploratory innovation. *The Academy of Management Journal,* 53 (4): 890-913.

Porter, M. E., 1980. *Competitive strategy.* New York: Free Press.

Porter, M. E., 1990. *The competitive advantage of nations.* New York: The Free Press.

Porter, M. E., 1999. *Wettbewerbsstrategie. Methoden zur Analyse von Branchen und Konkurrenten.* Frankfurt/M.: Campus Verlag.

Repetzki, B., 2010. Germany Trade and Invest. Polen kaufen mehr Haus-, Audio- und Videogeräte [online]. [cited 18.07.2010]. Available from World Wide Web:<URL:http://www.gtai.de/fdb-SE,MKT200710238001,MSN.html>.

Richardson, J., 1993. Parallel sourcing and supplier performance in the Japanese automobile industry. *Strategic Management Journal,* 14 (5): 339-350.

Ritter, T., Wilkinson, I. F. & Johnston, W. J., 2004. Managing in complex business networks. *Industrial Marketing Management,* 33: 175-183.

Rugman, A. M. & Collinson, S., 2009. *International business.* Essex: Pearson Education Limited.

Samiee, S., 2006. Supplier and customer exchange in international industrial markets: an integrative perspective. *Industrial Marketing Management,* 35: 589-599.

Schwartz, S. H., 1994. Beyond individualism/collectivism. New cultural dimensions of values. *Individualism and collectivism, theory, method and applications.* Thousand Oaks: Sage.

Stirling, A., 2007. A general framework for analysing diversity in science, technology and society. *Journal of the Royal Society Interface,* 4: 707-719.

Teece, D. J., 2000. *Managing intellectual capital.* New York: Oxford University Press.

Teece, D. J., Pisano, G. & Shuen, A., 1997. Dynamic capabilities and strategic management. *Strategic Management Journal,* 18 (7): 509-533.

Theisen, P., 1970. *Grundzüge einer Theorie der Beschaffungspolitik.* Berlin: Duncker & Humblot

Trompenaars, F., 1993. *Riding the waves of culture: understanding cultural diversity in business.* London: McGraw-Hill.

Unctad, 2009. United Nations Conference on Trade and Development - Statistics [online]. [cited 17.8.2009]. Available from World Wide Web:<URL:http://www.unctad.org/sections/dite_fdistat/docs/wid_cp_hu_en.pdf>.

Unctad, 2010. Inward and outward foreign direct investment stock, annual, 1980-2009 [online]. [cited 12.12.2010]. Available from World Wide Web: <www.http://unctadstat.unctad.org>.

Union, A. E., 2010. Automotive Cluster - West Slovakia [online]. [cited 18.07.2010]. Available from World Wide Web:<URL:http://www.autoclusters.eu/index.php/partner/127-automotive-cluster-west-slovakia>.

United_States_Labor_Department, 2010. Bureau of Labor Statistics. Employment situation summary [online]. [cited 15.10.2010]. Available from World Wide Web:<URL:http://www.bls.gov/news.release/empsit.nr0.htm>.

Vollmann, T. E., Berry, W. L., Whybark, D. C. & Jacobs, F. R., 2005. *Manufacturing planning and control for supply chain management.* New York: McGraw-Hill/Irwin.

Welge, K. M. & Holtbrügge, D., 2010. *Internationales Management.* Stuttgart: Schäffer-Poeschel Verlag.

Wernerfelt, B., 1984. A resource based view of the firm. *Strategic Management Journal*, 5 (2): 171-180.

Wheelen, T. L. & Hunger, J. D., 2010. *Strategic management and business policy.* New Jersey: Pearson Education Ltd.

Wilkinson, I. & Young, L., 2002. On cooperating firms, relations and networks. *Journal of Business Research*, 55: 123-132.

Williamson, O. E., 1975. *Markets and hierarchies - analysis and antitrust implications.* New York: The Free Press

Williamson, O. E., 1985. *The economic institutions of capitalism. Firms, markets, relational contracting.* New York: The Free Press.

Wilson, A., Zeithaml, V. A., Bitner, M. J. & Gremler, D. D., 2008. *Services marketing. Integrating customer focus across the firm.* London: McGraw-Hill.

Wind, Y., Douglas, S. P. & Perlmuttter, H. V., 1973. Guidelines for developing international marketing strategies. *Journal of Marketing*, 37 (2): 38-46.

Wto, 2010a. Understanding the WTO: The GATT years from Havana to Marrakesh [online]. [cited: 05.10.2010]. Available from World Wide Web:<URL:http://www.wto.org/english/thewto_e/whatis_e/tif_e/fact4_e.htm>.

Wto, 2010b. *World trade report.* Geneva.

Wu, C.-F., 2006. The study of the relations among ethical considerations, family management and organizational performance in corporate governance *Journal of Business Ethics*, 68: 165-179.

Yolles, M., 2007. Exploring culture through knowledge cybernetics. *Journal of Cross-Cultural Competence and Management*: 19-74.

Zentes, J., Morschett, D. & Schramm-Klein, 2007. *Strategic retail management.* Wiesbaden: Gabler Verlag.

Zingales, L., 1995. What determines the value of corporate votes. *Quarterly Journal of Economics*, 110: 1047-1073.

7   Chapter: Consumer behavior in international markets

- Describe the notion of consumer behavior.

- List the types of consumer needs.

- Identify consumer risk in the market.

- Describe the stages in the consumer decision-making process.

- Characterize the types of consumer decisions in the international markets.

- Present the economic determinants of consumer behavior.

- Describe the role of socio-cultural and demographic factors in creating consumer behavior in the global market.

7.1   The notion and scope of consumer behavior

Issues of consumer behavior not only present an interesting theoretical subject, but also constitute a very important element of practical considerations in international marketing. In the economy currently undergoing globalization, it is becoming increasingly important to recognize the processes of decision making, define the roles of different household members, and learn about the conditions underlying these processes. Finding the answer to questions about consumer need hierarchy and consumer selection criteria in the market will allow for formulation of conclusions about the future behavior of consumers, even in times of great economic turmoil.

Consumer behavior is based on **consumer needs**, precisely consumption needs. A need is a bodily condition evoked by lack of something (or a harmful excess) that is indispensable to the life of an individual on account of his or her bio-psychical structure and/or necessary for his/her functioning in the society. A need as a condition disturbs the individual's psychophysical balance producing discomfort (tension), which, in turn, works as a motivation to overcome this negative state (Arnold et al., 2004; Harris, 2010). The definition presented above includes the important element of combining human needs with human actions, endeavors, and goals. In fact, consumer needs express consumer goals, although not all of them directly, since what is referred to as 'tension' is not always clearly defined right at the moment of a need arousal. First, there appears an imbalance or disturbance of homeostasis, which is next followed by recognition of all previous experiences and conceptions about the means and possibilities of satisfying a given need. This brings the individual towards definite goals, i.e., objects capable of restoring the balance (Raymond, 2003; Bywalec, 2007). As a result, a need refers to a concrete object or objects that ensure certain benefits (Jachnis and Terelak, 1998; Foxall and Goldsmith, 1998; Hawkins and Best, 2004).

The literature distinguishes general (primary) needs and particular (secondary) needs (Antonides and van Raaij, 2003; Foxall and Goldsmith, 1998). **Primary needs** are of an abstract character and of a limited number. They do not refer to concrete objects, but to general conditions of human existence. General needs include, for example, hunger, entertainment, prestige, and safety. **Secondary needs** are of an infinite number and constitute wants of particular goods and services that serve as satisfiers of primary needs. In the process of evolution, abstract needs have formed into functional groups and have been defined as needs for definite goods (as well as of actions). For some people, the process takes place at such an advanced level that general needs are not revealed at all, because at the very moment of a need arousal, there appears a vision of satisfying it in one concrete way, by means of one type of product (Evans et al., 2009). Hence, right at the start, one is faced with a secondary need.

In order to bring these considerations into the area of consumer behavior, it is indispensable to develop a more precise concept of consumer needs. The specificity of consumer needs is tightly linked to their economic character (Blackwell et al., 2001), which means that the needs are satisfied by means of goods and services (unlike other needs that, in order to be satisfied, require verbal declarations, attitudes, and behavior) without involving a direct production result (like needs that are focused not on consumption, but on production of other products). It is hard to draw a line between consumption needs and other types of needs, as the same need may be of both an economic and noneconomic character. Nevertheless, for the sake of the discussion in the following pages, the term 'need' will denote consumption needs (Raymond, 2003; Schiffman and Kanuk, 2006). There are three sources of needs (Gajewski, 1994; Solomon et al., 2010):

- physical (biological) requirements of the human body (biological needs) – needs of this origin, are of an innate character, as people are born with a definite need structure imposed by their body and its requirements. With individual development, these needs are subject to modifications;
- spiritual qualities of an individual (psychical needs) – these give rise to needs that are related to a human personality structure (e.g., the need for self-esteem, the need for acceptance and love). Some of these needs are of an inborn character and are common to all people (e.g., the need for safety); and
- social cohabitation (social needs) – these produce needs related to the functioning of an individual in human communities. Additionally, these needs are connected with the social role played by an individual (e.g., the role of a student, a manager, a father). Social needs are adapted and developed by an individual throughout his/her entire life and involve dependence on other people and on the products of human culture. As a result, these needs are differentiated according to environmental features, the position of an individual in the environment, the level of individual intellectual development, and so forth.

Biological, psychical, and social features are strongly interdependent, which is demonstrated by the fact that even the most basic bodily needs (physiological and psychical) are satisfied by means of material objects that are a product of human culture and in a specific way determined by social factors (Gajewski, 1994; Evans et al., 2009). To provide an example, a sofa in a living room is intended to satisfy a human physiological need for rest. However, it can also serve as an object that allows the consumer to conform to certain social norms of a given environment, as well as to follow the aesthetic canons of fashion trends. Hence, biological needs and the way of satisfying them are modified by needs of a social character.

Determination of the sources of needs provides an excellent basis for a division of needs into their types. Nevertheless, the variety of needs and their qualities opens the way to many systems of need classification. Figure 61 presents the most popular division criteria and need groups together with their application.

By source				
biological	physiological	biogenic	inborn	real
psychical	emotional	sociogenic	acquired	extended
social	intellectual			apparent
	spiritual			

By intensity of experience – urgency	By subject	By character
Basic	individual	primary
Higher	collective	secondary

By object
distinction of need groups based on the types of means for satisfying a need – e.g., needs connected with food, accommodation, clothing, resting, education, communication, medical treatment, culture, etc.

Source: Evans et al., (1996), p. 23; Kiezel (2010), p. 36

Figure 61. Classification of consumption needs

In view of the abundance and variety of needs, it is extremely important to determine basic features characteristic of needs (Blackwell et al., 2001), including

- uncountability and infinity of needs in time – they cannot be counted; but at the same time, they refer to the whole of mankind without any exception and to each period of human existence;
- unlimited character of needs – satisfaction of a need leads to its temporary 'sedation', soon followed by another experience of a lack;
- changeability in time (historic nature) – needs change and evolve;
- certain physiological needs are of a limited scope and capacity, such as hunger;
- various intensity in certain need groups – the human body is more sensitive to unsatisfied needs, and less sensitive to satisfied needs;
- appearance of higher-level needs after satisfaction of lower-level needs;
- low level of substitution between need groups (types), slightly higher within one need group, i.e., with respect to different ways of satisfying the same need;
- complementary character of needs at the same level;
- synergism (mutual stimulation, need multiplication), particularly in the case of higher-level needs, e.g., a higher level of satisfaction of educational needs fosters development of cultural needs and vice verse; and
- competitiveness (mutual exclusion) of needs means that meeting one need requires not satisfying other needs. This phenomenon is caused by the limited capacity of the human body as well as by time limits and a restricted number of need satisfaction means.

All consumers have a similar need structure. Nonetheless, different needs will take priority in different people depending on time, circumstances, socio-cultural factors, and so on. This leads to the problem of a need hierarchy, which assumes prioritization (ordering) of needs based on the criterion of the urgency of need satisfaction. The critical feature of need urgency is how much the need is wanted, i.e., intensity and the strength of the desire for the benefits represented by the goods or services that are the object of a need. In the process of need satisfaction, certain benefits are desired more intensely than others (Schiffman and Kanuk, 2006). Need intensity is not determined in an absolute way, but in relation to other needs. (Intensity is a relative feature.) Moreover, intensity depends on the strength of the experience of a lack, which is being gradually eliminated in the course of need satisfaction (Blackwell et al., 2001; Hawkins and Best, 2004).

Classification of needs based on the criterion of urgency enjoys great popularity, since, as mentioned before, this classification scheme allows for establishment of a certain sequence, a hierarchy of need satisfaction. This hierarchy, in turn, helps distinguish basic (lower-level) and non-basic (higher-level) needs. The first group comprises physiological needs (hunger, thirst, sleep), as well as needs that are indispensable for living and functioning in society (e.g., educational needs). More importantly, this group includes needs whose satisfaction is considered to be conventionally indispensable in a society that has reached a particular level of social and economic development and a particular level of civilization (e.g., hygienic needs). Higher-level needs, on the other hand, represent the group of needs whose satisfaction is not necessary for routine functioning in society – it is possible to defer satisfaction of these needs, since delaying their fulfillment does not have any negative consequences for human health or life (Harcar et al., 2005). Additionally, delaying their fulfillment does not pose any threat to the functioning of an individual in society (Kotler et al., 2002).

The discovery of a sequence of need satisfaction typical of individual people, groups, and societies is very important for both cognitive and practical reasons. Thus, many scientists have attempted to develop a **need hierarchy**. The most well-known attempt was made by A. Maslow, who divided needs into five groups. In Maslow's theory, when satisfying a lower-level need is not possible, the result is a situation where the need begins to dominate a person's behavior (Schiffman et al., 2008). However, if the need is adequately met, another higher-level need is activated. Hence, progress to another level of need is possible only after satisfaction, at least partially, of lower-level needs. The five levels proposed by Maslow are the basis for the ERG model (Figure 62), in which three need categories are proposed. The first level consists of needs relating to the human body, physical existence, and safety. If unsatisfied, a human life may be at risk. Since a person is a social being, the next level focuses on relationships with other people and refers to needs that are met through social contacts, a sense of belonging and love, and assistance offered by other people. Finally, the third level is referred to as development (growth), because it is connected to achieving positive effects from actions taken by an individual, such as social respect, recognition, personal satisfaction with how talents and personal predispositions have been used, and fulfillment of dreams and one's own potential (Evans et al., 1996; Antonides and van Raaij, 2003).

Need for self-fulfillment living in accordance with one's own voca- tion and nature	
Need for respect and recognition connected with recognition and understanding of one's own value, with reinforcement of self- esteem; need for prestige and respect as well as independence	**Growth (G)**
Need for belonging and love awareness of being loved and accepted; of being someone important for the dearest ones; possibility of loving others	**Relations (R)**
Need for safety a sense of confidence, security, and order	**Existence (E)**
Physiological needs satisfaction of hunger and thirst; need for rest, physical protec- tion, etc.	

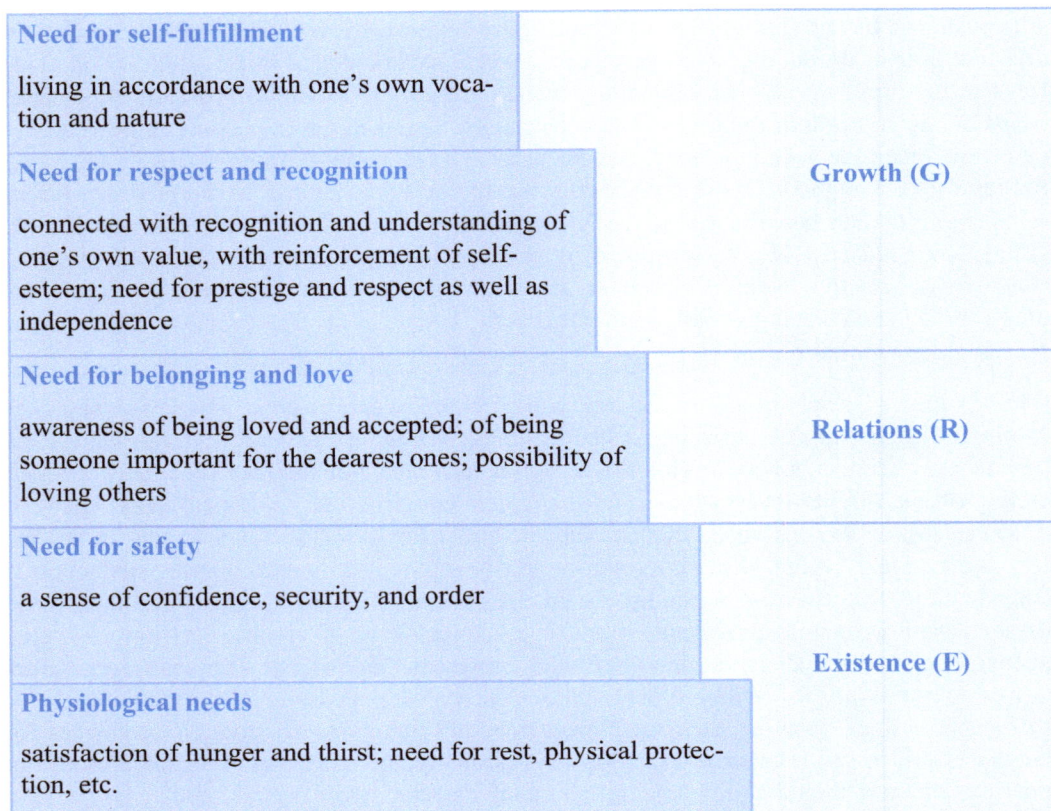

Source: Evans et al. (1996) p. 24; Falkowski and Tyszka (2009) p. 61

Figure 62. Maslow's need hierarchy and the ERG model

Finding the very essence and nature of consumption needs is of fundamental significance for studies into consumer behavior, as needs determine and initiate all actions undertaken in order to eliminate a lack and, therefore, underlie consumer behavior. **Consumer behavior** should be regarded as one of the elements of a broad understanding of human behavior, which may be defined as 'any observable reaction to external stimuli or as a set of reactions and attitudes of a living creature to the environment' (Kiezel, 2010). In praxeological terms, human behavior is identified with reactions to external stimuli as well as to internal signals that result from the condition of the human body (Evans et al., 2009).

Consumer behavior refers mainly to a real dimension of activities undertaken by consumers. The activities focus on the means of satisfying consumer needs, and needs themselves are defined as indispensable motivators of behavior. Accordingly, following Blythe (1997) consumer behavior refers to the whole of an individual's activities, actions, and manners of conduct intended to obtain the means of need satisfaction. This behavior also comprises all possible ways of handling these means. Raymond (2003) defines consumer behavior as a way of consumer need prioritization, a way of selection of goods and services to satisfy the needs, and a way of consumption of possessed goods. According to Kiezel (2010), consumer behavior is a coherent whole of activities, actions, and manners of conduct connected to choices made in the process of consumer need satisfaction in certain cultural, social, and economic conditions. Thus, the behavior is a set of activities that are meant to obtain the means of consumption, and to use them for need satisfaction together with assessment of the rightness of the decisions that are made (Raymond, 2003; Schiffman and Kanuk, 2006).

Along with the basic components of behavior related to consumption needs, the means of need satisfaction, and real consumer activities, the literature also concentrates on the psychical aspects of consumer behavior. Although the mental processes related to motivation, perception, and decision making cannot be observed directly, they constitute an indispensable element of behavior complementing the real actions of an individual. Following this approach, Hansen (Evans et al., 1996) defines consumer behavior as a set of consumer actions and perceptions responsible for preparing to make a decision on product selection, for selection itself, and for consumption. Blythe (1997) maintains that consumer behavior is concerned with thoughts, feelings, and actions people take in the consumption process, as well as with the environmental factors affecting them.

The most complex definition has been proposed by Antonides and van Raaij (2003), who concluded that consumer behavior consists of

- psychical and physical activities (behavior);
- together with the motives and reasons behind them;
- followed by individuals and (small) groups;
- and concerning orientation, purchasing, using, maintaining, and disposing of a product (consumption cycle);
- as well as household production (DIY);
- enabling the consumer to function, reach goals, and pursue values;
- and thus, gain satisfaction and well being;
- with respect to short- and long-term effects;
- as well as individual and social consequences.

In short, consumer behavior comprises everything that occurs before, during, and after the act of purchasing (acquiring) goods and services (Falkowski and Tyszka, 2009; Harris, 2010). Consumer behavior is dynamic on account of changes in consumer thoughts, feelings, and real actions. These changes concern both individual people and consumer groups, as well as the whole society. The primary cause of changes should be sought in features of consumer needs themselves – in their capability of returning and in the continuous development of new needs (Doole et al., 2005). Consumer thoughts, feelings, and real actions, being elements of consumer behavior, are constantly interacting with the environment. This takes place in the process of market exchange, during which consumers spend their resources (money, time, knowledge, skills, work) in return for the means of satisfying their needs. At the micro level, consumer behavior is part of the communication process (Smyczek, 2007).

Consumer behavior regarded as a process or – to emphasize its circular (closed) character – as a cycle (Blackwell et al., 2001) can be divided into several stages, including product purchasing, product consuming, and product disposing (Harcar et al., 2005). At the **purchasing stage,** the consumer searches for all available information (Antonides and van Raaij, 2003; Diller et al., 2006), compares it, and finally makes a choice and buys a product. The **stage of consuming** a product (possessing) refers to the process of using products and to consumer feelings accompanying this process. The final stage, called **disposing**, relates to activities and mental processes following the consumption, which is particularly connected with consumer satisfaction as well as decisions about disposing of packaging and product leftovers (Kotler et al., 2002).

Consumer behavior occurs on two institutional planes: the market and the household (Rudnicki, 2000). According to this division, one can talk about **market (buying) behavior** and about individual consumer behavior at the stage of consumption of an obtained (purchased) product. Close relations between these two sub-levels of consumer behavior result in their constant and mutual interactions. Although it is impossible to draw a clear-cut boundary between the purchasing and consuming behavior at the consumption stage, they can be distinguished by means of certain generalizations. Consumer behavior comprises actions and activities that relate to choices about buying goods and services. These are actions and mental processes before and during a purchase. The **behavior at the consumption level** mainly consists of activities related to using the means of consumption (Harris, 2010). Thus, the behavior concerns actions and mental processes that appear right after the act of purchasing. Figure 63 below presents these relationships in a schematic way.

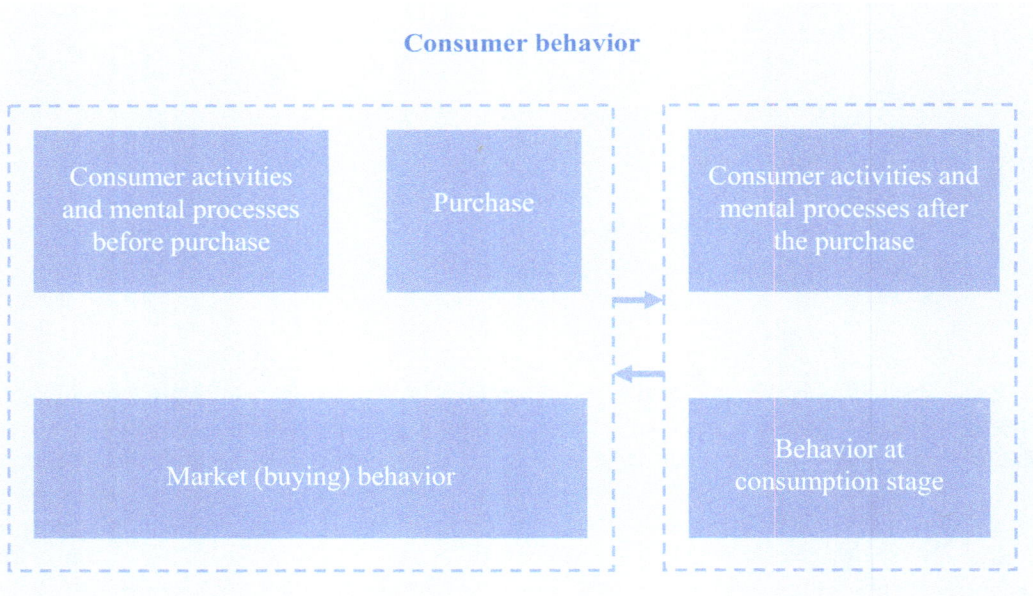

Source: Kiezel (2010), p. 44

Figure 63. Stages of consumer behavior

When considering market behavior, special attention should be directed towards differences between the consumer as the buyer, and the consumer as the user. The **consumer** is a person who has a consumption need, who buys a product (or 'acquires', obtains a product) and satisfies the need (consumes and uses the product). Thus, this person participates in all three stages of the process (cycle) of consumption (pre-purchase, purchase, post-purchase) (Solomon et al., 1999).

traditional consumer on local market	modern consumer on international market
looking for comfort	looking for authenticity
adapted to the market	individualist
uncommitted	engage
conformist	independent
less-informed	well-informed
low consumer awareness	high consumer awareness
little ethical market behavior	ethic in market behaviors

Source: Lewis and Bidger (2001), p. 172

Figure 64. Differences between traditional and modern consumer

It happens, though, that a product buyer is not always a product user, or else is not the only product consumer. To provide an example, a mother who buys her children toys does not satisfy her own consumer needs despite the fact that she is the buyer. Moreover, she may not even choose the product (if she buys a toy at her child's request). In this example, it is the child who is the user of the product, whereas the mother is the buyer. The child does not make a purchase, yet his or her needs are met. It can be concluded that the **buyer** is a person who buys goods on the market in order to satisfy his or her own consumer needs or other people's needs (Johnson, 1998; Kiezel, 2010). The **user**, then, is a person who satisfies his or her consumer needs (uses a product), no matter who has made a choice or a purchase. Consequently, the consumer is not identical to the buyer, and has a broader meaning than the user. The consumer, apart from the user, also performs other tasks: makes decisions, buys goods, and so on. Not every buyer is, in turn, the consumer: e.g., a social nurse buying food for her patients is a buyer who, with this purchase, does not satisfy her needs (Schiffman and Kanuk, 2010).

In the literature, the notion of the consumer usually appears exclusively with regard to the so-called **individual consumer** represented as purchasing goods and services for his/her own use, for the use of others, or for his or her household (Gefen and Straub, 2003). In this sense, the consumer is the ultimate product user, and may act both individually (the two first situations) and collectively (representing the household as in the third situation) (Chavda et al., 2005). The literature also makes a distinction between individuals and the so-called **institutional consumers**, which are companies, nonprofit organizations, governmental agencies, and institutions (schools, hospitals, etc.) for whom purchasing and consuming products is necessary for their proper functioning (Harris, 2010). Here, the point is made about products that are 'consumed' by subjects, but not used with the intention of bringing a direct production effect.

7.2   Consumer decision-making process

Contemporary international marketing literature analyzes consumer purchasing behavior from three perspectives (Harcar et al., 2005):

- the **perspective of decision making** – where the consumer is engaged in the process of problem solving, during which he or she goes through a sequence of stages;
- the **behavioral perspective** – which assumes that the behavior demonstrated by buyers is usually a reaction to different external stimuli; and
- the **perspective of experience** – which highlights the fact that consumers make purchases mainly to provide themselves with sensations, emotions, and experiences rather than to solve problems.

In fact, these perspectives are rather complementary as they point out different aspects of the buying process. Taking the decision-making perspective as a starting point, it should be noted that choosing a product is a complex and multi-level process. Apparently, particular stages of the process are very different, depending on the object of the purchase, the socio-economic situation of the consumer, and the stage of the consumer's family life. Additionally, during the **decision-making process,** changes occur in the roles played by other people. The whole consumer decision-making process with respect to buying products in the market can be broken into six stages (see Figure 65).

The experience of a need always comes first and activates consumer decision-making behavior. At this initial stage, the **need**, i.e., the sense of a lack, gives rise to tension, which comes from consumer awareness of a difference between reality and the desired state (Bendapudi and Berry, 1997). This sense of a lack produces in the consumer a wish for balance (a motivation that is strong enough to cause the process to continue). A need may be aroused by an internal impulse (hunger), but also by some external stimulus. The awareness of a lack becomes the beginning and, apart from some exceptional circumstances, the condition for actions undertaken to eliminate it by buying a desired product (Evans et al. 2009).

In his/her **search for possibilities** of need satisfaction, the consumer goes through the second stage of the decision-making process. Here, the consumer considers the possibilities and necessities of satisfying a need; analyzes the ways, time, and place of purchasing a product; counts out money to pay for it; and ponders over the type, color, and model of the product to be bought. At this point, the consumer may start to intensively focus attention or actively seek information, which is gained from personal, commercial, public, and experience-based sources (Kotler et al., 2002). The significance of particular sources varies depending on the personality of the buyer, the type of product, the type of purchase, and so on. (e.g., more significant and frequent changes in the market increase the probability of seeking additional information (Matysiewicz, 2010).

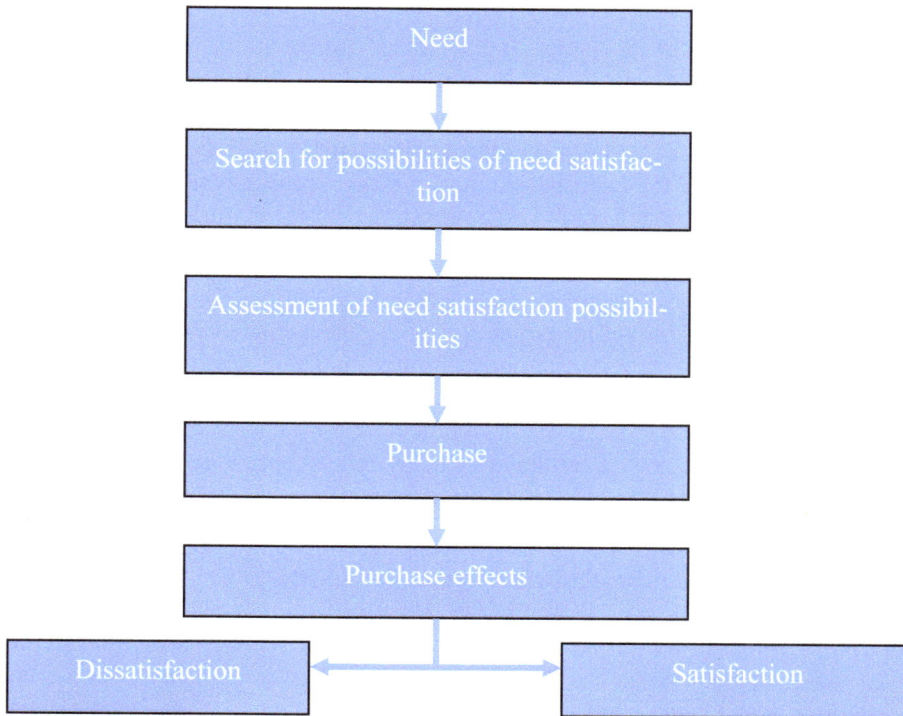

Source: Blackwell et al., (2001), p. 649

Figure 65. Consumer decision-making process based on EKB model

Consumer knowledge from the information obtained and processed provides sound grounds for the selection of **assessment** criteria for the possibilities for satisfying a definite need, namely the concrete product features most desired by the consumer. The assessment and selection are made only with respect to the physically and financially available means of need satisfaction. Sometimes the assessment is easy, but in the majority of cases, the comparison is made on many products with respect to numerous features; and the selection itself becomes extremely difficult and risky. The selection process is based on calculations of gain and loss from choosing one possibility and rejecting others. Consumers who are in search of definite benefits to be gained from using a product look upon the product as a cluster of attributes, which are, however, of different significance for every user. In addition, each consumer has a definite image of the product and assigns some utility function to its particular attributes (Evans et al., 1996). Different perceptions of definite factors determine the assessment of the same product by various people. During the process of selection, consumers reveal a tendency to make changes, which are determined by their preferences for one choice over the other (Kwai-Choi and Marshall, 1998). Ultimately, a particular order of purchase is established in accordance with the hierarchy of need importance and need urgency, as well as in accordance with the scale of preferences for and prioritization of different goods.

It may happen that as a result of an assessment, the consumer will come to the conclusion that none of the products is capable of satisfying his/her need. In such circumstances, the consumer is likely to look for additional information about products, which takes him/her back to the second stage of the decision-making process. If the assessment results in purchase withdrawal, the experience gained by the consumer is stored in the consumer memory and may be used in the future (Smyczek and Sowa, 2005).

A selection made by a buyer is based on optimization or simplification procedures (Grether and Wilde, 1994). With optimization procedures, the consumer makes an assessment of each product brand according to the criteria that he/she finds the most important. With simplification procedures, the consumer narrows down the range of attributes to be considered, making the final choice on the basis of the most crucial criterion, such as, for example, price. The type of selection procedure is determined by many factors, including type of product, the purchase situation, and consumer character (Falkowski and Tyszka, 2009).

Risk is a powerful determinant of consumer buying decisions. The main types of risk perceived by the consumer include the following (Arnold et al., 2004):

- functional risk – appears when a product does not fulfill the functions expected by the consumer (e.g., whether it is possible to withdraw cash with a particular banking card);
- financial risk – appears when a product is not worth its price (e.g., whether the interest rate on savings in one bank is more attractive than in others;
- physical risk – related to product safety and to ways of using a product (e.g., whether climbing equipment guarantees security);
- social risk – results from a consumer being a part of a certain social community. The consumer may fear that the purchased product will not be accepted by his or her environment (e.g., the husband and/or friends will not like a purchased dress);
- psychological risk – connected with consumer fears about whether a chosen product is appropriate for the consumer ego (e.g., whether the consumer will feel comfortable or be satisfied with the purchase of a high-risk investment fund); and
- risk of wasting time – appears when the time spent on searching for and choosing a service is wasted (or the time used is too great), especially if the service does not meet consumer expectations (e.g., the consumer has to make repeated efforts to buy a new insurance policy).

It is noteworthy that the consumer is affected by risks that are perceived as his/her risks. Risks that are not seen by the consumer are not taken into account in the process of choice making (as if the risk was nonexistent). Consequently, firms should define and understand factors that produce a sense of risk in consumers, and provide information that eliminates or considerably reduces these risk factors (Schiffman et al., 2008). Assessment of a purchase possibility may give rise to a consumer's purchase intention, which will turn into a real purchase unless other situational factors or other people's attitudes stand in the consumer's way. The act of purchase is followed by assessment of a product and the circumstances of a purchase with respect to fulfillment of consumer expectations. This comparison may produce a feeling of satisfaction, sometimes delight, or dissatisfaction and disappointment (Hawkins and Best, 2004). A greater difference between expectations and reality causes greater consumer dissatisfaction. Both discomfort and satisfaction are likely to become a subject of information exchange between consumers, as well as provide experience and knowledge for future decisions. However, the purchase is not the last step for the consumer. When the consumer makes an assessment of his/her decision during consumption of a product, this may lead to positive feelings, i.e., satisfaction, which, in the long run, may develop into brand loyalty (Chumpitaz-Caceres and Paparoidamis, 2007). The truth is, however, that the purchase often evokes negative feelings in the form of post-purchase cognitive dissonance. Cognitive dissonance is described as tension generated by reception of contradictory stimuli. With respect to a purchase, the dissonance appears as partial or total dissatisfaction with a product (e.g., as a result of noticing a fault or realizing that a rival product is somehow better) (Fey, 1994; Eggert and Ulaga, 2002). It should be mentioned that with more important purchases, the customer is more likely to confirm his/her choice by referring to various information sources, especially ones that can provide him/her with a valuable assessment.

It is noteworthy that purchase situations differ in terms of the significance attached to products by consumers and in terms of the degree of consumer involvement in the decision-making process. Hence, not all choices are made in the same way. The final shape of the decision-making process depends on the type and complexity of a consumer decision, which is determined by the following factors (Garbarski, 1999):

- factors related to a product purchase (product type, price differences between brands, purchase method, and purchase volume),
- factors related to the consumer (consumer experience and product knowledge, personal characteristics, financial resources, attitude toward a product), and
- factors related to the situation (time pressure, other purchase circumstances, product purpose).

All these factors determine the so-called degree of consumer involvement; in other words, they influence the consumer's time, energy, thoughts, and feelings connected with the choice of a given product. The degree of consumer involvement may indicate a different course for cognitive processes related to the purchase. In particular, it may determine the volume of information used by the consumer and the way the information is transformed. Consequently, there are two basic decision-making situations (Evans et al., 1996; Foxall and Goldsmith, 1998):

- situations requiring substantial consumer involvement in the purchasing process (of great significance for the consumer), and
- situations requiring slight consumer involvement in the purchasing process (of little significance for the consumer).

It should be emphasized that although research results confirm that the decision-making process consists of sequential stages, there are no explicit data revealing the real number of stages the consumer has to complete before making the ultimate decision (Kwai-Choi and Marshall, 1998).

The case: Number of stages in the decision-making process – Polish-Hungarian comparisons

Empirical studies demonstrate that the course of the decision-making process is determined by, among other things, the type of a product to be purchased. A comparison of the purchase of two basic products (sweets and fruit) in Hungary and Poland shows notable differences between the process of purchasing fruit and the process of purchasing sweets in both countries. It can be observed that not all stages of the decision-making process are completed by all consumers for either purchase. For example, in the case of the purchase of sweets, the most frequently omitted stage is collection of informal information and selection of a brand from an available brand offer, while these two stages are rarely omitted in the purchase of fruits. The comparison of the two ways of making a decision allows one to draw the conclusion that sweets and fruit are bought in two different ways: sweets are bought more impulsively, without consumer considerations about brand choice and without referring to information. In addition, in the case of sweets, the consumer more frequently assesses the purchased products than do consumers of fruits (Figure 66).

stages of the decision-making process	fruits		sweets	
	Hungary	Poland	Hungary	Poland
idea of buying product	0	0	9	3
collecting information about an available shopping offer from advertising, etc.	0	0	72	31
collecting information about product from other consumers	4	12	41	43
making a decision about buying product (a decision that it will be bought)	8	6	17	31
selecting one concrete type of product	5	6	87	43
choosing a place for product purchase	7	6	18	0
consuming product	72	63	84	54
assessing purchased product	31	28	17	22

Source: Molnar et al., (2006) p. 6; Burgiel and Sowa (2008) p. 52

Figure 66. Consumers decision-making process (data in percent)

Some researchers assume that consumer behavior and consumer decisions are preceded by a complex mental process of collecting and processing information, part of the buyer's rational problem-solving processes (Belch and Willis, 2002; Arnold et al., 2004). According to this understanding, buying processes are situations that require a substantial engagement of the consumer. It is also maintained that consumers are able to receive and interpret a considerable amount of information and to carry-out large-scale searches as well as make assessments before the purchase. Through this process, they develop long-lasting attitudes and beliefs. The buyer is engaged in collecting market information, is able to recognize important differences between types of the same product, and, by means of some special comparative procedures, chooses one product version (Foxall and Goldsmith, 1998).

Nonetheless, according to many researchers, the picture described above is unreal and takes too much consumer rationality for granted. In fact, a great deal of daily shopping takes place without any great consumer involvement or consumer conviction about the rightness of a particular choice. This is demonstrated by the results of empirical studies (Kassarjian and Robertson, 1991; Baumeister, 2002), which led to the hypothesis that most consumer behavior is not characterized by a high degree of involvement or arduous search for information. Instead, with low interest in mass media information and with a low level of identification with product brands, consumers try out a product of a certain brand to obtain information about it. Moreover, in their choice of a product and brand, consumers mainly refer to situational factors, their own experience, and information sources available in stores (Harcar et al., 2005).

Economists still disagree about the course of consumer decision-making processes, as well as the character and scope of the cognitive processes accompanying buying decisions (Lewis and Bidger, 2001; Dolinski, 2003). Acceptance of the fact that consumer involvement is often low does not exclude the existence of situations where it is high. Additionally, it does not thoroughly refute the concept of consumer cognitive involvement. This, however, necessitates defining areas of consumer market choices in which the two different approaches may apply. Consequently, three general methods of consumer decision making have been proposed (Harris, 2010):

- extended problem solving,
- limited problem solving, and
- routine problem solving.

The course of a decision-making process depends on the strength of a consumer's attitude towards the brands available in a given product category. When the consumer's attitude is weak (or else the consumer has no opinion about a certain group of products), a group of products to be considered by the consumer is not clearly defined, and available brands are not easily distinguishable, the consumer employs techniques of extended problem solving. This mainly applies to new and complicated products that lack very distinctive brand features. The consumer is in a situation of considerable involvement, which is connected with intensive cognitive processes. The consumer seeks information in order to get better knowledge about particular offers and thinks carefully before making final decisions (Geuens et al., 2003).

Another possible approach – limited problem-solving – is seen in situations where the consumer has some knowledge of a product and has some definite experience with product purchase and product consumption. The consumer has already tried out several brands in a given category and has assumed towards them a moderately strong attitude. This results in development of selection criteria for this type of product. In spite of superior knowledge of certain brands, the consumer still seeks additional information, especially when confused with respect to the qualities and possibilities of particular products (Garbarino and Johnson, 1999).

Finally, routine problem-solving becomes possible when the consumer has an established strong attitude towards brands. Having experience with several brands, the consumer is capable of distinguishing particular product variants (brands) and demonstrates stronger preference of one brand (or two) over the others. The consumer is not actively involved in a search for external information, as there is no need. As for unwittingly received information, it is perceived and interpreted in a selective way, as the consumer already has a clearly defined opinion about available product brands (Schiffman et al., 2008). The relationships are presented in Figure 67.

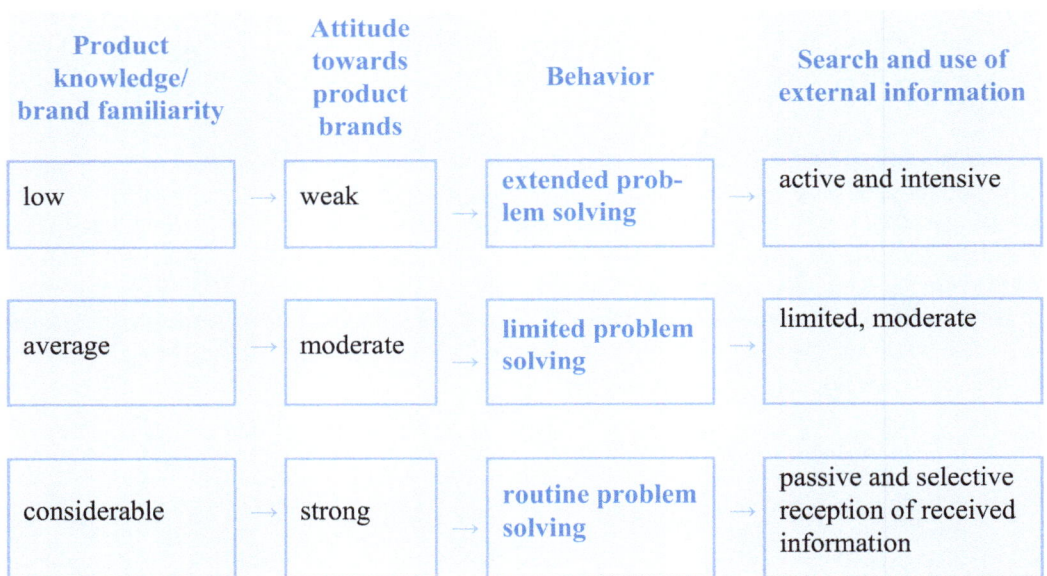

Product knowledge/ brand familiarity	Attitude towards product brands	Behavior	Search and use of external information
low	→ weak	→ extended problem solving	→ active and intensive
average	→ moderate	→ limited problem solving	→ limited, moderate
considerable	→ strong	→ routine problem solving	→ passive and selective reception of received information

Source: Foxall and Goldsmith (1998), p. 53

Figure 67. Types of consumer behavior and its determinants

Depending on the character and significance of a consumer decision, the decision-making process may be either extended or reduced in time. With respect to the latter, the reduction concerns the middle stages, which are connected with obtaining information to be used for identification and assessment of choice alternatives. All five stages of the decision-making process are responsible for behavior that is consciously monitored by an individual. Limitations concern automatic and unconscious behavior (Lambkin et al., 2001). The range criterion of conscious monitoring of one's own behavior makes it possible to distinguish and characterize general types of consumer decisions. On the one hand, market choices can be made in a conscious and reflective way. On the other hand, in his/her daily life, the consumer is faced with many decision problems that are solved in accordance with patterns of past behavior, or else under the influence of sudden emotions (Hawkins and Best, 2004). Hence, one can speak of behavior identified with decision types, including rational behavior (extensive rational decisions), rationally simplified behavior (rationally simplified decisions), routine behavior (customary habitual decisions), or impulsive behavior (impulsive decisions) (Graham, 2010).

Rational behavior follows an established plan and is supported with an active search for information from many sources. Rationally simplified behavior calls for considerable involvement on the consumer's part – an active search for information and creative transformation of information. Routine behavior, in turn, occurs when the consumer arranges consumption in a traditional way and according to his/her habits. With this behavior, the consumer does not seek extra information and new solutions and favors an individually elaborated formula. Finally, the smallest range of conscious consumer monitoring can be observed in the case of impulsive behavior, where decisions are made on the spur of the moment, as a result of sudden emotions. Here, the consumer does not seek information about a product and does not think much about a purchase. Impulsive behavior can be provoked by stimuli and conditions of a varied character (Beatty and Ferrell, 1998; Harris, 2010).

The case: Types of consumer decisions in Romania

Direct research shows that situations of extended problem solving and choices of great consumer involvement preceded by complex cognitive processes are very rare and concern goods that are bought either for the first time, rarely, or else are very risky. In the case of goods that are frequently purchased and that are widely available, decision-making processes are often characterized by low consumer involvement and by routine or limited problem solving. This happens due to the fact that both consumer possibilities and consumer willingness to transform information are limited. In addition, consumers have access to information that is stored in their memory and that is sufficient for decision making. Despite a limited search for information, the consumer does use information while making a buying decision, although some types of information are more preferred than others.

Source: Angheluta and Zaharia (2010)

Consumers are generally unable to consider all information available in a given decision-making situation. As a consequence, they refer to heuristic decisions in order to use some information and to choose a product. Decision heuristics represents simplified decision-making strategies, which increase the effectiveness of the process at the expense of greater uncertainty about choice correctness (Duhan et al., 1997). Consumer heuristics come in different forms, but the most important are those that involve the use of personal information sources, namely recommendation-based heuristics. Here, the decision maker uses recommendations (from different sources) in order to cut down on the amount of information to be considered in making a decision. Recommendations can be used as a way of reducing the number of considered alternatives (e.g., product brands). Another use of recommendations is to reduce the number of analyzed and compared product features. According to research results, it is the information from personal sources (mainly informal) that facilitates consumer buying decisions (Diller et al., 2006).

The case: Sources of information for customers in the Bulgarian clothes market

Results of research into consumer behavior during clothes shopping in Bulgaria show that half of consumers buy goods in the company of friends or relatives, who act as advisers and suggestion-makers. Forty-three percent of respondents claim they prefer to do shopping individually, without seeking anybody's advice. Only 6% of the questioned consumers say they ask a sales clerk for advice. At first glance, the results confirm, on the one hand, the existence of great possibilities for using personal sources for informal information, since 'the sources' accompany consumers during shopping. On the other hand, there are also great possibilities of exerting influence on the consumer by people who become such a source of information.

Source: Marinov et al., (2008)

In order to evaluate the use of personal sources instead of other types of information, the sources have been categorized into four major groups (Best, 2009):

- **marketing sources**, comprising media advertising, Internet pages of clothing companies, catalogs, and leaflets;
- **private sources,** including one's own experience and current observation of store offers and store window displays;
- **public sources**, including magazines and programs on fashion or other topics, as well as www pages on fashion and other non-commercial Internet pages; and
- **personal sources**, including three sub-groups:
  - informal sources based on strong relations with the consumer, including close family members, friends, acquaintances, and coworkers;
  - informal sources based on loose relations with the consumer, including relatives and neighbors; and
  - formal sources, including sales clerks.

In CEE countries, the purchase of financial services is most frequently made on the basis of a consumer's experience (see Figure 68). Other information sources, such as informal personal sources that are related to the customer and formal personal sources (sales person's support), occupy the second and third position respectively. The second group of personal sources of an informal character, including distant relatives and friends, is the least frequently used by consumers.

source	Czech Rep.	Hungary	Lithuania	Poland	Romania
own experience	84.5	79.4	89.2	87.2	92.1
family/friends	39.2	10.4	27.9	9.5	30.4
television	71.7	62.2	58.4	60.7	55.1
press	17.2	16.7	15.1	19.2	14.7
radio	19.0	21.9	13.3	24.3	12.1
internet	19.8	20.0	4.7	21.2	3.4
others	10.5	5.2	7.3	6.9	7.6

Sources: Smyczek and Sowa (2005), p. 164

Figure 68. Information sources for financial services (in percent)

The impersonal sources of information are, in the first place, responsible for providing consumers with information about the existence and availability of a new product (Evans et al., 1996). Other consumers and sales persons are consulted for information mainly at the stage of comparison and of alternative assessment, as well as while making a final choice. Information from these sources entails having consumers try out the actual innovation (Beatty and Farrell, 1998). However, a great deal of data shows that the role of personal information sources is also quite considerable in the initial stage of the decision-making process, specifically with respect to the diffusion of information about a novelty (Gilly et al., 1998).

Information from personal sources also plays a definite role at each stage of the decision-making process:

- a special role for this type of source in the diffusion of innovation is seen in a situation where personal information may determine consumer behavior right at the stage when a person becomes aware of a need. At such a moment leaders-innovators on the one hand, and sales people on the other, relay to consumers messages about novelties and their functions, thus arousing in consumers a desire for a new product; negative informal information also has significant influence on a purchase intention (Bone, 1995);
- although advertising is of primary importance for developing 'brand awareness' and informal communication is significant in later stages of product assessment and product acceptance (Jachnis, 2007), study results confirm that friends and relatives are one of the most crucial (sometimes the most crucial) sources of information about available products (Graham, 2010). By providing information about market offers, friends and relatives also affect consumers at the stage of searching for alternative ways of need satisfaction;
- word-of-mouth has a more powerful effect on product assessment than printed materials (Gilly et al., 1998), while negative personal information is capable of changing consumer attitudes towards a product (Bone, 1995); and

- finally, at the stage of product selection consumers are particularly responsive to information from personal sources (Gilly et al., 1998).

In the case of the purchase of electronic equipment, research conducted in Slovakia has revealed that personal, informal sources of information are most frequently used at the end of the decision-making process, i.e., at the stage of choosing a place of purchase and assessing a purchased product. However, the research also demonstrates that personal sources are significant throughout the whole process of decision making. Marketing sources are of equal importance to personal sources in the initial stages of the process but are less important at later stages (Kita, 2006). Figures on the popularity of source groups at subsequent stages of the decision-making process are presented in Figure 69.

stages of the decision-making process	source of information				
	personal (informal)	personal (formal)	marketing	public	experience
offer recognition	22.6	9.7	28.2	6.7	32.8
comparison of a choice possibility	20.6	9.7	23.7	10.0	35.9
choice of a place of purchase	23.7	5.2	18.0	10.6	42.5
final choice of product	18.5	8.4	14.6	4.5	54.0
assessment of purchased product	27.2	5.2	11.7	2.2	53.7

Source: Kita (2006), p. 148

Figure 69. Information sources and decision making in Slovakia (in percent)

The role and importance of various people in the decision-making process constitutes another problem. A considerable number of sources in the literature on consumer behavior used to concentrate on individual consumer behavior and individual consumer decisions. However, in most societies individuals live within smaller or larger organizational structures which, as groups, are themselves important decision-making subjects responsible for vital market choices. Decision-making processes inside these structures should be, and in fact have become, a subject of particular interest to researchers in different scientific fields.

The family, as the most basic decision-making subject, is an object of analysis. Researchers have studied the role of husbands and wives, and also, more frequently, children in decisions about buying various products (Solomon et al., 2010). Economists and market researchers show interest in the decision making of the household, as information about it can be useful in terms of forecasting and shaping consumer market choices as well as influencing consumer purchases (Hawkins and Best, 2004). Companies seek to understand the arrangement and assignment of roles in a family before being able to effectively affect consumer decision-making processes.

It appears that consumer buying decisions within families are of an increasingly mutual character, with participation of several family members who have different roles and different influence on the decision making. These roles are not constant for the whole lifetime and are not in conflict with each other. Moreover, the role of consumer played by a particular family member is likely to be different across families with respect to time and concrete decisions (Lackman and Lanasa, 1993).

I. concept (Kotler)	II. concept (Mowen)	functions related to a given role
purchase initiator (originator)	gatekeeper	process initiator, recognizes the need to buy a product, collects information about a product, and monitors provision of the information to the family
adviser	influencer	provides information about a product, thereby affecting the product choice
---	decision maker	makes decisions, resolves disputes, manages financial resources, makes the final decision of whether to buy something or not, what to buy, how much to buy, when and where to buy
supplier	buyer	makes a real purchase
---	preparer	transforms a product to make it useable/consumable
user	user	uses/consumes a product
---	maintainer	provides maintenance and repairs a product to ensure its constant efficiency and readiness to use
---	disposer	defines when to stop using a product and how to dispose of it

Source: Mowen (1987) p. 412; Kotler and Keller (2009) p. 237

Figure 70. Roles of consumers in the decision-making process

The roles assigned to particular family members in the decision-making process may vary, depending on the product to be bought; the wife may be the initiator of buying a dishwasher; the child, a TV set. However, in most relationships, it is possible to point out the person who plays the role of the so-called family financial director, i.e., a person who decides about the future of possible financial surpluses. In the case of young couples, this role is split equally between the two partners; yet, with time, one of the partners takes over the function. In some families (traditional ones as well as less-educated families), one can observe a certain 'specialization', with the man being the breadwinner and the wife the finance manager.

There are also two other dimensions of roles in the decision-making process. Davis (1994) suggests that there are roles of an instrumental and expressive character. The **instrumental role** comprises tasks that affect the ultimate buying decision, such as the time of purchase and amount of money to be spent on a given product. **Expressive roles**, in turn, consist in making sure the purchase expresses family norms in a way that ensures the social and emotional acceptance of a given decision. Such a role is exemplified by the choice of a product style or product color (Lackman and Lanasa, 1993).

Traditionally, the husband has been assigned the instrumental role, and the wife, the expressive one. However, according to the most recent research results, the nature of family 'role-playing' behavior is undergoing changes due to family transformations: women work more and in professional positions, which shifts husbands towards a greater role in the household (Doole et al., 2005). Simultaneously, the expressive role assigned to wives has decreased slightly in favor of the instrumental role (e.g., women pay bills and monitor expenses; they decide about the use of free funds). It is worth emphasizing, in addition, that children are beginning to play a significant role in decision-making processes (Palan and Wilkes, 1997; Belch and Willis, 2002). Their influence over household decisions is not independent of these families; on the contrary, children affect parental buying decisions based on what they have learned during the process of consumer socialization; and it is the family (mainly parents) that educates children and provides them with definite buying and consumption habits (Raymond, 2003).

Children, especially the youngest ones, exert indirect and passive influence on decision-making processes by informing their parents about their likes and dislikes. At the same time, though, their influence may be very indirect and active at moments when they demand concrete products by resorting to various pressure methods and strategies. The offspring may initiate the decision-making processes; collect information about alternative choice possibilities; and suggest a time, place, and the circumstances of a purchase. The older the child is, the greater the range and effectiveness of his/her influence. It should be noted that children in a family appear as a potential source of affecting not only the result of the decision-making process, but also the decision-making system (Lackman and Lanasa, 1993).

It is becoming more apparent that within consumer socialization not only children learn from their parents, but also parents learn from their children (re-socialization). It turns out that children shape parental behavior (and market choices) in terms of personal appearance, physical activity, home furnishings, or car purchases (Cowell, 2001). Children, affected by advertising and peer groups, persuade their parents to buy the latest and the most fashionable products, which are, however, often beyond the financial possibilities of a given household. A considerable role for children in the family decision-making process comes from their being an important and precious source of information about the market itself and market offers (Harris, 2010). It is even said that 'today the dominance of children over their families is so great that one can speak of child-led families'.

The role and significance of participants in the decision-making process may vary depending on the character of the product; a person may be assigned one role or several roles simultaneously. In addition, a given individual may take different roles in various decision-making processes: once being a purchase initiator; another time, a user; or sometimes, a supplier. All this is determined by the type of decision and by the decision-making model characteristic of a given family. Decisions that are made in a family are most commonly classified in the literature as follows (Hawkins and Best, 2004):

- **husband-dominated** – e.g., purchase of a car, alcohol, life insurance;
- **wife-dominated** – purchase of interior design articles, food items, domestic appliances, detergents, toys, medicine;
- **joint (syncretic)** – mostly connected with the purchase of a house, holidays, telephone service, or furniture; and
- **autonomous** – independent, made entirely by one family member.

The share of family members in the different decisions varies. According to study results from Hungary, it is the wife who is in charge of the greatest number of decisions, whereas the most important decisions are usually made jointly by both partners. The man makes decisions about sources for financing the largest purchases, but it is the woman who decides how to spend the financial resources and how to plan the biggest purchases. All banking and office matters are settled as frequently by men as by women, with 11% of families performing these activities jointly. Women are mainly in charge of decisions related to the purchase of interior design articles, furniture, and domestic appliances (91.8% of these decisions are made by women). Men, in turn, take over for the purchase of computer hardware as well as radio and TV equipment, but are less engaged in buying men's clothing. The share of children's buying decisions mainly concerns the purchase of computer equipment, 14%, and radio and TV equipment, 6%. Decisions made jointly by husbands and wives are highest in the purchases of domestic appliances, furniture, and radio and TV equipment.

decision maker	type of product					
	computer	radio & TV	husband's clothes	domestic appliances	furniture	interior design equipment
wife	18.9	20.0	38.2	54.7	71.2	91.8
husband	65.5	67.9	57.9	36.2	21.2	4.5
child/ children	14.1	6.3	1.0	1.7	0.7	0.6
husband and wife jointly	1.5	5.8	2.9	7.5	7.0	3.1

Source: Diller et al., (2006) p. 187

Figure 71. Share of family members in the purchase process in Hungary (in percent)

It should be recalled that these patterns in the divisions of decision making are becoming less valid. Changes are occurring partly because the recently observed growth in the number and variety of products, stores, and shopping centers, combined with the availability of alternative shopping methods (catalog and online shopping) have considerably increased the number of consumer choices and have complicated the decision-making processes (Schiffman et al., 2008). Women's professional involvement has also brought changes, which entail broadening of the range of family decision-making processes, with participation, or even dominance, of women. Due to the growing professional activity of women, it is becoming a commonplace that husbands take on household tasks and manage household finances together with their wives. It should be noted, however, that this observation refers only to some decisions, especially the high-risk ones, which tend to be resolved jointly. In the case of less risky choices, syncretic decisions are still less likely (Doole et al., 2005).

It should be emphasized that consumer behavior occupies a significant part of consumer market activity. This behavior refers to decisions concerning identification of consumer needs. It also entails search, purchase, consumption, and assessment of the products purchased. Currently, decisions made in an internationalized market are becoming more complex, which mainly results from access to many previously unknown products and from the diversity of the market offers. This, in turn, requires appropriate consumer knowledge and consumer involvement in decision-making processes.

Consumer behavior in the international market cannot be treated autonomously, without reference to other elements of the system within which the consumer operates, as the behavior takes definite forms influenced by numerous and diverse factors. The determinants of behavior can be classified in various ways using different criteria. The most general classification is based on the division of determinants into two groups according to the sources of origin. One group involves **genetic (hereditary) influence**; the other, **environmental influence** (Graham, 2010).

One of the most popular determinant classifications attaches less importance to economic influence; instead, it emphasizes the social, cultural, demographic and psychical determinants that influence consumer decisions (Solomon et al., 1999; Evans et al., 2009). Because of the financial crisis, the economic environment of consumers is not stable anymore. Thus economic determinants must be taken into consideration. Mowen (1987) proposes focusing on three basic groups: **economic factors** (including income, prices, supply, marketing information, and selling policy), **social factors** (socio-cultural, sociological – e.g., culture; social groups; and all types of interpersonal interactions, including family influence, the influence of opinion leaders, etc.), and **psychological factors** (internal, psychological, individual – e.g., processes of perception; memorizing; and learning, motives, attitudes, personality). These approaches, although very transparent and practical in terms of their usability for consumer behavior analyses, marginalize the significance of consumer descriptive variables such as the demographic features of age, gender, household population, family life cycle, and type and level of education.

In light of the considerations above, a compromise between various approaches is desirable. Ideally, all important groups of factors that directly or indirectly affect consumer behavior, economic determinants, socio-cultural and demographic factors as well as psychological determinants, would be included.

7.3 Determinants of consumer behavior in international markets

7.3.1 Economic

Economic determinants of consumer behavior can be divided into internal and external factors. The **internal economic factors**, dependent on the consumer, include, among others, income, loans, savings, household furnishing, the level and structure of consumption, and leisure. The **external economic factors** exist independently of the consumer and include supply, prices, trade and service infrastructure, selling policy, and the system of institutional information (Kiezel, 2010).

Income is the most potent factor determining consumer behavior, as it constitutes an essential element of a consumer's standard of living and allows for the satisfaction of basic and higher-level needs.

country	population (Mio.)	disposable income per capita (EUR)	average houshold size	expenditures for consumption per year (EUR/household)
EU 27	492.0	21,984	2.6	24,723
Austria	8.2	28,958	2.4	29,897
Germany	82.5	27,010	2.1	28,849
Poland	38.2	5,545	3.0	10,738
Portugal	10.5	13,787	2.8	21,281
Romania	21.6	2,940	2.9	5,024

Source: Eurostat (2009)

Figure 72. Income and population in selected European countries

In general terms, the dependence of consumption on income can be summarized in the following statement: the higher the income, the higher the level of consumption, and vice verse. This statement, however, refers only to global consumption and does not necessarily apply to consumption of particular goods. Changes in income level precipitate not only changes in global consumption, but also in its structure. The growth of income may result in an increase in the consumption volume of higher-level goods, both in qualitative and quantitative terms. The level of income defines the range of consumption independence, discouraging or encouraging people from selecting definite needs. Generally, an increase in income increases purchases accordingly, whereas a decrease hinders purchases. Income is an essential factor because (Csaba, 1995)

- it develops in the division of household budget sphere, thus being the primary factor in relation to others;
- it is a basic measurable, quantitative factor that determines supply and consumption and allows for their analysis according to many additional features that are distinctive for particular consumers; and
- it directly expresses changes in other economic and noneconomic factors.

Distribution of household income may take different directions depending on the source of origin. **Fixed income** is meant to satisfy basic needs, whereas periodic and **sporadic income** is used to purchase material goods and high-level services. An increase in consumer income level may lead to the following changes in consumption (Harris, 2010):

- quantitative growth of consumption within the same quality,
- qualitative growth of consumption within the same quantity,
- qualitative and quantitative increase in consumption of some goods,
- quantitative decrease in consumption with qualitative increase, and
- qualitative decrease within the same quality.

Income as a consumption determinant is closely related to demand. This relationship is defined as the **income elasticity of demand** (e_d). The demand for a given product may rise or fall as an effect of an increase in income. Consequently, the coefficient of income elasticity of demand may take either a positive or a negative value (Solomon et al., 2010):

- if $e_d > 1$, one can speak of a high demand elasticity in relation to income – such a situation is characteristic of the purchase of luxury or durable products as well as services;
- if $e_d = 1$, then demand is proportional – such a situation appears in the case the purchase of less luxurious (semi-luxurious) products;
- if $e_d < [0.\ 1]$, demand is slightly elastic (rigid for $e_d = 0$) in the case of basic need articles, mainly food items; and
- if $e_d < 0$, demand is inversely elastic, which is characteristic of low-level goods (the so-called mediocre, worse goods).

The case: Income as determinant of consumer behavior in transitional economies in Europe

During the transformational economic processes of Central and Eastern Europe, the income of citizens has changed mainly as a result of changes in the prices of consumer goods and services and changes in the socio-economic policies pursued by the countries of this region. Examination of the income level during the process of introducing a market economy shows that during the first twenty years of economic transformation, the highest income level was achieved by the households of individual entrepreneurs (self-employed people). In Poland, in 2009, the income of these households was 27.5% higher than the income level of households of employed people. A worsening income situation was observed in the case of agricultural households. At the beginning of the transformation, the income of this social group exceeded the income of employees, but by 1991, farmers' income level fell to levels below the income of employees.

During the transformational processes, important changes occurred in the structure of household disposable income in all households. An increase was observed, above all, in the share of income of self-employed people, from 6% in 1993 to 8.8% in 2009. The share of employee income also rose, to 53.8% in 2009. Between 1993 and 2006, there was a slight increase in the share from social security benefits (in 1993 they accounted for 32.5%, and in 2006, 33.5% of the whole disposable income), whereas in 2007 and 2009, the share decreased until it stabilized at 28.7%, which has been a positive change. Nonmaretheless, the share of income from social security benefits within the whole disposable income structure is still high. During the period between 1990 and 2009, the share of income in an agricultural household declined from 10.6% in 1993, to 4.1% in 2009.

Source: GUS (2010)

Supply and market infrastructure are other economic factors determining consumer behavior. Unlike income, supply and market infrastructure are of an external character. Understood as sales offers for definite goods and services in terms of assortment, quality, territory, and time dimensions, it marks clear-cut boundaries of need satisfaction. It is mostly determined by (Hawkins and Best, 2004) the following:

- **level of country production** – higher production volume fosters a higher level of supply,
- **foreign trade balance** – importation of goods in excess of exports stimulates supply on the domestic market so that supply goes beyond the volume of domestic production, and
- **distribution system** – availability of goods and services depends on a network of trading centers and on a transportation system that moves goods effectively.

These factors are mainly determined by the economic level of a country. On the one hand, supply sets a physical framework of consumption and allows for its qualitative changes. On the other hand, it determines the existence of regularities between consumption and the level of income and prices. Depending on its volume and its internal structure, supply can either restrict consumption or foster it through free consumer buying decisions. In a **seller's market** (Central and Eastern European countries from 1945 to 1989), the inability to buy goods produced not only a feeling of deprivation, but also precipitated a number of negative phenomena such as a **black market** (Bywalec and Rudnicki, 1999). Shortages of products on the market limited consumption and ultimately led to eliminating the satisfaction of some needs. In the case of a **buyer's market**, with an increasingly rich supply, supply not only extended the scope of needs, but also created new ones, thus determining consumer development (Evans et al., 2009).

The attractiveness of the supply of products and the market infrastructure often becomes a factor that stimulates both consumer aspirations and consumer motivations to undertake gainful employment and to increase income by means of performance. A sufficient amount and variety of goods on the market allows for the extension and attractiveness of need satisfaction. A commercial offer of consumer goods and services affects consumer decisions, either facilitating or complicating the decision-making process. Too varied and abundant an offer facilitates a purchase, but at the same time hinders making a decision (Csaba, 1995). Hence, one can say that supply enables the consumer to satisfy his/her needs, whereas needs themselves are determined by an available market offer. Therefore, it is necessary to tailor the market offer to a desired consumption pattern. The structure of supply and the quality of goods should be closely related to the level and distribution of income in the society (Evans et al., 2009).

country	hypermarkets	supermarkets	discount stores	other / small stores
Bosnia & Herzegovina	39	35	1	25
Bulgaria	10	34	0*	56
Croatia	19	47	2	32
Czech Republic	39	16	25	20
Hungary	29	16	22	33
Poland	29	11	31	29
Romania	42	18	17	23
Serbia	16	31	0*	53
Slovakia	30	23	9	38
Slovenia	29	41	10	20
Ukraine	13	48	-	39

* Below 1%

Source: Balan (2010), p. 231

Figure 73. Buyers of food per type of store in CEE countries (in percent)

Price is another significant economic factor that determines consumer behavior. Together with income level, the price of a product, being a monetary expression of product value, affects the choice of products in the market, and serves several principal functions that largely determine the rightness of consumer decisions (Blythe, 1997; Doole et al., 2005). They are referred to as income, informative, distributive, stimulating, and redistributive functions. The income function is responsible for shaping the real income of the consumer. Through the informative function, the price presents various choice options and constitutes the basis for the best of all consumer decisions. The distributive function of prices (balancing supply and demand) can be performed only by a market balance that excludes the presence of either excess or shortage and that ensures the purchase of goods and services by anyone who is willing to pay a definite price for them. Prices perform a stimulating function when the state regulates them so that they can become an incentive for an activity that is consistent with a general social interest. Finally, through their redistributive function, prices constitute a tool of income redistribution when they differ from the value of products. If consumers buy goods at prices higher than the value of the goods, the level of their real income decreases in relation to the nominal income and vice verse (Schiffman et al., 2008).

The demand reaction to price variation is best measured by **elasticity of the demand price** (e_p), whose value oscillates within the following ranges (Diller et al., 2006):

- if $e_p > 1$, demand is elastic, i.e., a price increase entails a demand decrease that is relatively larger than the price increase itself and vice verse; such a situation occurs in the case of the purchase of luxury and substitutable goods;
- if $e_p = 1$, change in the price produces a proportional change in demand;
- if $e_p < 1$, demand is slightly elastic, i.e., a price change causes a slight change in demand; such a situation occurs in the case of basic-need products and complementary goods.

The influence of the price of basic goods over the demand for related goods (substitutable, complementary) is measured by the coefficient of **cross elasticity of demand** (e_c). The coefficient helps determine how a change in the price of one product affects a change in the demand for another product. The value of a cross elasticity coefficient indicates the degree of relationship between goods. The higher the positive e_c value is, the stronger the substitutability, whereas the lower the negative value is, the stronger the complementarity of the relationship. Coefficient values approaching zero demonstrate a lack of 'relation' between goods (Blackwell et al., 2001).

Despite the fact that price is one of the most important elements of buying decisions, it should be emphasized that over the last couple of years, the role of price in consumer decisions has changed (Kahneman and Tversky, 2000). Changes have also occurred in researchers' attitude towards analyses of the relations between price and consumer decisions. More focus has been put on the psychological aspects of the influence of price and on additional variables that make the relations between price, income, and demand more complicated than the description in the literature. Research results indicate, among other things, that the general consumer knowledge of prices is declining. According to the latest findings, the majority of consumers not only do not remember the prices of recently purchased products, but also do not check prices as carefully as was previously assumed (Dickson and Sawyer, 1990; Hawkins and Best, 2004). A lower level of knowledge of product prices is a consequence of the two phenomena mentioned above: a higher financial status in the society means people lose 'interest' in price, whereas a wide assortment of products prevents people from learning the prices of such a multitude of products and greatly exceeds their cognitive abilities. Another factor differentiating possible consumer reactions to price is connected with the payer, i.e., whether it is the consumer or, for example, his/her employer who covers the costs of a company car. The research shows that consumers often 'guess' the price instead of verifying it, e.g., they assume that products bought on the market are cheaper than goods from a corner store, which is not necessarily true. At the same time, they use price as a basic determinant of product quality, especially when there is no other clear information about the standards for a given product (Schiffman and Kanuk, 2010).

Thaler (1985) has observed that while buying a product, the consumer achieves two types of satisfaction: one, already mentioned, is satisfaction with the product; another, the so-called satisfaction with the transaction, which translates into the sense of 'clenching a good deal'. Such a conviction develops when the consumer compares the price paid to the so-called reference price, i.e., to the cost of a competitive product regarded by the consumer as the best alternative to the chosen purchase item. This explains why sellers try, in many ways, to 'prove' that the price they offer is a good one, i.e., better than the reference price. For example, they compare their prices to the prices of other (more expensive) products or to a previous (higher) price of a given product. The theory of perspectives developed by Kahneman and Tversky (2000) formulated four principles of the so-called **consumer mental accounting** (mental calculations). These principles describe situations in which the consumer experiences greater satisfaction with a purchase. It turns out that satisfaction is greater when, instead of one larger profit, the consumer realizes several smaller ones, which leads to the conclusion that when paying a definite price, the buyer prefers to obtain a product with an added gift, rather than get a product of a higher value (Evans et al., 1996).

In the event of a decreased role for price, non-price forms of boosting the attractiveness of an offer gain increasing significance. These mainly include commercial services, especially warranties by which the guarantor ensures the quality of products. Another type of service influencing consumer market behavior relates to the services connected with goods or with a selling point, including the furnishing of the place, the assortment structure, and so on. Services that are independent and are not permanently related to a product constitute another type of service. They can be purchased separately from the product, e.g., delivery of goods to the home, assembly, and the like.

7.3.2   Socio-cultural

Social and cultural factors of consumer behavior belong to the group of noneconomic factors. Unlike economic determinants, they are more difficult to measure in terms of their role in affecting consumer behavior.

Cultural factors are of essential significance and exert the greatest influence on consumer behavior (Kotler and Keller, 2009). The factors include culture, subcultures, and social classes. Culture is a fundamental factor determining buyer's needs and behavior and is made up of subcultures (e.g., nationality, profession, race, geographic region) that also play a significant role in developing a buyer's behavior, as they have a direct effect on identification and the socialization of their members. The societies of particular countries are characterized by social stratification, most commonly revealed in the form of social classes. The latter also constitute an essential factor of a cultural nature that conditions consumer behavior.

According to Hofstede (2000), **culture** is a term that defines the programming of the human brain and is comprised of three levels: universal, collective, and individual. The universal level of the programming stems from human nature – elements that are hereditary and common to all people. (These are feelings related to happiness, fear, sadness, or love.) The way these feelings are expressed comes from the influence of the second, collective level of programming and is characteristic of certain social groups (e.g., nations, inhabitants of a given region, members of a given profession). The individual level of culture is closely related to the individual and to his/her hierarchy of values, interests, and behavior (Neymann, 2005). Culture is acquired, which means it is passed from generation to generation in a non-biological and non-hereditary way. Hofstede (2000) recalls four dimensions that distinguish one culture from another, i.e., distance to authority, individualism and collectivism, femininity and masculinity, avoidance of uncertainty).

Elements of cultural differences among societies are most frequently presented in a layered structure composed of a visible (external) layer, a middle layer, and the so-called core. The first two layers are derived from material, intellectual, and spiritual culture. The **external layer of culture** consists of language, cuisine, buildings, monuments, temples, art, farming, and clothing. The **middle layer of culture** is built of norms and values that may be observed in a given society (Solomon et al., 2010). These norms may appear in the written law (formal level) and in the form of customs and rituals (informal level under social control). Values determine the definition of good and evil and are closely associated with group ideals. Particular individuals behave in accordance with certain values, following the example of their parents, grandparents, and great-grandparents, without thinking about the sense and foundations of their behavior. The awareness of definite behavior, values, and beliefs grows from the internal layer through the middle layer, to the external one. The **core of culture** consists of basic assumptions referring to the roots of human existence, human attempts to survive, human struggles with natural forces, environmental adaptation, and so on. This layer-based approach to culture can be reduced to surface culture (made of visible, audible, and palpable elements) and depth culture (composed of invisible elements like values, religion, symbols, attitude, customs, and rituals) as the sources of the most distinct cultural differences (Evans et al., 2009).

Each culture is made up of many **subcultures,** which appear as patterns and norms of functioning in a social group that is part of a larger population. A subculture defines some life segment, and its culture may be distinguished on the basis of a certain criterion (ethnic, professional, religious, demographic) (Harris, 2010). The most common subcultures are racial, national, demographic, and religious subcultures. They form separate cultural groups, which function as separate market segments within a larger and more complex society, affecting consumer behavior in a direct and more significant way than culture itself. Subculture identification exerts strong and noticeable influence on the daily behavior of a consumer, defining consumer preferences with respect to diet, clothing, leisure, work ambitions, and so on. Knowledge of the needs and tendencies of subcultures makes it possible for a company to select an appropriate marketing strategy, whose effectiveness is expressed in acceptance of the values and style of living of a definite group (Solomon et al., 2010).

Integration and globalization processes have great impact on the mixing of cultures and may contribute to the disappearance of cultural differences in the area of consumption. This is partly explained by the convergence theory, according to which patterns of consumption behavior are becoming more similar through unification of the market systems among societies. However, the process of unification of consumer behavior is not occurring at a very fast pace. Convergence is accompanied by the opposite phenomenon of divergence, in which cultures distance themselves from one another and strive to preserve their identity (Raymond, 2003). Although symptoms of these phenomena can be observed at some analytical levels, there is no explicit proof either for cultural convergence or divergence. In the conditions created by globalization and integration processes, the encounters and confrontations of cultures as well as inclusion of particular countries into the system of the open economy appear as forerunners of, but without a guarantee of, total convergence (cultural, economic).

Cultural factors are very potent in shaping the decision-making processes of all market subjects, but keeping track of the tendencies of cultural changes is significant both from a theoretical and a practical point of view. The majority of change tendencies in a cultural environment revolve around two approaches (Harcar et al., 2005):

- observation of changes within particular national cultures leading either to cultural assimilation or serious cultural differentiation and
- identification of changes on an intercultural level in terms of cultural interrelations with special focus on the analysis of globalization tendencies.

The study into tendencies of cultural changes is difficult not only due to the multidimensional and multi-directional character of the tendencies, but due to their diverse dynamics. International cultural changes result from intensified international transfers and consist of the following processes (Doole et al., 2005):

- **mutual culture penetration** – elements of one culture penetrate another, culture coexistence;
- **shrinkage of the territorial dimension of cultures** – it is getting increasingly difficult to define culture on the basis of its territorial boundaries; national culture gets separated from a country's territory;
- **culture contamination** – the cultural identity of a nation undergoes specific transformations;
- **cultural pluralism** – combining home, local, and transnational customs; and
- **hybridization** – foreign influences are assimilated into a local culture, resulting in a fusion-type culture; hybridization is additionally reinforced by the marketing activity of global firms.

Intensified interpersonal contacts on an international scale contribute to the spread of cultural patterns across countries through the mechanism of intergroup imitation. Nowadays, a person is faced with separate cultural systems: some are determined by national and regional traditions that affect consumer tastes and preferences; and some are universal patterns determined by mass culture and brought about by the disappearance of cultural differences and globalization of consumption. A global culture or the so-called ethics of global consumption consists in identification of sets of common values respected by consumers on a global scale (i.e., pressure toward modernity, technology, freedom, individual choice, health, environmental protection, enforcement or observance of consumer rights) (Schiffman and Kanuk, 2010).

In addition to culture and subculture, social class is another significant determinant in the group of so-called cultural factors. Recognizing the predictive power of social class as a determinant of consumer behavior seems especially important from the perspective of class and income differences in a society (Hawkins and Best, 2004). Social class provides its members with social identification patterns and models of accepted behavior. It can be characterized by social status and prestige, among other things. Social status involves power exercised by one social class to influence members of other classes. Prestige, in turn, is the position of a social class in relation to other social classes. Due to their prestigious character, higher social classes provide a pattern to be followed by members of the lower classes of a society (Evans et al, 1996).

The case: Social classes in Europe

In Europe, social class, apart from objective determinants (i.e., profession, financial position, income, education), is based on subjective factors that include, among others, the opinion of an individual person about his/her own social position and the prestige of a particular job, or the prestige attributed to an individual by other social groups.

In France, social classes have been distinguished on the basis of four socio-professional categories defined by the INSEE agency:
-    upper class (A)
-    middle class/lower bourgeois (B)
-    lower class (C)
-    class of the economically weak (D)
In Spain, social classes have been divided into six groups:
-    higher middle class (A)
-    middle class (B)
-    lower middle class (C1)
-    qualified labor class (C2)
-    labor class (D)
-    class living on a very low level (E)
The Central and Eastern European countries have distinguished five classes in their societal structure:
-    upper class
-    upper middle class
-    middle class
-    peasant class
-    working class

Source: Karcz and Kedzior (2004)

It can be noted that the development of a consumer culture in countries in economic transition, such as Central and Eastern European states, has been temporarily restricted by loss of people's self-confidence and pride in their local culture, as well as by alienation and an increased level of frustration. Currently, in Central European countries that have become EU members, one can observe tendencies to adopt the symbols of Western material culture. Consumers in these countries have direct access to the culture of Western Europe. With the development of global consumption, consumer product preferences become gradually standardized. However, unification of the world culture and subordination of local cultures are rather unlikely to happen. It is, instead, probable that many consumer cultures will emerge; and a mixture of global and local values will evolve.

Social factors consisting of various types of social groups, including reference groups or opinion leaders, are another group of socio-cultural determinants of consumer behavior.

Reference groups denote groups of people that constitute a reference point for comparisons and assessments of an individual's own opinion and behavior, as well as for the formulation of values and attitudes (Blackwell et al., 2001). The groups have direct and indirect influence on individual behavior and attitudes. The direct-influence groups are groups that the individual belongs to or interacts with. They can be primary (family, friends, acquaintances – non-formalized, spontaneous) or secondary (religious, professional, trade unions, party groups – more formalized). There are also the so-called **aspirational groups**, i.e., groups the individual wants to be part of, and dissociative groups, i.e., groups whose values are rejected by the individual (Kotler and Keller, 2009). Moreover, literature on the subject distinguishes comparative benchmark groups (i.e., groups used by people for comparison and assessment of their own behavior, providing a basis for evaluation of beliefs, attitudes, values, and patterns of behavior), status benchmark groups (i.e., groups whose acceptance is sought by the individual, groups which the individual aspires to), and normative benchmark groups (i.e., groups whose values, norms, and standards of behavior are accepted by the individual and used in his/her judgment of various phenomena, identified with opinion groups) (Harris, 2010).

Reference groups affect buying behavior in a normative, informative, and evaluative way. **Normative influence** occurs when a group provides the individual with certain norms of behavior. **Informative influence** is connected to guaranteed provision of credible information by a benchmark group with respect to buying decisions. **Evaluative influence**, in turn, occurs when the consumer is aware of the values and attitudes accepted by a benchmark group and lets them affect him/her (Diller et al., 2006). In addition, one can distinguish influence exerted through roles, which means that each position occupied by the individual in society is related to a certain role. This role is restrained by acceptable and permissible behavior and has a concrete set of products/props, as well as is characterized by so-called group conformism. **Group conformism** is a change in behavior, attitudes, and opinions as a result of real or projected pressure from another person or a group of people (Evans et al., 2009). The influence of reference groups refers particularly to the choice of products, brands, preferences, ways of searching for information, sensitivity to economic factors, susceptibility to promotional activities, and so on.

Apart from reference groups, **opinion leaders** play another significant role as social determinants of behavior. Opinion leaders are people who informally, consciously, or unconsciously affect other people's motives, attitudes, and buying decisions (in one or in many areas). Their influence is connected with non-formal communication, which is gaining more significance in current market conditions (Schiffman et al., 2008). Within reference groups, there is still another vital factor, i.e., the **family,** which appears as the most potent primary reference group. A distinction should be made between the so-called family of upbringing and the family of procreation. The latter, i.e., the spouse and children, exerts the most direct influence on a buyer's behavior, as it forms the most important social unit that buys goods and services. Other family factors determining consumer behavior include stage of family life cycle, so-called life transformations, arrangement of roles, model of decisions made in a family, and family demographic features, i.e., place of residence, professional activity, personal composition, and so on.

Consumer behavior is becoming more strongly determined by new tendencies and socio-cultural transformations that are related to consumption, such as changes in the amount of free time, better education, heightened professional activity of women, extension of the life cycle, reduction in the number of household/family members, changes in role assignment, and so on. In global terms, these tendencies are of a similar character; yet, compared to other determinants, cultural factors are less susceptible to processes of unification (Evans et al., 1996). Hence, it can be concluded that these factors are of greater significance for activities undertaken by companies in the European market. Processes of integration and globalization bring about cultural, civilization, and custom changes revealed in the fast diffusion of consumer behavior patterns and in the development of homogeneous consumer segments on a European scale. This, however, is not tantamount to the emergence of a typical **European consumer**. One can only speak of the existence of similar consumer types in all EU countries.

7.3.3   Demographic

Demographic determinants are among the most essential objective determinants of consumer behavior. They comprise age, gender, household size, stage of family life cycle, profession, education, race, and nationality, among others. Despite the growing influence of social, cultural, and psychological determinants on consumer behavior within the last decades, demographic determinants still remain essential variables characterizing the consumer. First of all, they differentiate needs, stimulate or inhibit definite consumer behavior, and determine the conditions of the occurrence of behavior. Additionally, they are easy to identify and constitute one of the fundamental criteria of market segmentation and typology. Demographic factors allow divisions based on generations, including the **Silent Generation** (year 1909-1945), the **Baby Boomers** (1946-1964), **Generation X** (1965-1980) and **Generation Y** (1981-1995) (Graham, 2010). People of the Silent Generation (today accounting for 26% of the population of Europe) grew up in the difficult and turbulent times of world wars, which resulted in predictability and rationality in their decisions. Unlike the Silent Generation, Baby Boomers (30% of the population) are people who, since their birth, have been setting trends: they contributed to the dynamic development of the toy industry in their childhood; their adolescence marked the time of the expansion of fast food chain restaurants; and during their adult life, they shaped the real estate market. Currently – on account of their age – they make demands concerning their health, physical, and mental fitness. Generation X (about 17% of the European population) is a generation of discouraged people, frightened by the perspective of a crisis; or they reject the hunt for money, and traditional values. While growing up, they began to set up their own businesses and establish families (Solomon et al., 2010).

Age is of considerable importance among the variables of consumer behavior. It is particularly vital during the initial and final stages of human life. With age, changes occur in people's needs and consumption volume, market decisions, and roles in the buying processes (Harcar et al., 2005). Age also marks boundaries of buying possibilities: children, for example, have a limited ability to take legal actions, whereas more senior people, due to their heath condition, are limited in their abilities to compare goods and to make purchases.

The case: Children as buyers on the Lithuanian market

At present, children and young people are an important group of buyers of market products. In Lithuania, the population of children and young people is in decline, yet every fifth person is under the age of 19. The role of children in buying decisions is growing proportionately to their age. In the early years, their influence concerns the purchase of sweets, favorite snacks, or toys. Teenagers, in turn, press for purchases of clothes and holidays, as well as act as initiators of purchases of consumer durables, particularly electronic equipment. According to research results, children have the greatest impact on the purchase of products to be used by them. Their influence is rather moderate with respect to activities undertaken by the whole family (vacation, restaurants), and the lowest when it comes to the purchase of consumer durables and expensive goods. In the case of consumer durables, though, children's role is most prominent in the initial stages of the decision-making process (problem recognition, information search) and less important in the phase of a product purchase. Children can also decide about certain aspects of a purchase, leaving other aspects to parents. Consequently, they make a decision about a cell phone model, yet the choice of the operator or the place of purchase, as well as the type of contract remains in the parental power.

Source: DG SANCO (2007)

Adulthood is the period of the greatest market activity, which is mainly due to the fact that the age of 35-55 is the time of achieving the highest income level during the whole lifetime. Consumers aged 35-44 spend most on household maintenance, cars, and entertainment. People aged 45-54 spend 30% more on foodstuffs and clothing and 57% more on savings within pension schemes than those in other age categories (Solomon et al., 2010). The increased expenses in maturity are a factor differentiating consumer behavior at various stages of adulthood because uniformity of lifestyles in different age groups leads to standardization of consumption within each group. However, 'attributing' definite products or brands to a definite age group is no longer valid. On the contrary, seeing that more mature consumers are interested in offers targeted at younger people, producers may decide to expand their offer with products addressed to older people, without tarnishing the image of a youth brand.

Elderly people constitute a very special group of consumers (Lambkin et al., 2001). In the monthly budgets of seniors, savings reaches a slightly lower level than that of working people. Elderly people make their purchases in a more planned and organized way. Several times a week, they buy food in small local stores close to their home. They form their opinions of market offers mainly on the basis of their knowledge and experience. Average expenses of senior households are higher compared to working households, as well as to expenses of all households. The expenses mainly concern basic goods: according to observations, the expenses connected to satisfaction of nutrition, accommodation, and health needs account for the largest share of all expenses. Households of senior people have a higher level of consumption of food (by about 20-30%), but a lower level of purchasing durable products. Additionally, the equipment used by senior households is not new (Harris, 2010).

Gender is another determinant of consumer behavior. Gender differences affect consumer expectations of market goods and services, consumer ways of buying goods, and roles in the decision-making process. The comparison of male and female shares in decision making has revealed that women are more frequent decision makers with respect to shopping and big purchase planning, whereas men make decisions about ways of gaining the means of need satisfaction. With regard to definite goods, it turns out that male decisions chiefly concern all technical parameters of a purchased product and whether the product will be bought or not. Women, in turn, take the lead in decisions concerning the appearance of the product (Schiffman and Kanuk, 2010).

Household size also belongs to the group of demographic determinants, which, together with income, determines the way a given household is furnished with consumer durables – the higher the number of family members, the better the standard of household furnishing with consumer durables. The average monthly consumption of food per capita decreases with an increase in the number of family members. It turns out that the average food consumption per capita of a one-member household is 20 to 85% higher than that of a multi-member household (Hawkins and Best, 2004).

Finally, the stage of family life cycle appears as an especially significant determinant of decision-making processes. Generally, the older the family, the more autonomic are the decisions made by its members. Households run by 20-year-olds have a lower level of average spending than other families, as income in this age group is lower. In the course of maturing, consumers achieve higher income levels (until retirement); and therefore, in time, they can afford to increase their expenses on luxuries, higher-quality home furnishings, better services, and food. These changes, however, entail other types of decisions and different ways of making them. The analysis of the family life cycle assumes the existence of breakthrough moments that change consumers' previous priorities into new ones. These moments include the establishment of a family, the birth of a child, leaving home by the last child, the death of a spouse, retirement, or even divorce. These types of experiences provoke substantial changes in the level and structure of consumption expenses (Solomon et al., 2010), as well as in the ways and models of decision making.

The case: Way of spending free time by Finish consumers

Research carried out in the Finish market reveals that numerous families prefer to spend their leisure in an active way – by participating in sports or tourism. Two-member families (childless) also prefer to spend their free time outside the home, but by meeting friends or going to the theater or museum. Additionally, they like tourism or meetings. Three-member families most frequently choose entertainment that does not require leaving home – watching TV or taking care of the house, animals, and garden. The interest in computer games grows proportionately to the number of family members, but declines with respect to the cinema and social activities.

Source: DG SANCO (2009)

Education is considered to be another key factor that has a determining influence on consumer market behavior. Accordingly, people with basic education prefer to watch TV, tend to their house or garden, or look after their animals – generally activities that do not require leaving home or making a physical or intellectual effort. They like to relax together at home (Blackwell et al., 2001). Quite an opposite approach is seen in people with tertiary and secondary education – they go in for sports and tourism more often than people of other educational levels. People with a bachelor's degree spend their free time visiting friends; shopping; and going to concert halls, theaters, and museums. The higher the level of education is, the greater the people's interest in the cinema, tourism, and social activities outside the home. The degree of attractiveness of watching TV and tending to one's own home declines with the level of education. A higher level of education causes a rise in independent decision making by males and females and a fall in mutual decision making or decisions made by children (Evans et al., 2009).

Race and nationality are the most potent determinants with respect to consumer eating customs and habits, and slightly less important for consumption of consumer durables and services. As a result of migrations, many countries have seen minority groups foster the development of ethnic markets, stores, and service points (Raymond, 2003). Consequently, they affect the local society, leading to the mixing of cultures. Nevertheless, some groups live in isolation, trying to preserve their native character. Affiliation with a consumer ethnic group affects degree of vulnerability to a media message, type of message, food preferences, political views, type of leisure, and readiness to try out new products.

7.3.4 Psychological

Differentiation of consumer behavior is explained through an array of objective factors. It is obvious, however, that **psychological factors** are of equal or even greater importance for determining individual consumer decisions. Today, one can observe that these factors are gaining more significance in developing countries, as well as in emerging markets, because improvement in a consumer's material situation blunts his/her sensitivity to economic conditions, thus opening the way for more personal factors like motives, preferences, and attitudes. These and other determinants form a group of subjective factors defined as intervening variables that influence people's buying decisions. Objective factors provide certain foundations, mostly material ones, for definite consumer decisions. However, these objective variables and the individual's response come under the influence of other, subjective factors (intermediary) that are mostly responsible for the shape of the final consumer reaction (Schiffman and Kanuk, 2010). Psychological determinants that greatly affect consumer buying behavior consist of: perception, remembering, learning, motivation, emotions, attitude, and personality.

It is not a coincidence that **perception** begins the list of intervening variables, as perception processes, i.e., recognition, selection, and organization and interpretation of stimuli in order to give some meaning to the surrounding world (Foxall and Goldsmith, 1998) underlie all kinds of human behavior, not only market behavior. Through perception, the consumer becomes aware of the existence of certain products and their attributes and is able to see differences between the brands and places of purchase. Hence, perception is a condition of and an introduction to every buying decision (Graham, 2010). The process of perception consists of two stages: in the first stage the individual receives signals from the external world by means of the five senses (Doole et al., 2005), and in the second stage, based on previous experience and obtained information, he/she interprets the received stimuli. The second stage of perception is especially vital, as it determines the way a message is integrated with the whole human knowledge; and it categorizes the information included in the message. Moreover, it can influence the way the information is distorted.

country	white	red	green	blue
Austria	innocence	anger	hope	faithfulness
Denmark	purity	danger	boredom	quality
Finland	neatness	love	envy	luck of money
France	youth	modesty	youthful	fear
Portugal	freedom	passion	envy	faithfulness
Sweden	goodness	anger	inexperience	credulity
Italy	luck of suc-cess	danger	luck of money	fear

Source: Komor (2000), p. 61

Figure 74. Differences in perception of color in selected European countries

In both stages, there occur phenomena that are typical of perception such as tendentious perception, selective attention, selective distortion, and remembering (Blackwell et al., 2001). These cause the consumer to notice mostly the stimuli that are essential for the satisfaction of life needs and that reinforce the consumer's current vision of reality and of himself/herself (e.g., the consumer spots products that he/she is already familiar with, that are in his/her favorite color, or that are most needed, etc.). Subsequently, the consumer interprets the stimuli in a way that best fits his/her outlook on life and reinforces previous beliefs (e.g., the consumer interprets price promotion of a favorite product as something attractive, although objectively it is not). Selective perception comes from a consumer's desire to keep his/her views in harmony, but it is also a way of dealing with the excessive information that the contemporary person is bombarded with. That is why people often see what they want to see, and the same object or event may be perceived and interpreted differently by two independent persons (Raymond, 2003). Therefore, companies must check and examine the way buyers receive their offer, since consumers make choices not on the basis of what is real, but what they perceive as real.

Perception is extremely important for the consumer during the process of gaining informa-tion. However, for decision making, it is equally important to transform, order, keep, and properly use information stored in memory, in other words, to learn and to remember things. Processes of learning and remembering are strictly connected with perception, as the person learns and draws conclusions from what he/she perceives. However, without processes of remembering and referring to previous experience, it would be impossible to interpret the things that are continuously provided by the processes of perception.

Knowledge about the **processes of remembering and learning** may be used effectively in developing consumer behavior (Diller et al., 2006). The laws of psychology related to mem-ory organization are applied in marketing to define the conditions of remembering advertis-ing stimuli better, e.g., for establishing the frequency of message transmissions indispensable for message remembering, positioning a given message among many other messages, provi-sion of message background, type of a message, and so on (Doole et al., 2005). Classical conditioning is employed in building a brand image and in reinforcing positive emotions associated with a product. Instrumental marketing, in turn, is not only used in promotion strategies, but also in development of consumer brand loyalty. As for cognitive theories, they are most commonly used in the process of introducing complicated innovations, whose pur-chase requires deeper thinking. The theories are also referred to in pricing strategy because price is a significant selection criterion considered by buyers (Blythe, 1997).

Repeated behavior or decisions that provide the individual with a positive outcome result in the development of **habits,** which are another psychological determinant of consumer beha-vior. A habit is not an example of concrete behavior, but it is the ability (tendency) to react to a certain stimulus in a definite (regular) way. Habitual behavior is automatic and does not require concentration or thinking; whereby it belongs to lower forms of human behavior. Despite this, it plays an essential role in decision-making processes (mainly the routine ones), as it determines the purchase of just one specific item (Johnson, 1998).

Motivation is another example of a factor determining consumer behavior in the market. It is defined as an internal process that conditions human endeavors to reach certain goals or as activation, an incentive or a reason for initiation or continuation of a certain behavior (Ray-mond, 2003). Motivation has its own direction (it is oriented to reaching a certain goal) and intensity (Hawkins and Best, 2004). Intensification of motivation depends on the importance and intensity of the need that generated the motivation. However, the choice of a concrete direction and action as well as the ultimate goal is made on the basis of a consumer's mental (cognitive) processes and previous experience. It is worth mentioning the fact that motivation may be of a positive character (when the consumer seeks something worth the effort, when he/she wants to improve his/her current condition) or a negative character (when the individual, through a certain activity, wants to avoid negative phenomena, wants to protect himself/herself against something) (Schiffman and Kanuk, 2010). Along with these two types of motives, there exist some other types, including internal and external, innate and acquired, primary and secondary, general and selective, rational and emotional, and conscious or unconscious (Diller et al., 2006). Motives are most commonly distinguished on the basis of their characteristics – the description of what they refer to, i.e., a concrete need (e.g., hunger, safety, affiliation, etc.). Consequently, a practical classification of motivation is concurrent with a classification of needs.

The establishment of the motives and needs behind consumer needs is of key importance for an effective marketing policy designed to satisfy them. Nonetheless, it is a difficult task because the motives underlying certain behavior are generally quite varied. People buy products not only on account of their functional value, but also to impress other people, indulge their whims, improve their social position, or spend earned money. Nonetheless, even a very precise definition of consumer needs does not guarantee success, as the most difficult task for the manager is to transform a need into an actual motivation, i.e., to persuade the consumer who experiences some lack to take concrete actions. Moreover, one motive can spur actions aimed at different goals (objects). These actions are equally capable of satisfying the consumer's initial need (e.g., hunger may provoke the consumer to prepare a meal or order a pizza by phone), so it is difficult to predict possible consumer behavior upon generation of a certain motive. Despite these problems, attempts are made to apply the theory of motivation in practice, especially to develop effective promotional messages (Solomon et al., 2010).

Emotions have a great impact on consumer cognitive and decision-making processes. Sources in the literature distinguish between emotions, as consciously experienced, subjective psychical conditions accompanying daily experiences, and moods, as affective states of lower intensity and relatively short duration (Evans et al., 1996). Basic emotions consist of interest, joy, surprise, fear, anger, worry, disgust, contempt, shame, and feelings of guilt.

The greatest influence of emotions on a person is revealed in the way they determine the direction of human actions, as people tend to avoid objects and situations that bring displeasure, and choose those that bring pleasure. In terms of consumer behavior, emotions are especially important because they have a direct impact on market decisions (mainly impulsive decisions, often evoked by the buyer's good mood), as well as on other subjective factors by modifying their influence on consumer behavior. Accordingly, emotions determine perception, foster perception selectivity, and thus influence the processes of learning and remembering, as, according to research results, a positive mood stimulates active integration of incoming data with various information categories present in the human cognitive process. A negative mood, in turn, works the opposite way. It hinders the process of learning and remembering. Finally, emotions mold attitudes, one of their important attributes (Diller et al., 2006). The emotions experienced by the consumer at a given moment, as well as the emotions displayed in advertising, determine consumer reception of and consumer reaction to an advertisement. This fact is of particular importance from a practical point of view. Study results show that positive emotions improve susceptibility to advertising and facilitate remembering of the products and brands presented. At the same time, it was concluded that commercials should not be played at key moments during interesting films or during very aggressive programs, as this lowers the chance of reaching the viewer with a positive message while he/she is experiencing strong negative emotions (aroused by the program content or a commercial break) (Doole et al., 2005).

Attitude is another factor determining consumer behavior. Attitude is a relatively constant and coherent assessment defining a person's approach to a certain object, item, or idea (Kotler et al., 2009). Attitudes indicate the individual's knowledge and feelings, which reflect either positive or negative approaches towards a given object. Additionally, they reveal themselves in definite beliefs and behavior. All this is linked to the concept of a system of attitudes composed of the following components: a behavioral component comprising the intentions of behavior ('I plan to buy healthy food'), a behavior component ('I buy food items from healthy food stores'), a cognitive component ('I know that ecologically grown vegetables contain more antioxidants and fewer nitrates'), an emotional component ('I like eating healthy food'), and finally the attitude itself as a total evaluation including its other components ('I am for the development of ecological farming and the selling of healthy food') (Evans et al., 2009). Attitudes, including those concerning products, buying customs, and places of purchase, can be acquired by assimilation from other consumers (e.g., from parents, peers) or through one's own behavior and experience (e.g., as a result of trying our various products) (Graham, 2010).

Consumer attitudes towards products, stores, store clerks, promotional forms, and advertising media have apparent impact on consumer market behavior because the individual notices the positive features of an object that he/she is positively predisposed to. Consequently, a positive attitude towards product advertising is often reflected in a positive attitude towards a promoted product. Basing buying decisions on one's own established attitudes is comfortable for customers since consistent behavior towards similar products (e.g., loyalty to a footwear brand or a domestic appliances brand) saves time and energy needed for developing one's own opinion about other offers, and simultaneously reduces the risk of making a wrong decision. Therefore, changing long-established consumer attitudes is a very difficult task. Nonetheless, companies undertake actions to mold and modify them by resorting to persuasive techniques and messages (Hawkins and Best, 2004). On the other hand, there are factors that weaken the relationship between attitude and behavior (e.g., limited financial resources), which leads to a situation where even a very positive consumer attitude towards a product does not end in a purchase (e.g., in the case of a Volvo car).

Consumer personality is the last, but not least, subjective determinant of consumer behavior broadly discussed in the literature. In fact, it appears as the outcome of the existence and influence of all the previously discussed psychical factors. There are no unanimous definitions of this category. Most frequently, it is referred to as a relatively permanent psychical construction of individual features, which both determine and reflect the way the individual responds to the environment. Examples of such features – personality components – include self-confidence, autonomy, adaptability, dominance, order, emotional stability, independence, respect, sociability, shyness, and so forth (Solomon et al., 2010).

On the one hand, personality is the expression of the unique and different character of each individual person, who is capable of showing distinctive reactions to a particular stimulus. On the other hand, the fact that personality presents a set of certain features allows for recognition of similarities between people with respect to one or several characteristics (e.g., innovation). This provides an incentive for development of consumer typologies and market segmentation, and even for making forecasts about consumer behavior on the basis of research into personality. Unfortunately, it turns out that the possibilities of personality variables, both in market segmentation and in forecasting consumer buying decisions, are limited (Foxall and Goldsmith, 1998). Therefore, marketers have begun to refer to so-called psychography (psychographics), which presents a psychological portrait of the consumer, partially based on personality analysis and measurement of actual consumer behavior, interests, and opinions (Schiffman and Kanuk, 2010). This method is helpful in defining the individual's lifestyle by combining subjective variables with demographic features such as age, profession, and income. These characteristics are used to develop consumer profiles that are similar in terms of activities and ways of product consumption. Thus, psychography is useful from the perspective of market segmentation, product positioning, and elaboration of promotional campaigns.

To sum up, consumer behavior, especially analyzed from an international and a global perspective, appears to be a very complex and varied category. The research into consumer behavior constitutes a multi-faceted and multi-dimensional process, which makes it impossible for researchers to describe all consumer behavior issues in one single research event. This, however, should not prevent scientists from making attempts at a detailed description of selected issues. The collection of such research results will contribute to better knowledge about the consumer and to adaptation of market offers to consumer needs and expectations in the international market.

List of References

Angheluta, A-V. & Zaharia, R., 2010. Contribution of Romanian product and company brands to the creation and the development of Romanian's country brand. In: Smyczek, S. & Glowik, M., *Consumer behavior and marketing strategies of companies in the European market*. Katowice: UE.

Antonides G. & van Raaij, W. F., 2003. *Consumer behavior. European perspective*. New York: John Wiley & Sons, Ltd.

Arnold, E., Price, L. & Zinkhan, G., 2004. *Consumer*. Boston: Irwin.

Balan, C., 2010. New trends in distribution on FMCG market – case study of Romania. In: Smyczek, S. & Glowik, M., *Consumer behavior and marketing strategies of companies in the European market*. Katowice: UE.

Baumeister, R. F., 2002. Yielding to temptation: self-control failure, impulsive purchasing and consumer behavior. *Journal of Consume Research*, 28: 128-152.

Beatty, S. E. & Ferrell, M. E., 1998. Impulsive buying: modeling its precursors. *Journal of Retailing,* 74 (2): 4-27.

Belch, M. A. & Willis, L. A., 2002. Family decision at the turn of the century: has the changing structure of households impacted the family decision-making process? *Journal of Consumer Behavior*, 2 (2): 51-78.

Bendapudi, N. & Berry, L. L., 1997. Customers' motivations for maintaining relationships with service providers. *Journal of Retailing*, 73 (1): 129-149.

Best, R., 2009. *Market-based management: international version*. London: Pearson Higher Education.

Blackwell, R. D., Miniard, P. W. & Engel, J. F., 2001. *Consumer behavior*. Fort Worth: Dryden.

Blythe, J., 1997. *Essence consumer behavior*. New York: Financial Times Press.

Bone, F. P., 1995. Word-of-mouth effects on short-term and long-term product judgments. *Journal of Business Research*, 32: 72-98.

Burgiel, A. & Sowa, I., 2008. *Rola poszczegolnych czlonkow rodziny w procesie decyzyjnym*. Katowice: AE.

Bywalec, C. & Rudnicki, L., 1999. *Podstawy teorii i metodyki badan konsumpcji*. Krakow: AE.

Bywalec, C., 2007. *Konsumpcja w teorii i praktyce gospodarowania*. Warszawa: PWN.

Chavda, H., Haley, M. & Dunn, C., 2005. Adolescents' influence on family decision-making. *Young Consumers*, 6: 224-251.

Chumpitaz-Caceres, R. & Paparoidamis, N. G., 2007. Service quality, relationship satisfaction, trust, commitment and business-to-business loyalty. *European Journal of Marketing*, 41 (7/8): 409-428.

Cowell, P., 2001. Marketing to children: a quid for students and practitioners. *Marketing Review*, 2: 3-27.

Csaba, L., 1995. *The capitalist revolution in Eastern Europe. A contribution to the economic theory of systemic change*. Aldershot: Edward Elgar.

Davis, J. J., 1994. Good ethics is good for business: ethical attributions and response to environmental advertising. *Journal of Business Ethics*, 13 (11): 78-92.

DG SANCO, 2007. Consumers in Europe [online]. [cited 17.10.2010]. Available from World Wide Web: http://epp.eurostat.ec.europa.eu/cache/ITY_OFFPUB/KS-DY-07-001/EN/KS-DY-07-001-EN.

DG SANCO, 2009. The status of health in European Union [online]. [cited 24.10.2010]. Available from World Wide Web: http://euglorehcd.eulogos.it/IXT/_EXTREP/_INDEX.HTM

DG SANCO, 2010. Health program in Finland [online]. [cited 12.10.2010]. Available from World Wide Web: http://ec.europa.eu/dgs/health_consumer/finland/index_en.htm.

Dickson, P. R. & Sawyer, A. G., 1990. The price knowledge and search of supermarkets shoppers. *Journal of Marketing*: 54, 62-86.

Diller, S., Shedroff, N. & Rhea, D., 2006. *Making meaning: how successful businesses deliver meaningful customer experiences*. London: New Riders.

Dolinski, D., 2003. *Psychologiczne mechanizmy reklamy*. Gdansk: GWP.

Doole, I., Lancaster, P. & Lowe, R., 2005. *Understanding and managing customers*. New York: Financial Times Press.

Duhan, D., Johnson, S., Wilcox, J. & Harrell, G., 1997. Influences on consumer use of word-of-mouth recommendation sources. *Journal of Academy of Marketing Science*, 25 (4): 145-166.

Eggert, A. & Ulaga, W., 2002. Customer-perceived value: a substitute for satisfaction in business markets? *Journal of Business and Industrial Marketing*, 17 (2/3): 214-238.

Eurostat, 2009. Disposable Income – Real Terms [online]. [cited 10.11.2010]. Available from World Wide Web: http://epp.eurostat.ec.europa.eu/portal/page/portal/product_results/.

Evans, M., Foxall, G. & Jamal, A., 2009. *Consumer behaviour*. New York: John Wiley & Sons.

Evans, M., Moutinho, L. & van Raaij, W. F., 1996. *Applied consumer behaviour*, Harlow: Addison-Wesley Publisher.

Falkowski, A. & Tyszka, T., 2009. *Psychologia zachowan konsumenckich*. Gdansk: GWP.

Fey, C. J., 1994. Royalties from loyalties. *Journal of Business Strategy*, 4 (4): 42-65.

Foxall, G. R. & Goldsmith, R. E., 1998. *Psychologia konsumneta i reklamy*. Warszawa: PWN.

Gajewski, S., 1994. *Zachowanie sie konsumenta a wspolczesny marketing*. Lodz: UL.

Garbarino, E. & Johnson, M., 1999. The different role of satisfaction, trust and commitment in customer relationship. *Journal of Marketing*, 63 (2): 23-47.

Garbarski, L., 1999. *Zachowania nabywcow*. Warszawa: PWE.

Gefen, D. & Straub, D., 2003. Managing user trust in B2C e-services. *E-service Journal*, 2: 4-21.

Geuens, M., Pelsmacker, P. & Mast, G., 2003. How family structure affects parent-child communication about consumption. *Advertising and Marketing to Children*, January-March: 76-98.

Gilly, M., Graham, J., Wolfinbarger F. M. & Yale, L., 1998. A dyadic study of interpersonal information search. *Journal of Academy of Marketing Science*, 26 (2): 112-139.

Graham, J., 2010. *Critical thinking in consumer behavior: cases and experiential exercises*. New Jersey: Prentice Hall.

Grether, D. & Wilde L., 1994. An analysis of conjunctive choice – theory and experiments. *Journal of Consumer Research*, 4: 33-52.

GUS, 2010. *Badania budzetow gospodastw domowych*. Warszawa: GUS Publisher.

Harcar, T., Spillan J. E. & Kucukemiroglu, O., 2005. A multi-national study of family decision-making. *Multinational Business Review*, 13: 72-91.

Harris, E. K., 2010. *Customer service: a practical approach*. London: Pearson Higher Education.

Hawkins, D. I. & Best, C. R., 2004. *Consumer behavior: building marketing strategy*. Boston: McGrae-Hill.

Hofstede, G., 2000. *Kultury i organizacje*. Warszawa: PWE.

Jachnis, A. & Terelak, J., 1998. *Psychologia konsumenta i reklamy*. Bydgoszcz: Branta.

Jachnis, A., 2007. *Psychologia konsumenta*. Warszawa: Branta.

Johnson, M. D., 1998. *Customer orientation and market action*. New Jersey: Prentice Hall.

Kahneman, D. & Tversky, A., 2000. *Choice, values, and frames*. Cambridge: Cambridge University Press.

Karcz, K. & Kedzior, Z., 2004. Behaviour of market entities in Poland and the process of European integration. *Journal of Economics and Management*, 1: 69-80.

Kassarjian, H. H. & Robertson, T. S., 1991. *Perspectives in consumer behavior*. New Jersey: Prentice Hall.

Kiezel, E. (ed.), 2010. *Konsument i jego zachowania na rynku europejskim*. Warszawa: PWE.

Kita, J., 2006. *Nakup a predaj*. Bratislava: Ekonom.

Komor, M., 2000. *Euromarketing*. Warszawa: 2000.

Kotler, Ph., Armstrong, G., Saunders, J. & Wong, V., 2002. *Principles of Marketing*. New York: Pearson Higher Education.

Kotler, Ph. & Keller, K., 2009. *Framework for marketing management*. New York: Pearson Higher Education.

Kotler, Ph., Keller, K., Brady, M., Goodman, M. & Hansen, T., 2009. *Marketing management: first European edition*. London: Prentice Hall.

Kwai-Choi, L. C. & Marshall, R., 1998. Measuring influence in the family decision making process using an observational method. *Qualitative Market Research*, 1 (2): 17-32.

Lackman, C. & Lanasa, J., 1993. Family decision-making theory: an overview and assessment. *Psychology and Marketing*, March-April: 261-282.

Lambkin, M., Foxall, G., van Raaij, F. & Heilbrunn, B., 2001. *European perspective on consumer behaviour*. London: Prentice Hall Europe.

Lewis, D. & Bidger, D., 2001. *The soul of the new consumer*. London: Nicholas Brealey Publishing.

Marinov, M., Petrovici, D. & Marinova, S., 2008. Consumer attitudes toward advertising in Bulgaria and Romania. *Journal of Euromarketing*, 17 (2): 81-93.

Matysiewicz, J., 2010. Building relationship on healthcare market – Polish patients perspec-tive. In: Smyczek, S. & Glowik, M., *Consumer behavior and marketing strategies of companies in the European market*. Katowice: UE.

Molnar, A., Gellynck, X. & Felfoldi, J., 2006. Belgian and Hungarian producer organizations in the fruit and vegetable sector: comparison of experiences. In: Chadraba, P. & Springer, R., *Marketing and business strategies for Central and Eastern European countries*. Vienna: Vienna University of Economics and Business Administration.

Mowen, J. C., 1987. *Consumer behavior*. New York: Macmillan Publishing Co.

Neymann, M., 2005. *Komunikacja i kultura biznesu w Europie*. Warszawa: WSPiZ.

Palan, K. M. & Wilkes, R. E., 1997. Adolescent-parent interaction in family decision making. *Journal of Consumer Research*, 24: 3-24.

Raymond, M., 2003. *Tomorrow people: future consumers and how to read them*. New York: Financial Times Press.

Rudnicki, L., 2000. *Zachowania konsumentow na rynku*. Warszawa: PWE.

Schiffman, L. G., Bednall, D., O'Cass, A., Paladino, A., D'Alessandro, S. & Kanuk, L. L., 2008. *Consumer behaviour*. New Jersey: Prentice Hall.

Schiffman, L. G. & Kanuk, L. L., 2006. *Consumer behavior*. New Jersey: Prentice Hall.

Schiffman, L. G., & Kanuk, L. L., 2010. *Consumer behavior: global edition*. London: Pearson Higher Education.

Smyczek, S. & Sowa, I., 2005. *Konsument na rynku – zachowania, modele, aplikacje*. Warszawa: Difin.

Smyczek, S., 2007. *Modele zachowan konsumentow na rynku uslug finansowych*. Katowice: E.

Solomon, M. R., Bamossy, G. & Askegaard, S., 1999. *Consumer behaviour. A European perspective*. Paris: Prentice Hall Europe.

Solomon, M. R., Bamossy, G., Askegaard, S. & Hogg, M. K., 2010. *Consumer behaviour*. New York: Financial Times Press.

Thaler, R., 1985. Mental accounting and consumer choice. *Marketing Science*, 4: 61-79.

Urban, W. & Simieniako, D., 2008. *Lojalnosc klientow. Modele, motywacja i pomiar*. Warszawa: PWN.

8   Chapter: Consumer behavior application in international marketing

- Describe the process of international market segmentation.

- List the types of criteria used for segmentation in the international market.

- Identify the strategies of market targeting.

- Characterize the different types of loyalty programs.

- Explain the role of satisfaction in creating consumer loyalty.

- Present the process of increasing company profits through consumer loyalty

- Describe new consumer behavior trends in the international market.

- List the features of the modern consumer in the European market.

8.1 Market segmentation, targeting and positioning – an international approach

Contemporary consumer behavior in international markets is characterized by great complexity and dynamic change (Rugman and Collinson, 2009). In most cases, the needs and preferences of buyers who constitute a defined group and local market are very diverse. The so-called average consumer is nonexistent. Still, it is necessary to establish buyer profiles that can be used as a benchmark in evaluating corporate marketing activities and in developing new ones. Therefore, determining and examining differences between consumers and consumer groups, as well as dividing consumers into definite groups, constitute an essential element of the market segmentation process. Market segmentation is necessary for several reasons (Crane, 2000; Han et al., 2009).

- Not all buyers are the same.
- A group of buyers of a specific product consists of subgroups sharing similar behavior and value systems.
- Targeting activities aimed at a smaller number of similar consumers is easier and more effective.

Market segmentation is division of a potential target market into homogeneous groups of buyers (segments) according to some criteria. These buyers share similar needs and preferences, as well as reactions to specific marketing activities (Schiffman and Kanuk, 2010). According to Doole and Lowe (2001), market segmentation is the strategy by which a firm partitions a market into sub-markets or segments likely to manifest similar responses to marketing input. That is why a market segment consists of a large group of identifiable consumers within a market with similar wants, purchasing power, geographical location, buying attitudes, or buying habits (Kotler, 2000). Market segments refer to groups of consumers, in contrast to the widespread application of the term to industry product sectors.

However, it is important to note that many forms of consumer classification are not true segments either, i.e., they are not based on consumer needs, motivations, and resulting behavior but are 'profile' or 'characteristic' demographic variables, such as gender, age, income, occupation, and social class. These may sometimes appear to align with differences in buyer behavior but often do not cause or explain them (Clarke and Wilson, 2009; Blythe, 2009). To be useful, a market segment must be (Kotler, 2000)

- **measurable** – the size, purchasing power, and characteristics of the segment can be determined;
- **substantial** – the segments are large and profitable enough to serve; a segment should be the largest possible homogeneous group worth going after with a tailored marketing program;
- **accessible** – the segments can be effectively reached and served;
- **able to be differentiated** – the segments are conceptually distinguishable and respond differently to various marketing-mix elements and programs; and
- **actionable** – effective programs can be formulated for attracting and serving the segments.

The basic intention is that by segmenting a market, it may be possible to align a firm's offering more closely to the needs of a particular group of consumers than can a firm that does not recognize different segments. The firm that does this becomes a preferred supplier. Kotler (2000) maintains that segmentation is an approach midway between mass marketing and individual marketing. Ahmad and Buttle (2001) urge marketers to present flexible market offerings instead of a standard offering to all members within a segment. A flexible market offering consists of two parts: 1) a naked solution consisting of product elements that all segment members value and 2) options that some segment members value.

The problem of market segmentation is particularly relevant in international marketing. The need for international segmentation results from differences in conditions existing in foreign markets (Muhlbacher et al., 2006). Features of demographic, economic, political, legal, technological, or cultural conditions affect, among other things, the level of income, buying power, customer behavior patterns in the market, as well as customer needs and preferences with regard to products and other marketing activities. International market segmentation is a process of identifying specific segments as country groups and – within them – as groups of buyers representing potential customers with similar features and behavior (Doole and Lowe, 2001). The process of international market segmentation is more complex than domestic market segmentation, and it consists of five stages (Best, 2009; Wiktor et al., 2008; Hunerberg, 1994):

- macrosegmentation,
- microsegmentation,
- cross-border segmentation (transnational),
- selection of a target market, and
- market positioning.

The process of market segmentation in international marketing is presented in Figure 75. During Stage I, companies – through macro segmentation – divide international markets in terms of their geographic location and group countries into regions. For example, in Europe the regions are the following: Nordic Europe (Finland, Sweden, Denmark, Norway), Anglo-Saxon Europe (UK, Ireland), Mediterranean Europe (Spain, Portugal, Greece, Italy), and Central Europe (the Baltic States). The aim of the process is to evaluate the attractiveness of countries in terms of the threats posed and the opportunities countries offer as potential markets, and to select foreign markets that ensure the most favorable conditions for corporate expansion and development (Kotler et al., 2009). The Pareto law usually applies to international marketing segmentation with its full vigor. The most broad-based and well-established international firms find that 20 percent of the countries they serve generate at least 80 percent of the results (Doole and Lowe, 2001). Obviously these countries must receive greater managerial attention and allocation of resources.

When distinguishing country groups according to their geographic position, it has been assumed that neighboring countries share certain common features and elements of buying behavior (Doyle and Stern, 2006; Blythe, 2009). Nonetheless, there are some exceptions to this rule. Poland and the Czech and Slovak Republics, for example, share many similarities, including language. However, consumers of these countries greatly differ from neighboring Hungarian consumers in terms of their language and culture.

STAGE I – MACRO SEGMENTATION

1.Evaluation of political, economic, socio-cultural, legal, and other conditions.
2.Evaluation of threats and opportunities.
3.Sector and internal evaluation.

Country selection

STAGE II – MICRO SEGMENTATION

1.Demographic, psychographic, behavioral, and market potential criteria.
2. Internal conditions (corporate mission, corporate and marketing goals, know-how, etc).

Segment identification in particular foreign markets

STAGE III – CROSS-BORDER SEGMENTATION

Segment comparison in the international cross-section.

Identification of transnational segments

STAGE IV – SELECTION OF TARGET MARKET

Evaluation of particular segments.

Selection decision

STAGE V – MARKET POSITIONING

Evaluation of company position in particular segments.

Position identification

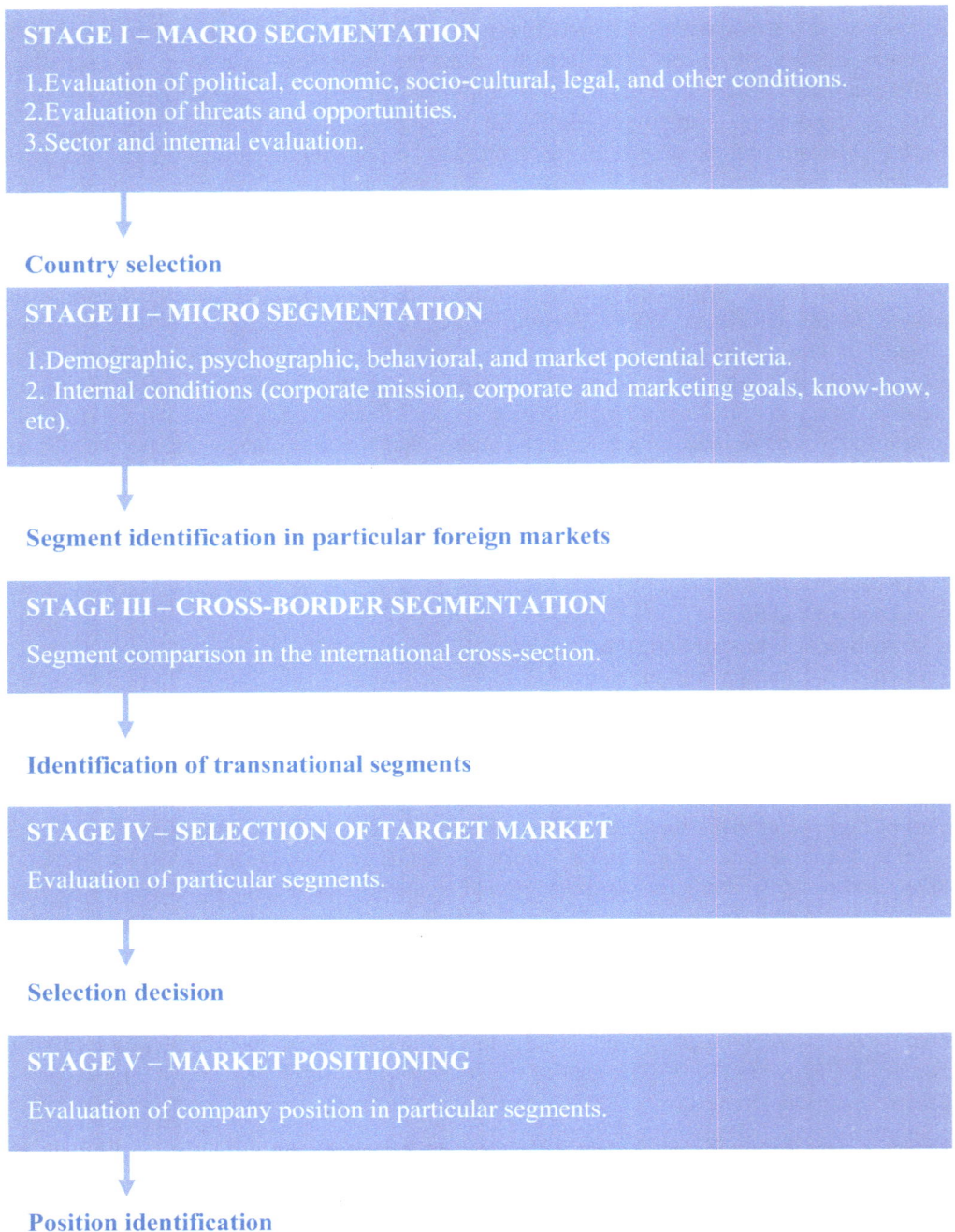

Source: Hunerberg (1994) p. 112; Wiktor et al., (2008) p.85; Best (2009) p. 109;

Figure 75. The process of market segmentation in international marketing.

When approaching macrosegmentation, a company should not only analyze and assess the general conditions of running a business activity in particular countries, but also look at the market situation with regard to a concrete product group. Here, it is important to analyze the threats and opportunities connected to the company's operation in a given country, examine sector conditions, and evaluate potential expansion markets in terms of the internal possibilities of the company's resources (de Mooij, 2010).

At Stage II of the international segmentation analysis, a company isolates market segments within national markets. Thus, it activates the process of **microsegmentation**. The internal segmentation analysis is especially useful for large countries and for countries with great market potential. From all possible segments, a company chooses one or several that, on the one hand, open up opportunities for the best possible use of the company's competitive advantage in its marketing strategy, and, on the other hand, ensure long-lasting maintenance of this advantage (Evans et al., 2009; Johansson, 2006).

At Stage III of the segmentation analysis, it is essential to establish whether the number of similarities displayed in the international cross-section of segments is sufficient for employing the same marketing program or only some of its elements across all the segments. Determination of a **transnational segment** or even a global market segment allows for standardization of marketing activities (Hatton, 2000; Johansson, 2006). Stage IV of the international market segmentation process involves assessing each particular segment, and then choosing one or more segments that a given company wants to be active in. Thus, a company chooses a **target market** (Usunie and Lee, 2009). Finally, at Stage V, the company needs to **position** products or brands into those segments.

Companies that intend to initiate marketing activities in different markets should conduct a comparative analysis of the demographic, economic, political, legal, techno-technological, natural, and cultural conditions of these markets. The purpose of the macrosegmentation analysis is to determine the best directions for foreign expansion. This involves evaluating both the current and future environmental conditions through analysis of threats and opportunities for a company's development in each particular market (de Burca et al., 2004).

Special attention should be paid to the criteria used for evaluating the environment in foreign markets. The criteria most commonly employed in the process of international segmentation include (Wiktor et al., 2008; Blythe, 2009)

- the demographic environment – the size of the population and the population growth rate, the structure of the population regarding age, the population density, the geographic distribution of the population, etc.;
- the economic environment – the rate of economic growth, price movements, changes in employment, payment balance sheet, total investment rate, sector investment rate, currency exchange rate, level of inflation, household income structure, etc.;
- the political and legal environment – confidence in the political system; legal regulations concerning setting up companies, company branches, and units in foreign markets; the customs and non-tariff instrument system; systems of foreign trade financing; the system of export insurance; the tax system; etc.;

- the technical and technological environment – the level of technological advancement in the country, especially of the technological sector; spending on research and development; inventions and patents; technical infrastructure; technical, technological, and organizational trends in a specific foreign market; etc.;
- the natural environment – the country surface area, climatic conditions, topographic features, natural resources, natural environment management, the condition of the natural environment, etc.; and
- the cultural environment – preferences, likes, and tastes of individuals, households, or social groups; customs and consumption traditions; religion; consumer ethnocentrism; education; attitude to foreign investors; etc.

The case: Cultural and lifestyle segmentation of the European car market

It has been possible to define six areas with respect to consumer attitudes towards cars sold across Europe: the Northern group (Scandinavia), North-Western group (Great Britain, Ireland, and Iceland), the Center group (the area of 'German mentality', covering Germany, Austria, and Switzerland), the Western group (French-speaking countries, including Belgium and Switzerland), the Southern group (the Mediterranean area, covering the area of Spanish, Italian, Portuguese, and Greek languages), and part of Central and Eastern Europe. Language areas reflect cultural and lifestyle communities of citizens in particular groups of countries.

For example, Central and Eastern European countries (like Slovakia or Romania) were chosen as the location for the plants of such companies as Peugeot, Citroen, and Volkswagen. These companies decided to invest in those countries on account of the good location, positive economic conditions, good development prospects, and low labor costs compared to the Western European countries.

Source: Samar (2011)

The market selection is most commonly conducted by means of analytical methods and portfolio analyses (Evans et al., 1996; Han et al., 2009). The analytical methods are based on a selection of indices characteristic of the countries under comparison, determination of the index border values, and elimination of less attractive countries from further analysis (Sagan, 2010). The procedure for the analysis consists of several stages:

- preparation of a list of selection criteria and development of a hierarchy of markets by means of value weights reflecting the significance of the criteria for potential expansion;
- determination of a point rating scale for particular criteria;
- evaluation of particular countries; this assessment is first rating-based, and then weight-based; and
- comparison of foreign markets according to their total points, and the choice of the most attractive markets on the basis of the largest number of points.

The traditional practice in international market segmentation is to use the business portfolio matrix. It is indicative of the approach taken by many companies. In this analysis, markets are classified into three categories (Doole and Lowe, 2001; Johansson, 2006).

- **Primary markets** – these markets indicate the best opportunities for long-term strategic development. Companies may want to establish a permanent presence and so embark on a thorough program.
- **Secondary markets** – these are markets where opportunities are identified but political or economic risk is perceived as being too high to make long-term irrevocable commitments. These markets would be handled in a more pragmatic way due to the potential risks that have been identified. A comprehensive marketing information system would be needed.
- **Tertiary markets** – these are the catch-what-you-can markets. These markets will be perceived as high risk and so the allocation of resources will be minimal. Objectives in such countries would be short term and opportunistic; companies would make no real commitment. No significant research would be carried out.

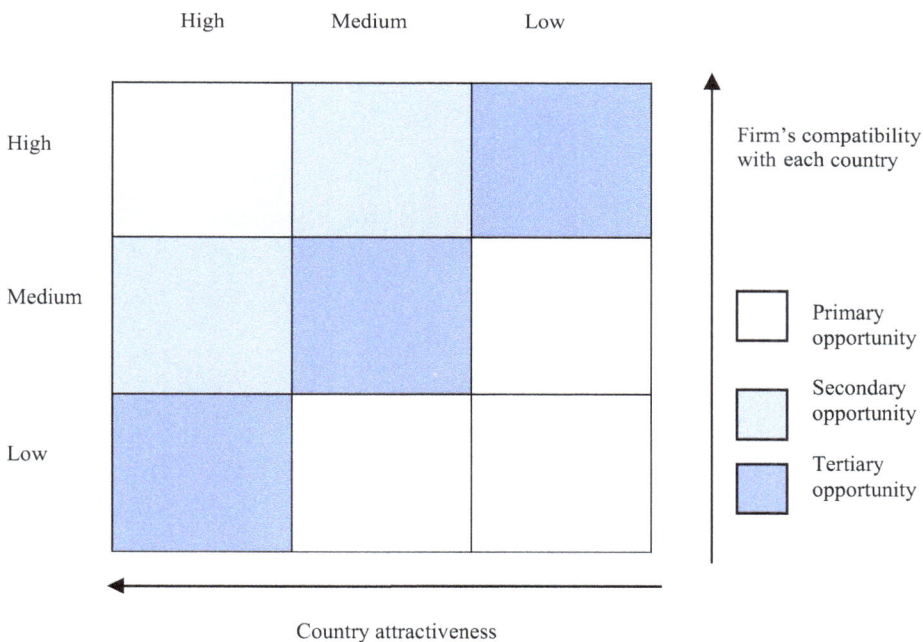

Source: Doole and Lowe (2001), p. 102

Figure 76. Business portfolio matrix in segmentation

Figure 76 shows the business portfolio matrix. The horizontal axis evaluates the attractiveness of each country on objective and measurable criteria (e.g., size, stability, and wealth). The vertical axis evaluates the firm's compatibility with each country on a more subjective and judgmental basis. Primary markets would score high on both axes. The next step in international segmentation is micro segmentation. It is based on the internal differentiation of markets within particular markets. The principle of selection of a segment within a country has been presented in Figure 77. Segmentation criteria applied in the internal analysis of national markets can be split into two groups: descriptive variables and behavioral variables.

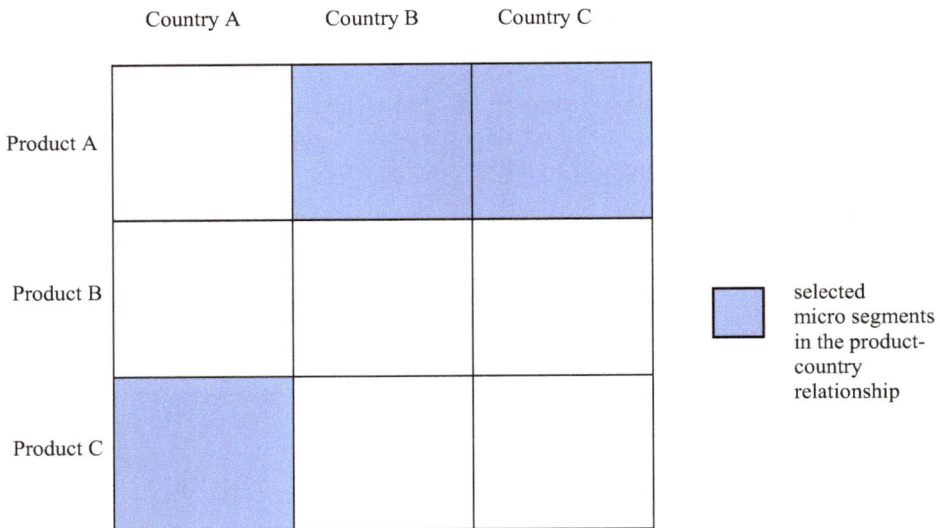

Source: Hollensen (2009), p. 121

Figure 77. Selection of product-country segments

The first group of criteria – descriptive variables – permits the identification of a potential buyer on the basis of the so-called general features or descriptive market segmentation variables, which include demographic, social, economic, and geographic criteria. Thanks to them, it is possible to answer the question of who the buyer of a given product is. The most common and relatively easy-to-measure variables are the following: gender, age, place of living, income, education, profession, family size, and social class (Schiffman et al., 2008; Johansson, 2006). It is most common for companies operating in foreign markets to use geographic criteria, as residents of specific countries or regions demonstrate similar demand and similar preferences.

The case: 'Singles' as an international segment

The 'single' segment is made up of unmarried, high-income people who live a life of consumption and are open to novelties. They are frequent buyers of high-quality products that either provide them with a sense of saving time or are associated with physical fitness or personal development. Products that are most popular with singles include fitness clubs, language schools, or dancing classes. Single people are more frequent users of laundry services, cleaning companies, and entertainment centers: pubs, restaurants, and cinemas. They are also attractive to travel agencies, banks, and cell phone networks.

Source: Wiktor et al., (2008)

For the second group of criteria – behavioral criteria – the main focus is on people's buying patterns and behavior mechanisms. The criteria help to establish what buyers buy as well as when, where, how, and why they buy, and to determine patterns of their reactions to marketing-mix instruments. Objective criteria describing consumer features are especially useful in the process of market segmentation of goods satisfying basic needs, whereas criteria describing consumer behavior are applied in the process of identifying buyers of higher-level goods and services. Many markets require application of both general and behavioral segmentation criteria (Solomon et al., 2010; Blythe, 2009).

The case: Multi-criteria consumer segmentation on the basis of WVS

The World Value Survey allows segmentation in which many criteria are used simultaneously in international markets. WVS concerns evaluation of value structures across a majority of countries. The segmentation is performed on the basis of the dimensions of a defining value, the so-called Schwart's motivating domain (Lubke and Muthen, 2005). The dimensions defining the system of consumer values consist of
- traditionalist values (good, ecology, conservative),
- materialistic values (innovations, wealth, entertainment, success, risk), and
- conservative values (safety, kindness).

To provide an example, a group of 4,064 of respondents, including 1,000 Poles (24%), 2,064 Germans (52%), and 1,000 Ukrainians (24%), was isolated from the 67,268 respondents in a WVS database and then subjected to a multi-criteria analysis. Three market segments were distinguished:
A) Germany:
- hidden class 1 – 882 (22%)
- hidden class 2 – 264 (7%)
- hidden class 3 – 917 (23%)
B) Poland:
- hidden class 1 – 427 (11%)
- hidden class 2 – 128 (3%)
- hidden class 3 – 444 (11%)

C) Ukraine:
- hidden class 1 – 411 (10%)
- hidden class 2 – 123 (3%)
- hidden class 3 – 466 (11%)

The analysis of segment profiles by value dimensions, with the first segment made up of 22% Germans, 11% Poles, and 10% Ukrainians, reveals a below-average level of traditional values among Poles and Ukrainians, and a relatively high level of a materialistic attitude. The second segment shows above average materialistic values among Germans, and a low level of conservative values (safety and tradition) among Ukrainians. The third segment displays a high level of materialistic values among Germans. Thus, the segment structure is characterized by a dominant position of materialistic value segments (wealth, risk, success), one representing Eastern Europe and another Germany. The application of mixed-factor models allows for model presentation of psychographic market segments with respect to heterogeneity of segmentation dimensions (criteria) and differentiation of examined populations. Thanks to this, it is possible to conduct the analysis, taking into consideration both hidden *post-hoc* segments and information about respondents' affiliation to pre-defined character categories (e.g., country or socio-demographic affiliation).

Source: Sagan (2010)

It is also worth paying attention to the phenomenon of the so-called Euro segmentation of buyers, i.e., homogeneous consumer clusters in the group of EU countries. Here, the main typology criterion is consumer lifestyle analyzed on the basis of consumer views (e.g., on politics, the economy, religion, and natural environment protection), consumer activity (e.g., social, professional, sports, leisure, buying behavior), and consumer interests (e.g., social, professional, hobbies, and fashion). The most important studies concerning Euro consumer typology based on consumer lifestyles were carried out by several research groups (Komor, 2000).

The case: Euro segments according to the Research Institute on Social Changes

In the Euro consumer segmentation elaborated by RISC, one can distinguish six segments:
1) traditional consumers, who are characterized by traditional thinking, recognition of conservative values, and identification with one's own national culture; here the family and respect for law and order occupy the central position;
2) homebodies, attached to their family and to the same group of friends, spending most of their time at home and in their local community, traveling rarely;
3) rational consumers, who, in all walks of life, demonstrate a rational approach towards life, ready to face new challenges, showing trust in science and new technologies;
4) hedonistic consumers, who lead a lifestyle according to their own beliefs, who follow sensual and emotional experience, attaching weight to their own appearance;

5) promotion-oriented customers, presenting a variety of attitudes corresponding to psychical development dynamics, pragmatists who try to enhance and develop their intellectual and physical abilities; and

6) trend-setters, characterized by spontaneity of actions, flexibility, a good education, active leisure, and creation of new trends.

Euro consumer segmentation takes consumer segmentation from the national dimension into the European one. Due to the homogeneous character of Euro consumers, companies are able to conduct their segmentation with respect to the whole European market, instead of only particular national markets.

Source: Komor (2000)

Segmentation of foreign markets entails making decisions about the choice of a company's **target segment**. This calls for evaluation of each specific segment and for identification of the company's key competencies. Assessment of segment attractiveness constitutes one of the main reasons for choosing a target foreign market that a company wants to be active in. If a company chooses an insufficient number of national segments or a segment that is too narrow, it is likely to fail to meet the planned turnover volume and profit or other measures of effectiveness. The choice of an area of activity that is too broad may, in turn, lead to a decrease in the benefits connected to a specialization (Hollensen, 2010; Blythe, 2009).

A list of possible attractiveness criteria for selecting segments might include size, growth rate, and stability of segments (e.g., resistance to seasonal, cyclical, or fashion fluctuation), price levels achievable, strength of competition, degree of concentration of consumers (i.e., a segment with a small number of larger consumers may offer economies of marketing but may also be risky), and degree of consistency with the overall competitive positioning of the firm (Clarke and Wilson, 2009; Han et al., 2009).

Taking into consideration the number of countries and foreign market segments that a company wants to operate in, one can define four strategies (Pierscionek, 2003):

1) double concentration strategy,

2) national concentration strategy,

3) segment concentration strategy, and

4) double diversification strategy.

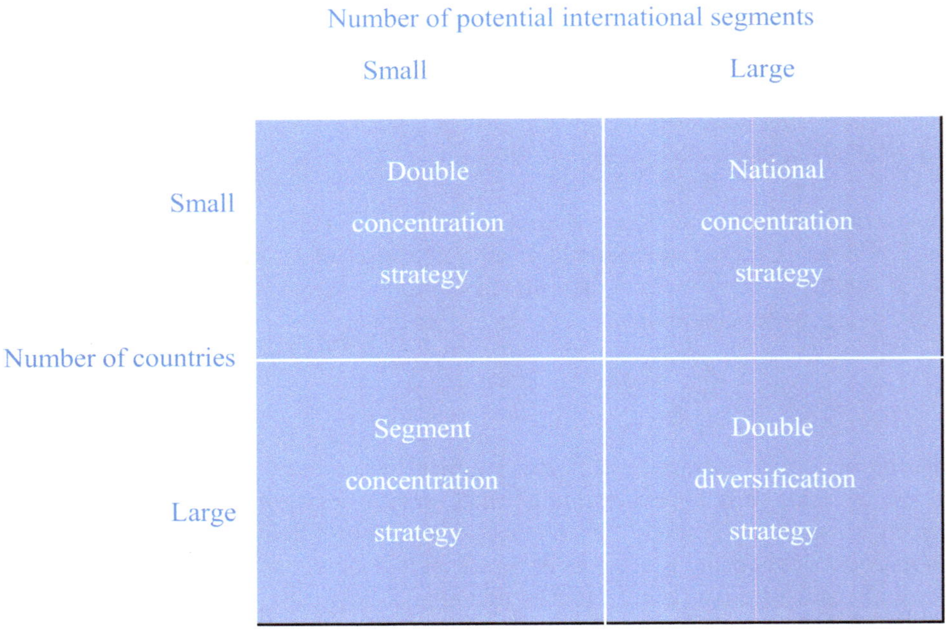

Number of potential international segments

| | Small | Large |

Source: Pierscionek (2003), p. 469

Figure 78. Strategies of market targeting the country-segment relationship

A **double concentration strategy** is based on a company's choice of a few countries and market segments, and thus reveals concentration of activities. This choice is a result of endeavors to reduce operational risk in foreign markets due to a company's limited resources and lack of experience functioning in a foreign context. Adoption of this strategy may be beneficial if market segments are large enough to ensure proper sales volume and achievement of the expected bottom line. A **national concentration strategy** involves running a company's activities in few countries, but in many market segments. This strategy is chosen by companies that have a wide product assortment and want to reduce the risk and costs connected with taking activities into new foreign markets. Therefore, companies decide to stay in a well-known foreign market, simultaneously preparing a wider offering of products for other market segments in a given country. A **segment concentration strategy** is characterized by selling products in many countries but in few market segments. Concentration on a few segments is most commonly pursued by companies specializing in the production of definite products for definite buyers. Since in these cases, the sales volume cannot be large in one foreign market, it is necessary to be active in many countries. In fact, marketing activities and the product itself are not diversified in the transnational dimension. A **double diversification strategy** is based on activities run in many foreign markets and segments. Employment of this strategy requires huge resources and experience, good knowledge of foreign markets, and a diversified product assortment. This strategy supports some markets at the cost of others in order to protect the company against unpredictable events in diverse markets, e.g., a slump in demand in one country, a change in economic policy, or the appearance of strong competitors. Additionally, it creates a good base for possible further expansion (Johansson, 2006; Wiktor et al., 2008). After selecting the proper target segment or segments in the international market, a company needs to position products or brands into those segments. A **positioning statement** defines the intended segment position of the product or brand. It describes the selected target consumers and the most important stakeholders, indicates the different benefits provided to those consumers and stakeholders, and defines the intended segment identity of the company (Muhlbacher et al., 2006).

International marketers are faced with four main options for positioning. The first offers the most scope for generating economies of scale and achieving consistency of brand image. The second recognizes that, for reasons already discussed, it may be necessary to target different or at least adapted segments. However, it may still be possible to retain the same positioning. The third option involves adjustments to positioning in different countries, even though the same segments are targeted. And finally, the last strategy involves adaptations to brand positioning and market segments (Albaum et al., 1998; Blythe, 2009).

Positioning may need adaptation for a variety of reasons. For instance, a brand market position will often differ among markets and this may mean some strategies are unavailable in some markets. For example, being able to claim market leadership may be seen as a desirable strategy, but a brand may be the leader in one country and a challenger or follower in another (Clarke and Wilson, 2009). Sometimes it is appropriate for a firm to change its positioning. This might be in response to changes in consumers' needs, a changing environment, or new strategies by competitors. Some of these are real changes, some are cosmetic, and others seek to change only consumer perception of the brand's positioning. Some options include changing the segment targeted, the breadth of segments targeted, or the basis of segmentation. Other options involve modifying functional attributes, customer perception of functional attributes, customer perception of competitors' products, or the personality of a brand (Bradley, 2005).

8.2   Creating consumer loyalty in the international market

In international marketing, consumer loyalty is growing in significance, as it presents an important corporate competitive factor and non-material company capital. The issue of consumer loyalty is particularly important with respect to the competitive position of companies in the international market and in terms of basic economic categories. Having a great number of loyal consumers is tantamount to company success. Many observers of marketing, and especially of the marketing environment, notice phenomena that indicate the need to develop corporate management oriented around building consumer loyalty. The phenomena include (Sroga, 2005)

• the increasing importance of information about a market, buyers, products, services, and competitors necessary for making proper corporate and consumer decisions;

- developing marketing, from local, through national, to the international and the global market;
- turning from mass marketing to individualized and diversified marketing;
- a need for rationalization of marketing and reduction of marketing costs; and
- a switch from satisfaction of consumer needs to satisfaction of consumer wishes, and a focus on non-price competition, mostly achieved through increasing product attractiveness as an expression of marketing methods and techniques.

Consumer loyalty can be defined as a consumer attitude toward a company and its products. This attitude is based on durability, longevity, and acceptance of goods and service conditions (Smyczek, 2001; Butscher, 1999). Consumer loyalty, i.e., consumer 'attachment' to a company is an expression of mutual understanding and mutual cooperation. Developing consumer loyalty (faithfulness) integrates all purposefully performed marketing activities, whereas being loyal is 'rewarded' by gaining preferential purchase conditions. A loyal consumer is one who is 'attached' to a company, is resistant to competitors' activities (i.e., a difficult-to-gain customer), and represents the interests of his or her company in the market (Schiffman and Kanuk, 2010).

Thus, consumer loyalty is tantamount to the consumer's full acceptance of a company's market offer. Such an attitude gets crystallized through emotional experiences and different states of consciousness (O'Dell and Pajunen, 1997; Stern and Hammond, 2004). A consumer becomes loyal to a company when a product delivers positive emotional experiences. Moreover, this loyalty is reinforced by showing the company's respect for and recognition of the customer, by proving its corporate integrity and transparency, as well as by ensuring competent service and meeting consumer needs and expectations. The level of consumer loyalty decreases when something negatively affects consumer perception of a product or a company.

Approaching loyalty as an attitude means presenting it as a function of an attitude demonstrated through some behavior (Dick and Basu, 1994; Lau and Lee, 1999). Attitudes are accompanied by close psychical constructs such as engagement and real entanglement. Iverson and Kuruvilla (1995) perceive customer engagement and customer loyalty as interchangeable concepts. Customer engagement is a key to advanced understanding of loyalty. According to Storbacka and Lehtinen (2001), loyalty appears as an intention of both parties to act and as willingness to interact with others. According to Reichheld (2003), loyalty emerges only if there is positive engagement. There is no place for loyalty in the case of passive and indifferent repeat buying by customers and when there are exit barriers imposed by a company or by other circumstances (e.g., lack of an alternative or the existence of purchase-resignation costs). Griffin (1995) points out two factors characteristic of customer loyalty: great involvement in a product or service in comparison to potential alternatives and buying behavior. Special attention should be drawn to the definition presented by Oliver (1999), in which the author argues that customer loyalty is a long-lasting customer engagement in making repurchases or in repeated consistent support of a preferred product or a brand in the future. As a consequence, the customer keeps on buying the same brand or the same set of brands despite situational influence or marketing activities designed to change such behavior (Urban and Siemieniako, 2008).

Another approach to the phenomenon of consumer loyalty is connected to a behavioral concept. The **behavioral approach to consumer loyalty** is presented in the literature as a repeated behavior supporting an object of loyalty, especially a repurchase. This loyalty is regarded as the quickest result of or as a visible demonstration of loyalty. Stum and Thiry (1991) distinguish four characteristic types of buying behavior of loyal customers:

- making repeated purchases,
- buying other goods and services,
- spreading a positive word-of-mouth, and
- low susceptibility to competitors' activities.

Other possible types of loyal behavior include

- giving advice to a company (Gruen and Gentry, 1995),
- accepting small problems on the part of a company (Tucker, 1964; Newman and Werbel, 1973), and
- intentions of repeated purchases (Soderlund, 1998).

The **behavioral concept of loyalty** was critically approached by Jacoby and Chestnut (1978) and Day (1969), who described weaknesses in its explanatory qualities. They suggest that consumer brand loyalty should be defined with reference to dimensions of customer attitudes and behaviors. According to these researchers, loyalty is a predisposition in a consumer towards a brand and represents a function of psychological processes; this predisposition consists of preferences and attitude-based engagement (Kassarjian and Robertson, 1991). The authors discuss six indispensable and sufficient conditions of brand loyalty. In a broader sense, loyalty (1) is biased (non-arbitrary), (2) appears as behavior that is a reaction (e.g., to a purchase), (3) is permanently expressed, (4) constitutes a process of decision making with regard to some elements, (5) is a distinction of one or more brands from the whole group of all available brands of the type, and (6) is a function of the evaluation process (Urban and Siemieniako, 2008).

In present market conditions, referring to brand loyalty strictly as a repurchase is, in most business situations, too superficial. It is learning about the motives of customer behavior that are becoming an increasingly significant factor in the loyalty reinforcement process. According to Reichheld (2003), loyalty is something more than repeat buying as it is tantamount to willingness, e.g., of a customer, a worker, or a friend, to make some investments or personal commitments in order to strengthen this relationship; for customers, this may be equal to staying with a seller who treats them properly and provides a long-term value, even if an offered price is not always attractive in particular transactions.

Customer loyalty may be demonstrated with reference to one or more objects connected to a company. With respect to the types of objects of loyalty, one can distinguish loyalty to a brand, a product category, a company's staff members, a selling point (e.g., a store), a group of objects within a community developed around the brand, and the organization (Blackwell et al., 2001; Blythe, 2009). Undoubtedly, the most favorable situation appears when the customer becomes loyal towards all objects of loyalty. This reduces the risk of customer defection as, in the case of some disloyalty towards one object, the customer may continue the relationship with a company on account of other objects.

Consumer loyalty is based on two types of motives: rational-functional and emotional-symbolic (Swiatowy and Pluta-Olearnik, 2000). The first concerns the analysis of loyalty with respect to the functional aspect of a product and is related to the analysis of the 'pros' and 'cons' of a purchase. The second comes from consumer feelings and values, the reflection of which he or she seeks in a product. Loyal consumers attach weight to the emotional-symbolic aspect, whereas disloyal consumers have little regard for it (Stern and Hammond, 2004). Additionally, the motives that differentiate consumers mainly relate to social and interpersonal aspects. In other words, through making purchases of definite products, loyal consumers want to convey a certain message about themselves to other consumers. Hence, they value highly the symbolic aspects of a product. It is noteworthy, however, that in the case of certain rational-functional motives, both groups of consumers (loyal and disloyal) have achieved similar results. Both types of consumers admit that when buying a specific product, they often take into consideration the utility value of a product, its price and convenience (Smyczek and Sowa, 2005).

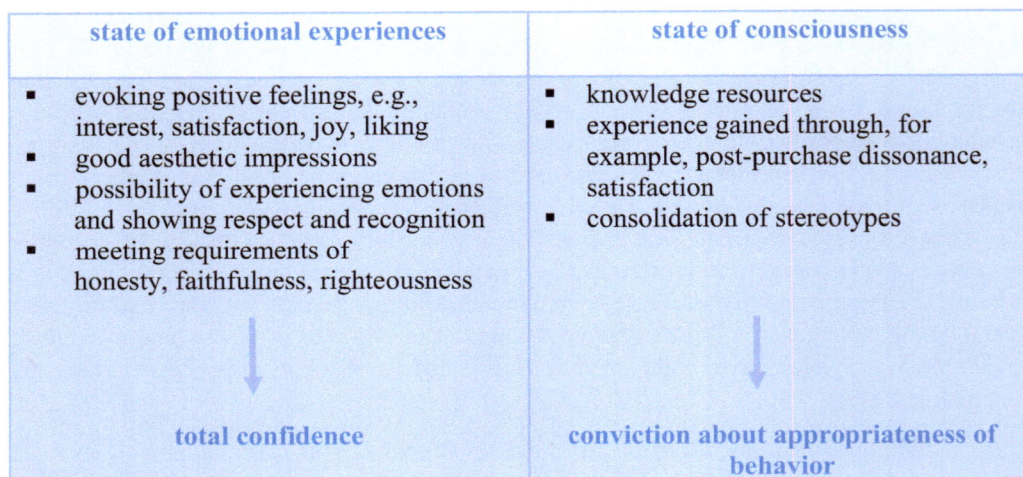

state of emotional experiences	state of consciousness
■ evoking positive feelings, e.g., interest, satisfaction, joy, liking ■ good aesthetic impressions ■ possibility of experiencing emotions and showing respect and recognition ■ meeting requirements of honesty, faithfulness, righteousness	■ knowledge resources ■ experience gained through, for example, post-purchase dissonance, satisfaction ■ consolidation of stereotypes
↓	↓
total confidence	**conviction about appropriateness of behavior**

Source: Swiatowy and Pluta-Olearnik (2000), p. 52

Figure 79. Basic attitudes of consumer loyalty

Among the many approaches to the motives of consumer loyalty, great significance is attached to models that attempt to define the phenomenon as a whole, the so-called models that define the factors and ways of loyalty development. Some of the proposed models reveal only a 'straightforward' relationship between several basic motives; others represent a complex description of relationships between different phenomena and motives. Some models have been verified through the process of empirical experiments, others not. The most common models of customer loyalty attitudes are

- customer satisfaction-based models (Oliver, 1999; Pong and Yee, 2001; Yu and Dean, 2001),
- brand-based models (McAlexander et al., 2003),
- corporate image-based models (Kandampully and Suhartanto, 2000; Zins, 2001),

- social factor-based models (Butcher et al., 2001), and
- customer attitude-based models (Huddleston et al., 2004; Sullivan and Adcock, 2003).

Customer loyalty can be classified as exclusive loyalty, also called undivided loyalty, and as multi-loyalty, or divided loyalty. **Exclusive loyalty** refers to buying one particular brand exclusively, which, in most cases, greatly benefits the company. **Multi-loyal customers** buy, at least, two brands that are equally acceptable or entirely substitutable, whereby brands are bought and consumed interchangeably (Oliver, 1999). Customers who stop or reduce the buying of brands, as a result of changes in their consumption needs, and who start buying non-substitutable products that provide them with other benefits do not display multi-loyalty, but exclusive loyalty. Recurrence of customer needs may lead to customer loyalty behavior towards the brand. In such a case, the customer reduces the frequency and/or value of purchases of a specific brand, but may remain in a relationship of exclusive loyalty (Reinartz and Kumar, 2002). Through building an image, a company is capable of creating consumer needs connected to a product category or a brand.

volume of spending on a brand within a category (purchase frequency and value)		volume of spending on a product category (purchase frequency and value)	
		high	low
high	exclusive loyalty	profitable customer – maintain *status quo* (lack of purchase growth potential)	nonexistent
	multi-loyalty	profitable customer – maintain *status quo* or increase support concentration (current brand support is rather high)	nonexistent
low	exclusive loyalty	nonexistent	low-profitability customer – create need connected with a brand or a product (an increased volume of spending on a brand will occur together with appearance of needs within a category, or development of a brand image will create the needs
	multi-loyalty	low-profitability customer – increase support concentration (current brand support concentration is low)	zero-profitability customer – minimize expenses (limited chance of brand building)

Source: Siemieniako and Urban (2005), p. 28

Figure 80. Types of consumer loyalty according to profitability

It happens that customers demonstrating exclusive loyalty buy less than multi-loyal ones, e.g., due to low buying frequency. Currently, research shows that exclusive loyalty customers account for no more than 20% of all buyers and show a downward trend (Ehrenberg, 2000). With respect to developing customer loyalty, it is important to note that the share of purchases by multi-loyal customers is growing in comparison to purchases made by exclusive customers.

Dick and Basu (1994) have distinguished different types of loyalty with regard to frequency and volume of purchases and in the customer attitude towards a company. In their typology, one can distinguish true loyalty, latent loyalty, spurious loyalty, and no loyalty. True loyalty is demonstrated both in the behavioral aspect – more frequent purchases – and in a positive attitude towards the objects of loyalty. Latent loyalty is an expression of a positive attitude toward specific objects of loyalty, but, at the same time, reveals lack of buying activity. Spurious loyalty, in turn, is characterized by intensive loyalty behavior, but also by a negative attitude. This type of loyalty may come from customer habits. Lack of loyalty appears in the case of low buying frequency and a low level of customer engagement. The customer may often be tempted into buying something by a competitive price (Griffin, 1995).

Jones et al., (1995) classified customers in terms of the level of their loyalty and the degree of achieved satisfaction. They distinguished loyalists/apostles, defectors/terrorists, mercenaries, and hostages (Figure 81). Apostles represent customers who are entirely satisfied and continue their relationship with the company. Here, customer needs as well as the company's products and services are perfectly matched. In their description of customer experiences and expectations, Jones et al., (1995) show some loyalists as individuals whose satisfaction and experiences have gone so far beyond their expectations that they are forced to share their strong emotions with others. They are true apostles. Defectors consist of not only dissatisfied or indifferent customers, but also satisfied ones. The authors of this typology emphasize the fact that it is necessary for companies to show much determination to keep this type of customer through better recognition of their needs and by paying attention to them. However, not all defecting customers can be retained, as some of their needs do not fit the value offered by the company. Terrorists are customers who, having undergone some negative experience with a company, share their anger and frustration with others. This can be exemplified by grocery store customers who buy a damaged product and whose complaint is not properly handled by the staff members. Pests' involvement in expressing negative opinions is likely to exceed that of apostles in sharing their positive views (Lau and Lee, 1999; Smyczek and Sowa, 2005). Mercenaries constitute another group of customers that are troublesome for a company, as their total satisfaction is not reflected in their loyalty towards a company. They are low-price hunters and impulse buyers. They track down new fashion trends or seek a change for the sake of it. Hostages experience a compulsion to continue their relationship with a company regardless of their level of satisfaction. A company that is in the position of a monopolist can keep hostages. Jones et al., (1995) point out two significant problems a company may experience in dealing with hostages. The first problem refers to a change in the competitive environment because of an increase in the number of competitors. This may cause a defection of hostages, who will turn into pests. The second problem concerns hostages themselves, who are very difficult to deal with owing to their readiness to make complaints and requests for service improvement (Storbacka and Lehtinen, 2001; Johannes, 2004).

types of customers	satisfaction	loyalty	behavior
loyalists/apostles	high	high	staying with the company and supporting it
defectors/terrorists	from low to medium	from low to medium	defecting from the company or intending to defect; dissatisfaction
mercenaries	high	from low to medium	coming to and leaving a company; low engagement
hostages	from low to medium	high	inability to make a change; the sense of 'being trapped'

Source: Jones et al., (1995), p. 6

Figure 81. Level of customer satisfaction and loyalty and types of behavior

For a company, there are many benefits that come from having loyal customers (Buchanan and Gilles, 1990):

- keeping present customers is cheaper than gaining new ones – loyal customers tend to be more frequent buyers of a larger number of a company's products, of complementary products or high-margin accessories;
- costs of handling loyal customers are lower;
- loyal customers accept higher prices for the same bunch of products;
- loyal customers act as advocates of their company for other market subjects; and
- the level of customer loyalty can be raised.

Reichheld (2003) distinguishes the following sources of profits generated by customers who have been with the company for many years: basic profit, profit from growth in purchases, profit from diminishing operating costs, profit from recommended customers, and profit from an increased price. According to Wansink (2003), some companies decide to take up activities aimed at strengthening customer loyalty with the simple conviction that it is far more expensive to gain a new customer than to keep and encourage the existing one to intensify his or her consumption. The benefits of having a portfolio of loyal customers motivate a company to make efforts to prevent defection by maximization of the customer retention index (Urban and Siemieniako, 2008). The influence of the customer retention index on the increase in a company's profits has been demonstrated by Reichheld and Sasser Jr. (1990), whose research showed that a 5% growth in the customer retention index contributes to a profit increase from 25% up to 85%, depending on the type of business (Figure 82).

branches	profit growth (in %)
car services	29.2
bank deposits	82.3
credit cards	73.4
bank guarantees	21.8
insurance	49.6
industrial goods distribution	43.1
laundry services	40.7
administration of office buildings	38.5
computer software	33.2

Source: Urban and Siemieniako (2008), p. 17

Figure 82. The effect of customer loyalty on profit in the Polish market

Companies carry out numerous activities aimed at gaining new customers, from strategy development, through product and service quality improvement, to higher standards of customer service, and to loyalty programs that are designed to bind the customer to a company. Following Dowling and Uncles (1997), companies that implement loyalty programs within their marketing strategy hope to

- maintain the current level of sales, profits and margins;
- increase consumer loyalty and the potential buying force of present customers;
- increase the level of cross-buying in present customers;
- diversify brand parity;
- prevent other brands from entering the market; and
- hinder the introduction of similar competitor loyalty programs.

However, not all loyal customers bring benefits to their company. Profitability from having some customers may even be of a marginal value, which has been demonstrated by Reinartz and Kumar (2002). They determined that

- it is not true that servicing every loyal customer is cost-effective;
- loyal customers do not always pay more for the same set of products; on the contrary, they often insist on getting price discounts; and

- not all loyal customers spread a positive word-of-mouth about their company and its products to their friends and family members; in fact, such behavior is demonstrated only by a part of the 'apostles'.

A company should identify customers who are 'real friends', i.e., customers who bring financial benefits and intend to stay loyal for a long time. According to Reinartz and Kumar (2002), customer loyalty and a company's influence on it appear to be a complex phenomenon; and profits from loyal customers cannot be taken for granted.

The effectiveness of influencing consumer loyalty is conditioned by selectivity in the ways of affecting different customers or customer groups. This, in turn, necessitates the possession of adequate knowledge about customers, both with respect to their attitudes and their buying behavior regarding a company's products. Moreover, it is equally important to know the economic value connected to purchases made by a customer (e.g., it is essential to know the service costs and the scale of price discounts with regard to particular customers or customer groups).The knowledge of customers is obtained in the process of collection, aggregation, and storage of information. Only effective and thorough knowledge of customers allows for effective development of customer loyalty. Gathering data about customers and undertaking selective activities towards them must be backed up with adequate IT tools (Wang et al., 2006).

The case: TRI*M method of identifying consumer loyalty in the international market

One of the most popular methods for diagnosing customer loyalty and developing a strategy for winning customer loyalty in the international market is the TRI*M method (Measure, Manage, Monitor). The method is proposed by TNS.

TRI*M consists of six different topical components and is customized regionally to focus better on the specific business challenges within regions and bring its global stakeholder management expertise to bear. In just the past three years, more than 45 percent of Fortune 100 companies have used TRI*M to measure and manage customer relationships.
TRI*M also provides a set of concise diagnostic tools and a benchmark database of more than 8,000 studies representing more than 12 million interviews across 120 countries. This knowledge database provides information about the business context of your organization within scalable geographic areas, industries, and sectors.
TRI*M determines the top priorities for addressing key issues affecting customer relationships. By identifying valuable lead indicators for future success and highlighting lag indicators that offer opportunities for improvement, the TRI*M method helps companies set gainful priorities and use their resources to obtain results in the most effective manner.

Source: TNS (2010)

Company activities that are designed to enhance customer loyalty take the form of investments that are expected to generate some financial return. It is possible, though, that some investments may not yield the required profit, especially when the customer demonstrates loyal behavior (even a very profitable one) only temporarily. Not all customers can be retained by a company despite consolidation of its various activities. Therefore, such customers should not be invested in as some of them are innately liable to change brands (Blythe, 1997; Johannes, 2004).

To form pro-loyalty strategies in order to build a stable relationship with customers, a company should focus on what follows the customer's first purchase of a given type of product. In order to form such a relationship a company needs to (Reichheld, 2003)

- identify buyers and gain knowledge on every one of them; this requires creating a database in which each individual customer will have his or her own unique place;
- constantly monitor information on buyers, which allows for estimating the value of every customer and establishing how attractive each one is for the company; and
- adjust its offer to every customer (based on the collected information on each buyer); a company should pay more attention to key customers, i.e., the most attractive customers to the company, and should develop a range of incentives to encourage them to remain faithful.

Creating a bond with a customer is a long-term process (Orchowski, 1999; Stern and Hammond, 2004). It requires a partnership approach and constant cooperation with the customer in order to form the best possible relationship based on mutual benefits. It is impossible to create and tighten bonds with a customer who cannot tell a particular brand from others. In such a situation, a company should act through promotion and should use informal communication to get to the customers and persuade them to buy a particular product (e.g., to try it out). These activities fall under the traditional understanding of marketing. If, however, a company wishes to establish a relationship with a customer, it needs to take another step, i.e., develop a customer habit of choosing a given brand over others (Cichosz, 2003).

When a company prepares a pro-loyalty strategy, the company first needs to clearly define its goals, namely the level of consumer loyalty that will be satisfactory. The goal(s) of pro-loyalty activities ought to be quantified and, most of all, presented to all the employees in the company, since the involvement of all personnel may guarantee the success of such activities (Lau and Lee, 1999; Johansson, 2006). The following coefficients may be helpful in quantifying the goals – on the one hand, they define consumer loyalty; on the other hand, they determine it (O'Dell and Pajunen, 1997).

- **New consumer turnover coefficient** is the ratio of the number of customers who make their first purchase to those who make their second purchase in a given period of time. The time is defined according to a typical purchase cycle (repurchase) specific for a given industry or product/service.
- **Consumer turnover coefficient** is the percentage of customers who have made a defined number of repurchases in a given period of time.
- **Consumer share coefficient** is the percentage of overall consumer purchases of a particular brand.

- **Average monthly number of new consumers** is the average number of consumers who have made their first purchase of a given brand in a given month.
- **Purchase frequency** is the average number of purchases made by consumers of a particular brand during one year.
- **Average purchase value** is the average value paid for goods/services at a single purchase.
- **Consumer defection rate** is the percentage of consumers who were lost to the company or have become inactive for various reasons in a given period of time.

Calculating these coefficients will not only allow for defining the goals of a loyalty-building strategy but will also facilitate the selection of appropriate tools for shaping consumer attitudes and will improve the process of monitoring the realization of the selected goals. In creating a pro-loyalty strategy, every company ought to conduct a thorough analysis of its customers and should group them according to the scheme presented above. Then a separate set of marketing activities should be prepared for every single group. These activities will allow for 'passing' from one group to another and will, at the same time, increase the level of consumers' loyalty to the company. We need to remember that the sign of increasing loyalty is a boost in the sales of a given brand. This ensures the growth of a company's profit. In this way a profit-generating system is established (Rudawska, 2005).

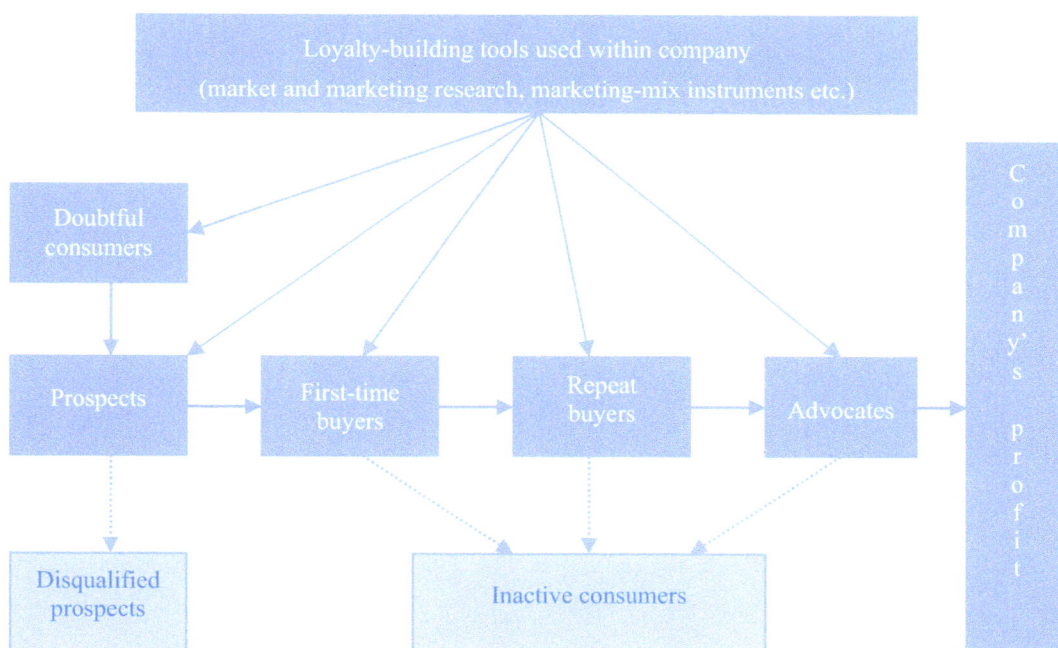

Source: Griffin (1995), p. 37; Smyczek (2001), p. 130

Figure 83. Profit-generating system in a company

Through marketing research, a company conducts an analysis of customers belonging to the 'doubtful' group. Then by using marketing activities, it tries to transform them into 'prospects' (Butscher, 1999). It is worth noting that persons of great potential (financial, intellectual, etc.) are subject to further actions undertaken by a company. In contrast, persons of low potential (thus classified by managers) are disqualified and removed from the system. The sooner a company rejects such customers, the faster its financial result will improve, since the loss of time and financial means spent on the 'doubtful' group (customers who do not or cannot buy products) is reflected in the amount of profit. Once 'prospects' are defined, a company should proceed to establishing a plan of marketing activities that will allow for transforming this group into first-time buyers and then into repeat-buyers, regular customers, and advocates (Marin et al., 2009; Schiffman and Kanuk, 2010).

It has to be remembered that when a customer goes through the profit-generating system, climbing to higher levels of loyalty, he or she should be encouraged by the company to regularly buy its products and give up other, competitive goods (Rudawska, 2005). Without a well-prepared set of marketing activities, the first-time buyers, repeat-buyers, regular customers, and advocates may turn into inactive customers. This causes significant loss to the company, which is reflected in a decrease in sales and lowered profit. It is worth noting that the higher we go in the profit-generating system, the smaller the number of customers (Buchanan and Gilles, 1990). This arises from the fact that every person reacts to a company's marketing activities in a different way, and not all consumers are affected by them (sometimes only a part of such activities reaches a customer). Such activities may also be hampered by the competition. This is why they should be diversified according to the target group. A set of such activities is included in Figure 84.

customer type	main goal	type of activity

doubtful customer / prospect	gain customers' understanding	1. listening to customers' voice.
		2. understanding customers' decisions.
		3. special activities:
		  - free consultation on how to use the product, etc. and
		  - guarantee of reliability.

first-time buyers	satisfy / increase customer expectations	1. increasing customer expectations. 2. creating a vision of further purchases. 3. thanking for cooperation. 4. inviting to repurchase.

repeat-buyers	provide additional values with every purchase	1. satisfying customers' needs through:
		  - additional value and
		  - cross-selling.
		2. sales of loyalty-building products.
		3. analysis of every purchase of competitive goods
		4. constantly prompting customers' reaction.

customers	adjust the offer to the needs of a particular customer	1. customer care. Looking for ways of activating the customer. 2. no continuation of cooperation with a customer 'for free'. 3. convincing the customer that further cooperation with the company is efficacious. 4. looking for methods to contact the customer systematically.
advocates	allow customers to 'sell' company's products	1. encouraging advocates, by sending them letters of appreciation and promises of reward, to recommend the company to others. 2. developing a regular communication with customer network and with influential individuals.
inactive	elaborate a good plan for customer 'return'	1. quick identification of inactive customers and show of interest in them. 2. preparing a special offer to induce customers to return to the company. 3. meeting the requirements of customers and communicating offer changes to them. 4. patience and systematic contact with inactive customers are of uttermost importance.

Source: Griffin (1995), p. 220

Figure 84. Activities undertaken under pro-loyalty strategy (per customer type)

One of the important tools used for building long-term bonds with customers in pro-loyalty strategies carried out by companies that operate in international markets is a loyalty program. Kotler (2000) defines **loyalty programs** as the process of identifying, keeping, and increasing all that the best customers provide for the company through the creation of long-term, interactive, and value-adding bonds with customers. We may, however, also define loyalty programs as a set of tools and undertakings related to the use of particular market-affecting instruments in order to build and uphold consumer loyalty (Schlegelmilch et al., 2001). Thus, we may say that the first approach to loyalty programs focuses on the process and the other on instruments.

What is essential in loyalty programs is the reward customers who often buy a given product or buy it in large quantities receive from the company. In a properly elaborated loyalty program, a company should define both the profits it wishes to gain and the benefits the program provides for the customers (Butscher, 1999; Bridson et al., 2008). We need to remember that loyalty programs do not have to give direct financial benefits to customers (such as discounts, gift cards, etc.). What is also important, and possibly even more important, is emotional gain ('I am reasonable when I buy my brand').

motives	France	Romania
material motives		
possibility to exchange points for awards	32.6	52.1
possibility to exchange points for free-of-charge goods or services	30.7	16.8
possibility to obtain discount for other goods or services	19.4	15.3
possibility to obtain discount for goods or services from other (partner) companies	11.2	7.9
emotional motives		
special services	5.6	2.1
possibility of belonging to program (elitism)	2.2	2.6
possibility to change points for charity goals	3.7	1.4
don't know	1.5	3.9

Source: DG SANCO (2010)

Figure 85. Participation motives in loyalty programs; France vs. Romania (in percent)

Dowling and Uncles (1997) indicate some of the factors that ought to maximize the chances of success in carrying out a loyalty program. They include the following:

- a loyalty program ought to be prepared in such a way that it adds value (attractiveness) to the offered product;
- the funds destined for program realization cannot use up the whole marketing budget because if the competition undertakes a similar action, some funds need to be available to counteract;
- the reward plan for loyal customers ought to maximize the buyer's motivation to repurchase; and
- before proceeding to the planning stage, a company needs to conduct a thorough analysis of the market situation.

company	Orlen	BP	Statoil	Shell	Lotos
name of program	Vitay	Partner Club	Premium club	Smart	Navigator
catalog	Yes	Yes	Yes	Yes	Yes
update of catalog	Quarterly	Once per year	Once per year	Once per year	Online
number of awards	101	258	232	138	10
awarding of points	Only for purchasing at station	Only for purchasing at station	For purchasing at station and partners	For purchasing at station and partners	Only for purchasing at station
validity of points	3 years	1.5 years	3 years	4 years	1 year
value of points	1l = 6 points	1l = 1 point	1l = 1 point	1l = 1 point	10l = 1 point

Source: Media and Marketing (2010)

Figure 86. Examples of loyalty programs in the Polish gasoline market

Loyalty programs used by companies that operate in the international market may be divided according to various criteria. If we take the manner of participation in a program into account, we may talk about the following types.

- **Marketing programs of participation** – their objective is to reward customers who often buy a given product or buy it in large quantities. The characteristic feature of this program is that the company that introduces it first, gains the most profit. This usually happens when the competition does not react quickly enough. If their reaction is fast, the program may become a burden for all the companies that offer it. After some time, most of the customers already 'belong' to some program and collect 'points', no matter which company's products they use. In this situation, the winner becomes the company whose program is the most effective or attracts the greatest number of customers (due to special benefits) or those companies that create the most sophisticated system, including attractive and convincing offers for particular customers (Kotler et al., 2009);
- **Consumer clubs** – created by companies around their product or products. The clubs offer a real and observable value to their members in the form of nonfinancial profits or an optimized combination of financial and nonfinancial profits; the purpose of such a club is to activate customers so that they buy more and/or recommend the company's products to others and so that they communicate their observations in the club (Butscher, 1999; Bridson et al., 2008). Consumer clubs are particularly recommended in those coun-

tries that have very strict regulations on such issues as, e.g., offering a given product to various customer groups at various prices – an example is Germany, where the law on these matters is very strict, and so consumer clubs are the most popular in this country. In such situations, the clubs mainly provide their members with emotional, nonfinancial profits and additional services (not connected with price reduction).

According to the number of participants, loyalty programs may be divided into the following groups.

- **Open programs** – every person who wishes to (e.g., who buys a given product) may participate. This type of program is characterized by a large number of participants, which enhances its effectiveness. The database obtained through such a program may become the basis for market segmentation. This program is most advisable for companies that do not have information on their present customers and potential buyers, operate in the mass market or market of individual customers, and have increased the budget for the realization of the program in the long-term (Smyczek, 2001).
- **Programs with a limited number of participants** – they are usually connected with paying some kind of membership fee. The fee partly covers the costs of the program, and the limited access to it makes the program more attractive and valuable to the customers. A well-defined member profile makes it easier to prepare appropriate tools of communication and persuasion. However, a membership fee increases the consumers' expectations for the program and requires that the managers systematically increase the values the program offers to its participants. 'Limited' programs are the best solution for companies that wish to win the most valuable customers and that have a very well-segmented market. It is extremely useful for companies with small budgets that prefer more concentrated activities and are active in the so-called non-consumer markets, such as the industrial goods and services market (Bridson et al., 2008).

According to their duration, the programs are divided into temporary programs and permanent programs. In terms of the medium used, they are divided as follows.

- Traditional programs and
- Internet programs (virtual) – here we may talk of commercial and corporate loyalty programs. Commercial loyalty programs are organized by particular web portals, and they are aimed at gaining profit. They use the point system to attract and reward customers for their loyalty, or they use their own 'internal currencies'. In commercial programs, there is a strict cooperation with advertisers. These programs are only present in the virtual world. On the other hand, corporate loyalty programs are prepared by particular companies in order to form long-term fidelity in their customers. Due to those programs, a company is able to contact directly and communicate with its customers in an interactive manner. The offers of value added are disseminated among the participants of the program via the Internet. Examples are the market loyalty program of Lufthansa (Miles&More) or Air France (Flyingbule).

Other types of loyalty programs include music and book clubs; fan clubs; user clubs, e.g., the Peugeot Owners Club; 'bonus' programs; discount clubs; and 'wholesale' clubs. Bearing the foregoing in mind, we should emphasize the fact that quickly developing competition in international markets will constantly force companies to introduce innovations and improve the already established strategies and loyalty programs. Many companies will have to change their activities and introduce completely new strategies.

8.3 Anticipation of new trends and future consumer behavior

The new market situation that has emerged because of globalization, the financial crisis, and so on has and will have a huge influence on changes in consumer behavior in the international market. Changes will consist not only of the consumption of new and more popular products or far-reaching modifications to products that are already in use but also of considerable changes in the level at which needs are satisfied and in consumer decisions in the market and in households. These changes take the form of specific trends – they intensify in some consumer groups, they penetrate other groups, they are subject to modifications, and they disappear with time. Some of the most important trends that occur in the market and can be observed in the international market are consumption globalization, consumer ethnocentrism, homogenization and heterogenization of consumer behavior, ecological behavior, servicization and dematerialization of consumption, virtualization of consumer behavior and cocooning, deconsumption and prosumption and also ethical consumption.

In the international market, some of the factors that stimulate changes in consumption and in consumer behavior and, at the same time, set new trends for them are (Hollensen, 2010)

- globalization of the economy and internationalization of business activities;
- development of democracy, enlarging areas of civil liberties, great ideologies disappearing, etc.;
- limited influence of religion and tradition on human behavior;
- development and spread of the Internet and mobile phones etc.;
- changes in production technologies and distribution of goods;
- advance of civilization, increasing levels of education (including market-related education) in society;
- longer life span, increasing numbers of elderly people and their economic emancipation; and
- changes in the family model, traditional family roles becoming obsolete, the loosening of social bonds etc.

Globalization of consumption manifests itself in intermingling consumption patterns observed on an international scale, in the spreading of consumption patterns, and in the creation of a global consumption culture (Bywalec, 2007; Johansson, 2006). Globalization leads to the creation of global sectors that are based not on location but on values, attitudes, and approach to objects and brands. In this context, creating becomes particularly important. It is usually an answer to the need to emphasize one's affiliation to the global sector (Zabinski,

2000). Globalization of consumer behavior arises from the so-called contemporary culture, which invokes such basic values as

- individual subject;
- activity-oriented attitude, as opposed to existence-oriented attitude;
- reification of time through economic thinking – 'time is money'; and
- future-oriented attitude and less interest in the past, but at the same time frustration caused by the small size of the 'here and now' (Bywalec, 2007).

It is impossible to evaluate the process of globalization of consumption since it has many advantages but also many drawbacks. The advantages mainly arise from the very essence of the process, namely the products and the ways they are used becoming universal throughout the world, regardless of local culture, climate, and so on. Such phenomena often facilitate life; increase human mobility in space; and most of all, stimulate the development of tourism and migration. On the other hand, globalization of consumption hinders the development of local cultures, products, and manners of consumption, which impoverishes regions and the whole world (Johansson, 2006).

A trend that is very much opposed to globalization is consumer ethnocentrism. Ethnocentrism is defined as an attitude according to which one's own group constitutes the center of the world, and all else is appraised and classified in reference to it (Solomon et al., 2010). Thus, consumer ethnocentrism is the conviction shared by consumers that they should and are morally obliged to buy domestic products. Ethnocentrism is manifested in ways of perceiving the world and evaluating it consistently in reference to one's own culture. In the sphere of consumption, ethnocentrism is observed as a belief that one needs to buy domestic goods either in order to support domestic industry, trade, and so on or because these products are of better quality than foreign goods. Consumers may also think that by supporting domestic production, they also protect, indirectly, their own jobs; so they do not act only for the good of the country, but for their own good. Therefore, we may say that consumer ethnocentrism is related to making choices on the basis of moral rather than on rational or emotional criteria. On the other hand, ethnocentric behavior requires some knowledge – a customer needs to be able to identify a domestic (or European) product and also needs to be familiar with and understand the benefits he or she gains by purchasing that product.

The power of an ethnocentric attitude depends on the following:

- the need to possess and use a product, as perceived and felt by an individual (this factor mitigates ethnocentrism) and
- economic threat related to foreign products, as perceived and felt by an individual or a group, and connected with such phenomena as decreased demand for domestic products, limited domestic output, unemployment, higher taxes, lower standard of living – this factor exacerbates ethnocentrism (Antonides and van Raaij, 2003).

Consumer ethnocentrism also depends on the demographic characteristics of consumers – their age, sex, education, earnings, and psychosocial characteristics, i.e., open attitude towards foreign cultures, patriotism, conservatism, and collectivism/individualism. In the sphere of consumer behavior, ethnocentrism is an effect of growing market awareness.

Non-ethnocentric consumers do not pay attention to a product's country of origin. Instead they use other criteria for selecting a product – their decisions are well considered and not based on moral aspects. Such an attitude is called 'consumer cosmopolitanism'. In some countries, there is another type of attitude that is referred to as 'consumer internationalism'. We may talk about such an attitude if consumers consciously choose to buy foreign products. Goods manufactured abroad are regarded as better and sometimes even as prestigious and a reflection of the status of the person who owns them. In the European Union, due to integration processes and the blurring of cultural and national distinctiveness, another phenomenon is observed, namely European ethnocentrism. We observe European ethnocentrism when consumers tend to buy goods manufactured in the European Union. This gives rise to a new type of consumer – a Euro-consumer (Raymond, 2003).

Sometimes conflicts occur between globalization and consumer ethnocentrism. These conflicts often end up with a compromise, the outcome of which is usually a global-local hybrid. Thus, we may talk about 'hybridization' of consumption or of its glocalization. When it occurs, a global product is accepted and adjusted to local systems of values and local methods of use. Otherwise it is manifested in global consumption of a 'local' product, e.g., champagne, pizza, whisky (Stiglitz, 2007).

Globalization and consumer ethnocentrism are the most wide-ranging and the most complex signs of changes that take place in the field of consumption and consumer behavior in modern, highly developed societies. Many factors overlap; they either enforce or weaken one another, and so we may simultaneously observe such tendencies in consumer behavior as homogenization and heterogenization of consumption.

Homogenization of consumption involves unification and assimilation of consumption patterns (Lambkin et al., 2001). It is manifested in the shifting and blurring of differences between life phases, in elderly people becoming economically emancipated and life styles of various age and social groups becoming similar, and so on. One of important factors that stimulates homogenization of consumption is a longer lifespan, which means that particular phases of life are longer and differences between them become blurred. Due to the development of education, the period in which we are at school (normally associated with youth) is prolonged to the age of 25-30 years; we are also active professionally for a longer period of time (Doole et al., 2005). Today, when medicine is advancing so rapidly and more people have access to health care, they are still in good shape when they retire and are able to live an active life. This is the reason that passing from one stage of life to another has become very smooth, and why differences between these stages are no longer so well defined. Also, the differences in behavior between men and women, inhabitants of urban and agricultural areas, and representatives of various social classes have become blurred (Raymond, 2003; Lambkin et al., 2001).

Homogenization stimulates detraditionalization of consumption, which means a decrease in the role of local family and job traditions. Detraditionalization may also have a completely different effect: it may cause diversification of consumption, i.e., lead to its heterogenization. Some factors that foster consumption heterogenization are (Bywalec, 2007; Blythe, 2009)

- development of democracy and a broader range of civil liberties,
- disappearance of great ideologies,
- individualized style of living and formation of subcultures,
- increasing mobility of people and of means of consumption,
- increasing ethnocentrism,
- changes in production technologies and distribution of goods, and
- development and spread of the Internet.

Developing democratization of consumers' lives induces many people to undertake unrestrained actions, including in the sphere of consumption, which they treat as ways of 'expressing themselves' or 'listening to their inner selves'. This approach is fostered by the huge diversity of goods available on the market and by a tendency toward as much product differentiation as possible (Graham, 2010). An example is the mobile phone market. It is true that consumers' requirements are increasing with respect to mobile phones – they are supposed to be multifunctional, unique, and stylized. They are to boost the owner's self-esteem and even express his or her personality. These expectations, however, are mainly created by manufacturers, who stress the fact that 'your product speaks for you', every time they launch a new one in the market.

Another phenomenon that can be observed in today's economy, especially in well-developed countries, is consumers' interest in environmental protection. This has an impact on the choices made by consumers. We feel more often the need to exclude the brands of manufacturers that do not care about the environment from the market, and so we choose other brands or producers. Thus we may talk about ecological consumption, i.e., a modification (and not limitation) of consumption such that the negative impact is the least possible (Smith and Wheeler, 2002; Lambkin et al., 2001). This phenomenon is sometimes referred to as 'green consumerism' (or new consumerism). Consumers who have adopted this attitude make wise, rational decisions on the market. They combine care for their own health with care for the environment. But even though they act in similar ways, their motives are diverse (Solomon et al., 2010; Johannes, 2004):

- consumers who rely on sound judgment – they choose products on the basis of solid knowledge and reliable information; their green behavior is based on their desire to gain prestige;
- personally well-oriented consumers – they purchase green products only out of consideration for their health; and
- eco-fanatics – they consider only green products to be valuable; they often initiate environmental protection activities.

The greening of consumption is manifested in (Doole et al., 2005)

- the rational use of goods;
- limited consumption of goods that use up scarce, non-renewable resources or that generate dangerous waste;

- decisions not to buy products that might be considered superfluous (such as fabric softeners, toothpaste boxes, etc.);
- buying goods that produce little waste;
- consuming organic food (with a limited amount of added substances);
- rational supplies management;
- choosing multiple-use goods, if possible;
- using and giving away used clothes, toys, etc.; and
- traveling by bike or by public transportation rather than by car.

The idea behind the green movement is to create a consumer who is rational and conscious enough to give priority to his or her health and security, and not to convenience, and who thinks about the future of everyday life. In other words, we may say the idea is to transform consumers from 'ego-consumption' to 'eco-consumption'. Such an attitude is also desirable among entrepreneurs, state bodies, and local authorities. It can be shaped; but it requires cooperation of particular entities in the market, responsible actions and decisions, clear motives, and good foresight.

Progressive servicization of the economy leads to the transformation of industrial societies into so-called service societies. One of the characteristics of such a society is an increase in the purchase of services – servicization of consumption. But we are not talking only about a simple servicization of consumption – i.e., replacing one's own consumption as a method of meeting one's needs with purchasing services on the market. What also changes is the quality of purchased services. This mainly refers to the group of services that is related to higher needs – the buyer does not want to 'have' but wants to 'be' or actually to 'survive'. That is why people tend to go on vacations to attractive, remote places or participate in extreme sports. This orientation also makes education or health-related services more popular. The main reasons for the occurrence of this phenomenon are (Lovelock et al., 2009)

- increasing production and use of goods for which services constitute complementary goods;
- substitution of some material goods and services, which means that some things can be replaced by services (car by taxi, summer house by hotel); and
- advance of civilization and advances in science and technology, which induces the need to develop the intangible services sector (education, culture, leisure, information).

The shift in emphasis to the quality of the consumed goods is connected with consumption dematerialization. Consumption dematerialization is defined as growing consumption of intangible goods, such as information, knowledge, aesthetic experiences, improvement of health and general condition, and so forth (Schiffman and Kanuk, 2010; Lambkin et al., 2001). On the one hand, it induces interest in goods (mostly intangible) that provoke emotions; but on the other hand, there is a growing need for material goods that also provide experiences. Therefore, the phenomenon of symbolic interaction already discussed is becoming more important (Lambkin et al., 2001).

When we bear the foregoing in mind, we may say that consumption has moved to the fourth phase of development, namely the post-material phase. As a reminder, in the first phase, the greatest share in the consumption structure (in value terms) was that of food; in the second phase, home and household equipment; and in the third phase, the means of communication and cultural media (Bywalec, 2007).

By **virtualization of consumer behavior** we mean satisfying consumer needs by means of electronic media, mostly the Internet and television. Due to the development of these media, the methods of satisfying many needs have changed radically – this concerns higher needs in particular. Virtualization in the sphere of consumer behavior is mainly manifested in (Lambkin et al., 2001; De Pelsmacker et al., 2010)

- more individual and democratized reception of cultural contents, due to which a consumer may select contents according to his or her preferences and may also become an author of cultural contents and offer them to others;
- replacing the 'culture of signs' with the 'culture of image' and the 'culture of sound' (the so called visualization and phonization of culture);
- shifting from public institutions to home as the place for satisfying cultural, educational, and even medical needs and satisfying them at any convenient time; and
- splitting human life into real life (the physical world) and virtual life (what we see on TV or on a computer screen).

Virtualization and the Gutenberg era

Some sociologists consider the increasing visualization of consumption to be a decline of the Gutenberg era, and they point to functional illiteracy as one of the symptoms of this process.

However, the prominent Polish writer and publicist Kapuscinski did not share this opinion. He said:

'In Third World countries, the problem is not the decline of the Gutenberg era, which is being replaced by the Internet and television; but the fact that the Gutenberg era has never reached them. There are many places in the world where the Gutenberg era is looked for; it is a dream. There are not many signs pointing to the decline of Gutenberg's invention, either. Quite the opposite – the number of books throughout the world is increasing. So is the number of publishing houses and of bookstores'.

Source: Kapuscinski (2000)

It is worth noting that rapidly increasing virtualization of consumer behavior may lead to a split of human life into real and virtual. It may also cause psychophysical addiction to the Internet, television, or mobile phones. These types of addiction may, with time, become a major social pathology, which is particularly dangerous since it affects mainly youth and children. Another characteristic trend present in the modern economy is **cocooning**. It develops due to technological progress, in particular the spread of the Internet, which allows for shopping, conducting bank transactions, studying, or even working without leaving one's home (Lambkin et al., 2001; Kiezel, 2010). Moreover, housing conditions are improving as well as the economic situation of households, which allows for equipping homes with appropriate devices that provide access to culture, information, or jobs. The development of cocooning is stimulated by progressive individualization of lifestyles and by escape to privacy. As a result, a large group of consumers, in particular women, disabled, and elderly people, are able to undertake all sorts of activities without giving up the raising of children or having to wait in stores and so on.

It is becoming clear that more and more people try to satisfy their cultural and leisure needs without leaving their homes – this is why homes are not only equipped with computers or TV sets, but also with home theatres or even gyms and other amenities. Obviously, this situation has some social consequences: on the one hand, human relationships are limited; people do not meet with friends or neighbors as often as before. On the other hand, we may observe a return to seeing the family as valuable. Family bonds are becoming stronger. This aspect of cocooning, however, refers to a limited number of households, since the role of the family in most cases decreases – young people become independent very quickly, and elderly people do not want to be dependent on their children. Thus, in highly developed countries, multigenerational families (at least of two generations) are becoming scarce. People get married at an older age, the number of single-person households is increasing, people are separated from one another, and this makes the process of decision making much more individualized (Bywalec, 2007).

The phenomenon of consumer cocooning is accompanied by another trend, namely **privatization of consumption**. This may be interpreted in two ways: we may either think of it as the process of commercialization, i.e., changing public consumption into private consumption or as the so-called process of consumption individualization. This phenomenon is mainly encouraged by (Lambkin et al., 2001; Schiffman and Kanuk, 2010)

- progressive escape to privacy and individualization of lifestyles (decollectivization);
- more and more households having their own means of transportation, modern information carriers, and cultural media;
- improving housing conditions and the possibility of installing all sorts of equipment that allows for communication at any distance; and
- shortening and modifying work time and the ways of doing jobs, thus increasing the amount of free time.

Cocooning and privatization of consumer behavior cause an increase in so-called informal consumption. **Informal consumption** (hidden consumption) may be defined as a very personal and individualized consumer behavior carried out at home, where the consumer does not have to follow the norms of the public sphere and where they can be themselves and act according to their nature as they are not observed or evaluated by anybody (Smith and Wheeler, 2002.). In highly developed countries, another tendency may be observed, namely **deconsumption**. This involves conscious limitation of consumption to a rational level, which means to a level that arises from the natural, individual, physical, and psychic characteristics of a consumer. There are four causes for this phenomenon (Bywalec, 2007):

- limiting consumption due to increasing instability of modern households (protective consumption);

- shifting from quantity to quality of the consumed goods;
- limiting consumption of material goods for the benefit of intangible goods; and
- limiting consumption to a rational level caused by:
  - growing fatigue and disappointment about high consumption and awareness of the need to rationalize it,
  - lowered ranking of consumption in the system of values (consumption becoming an instrument in accordance with the idea that 'you do not live to consume but consume to live'), and
  - environmental protection.

In view of the foregoing, we may say that the reasons for deconsumption are varied – first is the limitation of consumption out of necessity; the next two consist mainly of changing the manner of consumption. Only the fourth group of reasons lead to a conscious, deliberate, well-considered limitation of consumption based on a reconstruction of the system of values. Protective consumption arises from threats that modern households have to face, such as unemployment, illnesses, unstable situations, and military conflicts in the world (Kahneman and Tversky, 2000). Consumers deliberately limit the consumption of goods. They prefer saving to borrowing, which they hope will secure their future consumption in the event of a disadvantageous situation. It sometimes happens that buyers give up some goods in order to be able to buy goods of better quality – it is becoming very popular to buy highly aesthetic goods or those that are technologically advanced. Another step in this evolution of behavior is a shift towards immaterial spheres of consumption (Kiezel, 2010).

Deconsumption is a reaction to the excessive consumptionism that developed after World War II. Consumptionism is consumption that is not justified by biological, socio-cultural, or economic reasons. Still, many economists considered this phenomenon to be positive. They used the following supportive arguments (Stiglitz, 2007):

- it gives the possibility (together with a consumption life style) to spread the idea of freedom, democracy, security, and individuality and
- the phenomenon is treated as a worldwide leading idea, which integrates people and counterpoises growing fundamental religions and the terrorism based on them and even war.

In the literature, however, the most common attitude towards rapidly growing consumption is rather critical. It is even referred to as 'affluenza', derived from the words 'affluence' and 'influenza'. The symptoms of this disease are the feeling of continuous dissatisfaction, fatigue, nervous tension, rush; the feeling of permanent lack of something and the buying that follows, and so on (Bywalec, 2007). Some severe consequences of affluenza are also workaholism, permanent debt, excess of waste products, worse relationships with social surroundings, and so on. We may thus say that mass consumption (pertaining to large social groups), which is usually high, has not lived up to expectations. It has improved our daily existence, but it has not made our lives happier; it has not become an effective remedy for eternal problems, such as passing away, getting older, diseases, accidents, and others. That is the reason we feel fatigue and are disappointed with consumption, i.e., we experience the classic symptoms of affluenza (Lambkin et al, 2001; Johannes, 2004; Bywalec, 2007).

Another extremely interesting trend in consumption and in consumer behavior is **prosumption**. The term was coined from the words production (pro-) and consumption (-sumption). The term refers to a process of intermingling between consumption and production so that the difference between them becomes blurred. This may be the outcome of two tendencies: first when consumption 'enters' into the process of production and the manufacturer also becomes a consumer, and second when production is 'included' in consumption and the consumer also becomes a manufacturer (Stiglitz, 2007). Some of the main factors stimulating this process are the following (Lewis and Bidger, 2001):

- increasing amounts of free time due to automatization and robotization of production processes and the need to use this time in an attractive way;
- the possibility of working at home and intermingling home life with consumption activities;
- development and spread of education, in particular of so-called continuing education; and
- changes in work organization and redefining the role of work in human life (evolution of job towards creativity).

Modern consumption and consumer behavior are also, or even most of all, based on ethical premises. In this context, we introduce the notion of **ethical consumption**. The term has a very broad meaning. When we talk about ethics in consumption, we should first of all think about consumer behavior aimed at obtaining and using goods in a way that conforms to the basic rules of modern ethics (Antonides and van Raaij, 2003; Johannes, 2004). Such behavior can be manifested in the following ways (Brown, 2003):

- a person gives up the consumption of goods that are obtained as a result of killing animals,
- a person gives up the goods that were produced with the use of forced labor or child labor or for inadequate remuneration etc.,
- a person reacts to the unethical behavior of entrepreneurs, and
- a person does not participate in gadget consumption etc.

Ethical dilemma of consumers

The ethical dimension of consumption is visible in various activities aimed at diminishing the differences in the access to consumption of goods (which is manifested in poverty and social exclusion on the one hand, and as excessive wealth and luxury on the other hand).

The Swiss sociologist Ziegler thus comments on the phenomenon: '...*I have a sense of the utter absurdity of the world's situation. I am often angry because I have to live in a culture of excess, and I am aware of the fact that at this particular moment there is somebody who is paying for it with his or her life. It is high time we gave up that Malthusian talk about natural selection, which is only supposed to comfort our conscience while we are devouring our steak. If nowadays people die of hunger, it means they are murdered. And every person who does nothing but look is equally guilty'.*

Source: Bywalec (2007)

As has been shown, the changes we observe in consumption and in consumer behavior nowadays in international markets are not unified. Sometimes they oppose or exclude one another; they are divergent or synergetic. That is why the answer to the question – Quo vadis homo consumicus? – is not at all obvious. If we still wish to try to define a future consumer (a new consumer), we need to remember that this consumer will be characterized by (Graham, 2010):

- multiculturalism, since consumer's function in a multicultural environment;
- greater awareness of consumer rights and a more rational attitude toward market offers;
- a critical attitude; consumers will have doubts and will feel anxiety about economic and social policies, and about the functioning of various institutions;
- an evident need for social bonds that will differ from traditional community bonds;
- greater mobility in space and in social life;
- ability to see the value of human-nature relationships;
- seeking self-development, pursuing complete self-realization;
- replacing the prestige of having by the prestige of using, increasing the appreciation of free time, since it provides the conditions for achieving individual goals and values;
- looking for ever stronger experiences, pursuing the exotic, extraordinary; and
- growing attachment to such values as youth, health, good appearance, and physical fitness.

It is important to stress that without further growth of consumption, the development of the modern economy will not be possible. This development has become a sort of hostage of consumption. A possible stagnation or just a slow growth in consumption in highly developed societies accompanied by a high and growing supply pressure caused by quickly advancing economies will give rise to great tensions in the market and thus will paralyze the functioning of economies and of social life. The quickly increasing production potential and growing supply of consumer goods need to immediately find consumers in the market. Otherwise the consequences of the economic collapse that will follow will be difficult to imagine (Schiffman et al., 2008).

Socio-cultural, political, and economic changes that took place in the last decade in Europe and in the rest of the world caused a transformation of consumer mentality and adoption of particular consumption values (Mazurek-Lopacinska, 2002):

- customers reject the consumption civilization of the 20th century – based on increased quantities of consumption – and try to achieve better quality of consumption and of life in general;
- the critical attitude of customers is increasing, as well as their doubts and anxieties about the existing economic and social policies and the functioning of various institutions; people more often feel concern about the future and their insecure situation;
- consumers seek self-development, pursue complete self-realization; they pay more attention to emotions, feelings, individual tastes, likes, and dislikes; they more often appreciate their free time, since it provides the conditions for achieving individual goals and values;

- the social position of women is changing; they try to achieve self-realization at work and in other fields of activity rather than in the family community; and
- consumers exhibit growing attachment to such values as youth, health, good appearance, and physical fitness; they aim at buying healthy, safe, organic products, etc.; they recognize the importance of ecological problems.

These changes in consumption values give rise to the development of the following characteristics in the new consumer (Solomon et al. 2010):

- greater awareness of consumer rights and more rational approaches to market offers; we may assume that this will stimulate a tendency to be unfaithful to a product or brand;
- better strategic skills in managing one's own budget;
- a growing need for social bonds that differ from traditional community bonds; new forms of social bonds include bonds with small groups of friends, new families, and other relationships that satisfy the need to have one's own place in the world – hence the growing popularity of goods and services that get people together and thus facilitate social interactions;
- a feature of the new consumer that is particularly important for companies that operate in international markets is the consumer's multiculturalism arising from the fact of living in a multicultural world; on the one hand, we observe a tendency to yield to the global operational strategies of companies; but on the other hand, there is a tendency to retain identity and cultural specificity (in this case, it is the companies that need to adjust their strategies and mechanisms of operation);
- greater mobility of consumers in space as well as in social life, which favors the development of various forms of social communication; factors increasing customers' mobility in the labor market are system transformation processes that have taken place in the Eastern countries as well as growing liberalism in the economic policy of many countries;
- an appreciation of the importance of human-nature relationships, manifested in the approval of environmental protection activities and in purchasing and using green products; and
- a consumer more and more often participates in various forms of interpersonal integration, which focuses, to a smaller or larger extent, on the humanitarian aspects of social, national, and international life.

Clear consumer expectations towards enterprises as well as consumer organizations (Figure 87) pose a challenge to marketing companies. A more conscious and better prepared consumer is not so easily deceived by emotions, but rather expects accurate information on the product to have the choice made easier.

Consumers expect	
companies will provide	**consumer protection institutions will**
<ul><li>comprehensive and reliable information on products</li><li>a concept of solving consumption problems (design, ideas on how to dress, arrange home, etc.)</li><li>high quality products that are, most of all, healthy, safe, and natural</li><li>affordable and diverse prices</li><li>time-saving forms of sale</li><li>convenient methods of payment</li><li>polite and creative sales assistants</li><li>aesthetic interior decoration of places of sale that encourage customers rather than distance them</li><li>an appealing atmosphere in stores</li><li>convenient location of stores</li><li>commercial infrastructure that facilitates shopping for all types of customers</li><li>promotion benefits</li></ul>	<ul><li>enforce proper labeling of products</li><li>elaborate minimum quality standards</li><li>test products and make the results public</li><li>prevent false advertising</li><li>protect consumer safety</li><li>help consumers in drawing up claims and complaints</li><li>educate consumers</li><li>provide objective information on products</li><li>evaluate the level of customer service in companies</li><li>represent a customer in the event of litigation against a company</li><li>provide social/legal advice on consumer issues</li><li>evaluate the reliability of promotional activities</li></ul>

Source: Mazurek-Lopacinska (2002), p. 24

Figure 87. Consumers' expectations towards companies and consumer organizations

In their pursuit of a better quality of living, consumers will be more and more attentive to the uniqueness of the products they buy. Good examples that illustrate this trend are expensive personal products, which are extremely successful on the market, e.g., product lines launched by La Redoute on the French market. Companies also have to face another challenge, i.e., create services that can be used by consumers for self-realization. These include services related to higher needs in the various spheres of human activity, such as culture, tourism, do-it-yourself work, education, sport, research, creative activity, or pursuit of a hobby (Lambkin et al., 2001; Mazurek-Lopacinska, 2002).

Consumers try to live closer to nature. This opens the market to the organic food industry, green clothing, but also to healthy ways of spending free time (such as gardening, sport, and outdoor activities). This has led to a great expansion of health marketing in recent years. Anxiety about the future increases the demand for information and for the guarantees attached to products. This requires a considerable development of post-purchase services and puts great emphasis on being extremely professional in marketing management. This increases the demand for very well-qualified technology and publicity specialists. Growing expectations towards marketing should make marketing professionals more socially responsible for their activities and should lead to the elaboration of rules of professional ethics that ought to be observed (Kiezel, 2010). It is also important for marketing decisions to remain in harmony with ecology and the norms of social coexistence. Companies that adopt a socially responsible attitude include consumer affairs departments in their organizational structure. Their functions, as compared to the older customer relations departments, are broader – they are also responsible for maintaining relationships with customer organizations and for representing and defending consumer interests, not only those of present consumers, but also those of potential consumers and even of whole communities.

List of References

Ahmad, R. & Buttle, F., 2001. Customer retention: a potentially potent marketing management strategy. *Journal of Strategic Marketing*, 9: 67-94.

Albaum, G., Strandskov, J. & Duerr, E., 1998. *International marketing and export management*. London: Addison Wesley Longman.

Antonides G. & van Raaij, W. F., 2003. *Consumer behavior. European perspective*. New York: John Wiley & Sons, Ltd.

Best, R., 2009. *Market-based management: international version*. London: Pearson Higher Education.

Blackwell, R. D., Miniard, P. W. & Engel, J. F., 2001. *Consumer behavior*. Fort Worth: Dryden.

Blythe, J., 1997. *Essence consumer behavior*. New York: Financial Times Press.

Blythe, J., 2009. *Essentials of marketing*. London: Financial Times Press.

Bradley, F., 2005. *International marketing strategy*. New York: Financial Times Press.

Bridson, K., Evans, J. & Hickman, M., 2008. Assessing the relationship between loyalty program attributes, store satisfaction and store loyalty. *Journal of Retailing and Consumer Services*, 15 (5): 364-374.

Brown, M. T., 2003. *Ethical process: an approach to disagreements and controversial issues*. London: Pearson Higher Education.

Buchanan, R. & Gilles, C., 1990. Value managed relationship: the key to customer retention and profitability. *European Management Journal*: 8 (4), 38-55.

Butcher, K., Sparks, B. & O'Callaghan, F., 2001. Evaluative and relational influences on service loyalty. *International Journal of Service Industry Management*, 12 (4): 62-79.

Butscher, S. A., 1999. *Customer clubs and loyalty programmes*. Vermont: Gower.

Bywalec, C., 2007. *Konsumpcja w teorii i praktyce gospodarowania*. Warszawa: PWN.

Cichosz, M., 2003. Lojalnosc klienta wobec firmy. *Marketing i Rynek*, 8: 14-19.

Clarke, G & Wilson, I., 2009. *International marketing*. London: McGraw-Hill.

Crane, R., 2000. *European business culture*. New York: Financial Times Press.

Day, G. S., 1969. A two-dimensional concept of brand loyalty. *Journal of Advertising Research*, 9 (3): 36-51.

De Burca, S., Brown, L. & Fletcher, R., 2004. *International marketing: an SME perspective*. New York: Financial Times Press.

De Pelsmacker, P., Geuens, M. & van den Bergh, J., 2010. *Marketing communications: a European perspective*. London. Financial Times Press.

DG SANCO, 2011. Loyalty in Europe [online]. [cited 14.12.2010]. Available from World Wide Web: http://ec.europa.eu/dgs/consumers/loyalty/index_en.htm.

Dick, A. S. & Basu, K., 1994. Customer loyalty: toward an integrated conceptual framework, *Journal of Academy of Marketing Science*, 22 (2): 98-121.

Doole, I. & Lowe, R., 2001. *International marketing strategy*. London: Thomson Learning.

Doole, I., Lancaster, P. & Lowe, R., 2005. *Understanding and managing customers*. New York: Financial Times Press.

Dowling, G. R. & Uncles, M., 1997. Do loyalty customer programs really work? *Sloan Management Review*, 38 (4): 69-81.

Doyle, P. & Stern, P., 2006. *Marketing management and strategy*. New York: Financial Times Press.

Ehrenberg, A. S. C., 2000. Repeat buying – facts, theory and applications. *Journal of Empirical Generalisations in Marketing Science*, 5: 21-39.

Evans, M., Foxall, G. & Jamal, A., 2009. *Consumer behavior*. New York: John Wiley & Sons.

Evans, M., Moutinho, L. & van Raaij, W. F., 1996. *Applied consumer behaviour*, Harlow: Addison-Wesley Publi. Co.

Graham, J., 2010. *Critical Thinking in Consumer Behavior: Cases and Experiential Exercises*. New Jersey: Prentice Hall.

Griffin, J., 1995. *Customer loyalty. How to earn it, how to keep it*. London: Lexington Books.

Gruen, T. W. & Gentry, J. W., 1995. The outcome set of relationship marketing in consumer markets. *International Business Review*, 4 (4): 89-104.

Han, S. H., Shin, Y. S. Reinhart, W. & Moore, W. T., 2008. Market segmentation effects in corporate credit rating changes: the case of emerging markets. *Journal of financial Services Research,* 35: 141-166.

Hatton, A., 2000. *The definitive guide to marketing planning*. New York: Financial Times Press.

Hollensen, S., 2009. *Essentials of global marketing*. Harlow: Pearson Education.

Hollensen, S., 2010. *Global marketing: a decision-oriented approach*. Harlow: Pearson Education.

Huddleston, P., Whipple, J. & VanAuken, A., 2004. Food store loyalty: application of a consumer loyalty framework. *Journal of Targeting, Measurement and Analysis for Marketing*, 12: 140-159.

Hunerberg, R., 1994. *Internationales marketing*. Landsberg: Verlag Moderne Idustrie.

Iverson, R. D. & Kuruvilla, S., 1995. Antecedents of union loyalty the influence of individual dispositions and organizational context. *Journal of Organizational Behaviour*, 16: 142-165.

Jacoby, J. & Chestnut, R. W., 1978. *Brand loyalty: measurement and management*. New York: John Wiley & Sons.

Johannes, B., 2004. Looking at consumer behavior in a moral perspective. *Journal of Business Ethics*, 51 (2): 129-141.

Johansson, J. K., 2006. *Global marketing. Foreign entry, local marketing and global management*. Boston: McGraw Hill.

Jones, T. O., Sasser Jr., W. E. & Earl, W., 1995. Why satisfied customers defect. *Harvard Business Review*, 73 (6): 198-214.

Kahneman, D. & Tversky, A., 2000. *Choice, values, and frazes*. Cambridge: Cambridge University Press.

Kandampully, J. & Suhartanto, D., 2000. Customer loyalty in the hotel industry: the role of customer satisfaction and image. *International Journal of Contemporary Hospitality Management*, 12 (6): 176-192.

Kapuscinski, R., 2000. Dwa rozne swiaty. *Rzeczpospolita*, 150: 7.

Kassarjian, H. H. & Robertson, T. S., 1991. Perspectives in consumer behavior. New Jersey: Prentice Hall.

Kiezel, E. (ed.), 2010. *Konsument i jego zachowania na rynku europejskim*. Warszawa: PWE.

Komor, M., 2000. *Euromarketing*. Warszawa: PWN.

Kotler, P., 2000. *Marketing management*. New Jersey: Prentice Hall, Inc.

Kotler, P., Keller, K., Brady, M., Goodman, M. & Hansen, T., 2009. *Marketing management*. New Jersey: Prentice Hall.

Lambkin, M., Foxall, G., van Raaij, F. & Heilbrunn, B., 2001. *European perspective on consumer behaviour*. London: Prentice Hall Europe.

Lau, G. T. & Lee, S. H., 1999. Consumers' trust in a brand and the link to brand loyalty. *Journal of Market-Focused Management*, 4 (4): 341-370.

Lewis, D. & Bidger, D., 2001. *The soul of the new consumer*. London: Nicholas Brealey Publishing.

Lovelock, C. H., Wirtz, J. & Chew, P., 2009. *Essentials of services marketing*. New Jersey: Prentice Hall.

Lubke, G. H. & Muthen, B., 2005. Investigating population heterogeneity with factor mixture models. *Psychological Methods*, 10: 42-59.

Marin, L., Ruiz, S. & Rubio, A., 2009. The role of identity salience in the effects of corporate social responsibility on consumer behavior. *Journal of Business Ethics*, 84 (1): 65-78.

Mazurek-Lopacinska, K., 2002. *Orientacja na kienta w przedsiebiorstwie*. Warszawa: PWE.

McAlexander, J. H., Kim, S. K. & Roberts, S. D., 2003. Loyalty: the influence of satisfaction and brand community integration. *Journal of Marketing Theory and Practice*, Autumn: 164-181.

Media and Marketing, 2010. *Loyalty on gasoline market in Poland* [online]. [cited 23.12.2010]. Available from World Wide Web: http://media.com.pl/mmp/article/loyalty_index.htm.

De Mooij, M., 2010. *Global marketing and advertising*. Los Angeles: SAGE.

Muhlbacher, H., Leihs, H. & Dahringer, L., 2006. *International marketing. A global perspective*. London: Thomson Learning.

Newman, J. W. & Werbel, R. S., 1973. Multivariate analysis of brand loyalty for major household appliances. *Journal of Marketing Research*, 10: 126-143.

O'Dell, S. M. & Pajunen, J. A., 1997. *The butterfly customer*. Toronto: John Wiley& Sons.

Oliver, R. L., 1999. Whence consumer loyalty? *Journal of Marketing*, 63 (4): 41-58.

Orchowski, K., 1999. *Budowanie lojalności klientów w usługach doradztwa finansowego*. In: Rogoziński, K. (ed.), *Marketing usług profesjonalnych*, Poznan: AE.

Pierscionek, Z., 2003. *Strategie konkurencji i rozowju przedsiebiorstwa*. Warszawa: PWN.

Pong, L. T. & Yee, T. P., 2001. *An integrated model of service loyalty*. Brussels: Academy of Business and Administrative Sciences.

Raymond, M., 2003. *Tomorrow people: future consumers and how to read them*. London: Financial Times Press.

Reichheld, F. F. & Sasser Jr., W. E., 1990. Zero defections: quality comes to services, *Harvard Business Review*, 68 (5): 78-91.

Reichheld, F. F., 2003. The one number you need to grow. *Harvard Business Review*, 81 (12): 82-104.

Reinartz, W. & Kumar, V., 2002. The mismanagement of customer loyalty. *Harvard Business Review*, 80 (7): 214-232.

Rudawska, E., 2005. *Lojalnosc klientow*. Warszawa: PWE.

Rugman, A. M. & Collinson, S., 2009. *International business*. New York: Financial Times Press.

Sagan, A., 2010. *Mieszane modele czynnikowe w miedzynarodowej segmetacji psychograficznej – nowe podejscie do segementacji rynku*. In: Wiktor. J. W. & Zbikowska, A. (ed.), *Marketing międzynarodowy. Uwarunkowania i kierunki rozwoju*. Warszawa: PWE.

Samar, 2011. *European cars* [online]. [cited 07.01.2011]. Available from World Wide Web: http://www.samar.pl/__/__la/pl/__ac/sec,6/__Anisis-and-raports.html.

Schiffman, L. G. & Kanuk, L. L., 2010. *Consumer behavior: global edition*. London: Pearson Higher Education.

Schiffman, L. G., Bednall, D., O'Cass, A., Paladino, A., D'Alessandro, S. & Kanuk, L. L., 2008. *Consumer behaviour*. New Jersey: Prentice Hall.

Schlegelmilch, B., Keegan, W. J. & Stoettinger, B., 2001. *Global marketing management: a European perspective*. London: Financial Times Press.

Siemieniako, D. & Urban, W., 2005. Model zarządzania zorientowanego na lojalność klientów. in: Lewandowski, J. (ed.). Zarządzanie organizacjami gospodarczymi. Koncepcje i metody. Lodz: Politechnika Łódzka.

Smith, S. & Wheeler, J., 2002. *Managing the customer experience: turning customers into advocates.* New York: Financial Times Press.

Smyczek, S. & Sowa, I., 2005. *Konsument na rynku – zachowania, modele, aplikacje.* Warszawa: Difin.

Smyczek, S., 2001. *Lojalnosc konsumentow na rynku.* Katowice: AE.

Soderlund, M., 1998. Customer satisfaction and its consequences on customer behaviour revisited. *International Journal of Service Industry Management*, 9 (2): 68-89.

Solomon, M. R., Bamossy, G., Askegaard, S. & Hogg, M. K., 2010. *Consumer behaviour.* New York: Financial Times Press.

Sroga, G., 2005. Trendy w marketingu partnerskim. *Marketing w praktyce*, 2: 16-42.

Stern, P. & Hammond, K., 2004. The relationship between customer loyalty and purchase incidence. *Marketing Letters*, 15 (1): 5-19.

Stiglitz, J., 2007, *Globalizacja*, Warszawa: PWN.

Storbacka, K. & Lehtinen, J. R., 2001. *Sztuka budowania trwałych zwiazkow z klientem – Customer Relationship Management.* Krakow: Oficyna Ekonomiczna.

Stum, D. & Thiry, A., 1991. Building Customer Loyalty. *Training and Development Journal*, April: 64-81.

Sullivan, M. & Adcock, D., 2003. *Marketing w handlu detalicznym.* Krakow: Oficyna Ekonomiczna.

Swiatowy, G. & Pluta-Olearnik, M., 2000. *Kreowanie lojalnosci klientow poprzez marke i jakosc uslug.* Wroclaw: AE.

TNS, 2010. *Managing cutomer relationships profitability* [online]. [cited 28.12.2010]. Available from World Wide Web: http://www.tns-us.com/files/trim.pdf.

Tucker, W. T., 1964. The development of brand loyalty. *Journal of Marketing Research*, 1: 43-62.

Urban, W. & Siemieniako, D., 2008. *Lojalnosc klientow. Modele, motywacja i pomiar.* Warszawa: PWN.

Usunie, J-C. & Lee, J., 2009. *Marketing across cultures.* New York: Financial Times Press.

Wang, H. C., Pallister, J. G. & Foxall, G. R., 2006. Innovativeness and involvement as determinants of website loyalty: determinants of consumer loyalty in B2C e-commerce. *Technovation*, 26 (12): 166-173.

Wansink, B., 2003. Developing a cost-effective brand loyalty program. *Journal of Advertising Research*, September: 41-63.

Wiktor, J. W., Oczkowska, R. & Zbikowska, A., 2008. *Marketing międzynarodowy. Zarys problematyki.* Warszawa: PWE.

Yu, Y. & Dean, A., 2001. The contribution of emotional satisfaction to consumer loyalty. *International Journal of Service Industry Management*, 12 (3): 184-198.

Zabinski, L., 2000. *Modele strategii marketingowych.* Katowice: AE.

Zins, A. H., 2001. Relative attitudes and commitment in customer loyalty models. Some experiences in the commercial airline industry. *International Journal of Service Industry Management*, 12 (3): 160-183.

9 Chapter: International marketing in practice

Chapter learning objectives

- Describe the major elements of an export contract.

- Explain the contents of the Incoterms clauses.

- Identify common payment instruments in international business and their advantages/disadvantages.

- Identify the distribution channels used by companies in the international market.

- Describe the logistics performance of companies in the international market.

- Characterize the promotional tools in international marketing.

- Present the laws and cultural aspects of promotion in the international market.

9.1   The export contract

The requirements of the marketing mix in international business are extensive. The product needs to be modified more or less according to the design tastes, desired product features, and performance expectations of local customers. In general, the wider the international business scope, the broader the scope of managing the international product development, logistics, pricing, promotion, and communication. Business agreements, such as for example export contracts, vary according to the complexity of the product. First of all, there is the product description, the shipment quantity, the delivery date, and the address of the exporter and the importer to be provided in the contract. In addition, the transportation method should be clarified. Another important element in the export contract is devoted to the payment terms agreed upon by the parties. Delivery costs and the expenses associated with the payment agreements have a fundamental impact on the export sales price calculation. In the process of an export business, the exporting company is in close contact with the importer but needs to maintain many interfaces with other firms and institutions. The exporter must apply for the export allowance to the customs authorities. Further interfaces of the exporting firm are the bank, the carrier, and eventually an insurance company.

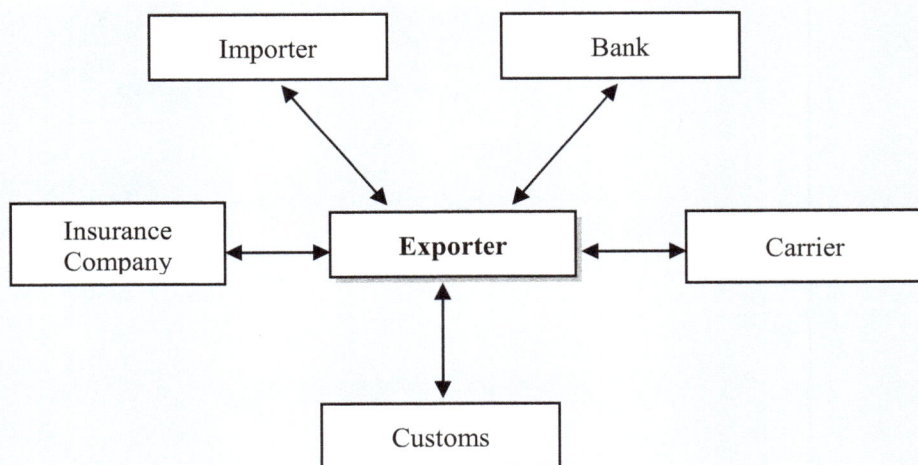

Figure 88. Important interfaces of the exporter

For each export contract, there are usually related documents provided by the exporter, who works together with the logistics firm and the customs office. Important documents provided by the exporting firm are

- a commercial invoice; (sample attached in the appendix of this publication);
- a packing list;
- export licenses approved by customs authorities;
- possibly, a shipment insurance certificate (CIF, CIP Incoterms);
- possibly, a Certificate of Origin; and

- possibly, technical and safety certificates.

The shipping documents, as prepared by the logistics firm upon delivery, are

- a Bill of Lading (B/L) for transportation by vessel; (sample attached in the appendix of this publication);
- a Convention Merchandise Routiere (CMR) for road shipment by truck; and
- an Air Waybill in case of air shipment.

In the following sections, major export contracting issues linked to the shipment and payment and their influence on the export price calculation are introduced.

9.1.1   International commercial terms (Incoterms)

In 1936, the International Chamber of Commerce first published international trade rules, which have been modified several times up to the latest version, International Commercial Terms 2010 (Incoterms 2010). Revisions have been made to ensure that the wording of the Incoterms rules clearly and accurately reflects present-day trade practices. Incoterms play a significant role in the operations of foreign trade businesses. In the context of export and import of goods, Incoterms provide a commonly accepted basis for regulating the duties of the seller and the buyer and dividing costs, such as transportation and border duties, between the parties. Moreover, they define the point where risks, such as damage, waste, and loss of goods, are transferred from the seller to the buyer. However, Incoterms do not have an impact on the payment conditions or the transfer of the property rights pertaining to the cargo. Incoterms are not applied automatically to the foreign trade partners. They are only applicable if both parties specifically agree on them in their contract. In general, Incoterms are divided into eleven codes as introduced below (Incoterms, 2010).

EX Works (EXW) . . . named place of delivery

EXW represents the minimum obligation for the seller; the buyer has to bear all costs and risks involved in taking the goods from the seller's premises. The seller fulfills its obligation when the goods are placed at the disposal of the buyer at the seller's premises or another named place (e.g., factory warehouse). They are not cleared for export and not loaded on any collecting vehicle. The seller must render the buyer, at the latter's request, risk, and expense, every assistance in obtaining an export license or other official authorization necessary for the export of goods.

'Free Carrier' (FCA) . . . named place of delivery

FCA means that the seller delivers the goods, cleared for export and at his own risk and expense, to the carrier designated by the buyer at the named place. If delivery occurs at the seller's premises, the seller is responsible for loading the cargo.

Free Alongside Ship (FAS) . . . named port of shipment

FAS indicates that the seller delivers the goods, which are placed alongside the vessel designated by the buyer at the named port of shipment. The buyer has to bear all costs and risks of loss or damage to the goods from that moment. The seller must obtain, at his own risk and expense, any export license or other official customs formalities necessary for the export of the goods.

Free on Board (FOB) . . . named port of shipment

FOB means the seller delivers when the goods pass the ship's rail at the named port of loading. This means that the buyer has to bear all costs and risks of loss or damage to the goods from that point. The vessel is designated by the buyer. The seller must obtain, at his own risk and expense, any export license or other official authorization and carry out all customs formalities necessary for the export of the goods. The FOB term can be used only for sea or inland waterway transport.

Cost and Freight (CFR) . . . named port of destination

CFR requires that the seller delivers when the goods pass the ship's rail at the named port of destination. The seller must deliver the goods to the vessel and must pay the costs and freight necessary to bring the goods to the named port of destination. The seller designates the vessel for the transportation to the port of shipment. The buyer bears all risks of loss or damage to the goods until such time as they have passed the ship's railing at the port of shipment. The seller must obtain, at his own risk and expense, any export license or other official authorization and carry out all customs formalities necessary for the export of the goods. The CFR term can be used only for sea or inland waterway transport.

Cost, Insurance and Freight (CIF) ... named port of destination

CIF stipulates that the seller delivers when the goods pass the ship's rail in the port of shipment. The seller must pay the costs and freight necessary to bring the goods to the named port of destination. The seller must deliver the goods on board the vessel and must obtain, at his own risk and expense, any license and customs formalities for the export of the goods. The seller designates the vessel for the transportation to the port of shipment. The seller bears all risks of loss or damage to the goods until such time as they have passed the ship's railing at the port of shipment. The seller must obtain, at his own expense, cargo insurance, as agreed in the contract, such that the buyer is entitled to make a claim directly to the insurer. The seller provides the buyer with the insurance policy. The CIF term can be used only for sea or inland waterway transport.

Carriage Paid To (CPT) . . . named destination

CPT means that the seller delivers the goods, at his own expense, to the agreed point of destination. The carrier is designated by the seller. The seller must obtain, at his own risk and expense, any export license and customs formalities necessary for the export of the goods. If subsequent carriers are used for the carriage to the agreed destination, the risk passes from the seller to the buyer when the goods have been delivered to the first carrier. The CPT term is used irrespective of the mode of transport, including multimodal transport.

Carriage and Insurance Paid (CIP) . . . named destination

CIP denotes that the seller delivers the goods, at his own expense, to the agreed upon destination. The carrier is designated by the seller, who also contracts for insurance and pays the insurance premium. The CIP term requires the seller to clear the goods for export. The buyer must bear all risks of loss or damage to the goods from the time they have been delivered by the seller to the carrier. If subsequent carriers are used for carriage to the agreed destination, the risk passes when the goods have been delivered to the first carrier. The term is used irrespective of the mode of transport, including multimodal transport.

Delivered at Terminal (DAT) . . . named terminal

DAT means that the seller delivers the goods, at his own expense, to the agreed upon terminal (e.g., railroad, air freight, and container terminal). The seller must obtain, at his own risk and expense, any export license and customs formalities necessary for the export of the goods. The seller has to bear all costs and risks of loss or damage to the goods until delivered to the named terminal. The term is used irrespective of the mode of transport, including multimodal transport.

Delivered at Place (DAP) . . . named destination

DAP requires the seller to deliver the goods, at his own expense, to the named place of destination. The seller must obtain, at his own risk and expense, any export license and customs formalities necessary for the export of the goods. The seller has to bear all costs and risks of loss or damage to the goods until delivered to the named place. The term is used irrespective of the mode of transport, including multimodal transport.

Delivered Duty Paid (DDP) . . . named destination

While the EXW term represents the minimum obligation for the seller, DDP represents the maximum. The seller delivers the goods to the buyer, cleared for import but not unloaded, at the named place of destination. The seller has to bear all the costs and risks of transportation, including all customs formalities necessary for the export of the goods and including costs for their transit through other countries and their import to the final place of destination. The seller must place the goods at the disposal of the buyer. The term is used irrespective of the mode of transport, including multimodal transport (Incoterms, 2010).

The case: The International Chamber of Commerce (ICC)

Founded in 1919, the International Chamber of Commerce is the largest, most representative business organization in the world. Its hundreds of thousands of member companies in over 120 countries have interests spanning every sector of private enterprise.

The ICC has three main activities: rules-setting, arbitration, and policy. Because its member companies and associations are themselves engaged in international business, ICC has unrivalled authority in making rules that govern the conduct of business across borders. These rules are observed in countless thousands of transactions every day and have become part of the fabric of international trade.

Setting rules and standards:

  * Arbitration under the rules of the ICC International Court of Arbitration is on the increase. Since 1999, the Court has received new cases at a rate of more than 500 a year.
  * The ICC's Uniform Customs and Practice for Documentary Credits (UCP 500) are the rules that banks apply to finance billions of dollars worth of world trade every year.
  * The ICC Incoterms are standard international trade definitions used every day in countless thousands of contracts. ICC model contracts make life easier for small companies that cannot afford large legal departments.
  * The ICC is a pioneer in business self-regulation of e-commerce. ICC codes on advertising and marketing are frequently reflected in national legislation and the codes of professional associations.

The ICC also provides essential services, foremost among them the ICC International Court of Arbitration, the world's leading arbitral institution. Another service is the World Chambers Federation, the ICC's worldwide network of chambers of commerce, fostering interaction and the exchange of best practices of chambers. Business leaders and experts drawn from the ICC's member companies feed their knowledge and experience into the crafting of the ICC stance on broad issues of trade and investment policy as well as on vital subjects. These include financial services, information technologies, telecommunications, marketing ethics, the environment, transportation, competition law, and intellectual property, among others. The ICC enjoys a close working relationship with the United Nations and other intergovernmental organizations, including the World Trade Organization, the G20, and the G8.

A world network of national committees works with its members to address the concerns of business in the countries and convey to their governments the business views formulated by the ICC.

Source: ICC (2010)

9.1.2   Payment instruments

The safest payment term from the exporter's perspective is 'payment in advance', which is typically used when (1) the importing firm is unknown or (2) the creditworthiness of the importer is doubtful or (3) potential payment restrictions within the country of destination may cause a considerable delay in the money transfer (Cateora et al., 2009). From the importer's view, payment in advance is obviously unpopular since it reduces the importer's liquidity before the goods are at its disposal. Moreover, the importer bears the risk that the payment has been made but the shipment will be delayed by the exporter or even cancelled, e.g., due to the exporter's bankruptcy. Another potential risk for the importer is that the cargo is shipped; but upon arrival, the importer recognizes that the quality standards agreed to in the product specifications of the contract are not met.

In contrast to payment in advance, the payment mode 'open account' transfers the risk from the importer to the exporter. Here, the exporter delivers its cargo to the importer, which pays the invoice amount upon receipt of the invoice (shipment) within the contractual period of time. However, the exporter bears the risk in case the importer is unwilling or unable to pay the shipment amount. The longer the agreed upon payment term, common periods are 30, 45, 60, 90, and 180 days after the invoice date, the higher the risk for the exporter. Therefore, business contracts based on open account should be agreed to only when exporter and importer know and trust each other. Another alternative is that the exporter sells its cargo against a draft issued by the importer. The draft can be used by the exporter, who can present it to his bank asking to receive cash upon presentation. The difference between the invoice (draft) value and the cash amount paid by the bank against the draft to the exporter depends on the importer's creditworthiness. In the worst case, the draft would not be accepted by the bank.

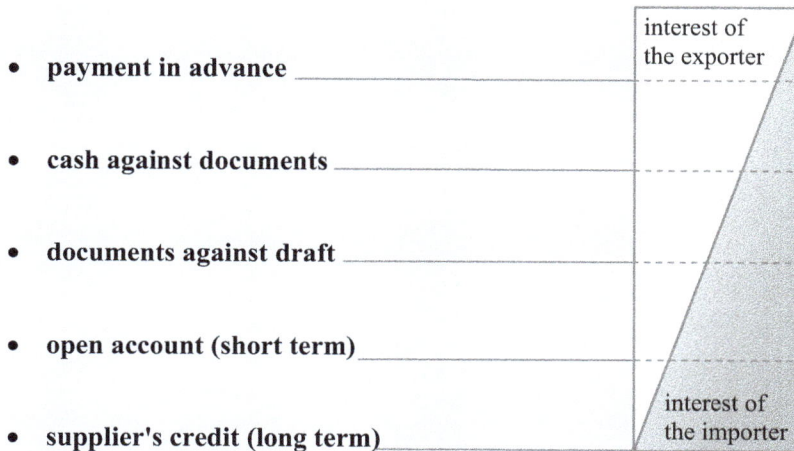

- **payment in advance** _____ interest of the exporter

- **cash against documents** _____

- **documents against draft** _____

- **open account (short term)** _____

- **supplier's credit (long term)** _____ interest of the importer

Figure 89. Payment conditions and related partners' interests

An exporter's ability to procure open account businesses can be enhanced by the use of credit insurance or factoring. **Credit insurance** protects the exporter from payment defaults by the importer in the context of an open account payment term. The premium paid by the exporter to the insurer depends on the importing firm's creditworthiness and the risk of the importer's country of residence. Large commercial credit insurance firms in Europe are Lloyd's, Euler-Hermes, and the Compagnie Française d'Assurance pour le Commerce Exterieur (Cofac). These firms, in addition to providing their clients with trade insurance, offer further services such as appraisals of the importer's creditworthiness and ratings of the exporter's trade receivables.

In the case of **factoring**, a third company (factor) purchases the accounts receivable from the exporting firm. Ideally, the exporter meets with the factor before any contract is signed and shipment procured in order to ensure its willingness to buy the receivable. The factor will investigate and evaluate the credit rating, and so forth, of the prospective buyer. In many cases, the factor has a correspondent in the importer's country in order to undertake the credit checking activities. The factor acts as a credit approval agency as well as securing the receipt of an outstanding payment for the exporter in case the importer becomes unable to pay its debts (Albaum et al., 2008).

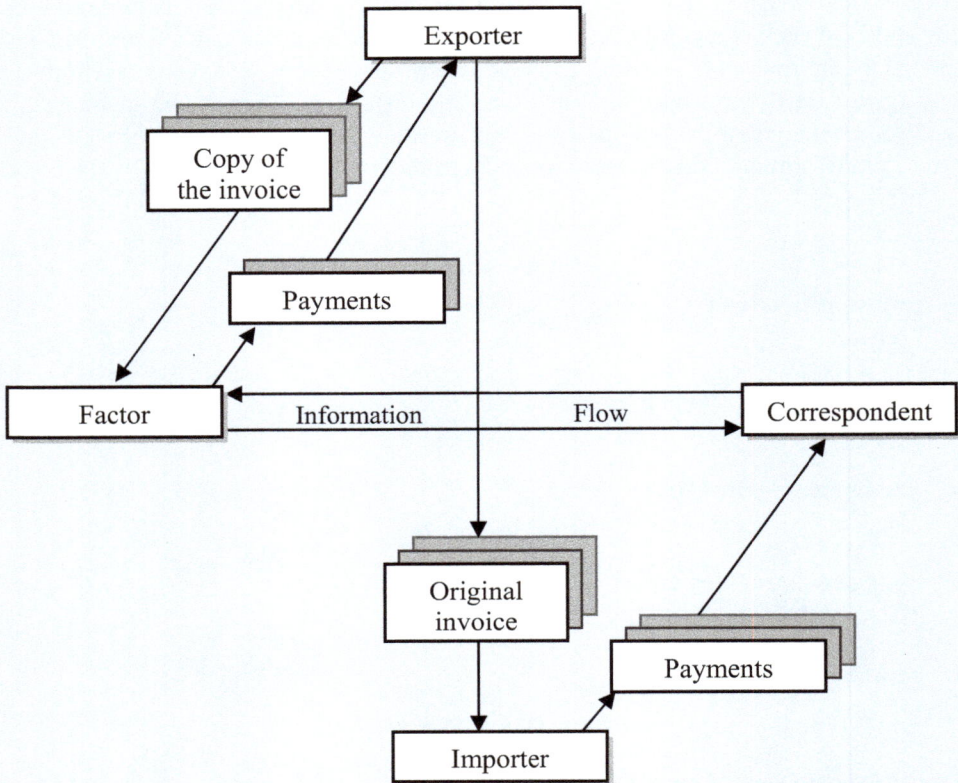

Source: Albaum at al. (2008), p. 513

Figure 90. Exporter's use of factoring

Nevertheless, factoring has two major disadvantages from the exporter's point of view. First of all, the introduction of a factoring firm (third party) does not provide a trustworthy basis for long-term business activities between the exporter and the importer since the factor directly contacts the importer in the context of the payment procedure. Second, depending on the buyer's individual risk and the country risk of the importer, the exporter may receive only a marginal part (up to 20 percent only) of the total invoice amount pending. These potential disadvantages are minimized when instead of factoring, a letter of credit as a payment term is agreed to by the seller and the buyer as discussed below.

Letter of credit

Assuming the buyer is unknown to the exporter (e.g., because of newly established business relations) and/or the importer does not indicate an excellent degree of creditworthiness, a

letter of credit (LC) serves as an instrument for securing the importer's payment. Exporter and importer have to agree on the use of the LC for payment in their contract (Fung, 2004). After the contract is signed with the exporter, the importer asks his bank to issue the LC. (A sample of a LC issuing form is attached in the appendix of this publication.) LC issuing charges are usually paid by the importer. In order to establish an LC, the importer has to provide corresponding securities to the LC issuing bank (e.g., real estate of the firm, cash, or the cargo itself to be imported).

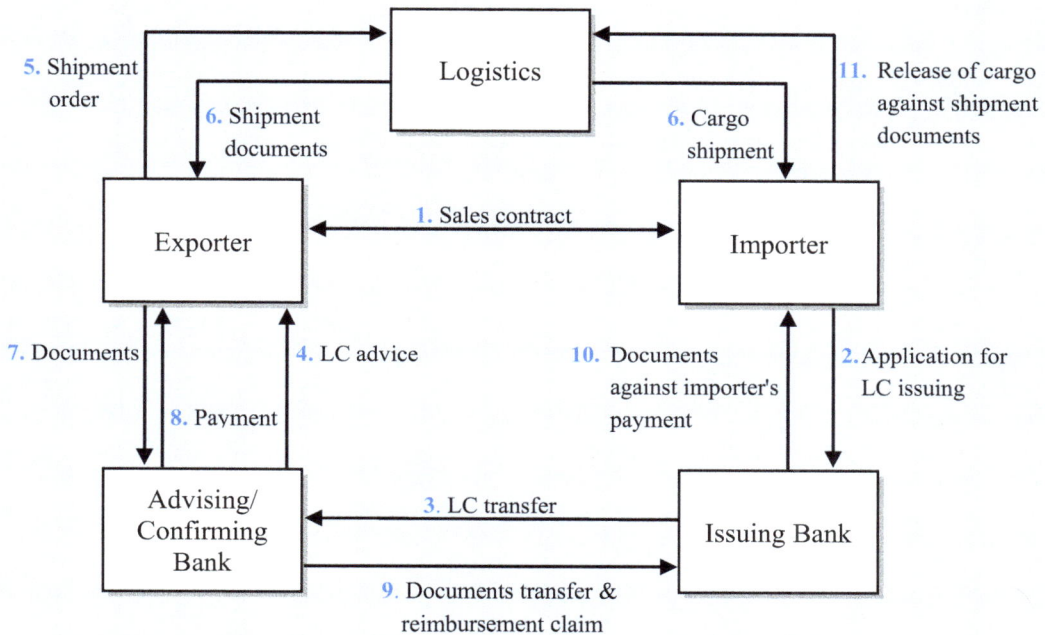

Source: modified from Albaum at al. (2008), p. 520

Figure 91. Export processing with letter of credit

1. A sales contract that determines the LC as the payment condition is signed by the exporter and importer.
2. A foreign bank issues the LC upon the application of the importer, who presents the signed contract and provides necessary securities to the issuing bank.
3. A valid credit line presumed, the issuing bank transfers the LC to the exporter's LC confirming bank.
4. The LC confirming bank notifies the exporter that the LC is in place.
5. The exporter contacts the logistics firm and the shipment is ordered.
6. The logistics firm ships the exporter's cargo to the importer and prepares and sends the shipping documents (e.g., Bill of Lading) to the exporter.
7. The exporter provides the delivery notification, commercial invoice, shipping documents, and, eventually, further documents (e.g., draft, a certificate of origin) strictly in accordance with the LC conditions to the confirming bank.

8. If the documents are in accordance with the LC requirements, the confirming bank pays the LC (contract) amount to the exporter.
9. The confirming bank transfers the documents to the LC issuing bank and makes a claim for reimbursement.
10. Upon receipt of the LC documents, the issuing bank makes a claim of the LC (contract) amount to the importer, at which point the documents are handed over to the importer.
11. The importer is able to release the cargo from customs upon presentation of the shipping documents.

In case that the importer does not pay, the LC issuing bank settles the claim of the exporter. In principle, it is possible to open an LC from one bank. Hence, the creditworthiness of the issuing bank as well as its geographical location (e.g., comparative country risk analysis) is important. It is possible that the issuing bank, at least temporarily, will interrupt its foreign payments, if, for example, an entire country is threatened by bankruptcy due to financial difficulties. Therefore, the involvement of a second LC confirming bank, often located in the exporter's home country, is desirable. Upon presentation of the documents (such as, for example, the invoice, shipping, and customs documents) by the exporter, the LC confirming bank becomes liable for the payment, if the importer and the LC issuing bank abroad are unable or refuse to make the payment to the exporting firm.

There are basically two LC alternatives: revocable and irrevocable. In the case of a **revocable LC**, the issuing bank can amend or terminate the issued LC at any time. The **irrevocable, confirmed LC** provides much higher safety for the exporter, since neither the importer nor the issuing bank is in a position to modify or withdraw the LC before its expiration date. Nevertheless, increased payment security is charged by the bank through higher issuing and LC confirmation fees. Confirmation fees vary, depending on the country risk and importer's creditworthiness, between 0.5 percent and 6.0 percent of the contract (LC) value. The processing of an export letter of credit involving two banks is illustrated in Figure 91.

LCs are issued as an '**LC at sight**' (prompt payment by the importer's bank upon receipt of the shipping documents) or as an '**LC with deferred payment**' clause. Common deferred payment terms are 30, 45, 60, 90, 180, and 360 days. In this case, the LC is used as a credit instrument by the importer. The longer the deferred payment period, the higher the risk (from the bank's perspective) and the higher the fees, called 'deferred payment charges', charged by the issuing bank to the importer. The exporter's advising bank charges its deferred payment confirmation fees according to its perceived risk. Subject to the contract, the advising bank's confirmation charges are usually paid by the exporter or, alternatively, by the importer. To summarize, the use of an LC as a payment instrument provides the following advantages for the exporter and the importer.

1. The exporter secures its receipt of payment because the importer's debt is assumed by the issuing bank against the receipt of the original shipment documents (**LC as payment security instrument**).
   Note: only with the original shipment documents is the importer able to initiate the procedure of customs clearance/import allowance in its home country.
2. The importer can be sure that the cargo has been shipped by the exporter upon receipt of the original shipment documents by the issuing bank (**LC as delivery security instrument**).

3. When the contracting parties agree on a deferred payment LC, the importer receives the cargo but takes advantage of the delayed payment. Because the importer can take advantage of credit, the exporter improves its competitive position because it is sure to receive the money from the bank (**LC as a credit instrument**). Even when there is a deferred payment agreed to by the contract parties, the exporter may use **'forfeiting'**. Forfeiting means the exporter can ask the LC confirming bank for immediate transfer of the invoice amount due by the importer. The bank may agree to transfer the money to the exporter who, in return, has to pay so-called forfeiting fees to the paying bank. The size of the fees depends on the payment period, the foreign importer firm's creditworthiness, and the risk of the importer's country of residence (Albaum at al., 2008).

Further LC variants are (1) a **transferable LC** and (2) **nontransferable LC** and (3) a **revolving LC**. A transferable LC allows the exporter (beneficiary) to transfer a partial amount or the whole amount of the LC to a third party. An LC is nontransferable to a third party unless the LC document expressively stipulates that it is transferable. There are several reasons that an exporter may request the importer to issue a transferable LC (Albaum et al., 2008).

- The exporter may actually be a 'middleman', who is purchasing the goods from someone else.
- The exporter may provide only a part of the cargo and/or value added activities linked to the product.

A **revolving LC** is suitable for firms whose business transactions are more or less regular but continue over a certain period of time (usually a minimum of one year). Thus, in order to ensure the safety of administrative efforts (costs), instead of issuing individual LCs for each business transaction, one revolving LC is set. There are two common types of revolving LCs. The first variant of a revolving LC has a maximum amount fixed, without explicitly mentioned monthly order (payment) volumes. If the buyer has used up the accumulated value of shipments from the seller, thus reaching the maximum LC amount, the importer needs to pay pending invoices to the LC issuing bank before placing new orders. In the second revolving LC variant, a specified maximum order (payment) volume is defined per month (or for other periods). The amount not used up by the buyer is not carried over to the next month. This variant is named a **noncumulative revolving letter of credit**. In contrast, a **cumulative letter of credit** allows unused shipment/credit amounts to be added to the amount allowed in the subsequent time period.

The **Stand-by Letter of Credit** (Stand-by LC) is another alternative. In this alternative, the payment condition 'open account' is agreed to by the exporter and the importer but simultaneously provides the exporter with a payment security. If the exporter does not receive the payment for one or several invoices based on open account payment by the importer, the beneficiary hands over the relevant shipping documents together with the pending invoice(s) to the Stand-by LC issuing bank and asks that the money be released. The Stand-by LC method saves some administrative costs because the exporter does not need to send its documents after each shipment is procured but only in the case of overdue payments or the importer's insolvency (Albaum et al., 2008). Nevertheless, the exporter should be careful not to exceed the Stand-by LC amount with running deliveries or to send in the documents to the issuing bank without double checking the importer's situation, e.g., payment delay caused by administrative problems or simply by errors of the operating staff. Why? Once, a Stand-by LC is activated by the exporter, it usually causes serious damage to the importer's reputation in the markets.

As an outcome of the worldwide financial crisis (2008-2010), firms involved in foreign trade have been confronted with hindrances to acquiring an LC from their bank. Mainly because of mistrust among the banks, which resulted in limited or interrupted credit lines among them, issuing procedures for LCs were delayed or even refused. This example underlines how the financial crisis caused and worsened a worldwide economic crisis.

As a summary, Figure 92 provides an overview of common payment instruments in the export business and related advantages and potential risks from the exporter's perspective.

payment instrument	advantages for the exporter	potential risks for the exporter
payment in advance	receipt of money before sending the cargo (minimum risk)	importer may refuse business or refuse the placing of an order
open account	minimum administrative efforts and support of customer satisfaction	partial or total loss of debt in case the customer does not pay
draft	draft can be used for the payment of own debts immediate cash when handing over the draft to the bank	draft might be refused by business partners or banks shipment (invoice) value reduced by discount, which depends on the importer's creditworthiness
letter of credit	payment receipt secured supposing the bank accepts the commercial and the shipment documents as 'strictly in accordance' with LC	importer may refuse because of limited resources (security) to issue an LC bank fees reduce the margin
credit insurance	payment risk reduction in the context of an open account business	insurance fees reduce margin greater administrative efforts required
factoring	prompt receipt of the payment by the factoring firm	higher costs depending on the importer's creditworthiness not recommended for long-term oriented business relationships

Figure 92. Payment instruments in export business

9.1.3   Export price calculation

When calculating the export price, in addition to the unit product cost, the exporter's margin, and the transportation method, the payment terms must be taken into consideration. The impact of the Incoterms chosen by the contracting parties in their agreement should not be underestimated when calculating the price. It makes a considerable difference, whether the exporter offers a price on an FCA or DDP basis. For example, in the case of a DDP, in addition to the freight costs, the customs clearance of the cargo at the country of destination has to be paid by the exporter. Simultaneously, a DDP means that the risk of cargo damage or its loss is transferred from the exporter to the importer when the goods reach the final place of destination. Whereas in the case of an FCA, freight expenses from the exporter's firm to the importer, the import tax in the country of destination, and the risk of loss or damage to the cargo is transferred to the importer at the premises of the exporter. Additionally, the payment terms are necessarily considered in the price calculation.

The case: Calculation of the export price

Assume there is a firm located in Berlin, Germany, that is negotiating with a potential client located in São Paulo, Brazil. The Brazilian importer wants to order one 40' container with automotive components. It is assumed that 800 pieces are stored in one 40' container. The parties agree to apply an irrevocable, confirmed LC. During the meeting, the price is negotiated considering the question as to who is responsible for the customs' formalities and the transportation from Berlin, Germany, via Hamburg to the port of Santos, and from Santos to São Paulo in Brazil. The alternative calculations below for an FCA and DDP display the cost. (A corresponding sample of the invoice, bill of lading, and an LC issuing form is presented in the appendix of this book.)

FCA Berlin – shipment of one 40' container

Exporter's model calculation

Manufacturing costs of goods	EUR 80,000.00
+ Exporter's margin 20 percent	EUR 16,000.00
= Total	EUR 96,000.00
+ LC fees (3 percent)	EUR 2,880,00
= Exporter's FCA price offer per one 40' container	EUR 98.880,00
Unit price (FCA Berlin)	**EUR 123.60**

DDP São Paulo – shipment of one 40' container

Exporter's model calculation

Manufacturing cost of goods	EUR 80,000.00
+ Exporter's margin 20 percent	EUR 16,000.00
+ Inland freight Berlin-Hamburg	EUR 1,200.00
+ Sea Freight Hamburg-Santos	EUR 2,100.00
+ Arrival costs Santos port	EUR 99,300.00
+ Import duty (18 percent of arrival costs)	EUR 17,874.00
+ Import tax (8 percent of arrival costs)	EUR 7,944.00
+ Inland 'product circulation tax' (18 percent of arrival costs)	EUR 17,874.00
+ Warehouse charge Santos port	EUR 645.45
+ Inland freight Santos- São Paulo	EUR 2,000.00
= Total	EUR 145,637.45
+ LC fees (3 percent)	EUR 4,369,12
= Exporter's DDP price offer per one 40' container	EUR 150,006,57
Unit price (DDP São Paulo)	**EUR 187.51**

Source: AHK Brazil (2010)

As the calculations above show, the difference in cost when the exporter offers a product unit price based on a DDP São Paulo (Euro 187.51) instead of an FCA Berlin (Euro 123.60) is considerable. Thus, careful calculation before offering the final export price is important.

9.2   International distribution and logistics

Distribution is the marketing tool that ultimately connects the products of a particular manufacturer with the consumer. Distribution constitutes an operation oriented around profit generation, and consists of planning, organizing, and monitoring ways of transferring finished products from their manufacturing plants to retail outlets, where they are sold to final recipients (Kotler et al., 2009). International distribution is distinguished by one specific feature, namely that the final recipient exists outside the borders of a company's country of origin. This does not mean that a product must physically cross country borders, as a company may produce its products – e.g., after making a direct investment – in another country. In such a situation, a company has to make decisions about the manner of delivery of products to consumers, but distribution itself is within the borders of one foreign country (Chan, 2006; Clarke and Wilson, 2009).

An effective system of product distribution permits a company to meet its marketing objectives. The system must be flexible to allow for modifications according to changing environmental conditions. Flexibility is especially important with respect to planning and building distribution networks in foreign markets, as this requires taking into account more variables than in the case of a home country (de Mooij, 2010). The number of variables grows proportionately to the number of countries that are entered by a company. Each country has different environmental conditions, which forces companies to modify the distribution solutions implemented elsewhere.

Key distribution decisions refer to selection of distribution channels. These **distribution channels** are the means by which goods are distributed from the manufacturer to the end user (Doole and Lowe, 2001). Some companies own their own means of distribution, some companies only deal with the most important customers, but many companies rely on other firms and agents to perform distribution services for them. Basic functions to be performed by agents in foreign markets involve (Bradley, 2005; Chan, 2006)

- coordinating and combining consumer demand in foreign markets with product supply; decreasing the cultural asymmetry in negotiations between buyers and sellers,
- protecting buyers and sellers against 'easy' solutions as a result of unfamiliarity with the cultural context,
- reducing transaction costs,
- assisting in making contacts between producers and buyers and in building consumer relationships, and
- organizing product distribution.

Distribution channels not only ensure physical transfer of products from a manufacturer to the consumer, but also play many other roles. Channel participants support the flow of (Kotler, 2000)

- market information concerning (e.g., present and potential buyers, competitors, or other channel participants),
- promotion (providing information about the products being offered in order to persuade buyers to buy),
- negotiations (seeking potential buyers and establishing prices and other transactional terms),
- orders (providing a manufacturer with information about a buyer's intention to purchase its products),
- financing (taking over and allocating the funds necessary for stock financing),
- service provision (e.g., shipping, transport, storage, sorting, compiling),
- payments (paying dues on behalf of the buyer),
- right of ownership (real transfer of the right of ownership to another channel participant and the final buyer), and
- risk (taking over the risk involved in, e.g., financing supplies or collecting liabilities).

Various characteristics of distribution channels help to distinguish different channel types. However, the most significant decision in the international market concerns whether a company should reach consumers individually or turn to intermediaries – hence, the choice is between direct and indirect distribution channels (Muhlbacher et al., 2006).

In **direct channel distribution**, manufacturers themselves are responsible for product distribution in the market, which is effected by means of the manufacturers' own employees (e.g., by organizing a chain network or commercial offices abroad) or by online selling. Direct distribution ensures that manufacturers have full control over prices and consumer service quality, easy access to market information, and the possibility of a quick response and market offer adaptation to accommodate changing demand. Direct channels facilitate development of a brand image and customer loyalty (Clarke and Wilson, 2009). Nonetheless, creating one's own sales network requires greater capital and personnel involvement; moreover, lack of distribution intermediaries makes it more difficult to reach a wider group of consumers in the international market.

In **indirect channels**, manufacturers use services rendered by other people or companies in order to deliver products to buyers (Chan, 2006; de Mooij, 2010). It is important to note that the inclusion of intermediaries in the process of distribution helps companies expand into foreign markets. Unlike manufacturers, intermediaries (particularly foreign ones) have generally better knowledge of local distribution conditions and consumer requirements and habits. Having distribution intermediaries allows a company to avoid the costs of developing its own channels. On the other hand, manufacturers lose at least part of their control of what is going on, and must be prepared for intermediaries' failure to meet contractual terms. The choice of indirect channels does not eliminate the possibility of a simultaneous use of direct selling channels, as they can be complementary to each other (Browersox and Cooper, 1992).

The choice of distribution channels is greatly determined by a company's foreign market entry strategy (Rugman and Collinson, 2009). On the one hand, each strategy imposes some limitations on developers of the distribution system; on the other hand, it can be concluded that all distribution channels available to a company (e.g., for financial or organizational reasons) are determined by a company's market entry strategy. If a company introduces direct export, in fact, it does not have to care about what products will be bought by the final buyers. Foreign investments based on the purchase of a company existing abroad may be connected either to development of new distribution channels or to simultaneous acquisition of existing ones.

The **selection of distribution channels** in foreign markets requires that marketers have a good understanding of the market and the goals to be achieved by the company. Distribution decisions are mainly determined by (Doole and Lowe, 2001; Borusiak and Slawinska, 2002)

- objectives of the marketing strategy and relevant objectives of the distribution strategy;
- types of products;
- consumer behavior with respect to distribution;
- the state of development of intermediaries (mainly trade and service companies, e.g., logistic);
- the material, personnel, and financial potential of the company responsible for the development of distribution channels;

- buyers' requirements and habits, as well as their geographic distribution and their buying force; and
- the range of the company's control over the channels.

Decisions about the length and width of distribution channels, as well as about the types of intermediaries should be made only after considering these factors. Generally, in the process of building distribution channels, it is necessary to take into consideration the same factors that determine the choice of domestic distribution channels. Here, one can distinguish external factors, having their origin in the environment, and internal factors, lying inside the company.

Identification and definition of the external factors that affect construction of distribution channels abroad force marketers to thoroughly examine laws, culture, and especially local patterns of product distribution and selling. Therefore, a company's decisions about distribution channels should be made with respect to the level of general economic development of a host country, consumers' buying behavior and buying habits, legal regulations, and the specificity of foreign distribution channels (Harrison et al., 2000; Chan, 2006).

The choice of distribution channels and of particular intermediaries is also determined by internal factors concerning a company's plans and needs, as well as its financial and personnel potential. These determinants make up a list of eight factors – company objectives, product character, capital, cost, coverage, control, continuity, and communication (Czinkota and Ronkainen, 2004). The analysis of these factors provides the basis for a company's development of foreign distribution channels. Thanks to this analysis, a company is able to define the types of channels (length, width, range of intermediary cooperation), as well as the type of functions to be performed by particular distributors. The choice of adequate intermediaries ensures efficient and effective product distribution.

The **types of agents in the international market** may vary. Differences between them mainly concern the functions provided by agents and the range of services offered. It is impossible to enumerate all the types of intermediaries that connect manufacturers to foreign buyers. Each category encompasses many different subjects; yet, in terms of international marketing, special attention should be drawn to intermediaries that support the export of goods. Conducting export-based foreign operations presents a special case, as products must cross at least one country border. Consequently, product distribution from a manufacturer's country to consumers in other countries is likely to pose additional problems such as a greater transport distance to be covered by the merchandise, the existence of customs tariffs, the need to maintain a larger volume of stock, prolonged order completion, and preparation of necessary documentation.

Export intermediaries are often divided in terms of the risk to be taken (Figure 93), and can be referred to as (Rymarczyk, 1996)

- intermediaries operating on somebody's own account and on behalf of others – commercial agents, cif-agents, brokers;
- intermediaries working on somebody's own account and on their own behalf – commission agents, consignees; and

- intermediaries operating on their own account and on their own behalf – wholesalers, retailers.

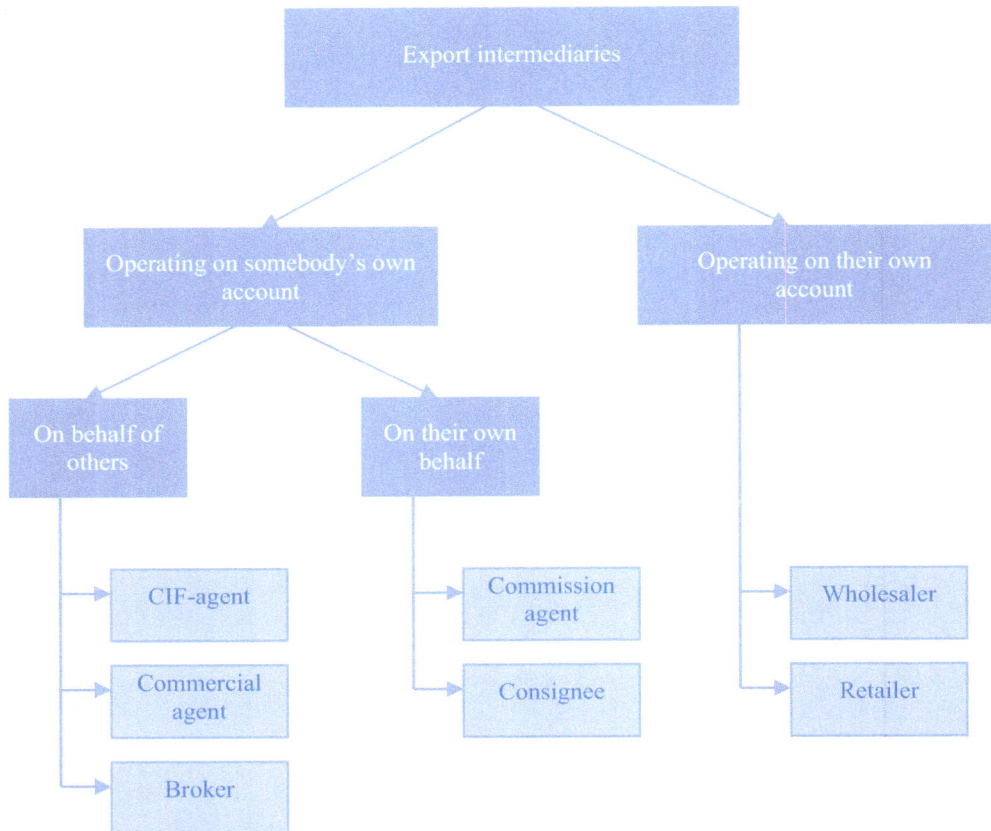

Source: Rymarczyk (1996) p.14; Wiktor et al., (2008), p. 264

Figure 93. The types of export intermediaries

The choice of foreign intermediaries and the initiation of effective cooperation with them should be preceded by considering the following issues (Rosenbloom, 1999; Keegan and Green, 2005; Chan, 2006).

- It is the manufacturer who chooses an intermediary and not vice verse, as it may turn out that an intermediary is also involved in collaboration with competitors and, thus, wants to take over control of the distribution of all product categories in a given market.
- It is better to seek intermediaries who are capable of expanding sales markets rather than those having contacts only with several customers.
- Intermediaries should be treated as long-term partners, and not only as facilitators of the market entry process.

- Investing in intermediaries, providing managerial or technical support, and sharing relevant marketing knowledge – all this displays a producer's involvement in the common enterprise. These investments are lower compared to expenses for the development of direct channels.
- A company should monitor an intermediary's marketing activities so as to keep them aligned with the company's strategy. An intermediary is allowed to tailor distribution to local needs, but on condition that a manufacturer approves of such practices.
- A manufacturer must be sure that the intermediary provides detailed knowledge of a market to be serviced (an intermediary may be the sole source of market information) and its financial results.
- A manufacturer's task is to quickly create bonds between intermediaries working in the same country. Exchange of experience among various channel participants is liable to enhance distribution functioning.

During the last few years, the distribution system in the international market has displayed several tendencies related to, among others, changes in consumer behavior. The most characteristic features of retailing in the contemporary world include providing buyers with purchase convenience, attracting customers by offering low prices, and going global with chain stores (Euromonitor, 2010). An increase in the number of households, long work hours, and a growing share of professionally active women contribute to consumer willingness to buy quickly and effectively. This constitutes one of the basic factors responsible for growth in retailers' product assortment (Doole and Lowe, 2001; Keegan and Green, 2005). Thanks to this, consumers are able to buy, at one time, goods that satisfy their various needs. To exemplify the latter, the French chain store Carrefour and the British Tesco, in addition to food products, have increased the volume of other nonfood products. Retailers also have enriched their offers with diverse services – customers can pay bills or use banking services. Consumers are even willing to pay more in return for a convenient location of a retail outlet (next to their place of work or home) and for convenient operating hours (e.g., until late at night or on weekends). Retailers themselves spend more funds for development of convenient stores, with hypermarkets, on the one hand, and smaller stores located closer to the customer on the other hand (Keegan and Schlegelmilch, 2001; Chan, 2006).

Growing consumer price sensitivity and intensive competition force many retailers to employ low-price strategies, which is most vivid in the case of the development of discount stores (e.g., Lidl, Plus Discount, Aldi). Hypermarkets, in turn, strive to attract customers by offering low prices on selected goods, mostly food products, while simultaneously improving the margins on other types of products (DG SANCO, 2010).

Retailing has been involved in the process of globalization, with large retailers entering developing markets (as a consequence of reduced possibilities of expanding into mature markets because of regulations that may be unfavorable). Internationalization of retail sales networks is partly fostered by advancing urbanization and by changes in the tendencies of consumer behavior in developing countries (although it is important to take into consideration local habits and to properly adjust marketing activities).

place	country	percent of international retail chains
1	Great Britain	55
2	Spain	51
3	France	49
4	Germany	47
5	Italy	45
6	Switzerland	42
7	Austria	42
8	United Arabic Emirates	41
9	China	40
10	Russia	39
11	United States of America	39
12	Netherlands	38
13	Singapore	38
14	Belgium	37
15	Poland	35

Source: Szymura-Tyc (2009) p. 231

Figure 94. Countries according to number of international retail chains

The significance of large **multi-surface chain stores** is continuously increasing in channel distribution, which results from concentration processes in the sector as well as from experience (also with respect to the use of marketing tools) gained in international markets. These chains have great possibilities for applying information technology in order to approach customers. Chains stores are adept at coordinating the flow of goods and managing distribution in a very cost-effective way; whereby they are able to comprise a considerable part of the market of consumer goods (Wilmanska-Sosnowska, 2002).

In the international market, it can also be observed that retailers have increased control over distribution channels (Domanski, 2005). The ever stronger position of chain stores is becoming more visible in distribution channels across international markets. The dominant role of manufacturers in the channels is becoming more limited, whereas intermediaries turn from passive distributors into active agents, not only considerably influencing distribution connections, but also determining which products will have access to the market. Thus, wanting to use a given sales network, manufacturers are forced to accept various conditions imposed by a retailer.

All decisions about the use of distribution channels and the types of intermediaries in the international market should be made with regard to the planned range of market distribution coverage. This criterion allows three types of distribution to be distinguished (Hatton, 2000; Doole and Lowe, 2001; Blythe, 2009):

- intensive distribution – products launched into the market through long and wide channels are available in many retail outlets (this mainly refers to frequently and commonly purchased goods);
- selective distribution – products (mainly selectable goods) are sold by a limited number of purposefully matched intermediaries, whose task is to provide customers with extra services (e.g., counseling, assembly); and
- exclusive distribution – products are offered by one or several intermediaries (luxury, specialist, or episodically purchased goods).

The case: Distribution strategies of luxury products

Rolex, Baume Mercier, Audemars Piguet, Chopard, and Patek Phillippe are a smattering of the very expensive watch brands that are prized for their exclusivity, beauty, artistic craftsmanship, and perceived value. They are sold in very few retail stores. The very fact that they are hard to find, expensive to buy, and have a limited production makes each of these watches highly desirable.

Cosmetics houses at the highest end of the market differentiate themselves by limiting distribution to a select few stores in any given trading area. Clarins, La Prarie, Guerlain, and Crème de la Mer are very choosy about where their products are placed. This insures that consumers recognize that by their very lack of availability these products are special and, therefore, have justifiably higher retail price points.

Source: Ezine (2010)

In the international market, a very important role is played by logistics. **Distribution logistics** (physical distribution) encompasses decisions and activities related to organization of product and information transfer from the production plant to the point of an ultimate purchase. Physical distribution engages manufacturers, agents, and logistics companies (including transport, shipping, and storage). In international terms, logistics is the organization of product transfer to foreign consumers (Keegan and Green, 2005; Blythe, 2009). The basic areas of physical distribution include order completion, storage, stock management, and transport (Kotler, 2000).

Distribution logistics in international marketing entails a set of specific activities with regard to product export. However, in situations where a company uses other forms of entering foreign markets, such as producing abroad, logistic operations will be similar to those conducted in the domestic market. Of course, it is necessary to take into account local conditions, especially infrastructure development (transport, technical development), legal regulations, or access to logistic services (Skjoett-Larsen, 2000; Hollensen, 2009). Nonetheless, export of goods poses new challenges, unknown to companies whose products are sold in the country of origin. Here, it is important to consider customs clearance, which can considerably lengthen the time of product delivery, and thus impact consumer dissatisfaction and lead to cost increases.

Organization of distribution logistics in the international market requires that the conditions of cooperation between exporters and importers be determined. These conditions may include (Stepien, 2004)

- identification of the duties of the parties involved with respect to commodity transport and delivery;
- division of costs related to transport, insurance, and customs clearance;
- division of duties connected with obtaining the necessary documents (transport or customs documents, certificates, etc.);
- content of documents that stand for goods; and
- forms of payment.

The case: Supply chain consolidation of Nestlé in Great Britain

In Great Britain, the Nestlé business has traditionally operated from three separate distribution sites: Bardon in Leicestershire, Scunthorpe in Lincolnshire, and York in North Yorkshire. Because one of the contracts was approaching review and lease agreements at two of the sites were expiring, Nestlé decided to take the opportunity to review its warehousing and distribution strategy in the UK, turning to Total Logistics to undertake a thorough and independent assessment of its current and future supply chain needs.
The main task facing the Nestlé team and Total Logistics' consultants was to develop a meaningful model by which to fully understand the pros and cons of every option that was available. This already complex scenario was made even more challenging due to the diverse and expansive nature of Nestlé's product range and large number of end markets. While the York, Bardon, and Scunthorpe sites handled foodstuffs, including water, confectionery, cereals and coffee, the latter also coped with the huge seasonal demands for confectionery products during periods such as Easter and Christmas. To add to the complex picture, Scunthorpe also used different technologies to service the international export market, dispatching products to Europe and further afield via deep-sea routes. Whereas Scunthorpe was characterized by high density, drive-in racking with temperature and humidity controls, Bardon and York used automated high-bay storage units that did not require as sophisticated an environmental management. Total Logistics set to work developing an assessment tool to look at the impact of putting different business streams into the same or new facilities. A further element to the assessment model included an analysis of transport and warehousing costs, including inbound and outbound flows. Particular attention was paid to the potential synergies that could be obtained by combining different streams to increase drop size, thus reducing the number of road miles and journeys required.
In the final analysis, it was decided that a twin site solution provided the greatest cost savings to Nestlé, while enabling it to improve flexibility and delivery performance to

supermarkets and other key retailers in the UK and further afield. Although its delivery performance was already at 99.4 percent, Nestlé was confident that concentration in two locations would allow the already high customer service levels to be improved. Due to its central location and existing potential for development, it was decided that the Bardon site was the obvious choice to centralize supply chain operations. However, this decision has meant closing the Scunthorpe site and a major investment program at Bardon, which will increase its pallet capacity from 50,000 to 110,000. While there have inevitably been some job losses due to the closure of the Scunthorpe site, it is expected that up to forty new jobs will be created initially at the Bardon site, with the possibility of more to follow in associated co-packing operations on site. Considerable investment has now gone into the Bardon site to enable it to handle the array of Nestlé food and drink products – including Kit-Kats, Carnation, Buxton and Nescafé. In addition to this focus, the area of risk management has been key to the team's thinking as the site is updated and fully commissioned.

Accordingly, Nestlé has worked hard to ensure the design of the new Bardon site takes issues such as fire protection and security very seriously. The communications infrastructure at the site has also been a key consideration during the implementation phase that saw the successful commissioning of the extension in May 2009 and completion to fit for purpose in July of that year.

Source: Nestlé (2010)

Another important issue concerning distribution logistics in the international market is connected to transport. Transport-related issues mainly concern the choice of a proper means of transport, which also affects the final price of exported products. It has been estimated that transport accounts for 10-15% of the price to be paid by a foreign consumer (Hollensen, 2009). Exporters can choose from a plethora of transport means, including railway, sea, car, air, water, land, or multi-mode transport (Neider and Marciniak-Neider, 1997). The decision about the choice of a transport facility is determined by many factors, including cost of transport means, distance, frequency of delivery, product type, value of delivery, and accessibility of particular means of transport (Skjoett-Larsen, 2000; Hollensen, 2009). However, it should be emphasized that computer software and the Internet permit activities related to the physical transfer of goods to be speeded up.

9.3   Promotion in international marketing

International marketing promotion is connected to communication on an international scale. Generally, promotion includes all the activities the company undertakes to communicate and promote its products to the target market (Kotler, 2000). The basic assumptions concerning goals, tools, and communication in the international market are the same as for the domestic market. However, communication in international marketing, which is a specific form of 'cross-cultural encounter' between an enterprise and selected target groups of receivers in other countries, is very characteristic in terms of the communication system, legal regulations, and social and cultural methods of dealing with dilemmas: standardization or adaptation (Russell and Lane, 2000; Blythe, 2002).

The basic premises for **standardization of marketing communication** include (Belch et al., 2003; de Mooij, 2010)

- observable convergence of national markets in terms of the acceptance of global products;
- customers' susceptibility to standardized advertising campaigns;
- the possibility of using similar media to reach particular national segments of consumers;
- the possibility of communicating a single, coherent corporate image and vision of a company's products in the international market;
- the possibility of transferring advertising ideas to other countries and their cultures;
- similar power and capital of the advertized brand in particular national markets; and
- lower costs for designing and carrying out a campaign.

On the other hand, the premises for **adapting marketing communication** to local conditions include the following (Sethuraman and Tellis, 2002; de Mooij, 2010):

- the social and cultural diversity of particular national markets;
- differences between legal systems, including the laws regarding advertising in national markets; and
- economic diversity (standard of living and other components that have an impact on patterns of consumption, habits and purchasing capacity, appropriateness of advertising slogans, etc.).

The system of promotion includes a collection of means and instruments through which an enterprise conveys information on products/company to the market, shapes buyers' needs, stimulates and directs demand as well as decreases its price elasticity. The characteristic elements of a marketing communication system are functions and tools (promotion-mix) and the manner in which they are combined.

There are many different **functions of promotion** when a company is active in international markets. The basic marketing tasks of promotion are referred to as the **function of securing a permanent presence in the market** for a company. This constitutes a sort of mission for the marketing communication system. The mere physical presence of a product on the competitive international market is not enough for a company to be successful. What is absolutely necessary is continuous communication with the market (Belch et al., 2003; Golan, et al., 2010). And here promotion comes into play. Promotion makes customers well aware of a company, incorporates it into their map of perception, and provides them with arguments for buying a given product. Modern promotion cannot be only a set of incidental, periodical actions, undertaken particularly at the moment of entering a foreign market, but it should be a continuous process that provides a constant presence in a new, international market. Communication policy is vital in the realization of strategic market objectives, and it is expressed in its three basic functions: informative, persuasive (inducing), and competitive functions.

The informative function constitutes a certain type of foundation from which other functions of promotion emerge. It offers to current and potential buyers' information that is designed to break the barrier of market ignorance. Promotion in its informative function provides market education for customers in the new international environment of a company's operation (Kotler, 2000; Belch et al., 2003). This objective is achieved through presenting a set of more or less complex and objective information, including both particular data (dates, numbers, facts) on the company and/or product and information that, due to appropriate context, word choice, and presentation of the scale of potential benefits, makes consumers aware of the existence of a company or brand.

The persuasive function (inducing, encouraging, activating, etc.) is aimed at provoking and upholding intended activities and consumer behavior. The dynamics of the international and global market and its competitive structure force companies to conduct active promotional policies based not only on objective information but also on selective information that is oriented towards the shaping of needs and demand (Golan et al., 2010). The persuasive function conveys the encoded intentions of the sender of the promotional message. It uses incentives that are rational by nature, but also emotional.

The competitive function is manifested in the creation of non-price instruments of market competition. At the present stage of economic development and because of the observed changes that take place in the competition mechanism, it is not enough to offer a mere service at an attractive and 'competitive' price to win customers. What is needed is a bundle of attractive information and strong incentives that will influence buyers' motivations and their tendency to make a particular decision concerning a purchase (Sethuraman and Tellis, 2002; Golan et al., 2010). The effects of the competitive function of promotion are visible in two areas. The first is related to the fact that a company has to make its instruments and promotional programs attractive and powerful. The other focuses on the possibility of hampering the promotional campaigns conducted by the competition. The competitive function of promotion may be observed if a company is more frequently present in the media than its competition; has more air-time and occupies more space; uses the strategy of copying the competition; or quite the opposite, tries to make its campaign as unique as possible, which is based on the strategy of diversification.

The other important element of a marketing communication system is promotional tools. The most popular composition of promotion tools is (Belch et al., 2003; Keegan and Green, 2005; Wiktor et al., 2008)

- advertising – an impersonal, payable, addressed to mass receiver form of conveying market information aimed at presenting and supporting the sales offer of a particular sender;
- sales promotion (complementary) – a collection of instruments used for evoking unusual, additional, strong, and usually short-lived incentives that increase the level of attractiveness of an offer of services and stimulate the tendency (readiness) to make a purchase;
- personal promotion – presenting a company's offer and activating sales by means of direct interpersonal contacts between a company's employees – its representatives – and buyers and other stakeholders; and

- **public relations** – activities the aim of which is to create, uphold, and extend social trust and the positive image of a company.

Advertising is the basic form of promotion. In international marketing, advertising is of particular importance in the process of launching a product in a new foreign market (launch and image campaign). In situations where the product is unknown and there is little information on it, the campaign should include informative elements and ought to perform educational functions, emphasizing, at the same time, the advantages of the product, the features of novelty, originality, and quality as compared to the already familiar competitive products. Through the informative function, which is dominant in the process of entering the market of a new country, advertisement shapes brand awareness: it educates consumers, activates them, and directs their needs and, at the same time, their method of satisfying those needs (Belch et al., 2003; Bradley, 2005). As a result, the market is prepared for the introduction of a new product and for the presence of a new company.

Enterprises that operate in international markets employ various media for the purposes of marketing communication. These media constitute information flow channels (transmission of message): the press, radio, television, movies, mail, billboards (outdoor carriers), and the Internet. In their advertising campaigns, companies also make use of all the other possible means and places to publicize the message. Decisions about which communication channel is the most suitable for a company's needs depend on many factors, including characteristics of the target group of buyers, scope and method of using the media, the size of the advertising budget, and service prices offered by the media (Blythe, 2002).

The decisions do not usually concern only the selection of a given media from among the whole available range but also the creation of an optimum composition of media. Such a composition is determined on the basis of detailed characteristics of particular media, especially their basic features, such as selectivity and area of activity and the profile and size of the potential audience (viewers, listeners, readers) in particular foreign markets as well as media's readiness to provide additional services. The media that are of crucial importance in advertising are those that operate across borders – the Internet, satellite radio and television, and certain international press titles.

Sales promotion in the international market includes a range of instruments that boost the level of attractiveness of a given service for a buyer and increase in buyers the inclination to make a purchase. Sales promotion creates and offers noticeable profits (utilities) that are economic and psychological by nature (Pauwels, 2007; Srinivasan et al., 2004). It adds 'something special and unique' to the product. Thus, the means of promotion may constitute a form of expanding a product, adding some new value to it, and in this way, making it distinct as compared to other, competitive offers that attract more buyers. The means used in sales promotion encourage customers to buy a product at a strictly defined time and/or in a specified place (Bell and Dreze, 2002; Usunie and Lee, 2009).

The importance of sales promotion in international marketing is growing. The increase in the BTL (below the line) budget that is destined for financing this type of promotion results from many factors, especially from the saturation of particular markets and difficulties with sales, the pressure of the competition, a systematic increase in the number of newly launched products, a clear acceleration and shortening of the average product life cycle, the increase of self-service sales, consumers' desire to save at least a little money, and also the decreasing effectiveness of classic advertising and the growing costs of its production and transmission (Schlegelmilch et al., 2001; Sethuraman and Tellis, 2002).

Sales promotion uses separate sets of tools for different target groups. The basic instruments of consumer promotion are price-cutting, gift vouchers, free samples of goods, reimbursed offers, shopping bonuses, competitions, lotteries, games, and exhibitions in the places of sale of goods and services (Bell and Dreze, 2002; Pauwels, 2007).

The case: Mobile sales promotion of Strongbow in Great Britain

In 2008, Strongbow launched a mobile campaign based in Great Britain called 'Bowtime', wherein people could text a short code and in return receive a voucher that could be exchanged for a pint at local pubs during Bowtime (5-7 p.m.) every Tuesday. Samples were distributed on the first day, and photos of users with their drinks were made available to take away and were posted after the event on Facebook. Virtual pints were also made available to people through 'Flirtomatic'.

The objective was to reach out to 18-35 year-old manual workers and get them to have a drink after a hard day's work. The campaign resulted in 90,000 new users being added to the brand's userbase, 112,225 pints ordered via mobile coupons, 300k ad impressions served on Flirtomatic, and 30,000 virtual pint gifts. Strongbow sales peaked in 2008.

In 2009, the campaign was relaunched with a website and the tag line 'Hard earned' was used. Strongbow also launched a spoof viral on its own. In this ad, workers were celebrated and bankers were picked on. Further activity included mobile barcodes, a pub locator, pack promotions, and virtual pint promotions. Participants were also entered into a four month CRM campaign featuring free pint and festival ticket offers, MMS animations, and wind-up-a-mate promotions. There were also sixty prizes a day for sixty days. The campaign prompted a 39% response rate and led to a claimed purchase increase of 44% and a brand preference increase of 8% in those who had received the CRM activity.

Source: Strongbow (2010)

When instruments target a company's own sales staff (staff promotion), the major promotional tools are employee remuneration systems, sales-related bonuses for the most effective sales personnel, meetings with personnel, and training and enhancing the professional knowledge of sales staff (through providing, on a constant basis, documents related to trading, including analyses, reports, documents on planning, guide-books, instructions, company and product guides, promotional gadgets, etc.). Some instruments that are used in promotions addressed to a company's agents in distribution channels are variable price, discounts, and bonuses for selling a particular amount of services within a given period of time. An important issue in dealer promotion is the policy of supporting a company's agents in activities related to activating sales. It is essential to create a common plane of communication with agents operating in foreign markets (Pauwels, 2007; de Mooij, 2010). This is related to the rules of corporate culture, mission acceptance, observing the rules, promotional codes, and continuous elements that constitute reference points for a company's identity.

Personal promotion is a special form of international marketing communication. It consists of presenting a company's offer and activating sales by means of direct contact between the company's employees and potential buyers. It is direct by nature and flexible to a large extent. The contact between the company's employee and a customer allows for the realization of feedback and for a flow of information in both directions. The flexibility of this form of promotion is manifested in the possibility of reacting quickly and adapting communication policy to the changing needs and expectations of the market. The enterprises that operate in international markets need to conduct special education programs for their staff in order to achieve their goal (Belch et al., 2003; Kotler et al., 2009).

An important element of personal promotion in the international market is the personality of a company's employee. The employee should express attachment to the institution's mission; great cogency; communication skills; ease in making contact with people; and negotiating skills such as tact, politeness, courtesy, honesty, mental strength, initiative and creativity in solving customers' problems, persistence, reliability, and other attributes essential for 'doing business'; as well as knowledge of cross-cultural differences among customers (Zabinski, 2000; Srinivasan et al., 2004). These features are vital elements that affect the way consumers perceive the quality of services provided by a given company. The seller ought to always remember that his or her work directly influences the way the company is seen by consumers; and it very often constitutes one of the major criteria for evaluating alternative choices and determines the future behavior of a consumer, especially in terms of his or her loyalty to a given brand, enterprise, or point of purchase.

In international marketing, a vital position is occupied by public relations. **Public relations** is one form of an enterprise's communication, the scope of which is to affect the emotions, opinions, and beliefs of stakeholders – customers, present and potential; shareholders; suppliers; workers; and other target groups. The essence of PR is to inform the public – every social group potentially interested in buying a product or that may influence the actual capacity of the enterprise to achieve complex objectives – of such events (facts, processes) in the company that are important not only to the company's situation but that may arouse particular social interest as well (Kotler, 2000; Belch et al., 2003). These may include a company's in-house performance related to its marketing situation (e.g., an increase in market share, gaining an important strategic investor, winning a prestigious award at an international fair) but also activities expressing a company's social responsibility (e.g., funding grants for artists, supporting environmental protection activities, donations to victims of natural disasters, sponsoring a leading football team).

The case: Lego 'Builders of Tomorrow' worldwide PR campaign

Lego enlisted 360 PR to help reestablish the iconic plastic brick as a leading children's entertainment brand with parents of iPod-toting, overscheduled kids who have little time for unstructured, open-ended play. 360 PR created Lego Builders of Tomorrow™, a platform from which to talk to parents about the importance of fostering creative play early and often, the benefits of which children would reap immediately and also well into the future as creative, successful adults – our 'Builders of Tomorrow'. Central to the PR campaign was communicating with parents directly and providing them with tools to help foster creative play. This was accomplished through a variety of online tools that 360 PR recommended and then created, including

- a website for parents, www.legobuildersoftomorrow.com, to deliver practical play tips and inspirational stories from parents (including celeb dad Matthew Broderick) and educators;
- a podcast series, called Lego Playtime Podcasts; and
- the blog, www.dadinprogress.com.

Providing helpful online tools to aid parents in their playtime choices became an integral strategy in the broader Lego Builders of Tomorrow campaign (which also had several offline, traditional media components). First, Lego created the Builders of Tomorrow website as a central place where parents could go for tips and advice on playtime. Lego assembled a panel of child development experts, educators, and real parents to provide compelling, useful content for the site. To keep the site fresh and provide tips for on-the-go parents, Lego scripted and produced a podcast series called Lego Playtime Podcasts.

The Builders of Tomorrow website has been featured in dozens of media outlets, including parenting, kids, and classroom publications; newspaper and magazines; and online outlets as well as in audio releases. The total circulation of media that featured the website is 46,567,247 translating to 92,186,083 impressions with pass along. Just six months into the website's life, the site is attracting more than 5,000 unique monthly visitors (based on the most recent month available), with more than 17,000 pages viewed. 360 PR submitted the Playtime Podcast series to several of the top podcast directories. Currently, the series is listed on iTunes, podcast.net, and manicmommies.com.

Source: Lego (2010)

From an international perspective, public relations serve diverse functions. Apart from the basic informative, sale-activating (on the basis of recognition, image, and reputation) functions of PR, there are other functions, namely shaping contacts with all institutions and elements of the environment located in the area of a company's interest (various groups of stakeholders); creating a corporate image (forming, altering, and/or upholding a positive picture and opinion of the company); stabilization of the enterprise in situations of crisis; securing unity in the direction of activities, which is based on the principles of the corporate culture; protection of corporate identity inside and outside the company as well as others (Zbikowska, 2005).

The realization of PR functions requires assuming certain principles on the basis of which the 'social relationships' of the company and its environment will be formed. These principles include reliability, openness, and readiness to provide information; attractiveness and originality of activities; a friendly attitude; tact; good manners in personal contacts; continuity and consistency in operation; and professionalism at the planning stage of activities as well as in their realization (Aniszewska, 2007).

The PR activities most frequently used by corporations operating in international markets are connected to (Belch et al., 2003; Wiktor et al., 2008; Blythe, 2009)

- establishing and keeping good contacts with the media through press conferences presenting a company's mission, philosophy, and the particular activities carried out by the company, in particular those for the benefit of the community; organizing interviews with the management for the media; preparing sponsored articles; elaborating information for journalists on the current events in the company; compiling information on particular issues, accounts, reports, communications, including information for investors; and developing explanations and responses to criticism from the media;
- organizing open-access lectures, presentations, and talks promoting the company and its activities; publishing anniversary materials; and organizing 'open days' in the company;
- financing charity activities;
- lobbying; and
- sponsoring sport, culture, education, TV programs, artistic events, and other important spheres of social life; sponsoring is a form of financial (material) support provided by a company to particular endeavors (organizations, projects, etc.) in exchange for the possibility of using the social significance and reputation to shape, improve, and/or consolidate the corporate image of the sponsor. Nowadays, in international communication, sponsoring sports plays a crucial role. This includes all kinds of sport events on a continental, international, or global scale; continental and world championships in particular sport disciplines; the Summer and Winter Olympic Games – all these attract a broad, international, and even global audience to stadiums but also to the media (television, the Internet, press, radio); and thus they fulfill the functions of range, reputation, and promotion for the sponsoring companies.

All of these promotional instruments are traditional and modern at the same time. They indicate the possibilities of companies for promotion in the network environment (hyper-media computer environment, on-line promotion). Regardless of the particular conditions, their intensity, and the diverse character of particular companies operating in various international markets, all the components of this system should be combined and should constitute a harmonized, coherent whole. This requirement is expressed in the integrated marketing communications concept (Schultz et al., 1993; Rossiter and Bellman, 2005). Its essence may be presented in the form of the following attributes of communication (Pickton and Broderick, 2000):

- the point of reference in shaping a company's promotional activities is the buyer together with his or her needs, preferences, and available purchasing capacity and, in a broader perspective, a clearly identifiable segment constituting a company's target market;

- the major criterion for effectively assessing promotion is the level of satisfying the needs of customers who create distinct international market segments;
- promotional programs are formed on the basis of market and marketing research; they allow, e.g., for the formation and updating of databases of consumers and all of the other variables in the environment (relating to both the current situation and the tendencies for changes) that have considerable impact on the shape of the marketing communication process (e.g., legal regulations in particular countries or regions that concern advertising, media market, promotional campaigns of the competition, IT development, etc.);
- the selection of particular forms and instruments of promotion is dependent on the requirements and expectations of particular segments of the international market; the IMC concept emphasizes the necessity of using all possible forms of personal, interpersonal, and mass communication in the process of communicating with the market; and it involves traditional methods as well as modern ones related to the hyper-media computer environment;
- the process of communication uses all available means and instruments; refers to all of them together in various configurations; treats them as the basic premise of the synergistic effect of promotion; and, in a broader sense, as the premise of the whole marketing concept of a company;
- IMC puts great emphasis on dynamic and interactive media; it assumes a clear, though cautious reevaluation of the significance of traditional media and an increase in the importance of electronic, interactive, and mobile media;
- communication is targeted at the creation and constant stimulation of interaction between the participants in the process; this activity does not focus only on current customers, but its objective is also to win new customers; and
- all forms of communication in the international and cross-cultural environment are expected to carry out the functions of the system – informative, persuasive, and competitive functions; their direct task is to form long-term company-buyer relationships, which are typical for partnership marketing. This objective, which can be achieved through a systematic and constant process of communication, is connected to an understanding of the most important function of promotion, namely the function of securing the permanent presence of a company in the market.

Integrated marketing communication in the international market is determined by many factors. However, the two most important issues are the law and the culture. These factors determine the possibilities for standardizing or adapting promotional activities, which means they determine the actual shape and character of a company's marketing communication in the international environment.

The legal system of a given country, its construction, norms, and nature and manner of law-making, is one of the fundamental components of the macro environment of a company. It provides a framework for legal, acceptable behaviors in the social and economic life of the country. Marketing communication is one of the most important instruments used by a company to shape the market (Belch, et al., 2003; Blythe, 2009). That is why today there are many countries in which marketing communication is subject to legal regulations, referred to as 'advertising law'. Even though there are differences among countries or groups of countries (e.g., the European Union) as to particular legal solutions, we may say that in general, advertising law governs the following issues (Wiktor et al., 2008):

- legal admissibility of advertisements,
- the contents and form of an advertisement communication,
- the process of advertisement realization,
- the scope of using the media for the purpose of conveying advertising messages, and
- possible bans on certain promotional activities.

The case: Advertising law regulations in the EU market

In the European Union, advertising law is undergoing harmonization at the community level. The premises for this process are the concept and rules of functioning in the single market including, in particular, regulations on consumer protection and competition. The existing national differences arise from the diversity of national regulations related to health care systems – including the approach to the problem of alcoholism, market and competition protection, anti-trust regulations, protection of minor consumers, and so on. Restrictions in EU advertising law are connected to the issue of health protection; protection of the economic interests of consumers; basic rules of social coexistence and good manners; respect for human dignity; and considerations of gender, skin color, religious beliefs, politics, and so forth.

The most important regulations in advertising law include rules for advertisements of products like alcohol, tobacco products, prescription drugs, some games of chance and gambling games, and some products for children. Such regulations are accompanied by a complete or partial limitation on the use of some media to advertise particular products, such as alcohol, tobacco, and pharmaceuticals. In France, for example, there is a ban on TV commercials advertising gas stations, some alcoholic beverages, the press, and literary works. A French petrol distributor – Leclerc-Siplec – was refused a permit for transmitting his commercials on TV 1 Publicité and TV 6 Publicité on the basis of a relevant decree; and the European Court of Justice (ECJ) upheld this ban. On the other hand, a ban on TV advertising of certain alcohols in France that were produced in other EU Member States was recognized by the European Court of Justice as a form of concealed discrimination against foreign products.

The other areas of advertising covered by special interest law are misleading advertising, comparative advertising, access to television, conditions for carrying out sales promotions, advertorials, and product placement.

Source: Wiktor et al., (2008)

Apart from the law, another important element that affects the promotional activities of an enterprise in international markets is culture. Culture is the plane of international marketing where a company experiences 'cross-cultural encounters', and the awareness of the cultural distinctness of the new market and of the cultural distance is crucial for realizing a company's international goals.

Diversity in the cultures of particular nations is evident, and so is the distinctiveness of cultural characteristics of the particular markets that are subject to expansion and corporate marketing activities. This diversification of cultures, i.e., of the soft element of the environment that is not easily quantified, determines the effectiveness of communication to a large degree. It influences the process of encoding and decoding the message, the perception and understanding of advertising slogans, activities undertaken as part of public relations, the language of nonverbal communication, style of negotiations and behaviors, and so forth (Doole and Lowe, 2001; Belch et al., 2003; Keegan and Green, 2005).

An awareness of the diversity of cultures and the ability to distinguish between Western and Eastern cultures is essential for success. Hofstede's five dimensions of culture – high context cultures and low context cultures, monochromic and polychromic cultures, and cultures differing in their approach to humans, time, and surroundings (Trompenaars and Hampden-Turner, 2002) – are vital for analyzing, designing, and carrying out not only promotion but all marketing activities in international markets. Cultural differences among particular countries are an undeniable fact and are of great importance. They ought to constitute the basis for the creation of rational marketing strategies in international and global markets. Cultural differences can be addressed by using an integrated system of marketing instruments.

List of References

AHK, 2010. Cãmara Brasil Alemanha, São Paulo Brazil.

Albaum, G., Duerr, E. & Strandskov, J., 2008. *International marketing and export management*. Essex: Pearson Education Limited.

Aniszewska, G., 2007. *Kultura w zarzadzaniu*. Warszawa: PWE.

Belch, G. E., Belch, M. & Guolla, M. A., 2003. *Advertising and promotion*. Toronto: McGraw-Hill Ryerson.

Bell, D. R. & Dreze, X., 2002. Changing the channel: a better way to do trade promotion. *MIT Sloan Management Review*, 43: 42-49.

Blythe, J. 2002. *Komunikacja marketingowa*. Warszawa: PWE.

Blythe, J., 2009. *Essentials of marketing*. London: Financial Times Press.

Borusiak, B. & Sławińska, M., 2002. Nowe trendy w procesach dystrybucji. *Swiat Marketingu*, 9: 3-7

Bradley, F., 2005. *International marketing strategy*. New York: Financial Times Press.

Browersox, D. J. & Cooper, M. B., 1992. *Strategic marketing channel management*. New York: McGrew-Hill.

Cateora, P. R., Gilly, M. C. & Graham, J. L., 2009. *International marketing*. Boston: McGraw-Hill Irwin.

Chan, F. T. S., 2006. Design and performance evaluation of a distribution network: a simulation approach. *International Journal of Advanced Manufacturing Technology*, 29: 814-825.

Clarke, G. & Wilson, I., 2009. *International marketing*. London: McGraw-Hill.

Czinkota, M. R. & Ronkainen, I. A., 2004. *International marketing*. Mason: Thomson- South-West.

De Mooij, M., 2010. *Global marketing and advertising*. Los Angeles: SAGE.

DG SANCO, 2010. The consumer markets scoreboard [online]. [cited 19.12.2010]. Available from World Wide Web: http:// http://ec.europa.eu/consumers/strategy/sec_2008_87_en.pdf

Domanski, T., 2005. *Strategie marketingowe dużych sieci handlowych*. Warszawa: PWN.

Doole, I. & Lowe, R., 2001. *International marketing strategy*. London: Thomson Learning.

Euromonitor, 2010. The world market for retailing [online]. [cited 06.01.2011]. Available from World Wide Web: http://www.gmid.euro-monitor.com/reports.aspx

Ezine, 2010. Exclusive strategy [online]. [cited 20.12.2010]. Available from World Wide Web: http://ezinearticles.com/?An-Exclusivity-Strategy-Can-Be-Crucial-to-Successful-Brand-Marketing&id=1605519

Fung, K. T., 2004. *Leading court cases on letters of credit*. Paris: International Chamber of Commerce.

Golan, G. J., Johnson, T. J. & Wanta, W., 2010. *International media. communication in a global age*. New York: Routledge.

Harrison, A., Dalkiran, E. & Elsey, E., 2000. *International business. Global competition from a European perspective*. New York: Oxford University Press.

Hatton, A., 2000. *The definitive guide to marketing planning*. New York: Financial Times Press.

Hollensen, S., 2009. *Essentials of global marketing*. Harlow: Pearson Education.

Icc, 2010. About ICC [online]. [cited: 04.01.2011]. Available from World Wide Web: <URL:http://www.iccwbo.org/id93/index.html>.

Incoterms, 2010. *Revised trade rules for an inter-connected world*. Paris: International Chamber of Commerce.

Keegan, W. J. & Green, M. C., 2005. *Global marketing*. Upper Saddle River: Pearson-Prentice Hall.

Keegan, W. J. & Schlegelmilch, B. B., 2001. *Global marketing management. A European perspective*. Harlow: Pearson Education.

Kotler, Ph., 2000. *Marketing management*. New Jersey: Prentice Hall Inc.

Kotler, Ph., Keller, K., Brady, M., Goodman, M. & Hansen, T., 2009. *Marketing management: first European edition*. New Jersey: Prentice Hall.

Lego, 2010. LEGO® Builders of Tomorrow campaign [online]. [cited 08.01.2011]. Available from World Wide Web: http://www.prfirms.org/index.cfm?fuseaction= page.viewpage&pageid=645

Muhlbacher, H., Leihs, H. & Dahringer, L., 2006. *International marketing. A global perspective*. London: Thomson Learning.

Neider, J. & Marciniak-Neider, D., 1997. *Transport intermodalny*. Warszawa: PWE.

Nestle, 2010. Supply chain consolidation: when less is more [online]. [cited 07.01.2011]. Available from World Wide Web: http://www.total-logistics.eu.com/logistics-clients/logistics-consultants-case-studies/NestleConsolidation.html.

Pauwels, K., 2007. How retailer and competitior decisions drive the long-term effectiveness of manufacturer promotions for the fast moving consumer goods. *Journal of Reailing*, 83 (3): 297-308.

Pickton, D. & Broderick, A., 2000. *Integrated marketing communication*. London: Prentice Hall.

Rosenbloom, B., 1999. *Marketing channels. A management view*. Hinsdale: The Dryden Press.

Rossiter, J. R. & Bellman, S., 2005. *Marketing communications*. London: Pearson Prentice Hall.

Rugman, A. M. & Collinson, S., 2009. *International business*. New York: Financial Times Press.

Russell, J. T. & Lane, W. R., 2000. *Reklama wedlug Ottona Kleppnera*. Warszawa: Felberg SJA.

Rymarczyk, J., 1996. *Handel zagraniczny. Organizacja i technika*. Warszawa: PWE.

Schlegelmilch, B., Keegan, W. J. & Stoettinger, B., 2001. *Global marketing management: A European perspective*. London: Financial Times Press.

Schultz, D., Tannenbaum, S. & Lauterborn, R., 1993. *Integrated marketing communications*. New York: NTC Publishing Group.

Sethuraman, R. & Tellis, G., 2002. Goes manufacturer advertising suppress or stimulate retail price promotions? Analitical model and empirical analysis. *Journal of Retailing*, 78 (4): 253-264.

Skjoett-Larsen, T. 2000. European logistics beyond 2000. *International Journal of Physical Distribution and Logistic Management*, 30 (5): 377-387.

Srinivasan, S., Keon, P., Hanssens, D. M. & Dekimpe, G. M., 2004. Do promotions benefit manufacturers, retailers, or both? *Management Science*, 50 (5): 617-629.

Stepien, B., 2004. *Transakcje handlu zagranicznego*. Warszawa: PWE.

Strongbow, 2010. Strongbow Bowtime [online]. [cited 20.12.2010]. Available from World Wide Web: http://hubpages.com/hub/Sales-Promotions.

Szymura-Tyc, M., 2009. *International marketing and business in CEE countries*. Katowice: AE.

Trompenaars, F. & Hampden-Turner, Ch., 2002. *Siedem wymarow kultury. Znaczenie roznic kulturowych w dzialalnosci gospodarczej*. Krakow: Oficyna Wydawnicza.

Usunie, J-C. & Lee, J., 2009. *Marketing across cultures*. New York: Financial Times Press.

Wiktor, J. W., Oczkowska, R. & Zbikowska A., 2008. *Marketing międzynarodowy. Zarys problematyk*i. Warszawa: PWE.

Wilmanska-Sosnowska, S., 2002. *Przemiany w strategii dystrybucji wspolczesnych przedsiębiorstw*. In: Czubala, A. (ed.), *Dystrybucja w marketingowych strategiach przedsiebiorstw*. Krakow: AE.

Zabinski, L., 2000. *Modele strategii marketingowych*. Katowice: AE.

Zbikowska, A., 2005. *Public relations. Strategie firm międzynarodowych w Polsce*. Warszawa: PWE.

Index

Appendix

INVOICE

Consignee Name:	José Pedro Gomez		Invoice No:	117-11/BS
Company:	Gomez East Import Company, Inc.		Date:	03-04-2011
Address:	Av. Alcântara Machado		No Of Pages:	1 / 1
	Sao Paulo		Account No:	KM 946 11 042
	03102-002 Brasil		Vat Number:	
Tel:	+55 11 5162 7841		Turn Number:	
Fax:	+55 11 5162 7849		Hawb:	
Vat Number:			Shipped Via:	Hamburg - Santos Port

No of Items	Weight KG	Commodity Code	Description Of Goods	Unit Value	Total Value
800	23.500	8501.43	hydraulic control elements, automotive brake mechanism	100	80.000,00
				Total	80.000,00
				Currency	EUR

Terms Of Delivery:	Berlin - Sao Paulo via FCA
Reason For Export:	purchase agreement
Country Of Origin:	GERMANY

I DECLARE THAT AS THE EXPORTER OF THE PRODUCTS COVERED BY THIS DOCUMENT, DECLARE THAT, EXCEPT WHERE OTHERWISE CLEARLY INDICATED, THESE GOODS ARE OF EC PREFERENTIAL ORIGIN.

Signature of Shipper:	*J. D. Gomez*
	José Pedro Gomez
Print Name:	United Carrier Lines, Hamburg

Date	BILL OF LADING – SHORT FORM – NOT NEGOTIABLE		Page 1 of 1

SHIP FROM		Bill of Lading Number:
[Name] [Street Address] [City, ST ZIP Code] SID No.	United Carrier Lines Brooktorkai 3 20457 Hamburg	**K - 854 - M1**

SHIP TO		Carrier Name:	AMT Logistic & Co. KG
[Name] [Street Address] [City, ST ZIP Code] CID No.:	R. Xavier da Silveira Santos - São Paulo 11013-050, Brasilien	Trailer number: Serial number(s):	Hansestraße 48 28217 Berlin

THIRD PARTY FREIGHT CHARGES BILL TO		SPAC:
[Name] [Street Address] [City, ST ZIP Code]	Schneider Int. Automobile GmbH Naumannstraße 167 10829 Berlin	Pro Number:

Special Instructions:

Freight Charge Terms (Freight charges are prepaid unless marked otherwise):

Prepaid ❑　Collect ❑　3rd Party ❑

❑ Master bill of lading with attached underlying bills of lading.

CUSTOMER ORDER INFORMATION

Customer Order No.	# of Packages	Weight	Pallet/Slip (circle one)		Additional Shipper Information
983 61 213	40	23.5	Ⓨ	N	stored in a 40't Container
			Y	N	
			Y	N	
			Y	N	

Grand Total

CARRIER INFORMATION

Handling Unit		Package		Weight	HM (X)	Commodity Description Commodities requiring special or additional care or attention in handling or stowing must be so marked and packaged as to ensure safe transportation with ordinary care. See Section 2(e) of NMFC item 360.	LTL Only	
Qty	Type	Qty	Type	Weight	HM (X)		NMFC No.	Class
1	40't Con.	40	DIN 3	23.5		said to contain:		
						40 Packages of hydraulic control elements,		
						automotive brake mechanism		
						Skid dimensions: 28 x 40 x 16 Inches		

Where the rate is dependent on value, shippers are required to state specifically in writing the agreed or declared value of the property as follows: 'The agreed or declared value of the property is specifically stated by the shipper to be not exceeding _____ per _____

COD Amount: $

Fee terms: Collect ❑　Prepaid ☒　Customer check acceptable ❑

Note: Liability limitation for loss or damage in this shipment may be applicable. See 49 USC § 14706(c)(1)(A) and (B).

Received, subject to individually determined rates or contracts that have been agreed upon in writing between the carrier and shipper, if applicable, otherwise to the rates, classifications, and rules that have been established by the carrier and are available to the shipper, on request, and to all applicable state and federal regulations.

The carrier shall not make delivery of this shipment without payment of charges and all other lawful fees.

Shipper Signature

Shipper Signature/Date	Trailer Loaded:	Freight Counted:	Carrier Signature/Pickup Date
This is to certify that the above named materials are properly classified, packaged, marked, and labeled, and are in proper condition for transportation according to the applicable regulations of the DOT.	☒ By shipper ❑ By driver	☒ By shipper ☒ By driver/pallets said to contain ❑ By driver/pieces	Carrier acknowledges receipt of packages and required placards. Carrier certifies emergency response information was made available and/or carrier has the DOT emergency response guidebook or equivalent documentation in the vehicle. Property described above is received in good order, except as noted.

Instructions for opening of an Irrevocable Letter of Credit

PLEASE FORWARD THESE INSTRUCTIONS TO YOUR BANKERS

Please arrange the issuance of an irrevocable documentary credit according to the instructions stated below:

Advising Bank:	Beneficiary:
	Schneider Int. Automobile GmbH Naumannstraße 167 10829 Berlin

Currency/ Amount: EUR 96.000,00	Credit to be **available with** **Advising Bank** by: ☒ payment at sight ☐ deferred payment ☐ _____ days after sight ☐ negotiation ☐ _____ days after shipment ☐ acceptance against presentation of the documents detailed below

| Account with:

Exporter's Bank Germany
Taunusanlage 71, 60325 Frankfurt a. Main | |

Date and Place of expiry: 23-08-2011 **Berlin**	**Partial shipments** are ☒ allowed ☐ not allowed
Latest date of shipment: 01-08-2011	**Transshipment** is ☒ allowed ☐ not allowed
Shipment/dispatch/taking in charge from/at: Berlin	For transportation to: São Paulo

Description of goods:

hydraulic control elements, automotive brake mechanism

As per Contract / Sales Confirmation / Proforma Invoice No. 117-11/BS

Terms of delivery: delivered via FCA   as per INCOTERMS (latest edition in force)

Documents required:

☒ Signed Commercial Invoice: 3   -fold
☒ Full set clean on board marine Bills of Lading made out to order and blank endorsed

☐ Air Waybill
☐ CMR
☐ Forwarding Agents Certificate of Receipt (FCR)
☒ Certificate of Origin
☐ Packing List: _____ -fold
☐ Insurance Policy / Certificate covering risks as per Institute Cargo Clause (A)/Air

☐

Special instructions :

Documentary credit to be confirmed by Advising Bank.	☒ yes	☐ no
All commission and charges arising in Germany are for account of:	☐ Buyer	☒ Seller
Documentary credit to be transferable:	☐ yes	☒ no

Documents to be presented within 5____ days after date of shipment but within the validity of the credit.

This Documentary Credit should be subject to the Uniform Customs and Practice for Documentary Credits (UCP) – latest edition in force – as published by the International Chamber of Commerce, Paris .

1/1

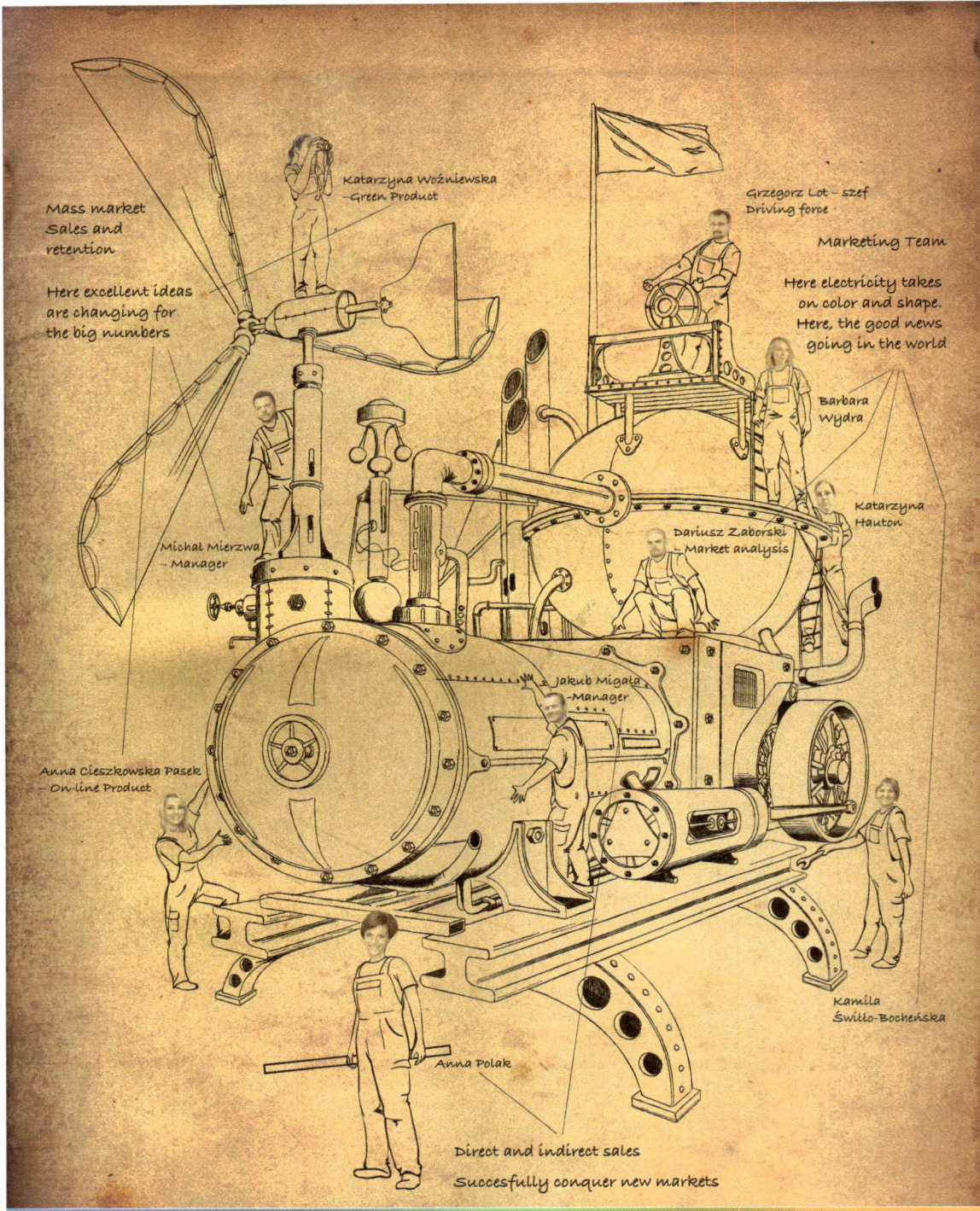

Mass market
Sales and
retention

Here excellent ideas
are changing for
the big numbers

Katarzyna Woźniewska
– Green Product

Grzegorz Lot – szef
Driving force

Marketing Team

Here electricity takes
on color and shape.
Here, the good news
going in the world

Barbara
Wydra

Katarzyna
Hauton

Michał Mierzwa
– Manager

Dariusz Zaborski
– Market analysis

Jakub Migała
–Manager

Anna Cieszkowska Pasek
– On-line Product

Kamila
Światło-Bocheńska

Anna Polak

Direct and indirect sales

Succesfully conquer new markets

VATTENFALL